U.S. Immigration and Migration
Almanac

U.S. Immigration and Migration
Almanac

Volume 1

Sonia Benson

Sarah Hermsen,
Project Editor

Detroit • New York • San Diego • San Francisco • Cleveland • New Haven, Conn. • Waterville, Maine • London • Munich

U.S. Immigration and Migration: Almanac

Sonia Benson

Project Editor
Sarah Hermsen

Editorial
Lawrence W. Baker

Permissions
Shalice Shah-Caldwell, Lori Hines

Imaging and Multimedia
Dean Dauphinais

Product Design
Kate Scheible

Composition
Evi Seoud

Manufacturing
Rita Wimberley

LIBRARY OF CONGRESS CATALOGING-IN-PUBLICATION DATA

Benson, Sonia.

    U.S. immigration and migration almanac / Sonia G. Benson.

      p. cm. — (U. S. immigration and migration reference library)

    Includes bibliographical references and index.

    ISBN 0-7876-7732-9 (set hardcover : alk. paper) — ISBN 0-7876-7566-0 (vol. 1) — ISBN 0-7876-7567-9 (vol. 2)

    1. United States—Emigration and immigration—Juvenile literature. 2. Immigrants—United States—Juvenile literature. [1. United States—Emigration and immigration. 2. Immigrants.] I. Title. II. Series.

JV6450.B46 2004
304.8′73—dc22

2003027833

Contents

Reader's Guide

The U.S. Constitution, signed in 1789, gave Congress the right to create laws involving immigration and citizenship. When the first Congress assembled, it created a loose idea of what it meant to be a citizen of the United States: all "free white persons" who had lived in the country for a couple of years were eligible. But the concept of citizenship was still vague. The naturalization process—the set of rules for becoming a citizen—was initially quite simple. The young nation actively sought immigrants to bring their professional skills and labor and to take part in expanding the borders of the nation from the Atlantic Ocean to the Pacific Ocean. There were initially no immigration agencies or border patrols—no passports or green cards. But not everyone was allowed to become a citizen or afforded the same rights. Issues of race for non-whites and Hispanics as well as a historical preference for the northwestern European immigrants led to inequalities and discrimination from the start.

Legislations and policies have continually added to or changed the original vague requirements, rights, and responsibilities of citizenship and immigration. Through the Fourteenth and Fifteenth Amendments, after the American Civil War (1861–65), the concept of the "free white persons" eligible to become citizens was amended to include African Americans. Women's citizenship generally was dependent on their husband or father's citizenship until 1920. Until 1943, most Asians were not included in the definition of someone who could become a citizen.

American sentiment toward immigrants has always gone back and forth between positive and negative for a number of reasons. During good economic times when labor is needed, immigrants usually receive better treatment than during economic downturns when people fear the competition for employment. When mass migrations from particular areas begin, there is often hostility in the United States toward the latest group to arrive. They are often perceived as different and as a threat to "American values," values leaning more toward Western European traditions. Immigration has almost always been at the center of political controversy in the United States. In fact, the first anti-immigrant government policies began to arise within only a few years of the signing of the Constitution.

Immigration restrictions brought about by nativist (favoring the interests of people who are native-born to a country, though generally not concerning Native Americans, as opposed to its immigrants), racist, or anti-immigrant attitudes have had a very major impact on the U.S. population, dictating who entered the country and in what numbers. The Chinese, for example, were virtually stopped from immigrating by the Chinese Exclusion Act of 1882 until it was repealed in 1943. Many families were separated for decades because of the severity of U.S. restrictions. Immigration from many other countries was significantly reduced by the immigration quota (assigned proportions) systems of 1921 and 1924.

Most immigrants, since the first English settlers landed at Jamestown, have had to pay tremendous dues to settle in North America. There has been a long-held pattern in which the latest arrivals have often been forced to take on the lowest-paying and most undesirable jobs. However, many historians of immigration point out that the brightest and most promising professional prospects of the nations of the world have immigrated to the United States. A daring spirit and the ability to overcome obstacles have always been, and continue to be today, qualities common to the immigrants coming into the nation.

The United States differs from many other countries of the world in having a population made up of people descended from all of the world's nations. Immigration controversy continues to confront the United States in the early twenty-first century, posing difficult questions from concerns about regulating entry and controlling undocumented immigration, to providing public services and a decent education to recently arrived immigrants. In the early years of the twenty-first century, the U.S. Marines intercepted refugees from the civil uprising in Haiti and sent them back to their country, where they feared for their lives. When does the United States provide refuge and what makes the nation deny others who are in need? These concerns are not likely to be resolved in the near future. The value of studying the historical and cultural background of immigration and migration in the nation goes well beyond understanding these difficult issues.

Why study immigration and migration?

As a chronicle of the American people's roots, the history of immigration and migration provides a very intimate approach to the nation's past. Immigration history is strongly centered on the people of the United States rather than the presidential administrations or the wars the nation has fought. Learning about the waves of immigration and migration that populated the continent and seeing the American culture as the mix of many cultures is central to understanding the rich diversity of the United States and appreciating it as a multicultural nation.

The two-volume *U.S. Immigration and Migration: Almanac* presents a comprehensive overview of the groups of people who have immigrated to the United States from the nations of Africa, Europe, Asia, and Latin America, as well as those who migrated within the country to unexplored lands or to newly industrialized cities. The first two chapters in the set present general information on immigration and migration—the eras, the means of transportation, and the anti-immigrant movements.

Seventeen chapters in the *Almanac* are devoted to a group or cluster of groups of immigrants from other nations and cultures. They are presented in a pattern of chronological order, beginning with those first mysterious migrations of peoples to North America thousands of years ago. National groups are presented roughly in the order that their first major waves of immigration occurred, as follows: Pre-Columbian; Spanish; English; Scots and Scotch-Irish; French and Dutch; Africans; German; Irish; Scandinavian; Chinese, Japanese, and Filipino; Jewish; Italian and Greek; Eastern European; Arab; Asian Indian, Korean, and Southeast Asian; Mexican; and other Latino and Caribbean groups. Although it is not possible to include every nation of origin in these volumes, many readers will be able to find their cultural roots in one or more of these chapters.

Most immigration chapters in these volumes begin with the historical background of the old country, leading to the reasons behind the mass migrations in U.S. history. The history of that national or ethnic group in the United States follows. The second section of the chapter presents current population statistics and some selected descriptions of cultural contributions and traditions, with the main focus on the immigration experience itself rather than on the contributions of those whose families have been in the country for several generations.

U.S. Immigration and Migration: Almanac also includes three chapters on internal migration. One focuses on westward expansion—the Oregon Trail, the California Gold Rush, settling the Great Plains, and much more. Another migration chapter chronicles a few of the forced migrations on the continent—the exile of the Acadians from Nova Scotia, which led to an Acadian culture in Louisiana; the Cherokee Trail of Tears; the Long Walk of the Navajo; the flight of the Nez Perce; and the internment of Japanese Americans during World War II. A third migration chapter provides an overview of industrialization and urbanization, the Great Migration of African Americans from the rural South to the cities of the North, and the urbanization of some Native Americans.

Each chapter in both volumes of *U.S. Immigration and Migration: Almanac* contains three types of sidebars: "Words to Know" boxes, which define important terms discussed in the chapter; "Fact Focus" boxes, which have a comprehensive overview of specific and noteworthy events from the chapter; and other boxes that describe people, events, and facts of special interest. Each chapter concludes with a list of additional sources students can go to for more information. Over 150 black-and-white photographs and maps help illustrate the material.

Each volume of *U.S. Immigration and Migration: Almanac* begins with a timeline of important events in the history of U.S. immigration and migration; a "Words to Know" section that features important terms from the entire U.S. immigration and migration era; and a "Research and Activity Ideas" section with suggestions for study questions, group projects, and oral and dramatic presentations. The two volumes conclude with a general bibliography and a subject index so students can easily find the people, places, and events discussed throughout *U.S. Immigration and Migration: Almanac.*

U.S. Immigration and Migration Reference Library

U.S. Immigration and Migration: Almanac is only one component of the three-part U.S. Immigration and Migration Reference Library. The other two titles in this set are:

- *U.S. Immigration and Migration: Biographies:* This two-volume set presents the life stories of fifty individuals who either played key roles in the governmental and societal influences on U.S. immigration and migration or are immigrants who became successful in the United States. Profiled are well-known figures such as German-born physicist Albert Einstein; Scottish-born industrialist Andrew Carnegie; Czech-born Madeleine Albright, the first female U.S. secretary of state; and English-born comedic actor Charlie Chaplin. In addition, lesser-known individuals are featured, such as Kalpana Chawla, the first female astronaut from India; Mexican-born Antonia Hernández, a lawyer and activist for Latino causes; and folk singer Woody Guthrie, whose songs focused on the plight of victims of the Great Depression and the Dust Bowl of the 1930s—migrants who left the Midwest in search of a better life in the West.

- *U.S. Immigration and Migration: Primary Sources:* This volume tells the story of U.S. immigration and migration in the words of the people who lived and shaped it. Eighteen excerpted documents relating to immigration and migration provide a wide range of perspectives on this period of history. Included are excerpts from presidential vetoes; judicial rulings; various legislative acts and treaties; personal essays; party platforms; and works of fiction featuring immigrants.

- A cumulative index of all three titles in the U.S. Immigration and Migration Reference Library is also available.

Acknowledgements

The author and editor would like to thank James L. Outman of Lakeside Publishing Group for his editorial efforts and the Arab Community Center for Economic and Social Services (ACCESS) for their contributions to *U.S. Immigration and Migration: Almanac*. Thanks also to copyeditor Theresa Murray, proofreader Amy Marcaccio Keyzer, indexer Trish Yancey, and typesetter Jake Di Vita of the Graphix Group for their fine work. Additional thanks to Julie Burwinkel, media director at Ursuline Academy, Cincinnati, Ohio, and Janet Sarratt, library media specialist at John E. Ewing Middle School, Gaffney, South Carolina, for their help during the early stages of the project.

Comments and suggestions

We welcome your comments on *U.S. Immigration and Migration: Almanac* as well as your suggestions for topics to be featured in future editions. Please write to: Editor, *U.S. Immigration and Migration: Almanac,* U•X•L, 27500 Drake Road, Farmington Hills, Michigan, 48331-3535; call toll-free: 800-877-4253; fax to 248-414-5043; or send e-mail via http://www.gale.com.

U.S. Immigration and Migration Timeline

c. **13,000** B.C.E. The first immigrants arrive on the North American continent and gradually migrate in groups throughout North and South America. Neither the timing of the first migrations nor their origins are known.

c. **400** C.E. The Anasazi culture emerges in the Four Corners region of present-day Arizona, New Mexico, Utah, and Colorado. The Anasazi, thought to be the ancestors of the Pueblo, Zuni, and Hopi Indians, were known for their basketry and pottery as well as their elaborate mansions built into high cliff walls.

c. **700** People of the moundbuilding Mississippian culture build the city of Cahokia near present-day East St.

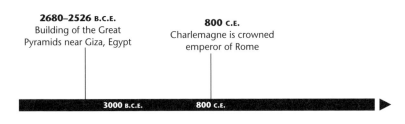

2680–2526 B.C.E.
Building of the Great
Pyramids near Giza, Egypt

800 C.E.
Charlemagne is crowned
emperor of Rome

3000 B.C.E.   **800** C.E.

Louis, Illinois, about five square miles wide, and containing about a hundred mounds situated around central plazas.

1000   Norse explorer Leif Eriksson sets out from Greenland and apparently sails to Vinland, in present-day Newfoundland, Canada.

1492   Navigator Christopher Columbus arrives in the Caribbean while searching for a route to Asia on an expedition for the kingdom of Spain. He returns to Hispaniola (the island which today is home to Haiti and the Dominican Republic) with settlers the following year.

1565   Spanish explorers and settlers establish Saint Augustine, Florida, the oldest permanent European settlement in the United States.

1607   The Jamestown settlers from England arrive in Virginia and establish a colony.

1618–1725   From five to seven thousand Huguenots flee the persecution in France and sail to America to settle in the British colonies.

1619   A Dutch warship brings twenty African slaves to Jamestown, Virginia, the first Africans to arrive in the British colonies.

1620   The Pilgrims and other British colonists aboard the *Mayflower* land in Plymouth Harbor to found a new British colony.

1624   The first wave of Dutch immigrants to New Netherlands arrives in what is now New York. Most settle at Fort Orange, where the city of Albany now stands.

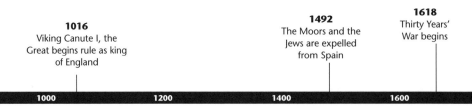

1016
Viking Canute I, the
Great begins rule as king
of England

1492
The Moors and the
Jews are expelled
from Spain

1618
Thirty Years'
War begins

1000   1200   1400   1600

1630–40 In the Great Migration from England to New England, about twenty thousand men, women, and children, many of them Puritans, migrate.

1718 The vast territory of Louisiana becomes a province of France; the European population of the colony numbers about four hundred.

1769 Two Spanish expeditions—one by land and one by sea—leave Mexico to colonize Alta California, the present-day state of California.

1790 Congress passes an act providing that "free white persons" who have lived in the United States for at least two years can be naturalized (become citizens) in any U.S. court. Along with non-white males, this also excludes indentured servants, slaves, children, and most women, all of whom are considered dependents.

1803 The United States buys Louisiana Territory from France in the Louisiana Purchase. The purchase more than doubles the size of the United States, adding to it what are now the states of Louisiana, Oklahoma, Arkansas, Missouri, Kansas, Nebraska, Iowa, Minnesota, and North and South Dakota, as well as a large part of Wyoming, most of Colorado, and parts of New Mexico and Texas.

1804 Meriwether Lewis and William Clark set out on their overland trip across the continent to the Pacific Ocean, forging a path never before explored by European Americans.

1808 Congress prohibits the importation of slaves into the United States, but the slave trade continues until the end of the American Civil War in 1865.

1815–45 About one million Irish Catholics immigrate to the United States.

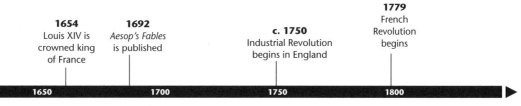

| **1654**
Louis XIV is crowned king of France | **1692**
Aesop's Fables is published | **c. 1750**
Industrial Revolution begins in England | **1779**
French Revolution begins |

| 1650 | 1700 | 1750 | 1800 |

1825 A group of Norwegians immigrate to the United States, eventually settling in Illinois, where they begin the Fox River settlement. This serves as the base camp for future Norwegian immigrants to the United States.

1830s Many tribes from the Northeast and Southeast are forcibly moved to Indian Territory (present-day Oklahoma and Kansas). Southern tribes to be removed include the Cherokee, Chickasaw, Choctaw, Creek, Seminole, and others. In the North, the Delaware, Miami, Ottawa, Peoria, Potawatomi, Sauk and Fox, Seneca, and Wyandot tribes are removed. The government is not prepared to provide supplies for so many Indians along the trails and in new homes, causing great suffering and death for the Native Americans.

1830s The mass migration of Germans to the United States begins.

1836 The Mexican province of Texas declares its independence from Mexico. Texas will become a state in 1845.

1836–60 The Jewish population of the United States grows from fewer than 15,000 to about 160,000. Most of the Jewish immigrants during this period are from Germany.

1841 The first wagon trains cross the continent on the Oregon Trail.

1845 The potato crop in Ireland is hit with a mysterious disease, beginning the Irish potato famine. By the winter of 1847, tens of thousands of people are dying of starvation or related diseases. An estimated one to one and a half million Irish Catholics leave Ireland for the United States over the next few years.

1804
Napoléon Bonaparte is crowned emperor of France

1812–15
War of 1812

October 26, 1825
Erie Canal opens

1835–42
Seminole War

1810   1820   1830   1840

1848 After the Mexican-American War, the United States acquires the Mexican provinces of New Mexico, Arizona, California, and parts of Nevada, Colorado, and Utah. Between 80,000 and 100,000 Mexicans suddenly find themselves living in the United States. Those who choose to stay in their homes automatically become citizens of the United States.

1848 Gold is discovered in the foothills of northern California's Sierra Nevada Mountains. In the next few years, hundreds of thousands of people from all over the United States and around the world migrate to California hoping to strike it rich.

1848–1914 An estimated 400,000 Czechs immigrate to the United States from Austria-Hungary.

1850s Anti-immigrant associations, such as the American Party (also known as the Know-Nothing Party), the Order of United Americans, and the Order of the Star-Spangled Banner, are on the rise. Their primary targets are Catholics, primarily Irish Americans and German Americans.

1851–1929 More than 1.2 million Swedish immigrants enter the United States.

1855 Castle Island, operated by the State of New York, becomes the first central immigrant-processing center in the United States.

1862 Congress passes the Homestead Act to encourage people to settle west of the Mississippi River. Under this act, a person can gain ownership of 160 acres simply by living on the land and cultivating it for five years.

1864–69 Thousands of Chinese laborers work on the first transcontinental railroad in the United States, cutting a path through treacherous mountains.

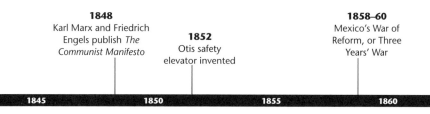

1848
Karl Marx and Friedrich Engels publish *The Communist Manifesto*

1852
Otis safety elevator invented

1858–60
Mexico's War of Reform, or Three Years' War

1845　　　　1850　　　　1855　　　　1860

1866–1914 More than 600,000 Norwegians immigrate to the United States.

1867–1914 About 1.8 million Hungarians immigrate to the United States.

1868 The Fourteenth Amendment of the Constitution provides citizenship rights to African Americans.

1869 The first transcontinental railroad in the United States is completed.

1870 The Fifteenth Amendment gives African American citizens the right to vote.

1870 Polish serfs are given their freedom and begin to emigrate. Up to two million Poles will immigrate to the United States between 1870 and 1914.

1870–1920 About 340,000 Finns immigrate to the United States.

1880–1920 About 35 million people, mainly from southern and eastern Europe, arrive on U.S. shores.

1880–1920 About 4 million people leave Italy for the United States, making Italians the single largest European national group of this era of mass migration to move to America.

1880–1924 About 95,000 Arabs immigrate to the United States, most from the area known as Greater Syria—present-day Syria, Lebanon, Jordan, Palestine, and Israel.

1881–1914 About 2 million Eastern European Jews arrive in the United States.

1882 The Chinese Exclusion Act prohibits the naturalization of Chinese immigrants for ten years and prohibits Chinese laborers from entering the country. For the Chinese already in the country, it denies hope of

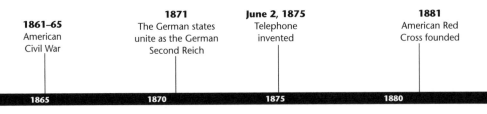

1861–65
American
Civil War

1871
The German states
unite as the German
Second Reich

June 2, 1875
Telephone
invented

1881
American Red
Cross founded

1865   1870   1875   1880

gaining citizenship and for many Chinese men it meant that their wives or families would not be able to join them. The act, the first major restriction on immigration in the United States, is extended twice and becomes permanent in 1902.

1885–1924 About 200,000 Japanese people immigrate to Hawaii.

1890 The Superintendent of the United States Census issues a statement that the American frontier has closed— that is, it has become populated and is therefore no longer a frontier.

1891 The Immigration and Naturalization Service (INS) is created as the department that administers federal laws relating to admitting, excluding, or deporting aliens and to naturalizing the foreign-born who are in the United States legally. It remains in operation until 2003.

1892 The federal government takes over the process of screening incoming immigrants at the Port of New York and creates an immigration reception center at Ellis Island, one mile southwest of Manhattan. Before it closes in 1954, more than 16 million immigrants will pass through Ellis Island.

1900 In this one year, one-tenth of Denmark's total population immigrates to the United States.

1907 The Dillingham Commission, set up by Congress to investigate immigration, produces a forty-two-volume report. The commission claims that its studies show that people from southern and eastern Europe have a higher potential for criminal activity, are more likely to end up poor and sick, and are less intelligent than other Americans. The report warns that the waves of immigration threaten the "American" way of life.

1886
The Chicago Haymarket Riot occurs

1891
Escalator invented

1898
Spanish-American War

1885   1890   1895   1900

1907 As anti-Asian immigrant sentiment rises in the United States, Congress works out the "Gentlemen's Agreement" with Japan, in which the United States agrees not to ban all Japanese immigration as long as Japan promises not to issue passports to Japanese laborers for travel to the continental United States.

1910 To enforce the Chinese Exclusion Act, an immigration station is built at Angel Island in the San Francisco Bay. Any Chinese people arriving in San Francisco go through an initial inspection upon arrival; many are then sent to Angel Island for further processing and thousands are held there for long periods of time.

1910–1920 Between 500,000 and 1,000,000 African Americans migrate from the southern United States to the cities of the North.

1913 California passes the Alien Land Laws, which prohibit Chinese and Japanese people from owning land in the state.

1917 Congress creates the "Asiatic barred zone," which excludes immigration from most of Asia, including China, India, and Japan, regardless of literacy.

1920s–30s More than 40,000 Russians come to the United States in the first few years after the Russian Revolution of 1917. Many Russians go into exile in other European cities. In the 1930s, those in exile in Europe begin fleeing the rising Nazi movement. More than a million people who had been born in Russia but were living elsewhere in Europe immigrate to the United States in the 1930s.

1921 Congress passes the Emergency Quota Act, which stipulates that each nation has an annual quota (proportion) of immigrants it may send to the United

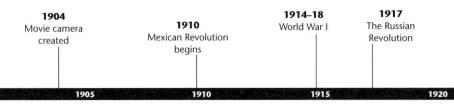

1904
Movie camera
created

1910
Mexican Revolution
begins

1914–18
World War I

1917
The Russian
Revolution

1905   1910   1915   1920

States, which is equal to 3 percent of that country's total population in the United States in 1910. Because the majority of the U.S. population was from north-western Europe in 1910, this method favors north-western Europeans over other immigrants.

1924   Congress passes the National Origins Act, which restricts the number of immigrants even beyond the Emergency Quota Act of 1921. Under the new act, immigration is decreased to a total equaling 2 percent of the population in 1890. Under this act, each country may only send 2 percent of its 1890 population in the United States per year. The new act skews the permitted immigration even further in favor of Western Europe, with the United Kingdom, Germany, and Ireland receiving more than two-thirds of the annual maximum quota. This legislation ends the era of mass migrations to the United States.

1924   The Oriental Exclusion Act prohibits most Asian immigration, including the wives and children of U.S. citizens of Chinese ancestry.

1924   Congress creates the Border Patrol, a uniformed law enforcement agency of the Immigration Bureau in charge of fighting smuggling and illegal immigration.

1925   One out of every four Greek men between the ages of fifteen and forty-five have immigrated to the United States.

1934   The Tydings-McDuffie Act sets the date and some of the terms of independence for the Philippines on July 4, 1946. Since the United States had acquired the Philippines from Spain in 1898, Filipinos had entered the United States as nationals (people who live in a country legally, are loyal to the country and protected

1921
Insulin
discovered

1922
Harlem
Renaissance

September 1924
First modern highway
opens in Italy

1921   1922   1923   1924

by it, but are not citizens). The act takes away status of Filipinos as U.S. nationals, reclassifying them as aliens, and restricts Filipino immigration by establishing an annual immigration quota of 50.

1942   The United States, heavily involved in World War II, needs laborers at home and turns to Mexico. The U.S. and Mexican governments reach an agreement called the Mexican Farm Labor Supply Program, or the *bracero* program. The program permits Mexicans to enter the country to work under contract as farm and railroad laborers. The program continues for twenty-two years and brings 4.8 million Mexicans to work on U.S. farms and in businesses.

1942   During World War II, President Franklin D. Roosevelt signs Executive Order 9066, which dictates the removal and internment of Japanese Americans. More than 112,000 Japanese Americans living along the Pacific coast are taken from their homes and placed in ten internment camps for the duration of the war.

1943   Congress repeals the Chinese exclusion acts. Immigration from China resumes. Most of the new immigrants are females, the wives of Chinese men who have been in the United States for decades.

1945   As World War II ends, more than 40,000 refugees from Europe flee to the United States. Because the quota system does not provide for them, they are admitted under presidential directive.

1945   The War Brides Act allows foreign-born spouses and adopted children of personnel of the U.S. armed forces to enter the United States. The act brings in many Japanese, Chinese, and Korean women, among other groups.

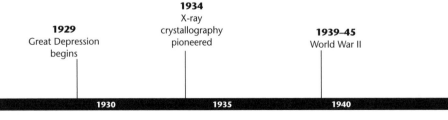

1929
Great Depression
begins

1934
X-ray
crystallography
pioneered

1939–45
World War II

1930   1935   1940   1945

1948 The first U.S. refugee policy, the Displaced Persons Act, enables nearly 410,000 European refugees to enter the United States after World War II.

1950 The Internal Security Act forces all communists to register with the government and denies admission to any foreigner who is a communist or who might engage in subversive activities.

1952 Congress overrides President Harry S Truman's veto of the Immigration and Nationality Act, which upholds the quota system set in 1921–24 but removes race as a bar to immigration and naturalization and removes discrimination between sexes. The act gives preference to immigrants with special skills needed in the United States, provides for more rigorous screening of immigrants in order to eliminate people considered to be subversive (particularly communists and homosexuals), and allows broader grounds for the deportation of criminal aliens.

1954 As jobs in the United States become harder to find, Mexican workers are viewed as unwanted competition by many. Under Operation Wetback, a special government force locates undocumented workers and forces them to return to Mexico. In one year alone, about one million people of Mexican descent are deported.

1959 The Cuban Revolution initiates a mass migration from Cuba to the United States—more than one million Cubans will immigrate after this year.

1960–80 The Filipino population in the United States more than quadruples, from 176,130 to 781,894.

1960s Between 4 and 5 million African Americans have migrated from the South to the North since the turn of the century.

1946
Cold War between the
United States and the
Soviet Union begins

1950
Korean War
begins

1957
The Soviet Union
launches *Sputnik I,* the
first Earth satellite

1946   1951   1956   1961

1965 In a new spirit of immigration reform, Congress repeals the national-origins quotas and gives each Eastern Hemisphere nation an annual quota of 20,000, excluding immediate family members of U.S. citizens. The Eastern Hemisphere receives 170,000 places for immigrants and the Western Hemisphere 120,000. (In 1978, Congress creates a worldwide immigration system by combining the two hemispheres.)

1966–80 About 14,000 Dominicans per year enter the United States, most seeking employment they cannot find at home.

1972–81 Sailboats carrying Haitians begin to arrive on the shores of Florida. More than 55,000 Haitian "boat people"—and perhaps more than 100,000—arrive in this wave.

1975 Saigon, the South Vietnamese capital, falls to the communist North on April 30; at least 65,000 South Vietnamese immediately flee the country.

1975–81 About 123,600 Laotian refugees enter the United States.

1979 In the aftermath of the Vietnam War, the Orderly Departure Program (ODP) is established to provide a safe alternative for Vietnamese people who are fleeing the country in large numbers, often risking their lives in overcrowded old boats. Under the ODP, refugees are allowed to leave Vietnam directly for resettlement in one of two dozen countries, including the United States. There are about 165,000 admissions to the United States under the ODP by 1989, and new arrivals continue into the 1990s.

1980 More than 125,000 Cubans flee to the United States during the Mariel Boat Lift.

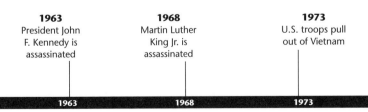

1963
President John
F. Kennedy is
assassinated

1968
Martin Luther
King Jr. is
assassinated

1973
U.S. troops pull
out of Vietnam

1963   1968   1973   1978

1980–86 Tens of thousands of Cambodian refugees enter the United States annually.

1981–2000 The United States accepts 531,310 Vietnamese refugees.

1986 The Immigration Reform and Control Act (IRCA) provides amnesty (pardon to a group of people) to more than 3 million undocumented immigrants who had entered the United States before 1982, allowing them to become legal residents. The measure outlaws the knowing employment of undocumented immigrants and makes it more difficult for undocumented immigrants to receive public assistance.

1988 Congress passes the Amerasian Homecoming Act, which brings thousands of children—most are the offspring of American servicemen and Asian mothers—to the United States.

1991–93 Some 43,000 Haitians try to reach the United States by boat. Many of their boats are intercepted by U.S. officials and those emigrants are taken to Guantánamo Bay, a U.S. naval base in Cuba.

1994 In an effort to stop undocumented workers from illegally crossing the border, the government adopts Operation Gatekeeper, an extensive border patrol system at Imperial Beach at the border between Mexico and southern California. The number of border agents is increased and new hi-tech equipment is put to use, costing billions of dollars over the next few years. Illegal immigration moves further inland where the climate is more severe, proving to be deadly in some cases.

1994 The United States enters a Wet Feet–Dry Feet agreement with Cuba under which, if fleeing Cubans trying to reach the United States are caught at sea, U.S. authori-

1979–80
52 Americans
are held hostage
in Iran

1985
DNA
fingerprinting
developed

1989
Berlin Wall falls

January 1, 1994
The North American Free
Trade Agreement (NAFTA)
goes into effect

1980   1985   1990   1995

ties will send them back to Cuba. If the Cubans make it to U.S. shores, they will be admitted to the country.

1996 Congress passes the Illegal Immigration Reform and Immigrant Responsibility Act (IIRIRA). The IIRIRA creates a huge increase in funding for border patrol personnel and equipment. This act creates harsher penalties for illegal immigration, restricts welfare benefits to recent immigrants, and makes the deportation process easier for U.S. administrators. The IIRIRA also tries to make it harder for foreign terrorists to enter the United States.

1996 The bombing of the Oklahoma Federal Building at the hands of a terrorist (a U.S. citizen) in 1995 raises new fears about terrorism. The Anti-terrorism Act is passed, making deportation automatic if an immigrant commits a deportable felony (a grave crime), even if the immigrant has been in the United States since early childhood. By 2003, 500,000 people had been deported under the terms of this act.

1997 The Border Patrol initiates Operation Rio Grande, strengthening the Texas-Mexico border with more agents to deter people from crossing.

1998 California passes Proposition 227, a referendum that bans bilingual classroom education and English as a second language (ESL) program, replacing them with a one-year intensive English immersion program.

2000 The Immigration and Naturalization Service estimates the number of undocumented immigrants in the country at about 7 million, up from the estimate of 5.8 million in 1996. About 70 percent of the undocumented immigrants are from Mexico.

2001 Congress passes the USA PATRIOT Act ("Uniting and Strengthening America by Providing Appropriate

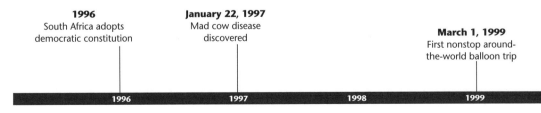

1996
South Africa adopts
democratic constitution

January 22, 1997
Mad cow disease
discovered

March 1, 1999
First nonstop around-
the-world balloon trip

1996   1997   1998   1999

Tools Required to Intercept and Obstruct Terrorism"). The bill calls for increased border patrol and tightened provisions for screening and restricting immigrants. It grants sweeping new powers to federal police agencies and permits indefinite detention of immigrants and aliens in the country for minor immigration status violations.

2001   Within weeks of the September 11 terrorist attacks on New York and Washington, D.C., approximately 1,200 immigrants are arrested by federal government agents as part of an anti-terrorist campaign. Most are from Saudi Arabia, Egypt, and Pakistan. Many are held without charges and without access to attorneys or their families. Many are deported. None are charged with terrorism.

2002   The Homeland Security Department requires the annual registration of temporary male immigrants from twenty-four predominantly Arab or Muslim countries as well as North Korea. People from the following countries are required to register: Afghanistan, Algeria, Bahrain, Eritrea, Iran, Iraq, Lebanon, Libya, Morocco, North Korea, Oman, Pakistan, Qatar, Saudi Arabia, Somalia, Sudan, Syria, Tunisia, United Arab Emirates, and Yemen. The following year, five more countries are added to the list: Bangladesh, Egypt, Indonesia, Jordan, and Kuwait. Of the 83,519 people who register with immigration officials in 2002, 13,799 are put in deportation proceedings. Others complain of terrifying or humiliating interrogations and harsh conditions. Immigrant and civil liberties groups protest the policy.

2001
Terrorists attack the
World Trade Center
and the Pentagon

2003
U.S. declares
war on Iraq

2000   2001   2002   2003

Words to Know

A

Alien: a person living in the United States who is not a U.S. citizen.

Amnesty: a blanket pardoning of a group of people.

Anabaptist: a category of radical Protestants, including the Mennonites and the Amish, the German Brethren, or Dunkards, and the Society of Friends, or the Quakers, who believe in nonviolence and in simple worship based on readings of the Bible. Anabaptists believe that knowledge of God must come from within oneself and that the rituals and politics of existing churches are a hindrance to true faith and worship. They also believe that an individual should decide to be baptized as an adult, when he or she fully understands what it means, rather than in infancy.

Anarchist: a person who believes that governments are unnecessary and should be eliminated, and that the social world should be organized through the cooperative efforts of the people within it.

Anthropologist: a scientist who studies human beings in terms of their relations with one another, race and ethnicity, populations, migrations, and culture.

Antimiscegenation laws: laws prohibiting marriage between races, usually between whites and any other race.

Anti-Semitism: hostility to, or discrimination against, Jewish people as a group.

Arctic: the northernmost region of North America, with its shores on the Arctic Ocean. It includes parts of Alaska, Canada, and much of Greenland.

Arctic Circle: A line of latitude at 66° 33' North that delineates the northernmost point at which the sun is visible on the northern winter solstice and the southernmost point at which the midnight sun can be seen on the northern summer solstice. In the Arctic regions, the winters are continuously dark and the summers are continuously light.

Aristocracy: government by the elite or a small class of the privileged.

Artifact: a product made by humans of an earlier period.

Artisan: craftsman; someone who is skilled at a trade or craft.

Assimilation: the way that someone who comes from a foreign land or culture learns to blend into and eventually becomes absorbed into the ways of the predominant, or mainstream, society in which he or she now lives.

Asylum: a status granted by a government or authority in which one is protected from persecution and not subject to arrest.

B

Band: a social and economic group of nomadic hunting people.

Barrio: a Spanish-speaking section of a U.S. city or town.

Bilingual: able to speak two languages fluently.

Bilingual education: in the United States, a system of education in which students who speak languages other than English are instructed at least partly in their native language.

Bird of passage: an immigrant who comes to the United States with the intention of returning home as soon as he or she had makes some money.

Boat people: people who flee their country in small boats not meant for this use, and often at great risk.

Bourgeoisie: the middle class.

Braceros: "guest" Mexican laborers who entered into contracts for temporary work in the United States, under a government program in place between 1942 and 1964.

C

Calvinism: the belief system of theologian John Calvin, which asserted that the human world was basically corrupt and only the Bible—not the church—could reveal the true religion.

Celtic: (pronounced KEL-tick) relating to an ancient race of European people—the Celts whose descendants live today in the Scottish Highlands, Ireland, Wales, and Brittany, a part of France. *Celtic* also refers to the language spoken by these people.

Chain migration: a process of immigration in which someone migrates to a new home and then begins to bring family and friends from the old country to the new home. They in turn bring over more friends and family, who all settle near each other, creating a neighborhood or village of people who were in some way connected in the country or area of origin.

Chiefdom: a society in which a person's rank and prestige is assigned by how closely he or she is related to the chief.

Citizen: someone who lives in and participates in a political community or country, who has fulfilled the requirements for citizenship as set out by the government. Citizens can expect certain rights and privileges from their government, such as voting or military defense, and at the same time the government has a right to expect its citizens to obey its laws.

Civil disobedience: an act of protest against a questionable law through nonviolent acts of breaking that law.

Clachans: small, close-knit communities in rural Ireland.

Colony: a group of people living as a political community in a land away from their home country but ruled by the home country.

Commonwealth: a political unit, such as a state or a nation.

Communism: an economic theory that does not include the concept of private property. Instead, the public (usually represented by the government) owns the goods and the means to produce them in common.

Confederacy: a joining together of different groups of people for a common purpose.

Constitution: the document that sets out the laws and principals of a nation or state, defining the powers of the various government bodies and the rights of its citizens.

Continental United States: also called the mainland United States; the 48 states on the continent, excluding Hawaii and Alaska.

***Coureurs de bois*:** (pronounced KOO-ruhr deh bwa) the French term for "travelers in the woods," or fur trappers and traders.

Coyote: a person who smuggles immigrants across the borders into the United States for money.

Culture: a way of life shared by a group of people who have things such as art, religion, and customs in common with each other.

Czar: (also spelled tsar) the emperor or ruler of Russia.

D

Defect: to illegally renounce one's citizenship and request residency in another country.

Deportation: the act of sending an alien out of the country.

Discrimination: unfair treatment based on racism or other prejudices.

Displacement: involuntary removal from one's home or nation.

Dynasty: a series of leaders that are from the same family line and rule over a long period of time.

E

Ecosystem: a natural community of plants, animals, and microorganisms living in relation to each other in a particular habitat.

Emigration: leaving one's country to go to another country with the intention of living there. "Emigrant" is used to describe departing *from* one's country—for example, "she emigrated from Ireland."

Enclave: a distinct cultural or nationality unit within a foreign territory.

Encomienda system: a system in which the Spanish nobles, in return for taking part in a war, were granted a large section of land and the right to rule as lord over the infidels on that land.

Ethnic: relating to a group of people who are not from the majority culture in the country in which they live, and who keep their own culture, language, and institutions.

Ethnic cleansing: the killing of an ethnic minority group by the majority group.

Ethnic communities: sections of cities or towns in which people from a common racial, national, tribal, religious, or language group live together and practice their the customs of their homeland or cultural background.

Evacuate: to remove people from their homes during a military alert or other emergency.

Exiles: people who have been sent away from their homeland.

Expedition: a group of people making a journey together for a common purpose.

Extended family: A family with several generations all living together or acting as a unit. An *extended family* usually includes grandparents, their sons or daughters, and their children, and the term is used to differentiate the extended family from the nuclear family, which is only a married couple and their children.

Extermination: killing an entire group or population.

F

Feudal estate: a system in which a local lord who had received his land from the king ruled over the people in his area.

First-generation immigrant: those who were born in another country and then immigrated to the United States.

Forced migration: being moved from one's home to a new country or area against one's will.

Frontier: the area at the most remote border of a settled territory.

G

Gael: a Gaelic-speaking person from the Scottish Highlands, Ireland, or the Isle of Man.

Gaelic: the language spoken in the Celtic Scottish Highlands; Ireland; and on the Isle of Man.

Genocide: the systematic killing or destruction of a racial, ethnic, or cultural group of people.

Ghetto: an area within a city where members of a minority group live; frequently places where groups are isolated from the community due to discrimination or ethnic prejudice.

Grassroots: arising from common people, rather than politicians, corporations, or others in power.

Great Depression: 1929–41; a period, following a stock market crash in 1929, of depressed world economies and high unemployment.

Green card: documentation that allows an alien to live permanently and work in the United States.

H

Hellenic: relating to ancient Greek and Roman civilizations.

Hereditary: passed on from generation to generation along family lines.

Huguenots: French Calvinists.

I

Immigration: to travel to a country of which one is not a native with the intention of settling there as a permanent resident.

Indentured servants: servants in colonial times who agreed to work for a colonist for a set period of time in exchange for payment of their passage from Europe to the New World. At the end of the service term (usually seven years), the employer usually gave the indentured servant a small piece of land or goods to help set up a new life in the colony.

Indigenous: native to an area.

Industrialization: the historic change from a farm-based economy to an economic system based on the manufacturing of goods and distribution of services on an organized and mass-produced basis.

Infidel: non-Christian.

Internment camps: places in which people are confined in wartime.

Islam: the religion of the Muslims, who believe in Allah as the one supreme god and Mohammad as the prophet, or the interpreter the will of Allah; the religion is based on the Muslim holy book, the Koran.

Issei: foreign-born Japanese.

J

Joint stock company: a group that organizes an enterprise, such as trading in a certain overseas market, and then sells shares of this enterprise to investors.

L

Labor unions: organizations that bring workers together to advance their interests in terms of getting better wages and working conditions.

Laissez faire: (French for "let it be"); a belief that the government should not interfere in the economy more than absolutely necessary.

M

Mafia: an organized crime network in the United States that is organized in families and is thought to have important ties to the organized crime families in Sicily, Italy.

Manifest destiny: a belief that the United States had a special destiny, and therefore the right, to stretch out across the continent.

Mass migration: times in history when thousands—or even millions—of people from one country in the Old World have immigrated to the New World within a short period of time.

Mesoamericans: people from the cultural area that lies in present-day Mexico and most of Central America where civilizations such as the Mayans and the Aztecs lived before European contact.

Mestizo: a person of mixed Spanish and Indian descent.

Middle East: the part of the world that encompasses Southwest Asia and North Africa, extending from Turkey to North Africa and east to Iran.

Middle passage: the journey by slave ship from Africa to the Americas, the middle leg in the European traders' triangular system—the first leg was the trip from Europe to Africa, and the last was the trip from the Americas to Europe.

Migrant workers: workers who are not citizens of the United States but come to the country—legally or illegally— to fulfill temporary labor needs on farms and in construction, factories, and services.

Migration: to move from one place to another, not necessarily across national borders.

Mission: an organized effort by a religious group to spread its beliefs in other parts of the world. The word *mission* refers either to the project itself, or to the buildings built in a new area in order to spread the religious beliefs.

Moor: an African person of Arab and Berber descent, generally a member of the religion of Islam.

Mulatto: a person of mixed European and African descent.

Multiculturalism: a view of the social world that embraces, or takes into account, the diversity of people and their cultures within the society.

N

Nationalist movement: struggle for independence from the rule of another country.

Nativism: a set of beliefs that centers around favoring the interests of people who are native-born to a country (though generally not concerning Native Americans) as opposed to its immigrants.

Naturalization: the process of becoming a citizen.

Navigation: setting the course for ship travel.

New England: the northern colonies (later states) of Massachusetts, Rhode Island, Connecticut, and New Hampshire.

New World: the western hemisphere, including North and South America.

Nomads: people who travel and relocate often, usually in search of food and other resources or a better climate.

Non-quota immigrants: the spouses, children, and parents of U.S. citizens who wish to immigrate to the United States—non-quota immigrants are not counted by the United States as part of the sending nation's yearly quota, or their allotted proportion of U.S. immigrants.

Northwest Passage: a mythical water route through the American continent that the early Europeans hoped would lead to the Pacific Ocean and new trading with Asia.

Nostalgia: remembering one' home with longing; homesickness.

O

Old World: the regions of the world that were known to Europeans before they discovered the Americas, including all of the eastern hemisphere—Europe, Asia, and Africa—except Australia.

Oral traditions: history, mythology, folklore and other foundations of a culture that have been passed by spoken word, often in the form of stories, from generation to generation within a culture group.

Orthodox Jews: those who strictly adhere to the Jewish traditions and rituals.

Overlanders: people traveling west by land rather than sea.

P

Padrone: an Italian (or Greek) immigrant who was established in the United States and acted as a professional labor broker for more recent immigrants. The padrone was usually paid by both the employer and the employee.

Palisade: a defensive fence or wall made of stakes.

Papal States: political units ruled by the pope, the leader of the Roman Catholic Church.

Parish: local church community.

Patroonship: a system developed by the Dutch West Indies Company to promote emigration in which the company granted large parcels of land to any person of wealth who would commit to bring over a certain number of colonizers and house them on his land (usually fifty settlers within four years). In turn, the patroons owned the land and had great authority over their tenants.

Peasant: a person who tills the soil for a living, as a renter, a small landowner, or a laborer.

Persecution: abusive and oppressive treatment.

Pidgin language: a simple speech created to make trade possible between two groups that speak different languages.

Pilgrim: a member of the group of British Protestant colonists who sailed on the *Mayflower* and founded the colony of Plymouth in 1626.

Pogroms: state-sponsored massacres of innocent and helpless people.

Populist: oriented toward common people, or democratic.

Pre-Columbian: the time in American history before Spanish explorer Christopher Columbus arrived in 1492 and Europeans began colonizing the American continents.

Presbytery: a group of ministers and lay people that lead a Protestant church, as opposed to the bishops who head the Episcopalian churches, or the congregations, or members of the local church, who lead the Puritan churches.

Presidio: a military post or fort.

Primogeniture: a system of inheritance under which all of the wealth from one family is passed to the oldest son upon the father's death, ensuring that the estates of the wealthy did not get divided into small pieces.

Proletariat: the laboring class.

Propaganda: information spread to persuade or further a cause.

Protectorate: a dependent state under the authority of a stronger state.

Protestant church: a Christian church that denies the pope's authority and accepts the Bible as the only source of revealed truth.

Q

Quaker: a member of the Religious Society of Friends, a Christian group dedicated to social reform that rejects the rituals and preachers of formal churches, and instead holds open meetings at which all are free to speak.

Quarantine: enforced isolation of the sick or potentially sick from the public to prevent the spread of an infectious disease.

Quota: an assigned proportion.

R

Racism: a system of belief based on an assumption that important characteristics, such as intelligence, morality, or sophistication, of the different races are passed along from generation to generation and are determined by the ethnic group or race. This allows some people to assert that one race is superior to another.

Refugee: a person who has left the country in which he or she last lived and is unable to return to that country for fear of being persecuted due to his or her race or ethnic background, religion, group membership, or political beliefs.

Registered alien: a documented alien, meaning (in the United States) someone who has obtained from the government a permanent resident card, commonly known as a green card, which shows the holder's status as a lawful permanent resident, though not a citizen, of the country, with a right to live and work there.

Religious settlers and refugees: people who immigrate, often as a group, because they do not conform to the religion practiced by the majority in their home country and either face persecution or are not allowed to practice their religion in the way they choose. Some religious settlers create communities that are governed by the principles of their religion.

Removal policy: the government's systematic relocation of American Indians from the eastern United States to west of the Mississippi.

Repatriation: the act, usually by a government, of returning someone to their home country.

Republic: a country ruled by the people, rather than a king.

Reservation: land set aside by the government for the use of a particular Native American group or groups.

Ritual: a formal act that is performed in a ceremony or other religious observation, and usually done the same way each time.

S

Sabbath: the day of rest and worship; the Jewish Sabbath starts on Friday evening and ends Saturday evening.

Second-generation: born in the United States, but having parents who immigrated from another country.

Serfdom: a system of servitude in which a peasant is bound to the soil he tills and is subject to the authority of his lord.

Sharecropper: a tenant farmer who is usually provided with the land, seed, and equipment to farm, but owes the landlord a significant portion of his or her crops in return.

Shtetl: small towns and villages with a predominantly Jewish population.

Socialist: believing in a society in which no one owns private property, but rather, the government or public owns all goods and the means of distributing them among the people.

Sovereign: self-governing and free from outside rule.

Soviet: a government council in a communist country.

Steamship: a large vessel propelled by one or more steam-powered propellers or paddles.

Steerage: an area below the ship's deck. For a period of time in the mid-nineteenth century to the early twentieth century, steerage compartments of ships were over-crowded with immigrants, and conditions in steerage were notoriously bad.

Subsistence farm: a small farm that provides the goods for the survival of its tenants without producing extra crops for commercial use.

Syllabary: a system of writing that uses characters, or letters, to represent whole syllables or sounds.

Synagogue: a Jewish congregation, or the house of worship that the congregation meets in.

T

Talmud: a book of ancient writings of rabbis on Jewish law and tradition.

Temperance movement: the drive to stop people from drinking alcohol.

Theologian: one who studies religion.

Topography: the surface features of a region, such as its mountains, plateaus, or basins.

Torah: the first five books of the Bible—Genesis, Exodus, Leviticus, Numbers, and Deuteronomy; to an Orthodox Jew *Torah* means the entire body of Jewish law.

Trade embargo: prohibition of the trade of certain goods with a country.

Transatlantic: crossing the Atlantic Ocean.

Transcontinental railroad: a railroad that spans the continent.

Treaty: an agreement between two parties or two nations, signed by both, usually defining the benefits to both parties that will result from one side giving up title to a territory of land.

U

Undocumented alien: someone from another nation who is in the United States without a visa.

V

Vaquero: cowboy.

Viceroyalty: a state in which a viceroy governs as the representative of the king.

Visa: the official endorsement on a passport showing that a person may legally enter the country.

W

West Indies: islands in the Caribbean Sea on which explorer Christopher Columbus first landed in 1492, including Hispaniola—now Haiti and the Dominican Republic—Cuba, Jamaica, Puerto Rico, the Virgin Islands, Windward Islands, Leeward Islands, and the islands in the south Caribbean Sea north of Venezuela, usually including Trinidad and Tobago.

White-collar immigrant: a person from another country who has professional skills (doctors, computer specialists, academics, nurses).

Workhouses: institutions in which people in desperate poverty went to reside, and in which they worked for food and other aid.

Z

Zionism: the international movement seeking the return of the Jewish people to their ancient homelands in Palestine and the creation of a Jewish state there.

Research and Activity Ideas

The following research and activity ideas are intended to offer suggestions for complementing social studies and history curricula, to trigger additional ideas for enhancing learning, and to provide cross-disciplinary projects for library and classroom use.

Make a Map of Colonial America

Find or create a map of the United States (preferably one with the state borders and major rivers and mountains, but not much written detail). Using different colored pencils or crayons to distinguish between countries, color in the areas settled by England (the thirteen colonies), the Netherlands (New Netherland), France (Louisiana Territory and Illinois Country), Spain (Florida, New Mexico, Arizona, Texas, and California), and Russia (Alaska).

Read a Good Book

Read a novel, memoir, or biography about the experience of immigration or migration. Get together with a group of students who have read other books about the immigration experience and compare how people from different backgrounds describe the experiences. Here are some suggested readings:

- Mexican American: Victor Villaseñor, *Walking Stars: Stories of Magic and Power* (1996).
- Chinese American: Lawrence Yep, *Dragonwings* (1975).
- Palestinian American: Naomi Nye, *Habibi* (1999).
- Haitian American: Edwidge Danticat, *Behind the Mountains* (2002).
- Dominican American: Julia Alvarez, *How the Garcia Girls Lost Their Accents* (1991).
- Filipino American: Jessica Hagedorn, *The Gangster of Love* (1996).
- Asian Indian American: Bharati Mukherjee, *Jasmine* 1989.
- Puerto Rican: Esmerelda Santiago, *When I Was Puerto Rican* (1994).
- Korean American: Patti Kim, *A Cab Called Reliable: A Novel about Growing Up in America* (1998).

Create an American mosaic

As a nation of immigrants, the United States has long been described as a melting pot, in which people of all nationalities blend together to become one—American. In recent times, though, most people acknowledge the fact that not everyone blends in to the mainstream in the United States, and perhaps there is no such thing as one mainstream. In the Chinatowns, Little Italys, Pennsylvania Dutch country, Cajun parishes, and many other ethnic communities in the nation, many immigrants choose to keep some of their old traditions and language and raise their children with them. Even people who do not live in ethnic communities often strive to maintain their own ethnic and national roots. In the past few decades, Americans have embraced the wealth of ethnic and cultural differences that make up our nation. Many have begun to speak of the United States not as a melting pot, but as a mosaic of peoples, different and distinct—not blended, but joined together to make a whole. This view of society is called "multiculturalism."

Make a poster or collage that illustrates the American mosaic, showing some of the many elements of our society that come from all over the world to be joined together as Americans. Try to show the elements of the different national or ethnic groups that are common within your daily life. Clip pictures from magazines, labels from products, newspaper headings, print up words or phrases from other languages that are used in everyday English, find cloth from other countries, and use your own drawing, painting, or graphics to make a multicultural mosaic.

Push and pull factors

When there are mass migrations, there are always "push" and "pull" factors motivating them. The push factors are the things that make people want to leave their country, such as religious oppression or lack of job opportunities, and the pull factors are the things that draw them to the new country, such as land to farm or a democratic government.

Write a report describing some of the push and pull factors of immigrants from any two of the following groups:

- English Jamestown settlers: 1607
- Irish Catholics: 1847
- Norwegians: 1880
- Italians: 1900
- Russian Jews: 1910
- Japanese Americans: 1920
- Vietnamese: 1970
- Asian Indians: 2000

Write a letter

It is the year 1844 and your family is migrating across the country on the Oregon Trail in a wagon train. You said goodbye to a very good friend when you left home and now you wish to write to him or her. Write a letter to your friend and tell him or her all about your experiences and what daily life is like on the Oregon Trail.

Stage a multicultural festival

As a group, plan a feast day in which everyone brings international foods to share. Each participant should choose a national or ethnic group and then bring one of its traditional foods. Along with bringing the food, each participant should decorate the table from which they are serving and be prepared to discuss some of the traditional ways to celebrate holidays and special events among the selected culture group. They may also want to bring in recordings of traditional music.

U.S. Immigration
and Migration
Almanac

Introduction:
The Nation of Immigrants

Every resident of the United States, with the possible exception of Native Americans, descends from an immigrant. (An immigrant is someone who travels to a country of which he or she is not a native with the intention of settling there as a permanent resident.) The United States celebrates that it is a nation of immigrants; it is part of the country's identity and is incorporated into the stories that Americans tell about themselves. In fact, immigration is the basis of the legendary American dream, the belief that people from any background and any nationality can find in the United States the opportunity to work at a secure job, live in a nice home, get an education, and raise their standard of living through their own efforts.

Melting pot and mosaic

In order to maintain the sense that citizens of the United States are uniquely American in character even while millions of people keep pouring into its borders from every corner of the world, some distinctively American ideas have developed about the process of assimilation—the way that someone who comes from a foreign land becomes absorbed into American culture and learns to blend into the ways of its main society. For years the United States has been described as a melting pot, in which people of all nationalities who immigrated blended together like a stew—a single dish made out of many different ingredients. This is the message of the U.S. motto, seen on every dollar bill: "E pluribus unum": From many, one.

Like most stories that people tell about themselves, there is truth to the melting pot metaphor, but it does not tell the whole story. Not everyone blends in. The United States has a long-standing tradition of ethnic communities, sections of cities or towns in which people from a common racial, national, tribal, religious, or language group live together and practice their own customs. For example, many cities have a Chinatown or a little Italy and other ethnic sections within them. Certain cities draw particular immigrants; for example, Cuban immigrants have a large population in Miami's Little Havana, while many Vietnamese immigrants have gathered in Little Saigon in Westminster, California. Not every ethnic community is in a city: the Pennsylvania Dutch (Germans, actually) established distinctive cultures in rural Pennsylvania, as have the Cajuns (a group of exiled French Canadians) in rural Louisiana. These ethnic communities, or enclaves, are made up of people who choose to keep their traditions and language. Sometimes they even have the same neighbors they had in their country of origin. For newly arrived immigrants, ethnic neighborhoods often provide a safe place in the new surroundings.

In the past few decades, Americans have embraced the wealth of ethnic and cultural differences that make up the nation. American educators and media (television, newspapers, and radio) have begun to speak of the United States as a mosaic of peoples, different and distinct—not blended, but joined together to make a whole. This view of society is called "multiculturalism."

Nativism and discrimination

Almost every first generation of immigrants from a particular nationality experiences some amount of discrimi-

Fact Focus

- In 1883 Emma Lazarus won a poetry contest, and as a result her poem was selected to be inscribed in a bronze plaque at the base of the new Statue of Liberty. Her poem, "The New Colossus," depicts the United States as a haven for immigrants. At the time, although millions were arriving from Europe, few people had thought of the statue—or the nation—in quite that way.

- A large portion of the nation's immigrants came here intending to stay only long enough to make some money to take back to their families. Although many did return to their home country, many who had intended to return never did.

- Migrations during the first century of the colonial era were almost always undertaken by large groups, or expeditions, sponsored by a government or large trading company.

- In 1843 a group of one thousand pioneers began a journey west from Independence, Missouri, on the 2,000-mile-long Oregon Trail. This rugged journey was repeated by settlers annually until about 1870, when railroads took a large share of the westward traffic.

- Up until the 1880s, the United States had an open-door policy on immigration, allowing almost anyone to enter the country.

- The Great Migration of 1880–1920 brought twenty-seven million immigrants into the country from European nations such as Russia, Poland, Italy, Greece, and Austria-Hungary.

- In 1921 and 1924, the U.S. Congress passed the first generally applied immigration acts that limited new immigration by a quota (an assigned proportion) system. The result was a drastic reduction in the numbers of immigrants coming into the United States that lasted until the 1970s.

- The United States Border Patrol was established in 1924. Until the 1920s, the United States had not tried to stop undocumented immigration across the border.

- Between 1975 and 1988, after the war in Vietnam ended, some nine hundred thousand refugees from Vietnam, Cambodia, and Laos entered the United States.

- Approximately 70 percent of illegal aliens in 2000 were from Mexico. Other nations sending a high number of illegal aliens to the United States were El Salvador, Guatemala, Colombia, Honduras, China, Ecuador, Dominican Republic, Philippines, Brazil, Haiti, India, Peru, Korea, and Canada.

nation (unfair treatment based on racism or other prejudices) when it arrives in the United States. The early waves of German, Irish, Greek, Italian, Hungarian, and Russian immigrants met with hostility and sometimes even violent discrimination. Politics in the United States have revolved around immigration issues since the country was first formed. The Federalists, one of the first political parties in the newly formed Union, ran on a nativist platform—one that favors the interests of people who are native-born over the interests of immigrants. One nativist group in the mid-nineteenth century, the Know-Nothing Party, rose to power because of its anti-immigrant stand, particularly in regard to the Irish Catholic and the German immigrants. One of the most extreme organizations was the Ku Klux Klan. The Klan, formed after the American Civil War (1861–65) on the premise of white supremacy (the belief that white people are superior to people of other races), directed most of its violence and intimidation against African Americans and terrorized several immigrant groups as well.

Oddly, many of the nativists who were hostile to new immigrants were themselves descendants of immigrants with just a few more generations in the United States than the people they were antagonizing. For European immigrants, a pattern developed in which new immigrants generally met the fierce hostility of nativists for a few generations and then were assimilated into the U.S. mainstream, either by means of the melting-pot process, meaning that the second and third generations became indistinguishable from their neighbors, or by living successfully in an ethnic enclave that came to be an accepted part of a city or region.

But not everyone who works hard and gets an education has been given the same opportunities to succeed in the United States, even when they have been in the country for centuries. For some groups the exclusion and mistreatment by mainstream society in the United States has a long and ugly history. The reason for this extended discrimination is almost always racism. People of European descent formed the mainstream of American society early in the colonial days of its history. They started out as the predominant culture. Over time, those who wanted to assimilate into the predominant culture must, in the end, look and sound like the predominant, white, English-speaking culture. The institution of slav-

Words to Know

Alien: A person who is not a citizen of the United States.

Assimilation: The way that someone who comes from a foreign land or culture becomes absorbed into a culture and learns to blend into the ways of its predominant, or main, society.

Colony: A group of people living as a political community in a land away from their home country but ruled by the home country.

Discrimination: Unfair treatment based on racism or other prejudices.

Emigration: Leaving one's country to go to another country with the intention of living there. Loosely, the word "emigrant" is used to describe departing *from* one's country—for example, "she emigrated from Ireland." "Immigrant" is used to describe coming *to* a new country—for example, "she immigrated to the United States."

Enclave: A distinct cultural or nationality unit within a foreign territory.

Ethnic: Relating to a group of people who are not from the majority culture in the country in which they live, and who keep their own culture, language, and institutions.

Exiles: People who have been sent away from their homeland.

Immigration: To travel to a country of which one is not a native with the intention of settling there as a permanent resident.

Industrialization: The historic change from a farm-based economy to an economic system based on the manufacturing of goods and distribution of services on an organized and mass-produced basis.

Migration: To move from one place to another, not necessarily across national borders.

Multiculturalism: A view of the social world that embraces, or takes into account, the diversity of people and their cultures within the society.

Nativism: A set of beliefs that centers around favoring the interests of people who are native-born to a country (though generally not concerning Native Americans) as opposed to its immigrants.

New World: The Western Hemisphere, including North and South America.

Old World: The regions of the world that were known to Europeans before they discovered the Americas, including all of the eastern hemisphere—Europe, Asia, and Africa—except Australia.

Persecution: Abusive and oppressive treatment.

Pre-Columbian: The time in American history before Spanish explorer Christopher Columbus (1451–1506) arrived in 1492 and Europeans began colonizing the American continents.

Repatriation: The act, usually by a government, of returning someone to their home country.

ery, Jim Crow laws (a series of laws beginning in about 1877 that segregated African Americans from European-based Americans), the Chinese Exclusion Act of 1882 (which prohibited Chinese laborers from coming to the United States or becoming citizens), and racial segregation (separation along racial lines) in public schools are just a few of the many instances of widespread racism within the country's legal and political system. Native Americans, African Americans, Asian Americans, Hispanic Americans, and Arab Americans have all experienced institutionalized discrimination (discrimination that is part of the nation's laws and policies) as well as social discrimination. Patterns of discrimination have changed, and continue to change, throughout the nation's history, but they generally change slowly.

Who are the immigrants?

In 1883 a poetry contest was launched as part of a fund-raising effort for building the pedestal for the Statue of Liberty, a gift to the United States from France. The sculptor of the statue created the form of a woman holding a torch high in the air, intending that the torch signify the light of liberty. Poet Emma Lazarus (1849–1887) entered a poem called "The New Colossus." Her poem won the contest and was later inscribed on a bronze plaque at the statue's base. Lazarus added her own conception of the meaning of the statue in her poem by depicting the United States as a haven for immigrants. At the time, few people had thought of the statue in those terms. Lazarus calls the Statue of Liberty the "mother of exiles" (exiles are people who have been sent away from their homeland) who "from her beacon hand / Glows worldwide welcome." In the poem's most famous words, the statue beckons Old World countries to send their immigrants to American shores:

> Give me your tired, your poor,
> Your huddled masses yearning to breathe free,
> The wretched refuse of your teeming shore,
> Send these, the homeless, tempest-tost to me....

Lazarus, a fourth-generation American from a wealthy, educated Jewish family, lived a comfortable life within the rapidly growing city of New York. In the early 1880s, she witnessed the arrival of a massive wave of poor

Jewish immigrants from Russia, fleeing a new era of persecution (abusive and oppressive treatment) there. Disembarking in New York, many of the immigrants were impoverished and disoriented. People in New York viewed them with suspicion and contempt, and Lazarus knew they would not have an easy time in America. Her poem encourages the view of the United States as a compassionate land where the oppressed can find freedom and comfort.

Lazarus's image of the welcoming shores of the United States was certainly based on reality. Many immigrants who came from desperate circumstances—even some of those who faced discrimination and worked in the most undesirable jobs when they arrived—have been grateful for the refuge, or protection, provided to them in the United States. On the other hand, Lazarus's image is only part of the story. Many newly arriving immigrants expected better treatment and an easier life than the one they found in the United States. Some historians object to the poem's one-sided view of the immigrants as the "tired" and "poor" and as the "refuse" of the Old World. In fact, scholars who study immigration have shown that people who emigrate are almost never the poorest or weakest or least educated of their nation. The poorest people could not scrape together the funds to make the trip to the United States; the weak and uneducated would not have the determination, strength, or even the information they would need to make the decision to emigrate and carry it out. Many historians theorize that the people who emigrate are often the most motivated and determined of their lot.

The Statue of Liberty, the "mother of exiles" in Emma Lazarus's poem "The New Colossus."

The push and pull factors

Throughout history, many have immigrated to the United States to escape from political or religious oppression, wars and violence, major natural disasters, or an inability to make a living or feed their families in their home country. These elements are called the "push" factors, because they tend to push people out of their home countries. By far, though, the majority of immigrants have come to the United States seeking economic and professional opportunities. Available lands for farming, an abundance of jobs, higher salaries, a good market for entrepreneurs (people starting up businesses) and traders, and high-quality facilities for professionals, such as top-notch hospitals, laboratories, and universities, are some of the "pull" factors of immigration, because they have drawn, or pulled, people to the United States. One of the huge pulls has long been the almost unending need for labor in the ever-growing United States. Often both push and pull factors have been central to the decision to emigrate. Perhaps the only major group of immigrants who did not respond to push or pull factors was the Africans, who were captured and traded into slavery against their will.

Immigrants from colonial times forward have come with many different intentions. Although we usually study immigrants in terms of their mass migrations (times in history when thousands, or even millions, of people from one country in the Old World have immigrated to the United States), decisions to migrate are made one person or one family at a time. For a mass migration to take place, common push and pull factors among the group of immigrants are necessary. But many people who immigrated to America left their homes for personal reasons: a broken heart, a love of adventure, hopes of finding a husband, or escape from an overbearing parent. They did not always seek, or find, religious or political freedom, and many returned to their homelands. In fact, a large portion of the nation's immigrants came here intending to stay only long enough to make some money to bring back to their families. Before 1900 most immigrants were young men who had left families behind to seek economic opportunity in the New World. As time passed, women and children made up larger percentages of the number of immigrants who came to stay, as the young men established themselves and then sent for loved ones. Of

Examples of the Different Kinds of Immigrants Who Have Come to the United States

Bird of passage: An immigrant of the second wave (1880–1945) who came to the United States with the intention of returning home as soon as he or she had made some money. These immigrants were usually young males from eastern and southern Europe.

Boat people: People who flee their country in small boats, often at great risk. Large numbers of boat people fled from South Vietnam at the end of the Vietnam War (1954–75) from about 1975 through the 1980s. Many died, but thousands were rescued and brought as refugees to other countries, including the United States. Many have also fled Cuba in small crafts since Cuban dictator Fidel Castro (1926–) has ruled the country. Haitian boat people have been arriving in the early twenty-first century

and the United States has been returning them to their own country.

Braceros: "Guest" Mexican laborers who entered into contracts for temporary work in the United States, under a government program in place between 1942 and 1964. During World War II (1939–45), many U.S. men served in the military, causing a serious labor shortage. The U.S. government negotiated the guest-worker program with Mexico. In all, 4.8 million bracero contracts were signed between 1942 and 1964. When the contracts expired, the braceros were required to return to Mexico. The program ended in 1964 because of mounting protest against the poor working and living conditions the braceros were forced to endure.

→

the nineteenth-century immigrants, only European Jews, facing political persecution in eastern Europe, consistently remained in America.

Eras of migration

The pre-Columbian era

Pre-Columbian refers to the time in American history before Spanish explorer Christopher Columbus arrived in 1492 and Europeans began colonizing the American continents. Many Native Americans believe that their ancestors originated in the United States and have always been here. Most scientists do not believe that human beings evolved on

Chain migration: A process of immigration in which an initial group of people from one location in the Old World migrates to a location in the New World and then brings over more people from their home. In chain migration, a young single person or a young family travels to the United States and gets settled in a home and a job. Then the first immigrants write to family and friends in the home country, telling them about the new country and often sending money for close relatives' passage. The relatives come, settling close to the first immigrant. They write to more people back home and send money when possible for their close relatives to join them. In many cases, an entire neighborhood within a U.S. city, town, or farming region has been populated by people from one village or neighborhood in the old country.

Colonists: People who travel from their mother country to settle and live in a community in a faraway country, where they will remain citizens of and be governed by the mother country. In what would become the United States, the colonial period started with the Spanish in the sixteenth century and continued until the British colonies revolted and won their independence in 1783.

Forced migration: Being moved from one's home against one's will. Africans captured by slave traders came to the New World by force, rather than by making a decision to leave. Many Native American groups were forced to migrate to reservations or other new homes.

Indentured servants: Servants in colonial times who agreed to work for a colonist for a set period of time in exchange for payment of their passage from Europe to the New World. At the end of the service term, usually seven years, the indentured servant was given a small

the American continents because no remains of early forms of humans have ever been found here. They believe that emigrations from the Old World (eastern hemisphere, except for Australia) took place, probably starting about twenty thousand years ago, bringing people to the Americas from northeastern Asian areas, such as China, Siberia, and Mongolia, and possibly from other areas as well, including Southeast Asia and the southern Pacific.

After the mysterious first immigrants arrived in the Americas, centuries of migrations took place. (Migration differs from immigration in that it can take place within one

piece of land or goods to help set up a new life in the colony.

Mass migration: Times in history when thousands, or even millions, of people from one country in the Old World have immigrated to the New World within a short period of time.

Migrant workers: Workers who are not citizens of the United States but come to the country—legally or illegally—to fulfill temporary labor needs on farms and in construction, factories, and services. Migrant workers have historically lived and worked in very harsh conditions while they labored in the United States. They usually come with the intention of making some money to send or bring home to their families in their home countries. Most plan to return home. Because migrant workers often accept lower wages than most American citizens and receive fewer, or no, work benefits (such as health insurance or vacations), farmers and businesses profit from their labor. During economic downturns in the U.S. economy, however, fears about migrant workers competing with citizens for jobs often result in government measures to repatriate them (send them to their home country).

Nonimmigrant: A citizen of a country other than the United States who has a visa to enter the United States, but only for a specific amount of time and for a specific purpose.

Refugee: The Refugee Act of 1980 defines a refugee as a person who has left the country in which he or she last lived and is unable to return to that country "because of persecution or a well-founded fear of persecution on account of race, religion, nationality, membership in a particular social group, or political opinion." Once a person is determined to be

→

country, while immigration involves moving across national borders.) By about 11,500 years ago, there were hundreds of human settlements throughout both American continents. Responding to the climate changes, people had moved about the land, finding places where life was more stable. Groups developed their own habits and tools as was best suited to the particular region in which they settled. By the time Columbus arrived in the New World in 1492, Native Americans had settled and resettled throughout the American continents. Because the Europeans arriving in the sixteenth century carried deadly viruses that killed a huge part of the

a refugee in the United States, he or she is entitled to federal assistance in settling into a home and finding a job, and in getting English-language training, temporary cash loans, and necessary medical services.

Registered alien: A documented alien, meaning someone who has obtained from the government a permanent resident card, commonly known as a green card. The green card shows the holder's status as a lawful permanent resident, though not a citizen, of the United States, with a right to live and work there. It is also evidence of registration in accordance with United States immigration laws.

Religious settlers: People who immigrate, often as a group, because they do not conform to the religion practiced by the majority in their home country and either face persecution or are not allowed to practice their religion in the way they choose. Religious settlers have often tried, sometimes successfully, to create

Native American population, no one knows for sure how many American Indians there were at the time of contact, but a rough estimate is about fifty-four million people. At that time, there were about one thousand languages among the diverse Native American groups. There were large cities, villages, extensive trade and long-distance interaction, farming technology, fine arts, religions, astounding architecture, and hundreds of unique cultural traditions.

Colonial era: 1492–1776

During the more than two-and-a-half-century American colonial era, a few powerful European nations set up colonies in what is now the United States. A colony is a group of people who have traveled from their mother country to live in another country, where they are governed, at least officially, by the mother country. Migrations during the first century of the colonial era were almost always undertaken by large groups, or expeditions, sponsored by the government or a large trading company. The home governments wanted to have colonies in the New World for the purpose of

communities that are governed by the principles of their religion.

Undocumented alien: Someone from another nation who is in the United States without a visa. Use of the term "undocumented" to refer to people who are in the United States without proper immigrant papers was established by the International Labor Organization in 1974. It was meant to be descriptive and neutral, in contrast to the term "illegal," which implies criminality. Being an undocumented alien in the United States violates civil statutes but does not violate criminal laws. Some undocumented workers enter the country without legal authorization, while others enter with the authorization of temporary permits, but then extend their stay.

White-collar immigrant: A person from another country who has professional skills (doctors, computer specialists, academics, nurses) who immigrates to the United States. These immigrants are given a special status for obtaining visas to live in the country.

providing new trade opportunities, getting rid of unwanted elements of society, or staking a claim to territory that another country might take over.

The first country to begin colonizing in the New World was Spain, with its focus in the Caribbean, Mexico, and South America. The young men who arrived in the New World from Spain generally did not intend to stay; they searched for, and found, gold and silver, and forced the Native Americans in the area to work in their mines. Many then returned home. A significant number of these early Spanish colonists, though, were rewarded by the Spanish government with large tracts of land to farm. With the land they received authority from Spain to put the Native Americans in their area to work as laborers, often in circumstances similar to slavery. The Spanish were important in the European settlement of what are now the states of Texas, California, Arizona, and New Mexico. Spain also had an early presence in Florida.

Spain was a predominantly Catholic country and all its colonies were automatically created as Catholic provinces. Other West European countries that would send colonists in North America—the English, Dutch, French, Scots, Germans, and Scandinavians—all experienced a tremendous religious revolt in the sixteenth and seventeenth centuries. That revolt is now known as the Protestant Reformation. In the Reformation, a large number of converts to Protestantism opposed the Roman Catholic Church's rituals and powerful leaders. Protestants believed that the Bible should be accessible to everyone in their own language, rather than the Roman Catholic's Latin Bible, and they developed new ways of worshipping. There were many variations of Protestantism; some Protestants persecuted others. Since religion in sixteenth- and seventeenth-century Europe was the basis of the social and political world, the Reformation profoundly shaped everyday life and created sharp divisions among people in many European countries. The religious upheaval in Europe was a prime motivator of immigration to the United States.

Not all of the colonial immigrants were from Europe. African slaves came to the New World with the first Spanish explorers as early as 1493. Africans, both as slaves and as free people, began arriving in the Dutch and English colonies in the early seventeenth century. By 1790, there were 750,000 people of African descent in the United States; all but 60,000 of them were slaves. The involuntary labor of the African slaves was responsible for many of the successes in the European colonizing efforts and laid a foundation for the nation that was to come. Slavery stood in stark contrast to the ideals of justice, equality, and liberty upon which the United States was to be founded. It deprived African Americans of the most basic human rights and deeply divided the nation.

In 1610, the population of the English colonies of the Americas was only 350 people. In the first colonies, in Jamestown and New England, the death rate of the colonists was staggering. Especially in the early years in Jamestown, many more settlers died than survived as they attempted to establish the new colony. Disease, starvation, extreme conditions, and poor relations with local Indians led to thousands of deaths among the settlers. At the same time, the presence of the settlers led to thousands of deaths among the Native American tribes, particularly because the Indians had no natural resistance to the infectious diseases brought over from Europe. Life in the early colonies was often miserable and dangerous: It was difficult to get supplies, ministers, proper food, health care, and many other things most people take for granted in the twenty-first century. Many who managed to survive a winter or two fled back to their homelands. Only by sending more and more people into the colony could its corporate sponsors keep the population from disappearing altogether. Nonetheless, by 1650, it was becoming clear that the experiment of colonization in the New World was paying off. The European and African population of the North American colonies had reached about 50,000 and it would grow quickly and steadily from there. The thirteen British colonies had a population of about 2.75 million by the time of the American Revolution (1775–83). By that time, there were active cities with a flourishing trade and cultural arenas.

First wave of immigration: 1783–1880

Immigrants who came to the United States between the American Revolution and 1880 are considered to be in the "first wave" of immigration. First-wave immigrants are also called "old immigrants." Up until the 1880s, the United States had an open-door policy, allowing almost anyone to enter the country. Old immigrants were primarily Irish, German, and Scandinavian, with some Canadian and, later in the era, Chinese. Many were single young men who hoped to save up enough money to return home in better circumstances. Some did in fact return to their homelands, but the majority ended up settling permanently in the United States. These young men then encouraged their relatives and friends to join them in America, setting off a chain migration. The friends and relatives usually settled near the original immigrants, creating ethnic neighborhoods or farming communities.

The huge influx of Irish and Germans, in particular, rapidly changed the shape of the United States, as the immigrants poured into the large eastern cities and migrated out to the Midwest in large numbers. Between 1820 and 1880, nearly three million Irish entered the country, fleeing from the starvation brought about by the potato famine of 1846 to 1847 and by years of oppression under the British that had left many Irish peasants landless and without means of survival. From 1820 to 1880, more than three million people from the German states came to the United States, mainly in an effort to improve their economic situation. Germany, like many other European nations, had experienced a tremendous population growth. Along with other aspects of the approaching age of industrialization (the historic change from a farm-based economy to an economic system based on the manufacturing of goods and distribution of services on an organized and mass-produced basis), commercial farms, in which wealthy investors bought up big parcels of land to farm on a large scale, were becoming widespread. There was little available land for the former tenant (renting) farmers. While many rural Germans had no means to make a living, many craftsmen and tradesmen in the cities sought new opportunities to ply their skills.

The first wave of Chinese to immigrate to the West Coast arrived shortly after 1848. News of the discovery of gold in California reached China at that time, and many young men set off on the long journey in hopes of becoming rich in the gold fields. After most of the gold fields had been claimed or mined, Chinese were drawn to emigrate by the prospect of labor on the U.S. railroads. Railroad companies were glad to have their labor, paying them little and demanding long hours of back-breaking work with picks and shovels. By the 1880s, there were about one hundred thousand Chinese immigrants in the United States, most of them young men. They experienced strong discrimination from other Americans. In 1882 Congress passed the Chinese Exclusion Act, which prohibited Chinese people from immigrating to, or becoming citizens of, the United States. It was the first serious restriction on immigration and the only one to target a single ethnic group in U.S. history. The act stopped most Chinese immigration until 1943, when the Chinese Exclusion Act was repealed. For many young male Chinese immigrants who had come to the United States prior to the act, there was no hope of bringing over wives or families from China. Many Chinese American men remained single for a lifetime.

Second wave of immigration: 1880–1945

In the second wave of immigration, from 1880 to 1945, many of the "new immigrants" came from southern and eastern Europe and Japan. The southern and eastern Europeans arriving in masses, partly because of widespread economic problems throughout the region, looked quite different from the old immigrants. While the old immigrants were generally fair-skinned Anglo-Saxons, the new immigrants were

darker-skinned Slavic and Mediterranean peoples. Most old immigrants had spoken English or another Germanic language upon arrival in the United States, but the new immigrants spoke languages that sounded completely foreign to the old immigrant population. Many more Jews came during this period, along with Eastern Orthodox and Italian Catholics.

The representation of Asian Americans grew. An influx of Japanese to the West added to the anti-Asian sentiments already developing in response to the Chinese presence there. Filipinos were "imported" to work on the sugar plantations of Hawaii and in the agricultural industry of the West Coast.

The Great Migration of 1880–1920 brought 27 million immigrants into the country from Europe. In the 1880s and 1890s immigrants from the eastern European nations of Russia, Poland, Italy, Greece, and Austria-Hungary poured into the United States. From 1900 to 1909 alone, an estimated 2 million Austria-Hungarians, 2 million Italians, and 1.5 million Russians

Recently arrived immigrants awaiting processing at the Ellis Island immigration reception center in New York. *Courtesy of the Library of Congress.*

entered the country. The first wave of Arabs arrived between 1875 and 1920, mainly from Lebanon and Syria. The American public was generally very mixed about new waves of immigrants, benefiting from their labors but not trusting them. The westward expansion of the United States had neared completion, with Americans reaching the western borders.

The end of this era brought about dramatic changes in immigration policy in the United States. Americans had become alarmed by all of the new arrivals, prompting a widespread movement to drastically restrict immigration. In 1921 and 1924, the U.S. Congress passed the first generally applied immigration acts, limiting new immigrants by a quota (an assigned proportion) system. The Emergency Quota Act of 1921 stipulated that each nation could send a quota of immigrants equal to 3 percent of that country's total population in the United States according to the 1910 census. This method favored northwestern Europeans, who had a much larger population in 1910 than other immigrants. The act set a cap of 350,000 as the maximum number of legal immigrants to be admitted in any one year. The National Origins, or Johnson-Reed, Act of 1924 restricted the number of immigrants further. Under this act, each country could only send 2 percent of its population in the United States in 1890. Because of their large representation in 1890, the United Kingdom, Germany, and Ireland were allotted more than two-thirds of the annual maximum quota.

The effect of the quota system of restrictions was a drastic reduction in the numbers of immigrants coming into the United States. Prior to this legislation, the number of immigrants to the United States had increased every decade from the 1820s (0.1 million) until the 1900s (8.8 million), with the exception of the American Civil War years (1861–65). From the 1930s, the numbers decreased. The number of foreign-born people in the United States in 1930 was 14.2 million, but by 1950 it was down to 10.3 million, or 6.9 percent of the total population. In 1970 the population of foreign-born people in the United States was 9.6 million or 4.7 percent of the total population.

Great migrations within the United States

While hundreds of thousands of people continued to cross the Atlantic from Europe to settle in the United States, hundreds of thousands more who were already living on the

continent moved to its Western regions. New canals, steamboats, turnpikes, and railroads tied the nation together. Most Americans moved westward in pursuit of land or financial gain. Many were drawn westward by the very idea of the frontier as a place where they could create a new life, unhampered by existing societies. The destinations were spread out across the nation, as people left the populated eastern seaboard. As the years progressed, pioneers pushed further and further West. They moved onto lands that were inhabited by Native Americans or, in the former Mexican states like Texas and California in the 1848 war, by Mexican Americans, and into territories claimed by other nations. They were following a popular doctrine known as "manifest destiny," a belief that the United States had a special destiny, and therefore its citizens had the right, to stretch out across the continent.

In 1843 a group of one thousand pioneers began a journey west from Independence, Missouri, on the 2,000-mile-long Oregon Trail. The expedition consisted of more

Illustration of Oregon Trail Wagon Caravan. *Drawing by William H. Jackson. Reproduced by permission of © Bettmann/Corbis.*

than one hundred wagons, and a herd of five thousand cattle. This rugged journey was repeated by other settlers each year after that. Thousands made the move to the Pacific Northwest during the 1840s and 1850s. The California Gold Rush of 1849 also drew thousands more across the United States: In 1848, when gold was discovered, the population of California (newly acquired from Mexico) was fourteen thousand; by the end of 1849 the population was estimated at about one hundred thousand. The Homestead Act of 1862, offering small parcels of land to those who would turn them into farms, brought thousands more.

The incredibly successful and rapid expansion of the United States signaled disaster for the original inhabitants of the land. Across the western lands, the Native Americans attempted to fight wars and even to prevail in court against the movement of the pioneers onto Indian lands, but they did not succeed. In 1830 Congress passed the Indian Removal Act, which began the forced migrations of thousands of Native Americans off their lands and onto reservations. In one of the most famous removals, the Trail of Tears of 1838, about fifteen thousand Cherokee were forced to march from their lands in Georgia to Oklahoma. The journey was made mostly on foot. As winter came on, many of the Cherokee fell ill and approximately four thousand Cherokee died en route.

Westward expansion was virtually complete at the end of the nineteenth century, but other migrations within the country continued. In the last decades of the nineteenth century, the United States took its place as the top industrial nation of the world. The large cities with their huge factories and plants became a magnet for laborers, drawing people from the rural South and elsewhere. The new American cities had a host of problems, including poverty, gangs, overcrowding, lack of sanitation, and infectious diseases. But with their diverse immigrant populations, they had also become the centers of a host of new American cultures. The populations of cities exhibited an amazing number of backgrounds and languages, with Little Italys, Chinatowns, Greektowns, and Irish, Arab, Hungarian, and Russian Jewish enclaves and many others. For example, more than 70 percent of San Franciscans in 1916 spoke a language other than English as their first language, often Chinese or Japanese. Groups had separated by region. Slavs (some eastern Europeans) settled in the mining regions of the upper Midwest and dominated the slaughterhouse industry in Chicago. African Americans migrated by the thousands from the South to northern industrial cities beginning in 1910. The combination of the huge influxes of migrating immigrants, industrialization, and urbanization (the process of forming cities) profoundly changed the United States in the early twentieth century, laying the basis of the culture today.

Third wave of immigration: 1945 to present

Post–World War II immigrants are considered to be the "third wave." Immigration laws relaxed in the first decades of this era. The Chinese Exclusion Act was lifted in 1943. The McCarran-Walter Act, also called the Immigration and Nationality Act of 1952, upheld the quota system of 1924, but removed race as a barrier to immigration and naturalization. In 1965 the Hart-Celler Act further eased the immigration restrictions, particularly by removing racial or national biases. The act repealed the national-origins quotas and gave each Eastern Hemisphere nation an annual quota of twenty thousand. The new law encouraged family reunification, particularly encouraging citizens whose immediate family members (spouses, children under 18, and parents) lived outside the country to bring them to the United States. Since the 1970s, the number of immigrants has been rising every decade. The third wave of U.S. immigration has been characterized by a rise in the numbers of immigrants from Asia, Latin America, and the Caribbean.

Between 1975 and 1988, after the war in Vietnam ended, some 900,000 refugees from Vietnam, Cambodia, and Laos entered the United States. The South Vietnamese, supported by the United States, lost the war in 1975, placing many people in jeopardy as the North Vietnamese took over. Because of the need to assist refugees from Indochina and other parts of the world, the United States passed the Refugee Act of 1980, setting a special quota of 50,000 for refugees and allowing the U.S. president to accept more, if necessary. The annual limit for total immigration to the United States was also raised from 290,000 to 320,000 people.

In 2000 more than one-half of the immigrants in the United States were from Latin America, one-quarter were

from Asia, and about one-seventh were from Europe. Mexico accounted for by far the largest number of immigrants, at one-quarter of the total immigrant population. The other top countries sending people were China, India, Korea, the Philippines, Vietnam, Cuba, the Dominican Republic, and El Salvador. There were 28.4 million foreign-born people living in the United States in 2000, making up about 10.4 percent of the total population.

Registering as an immigrant

In the 1930s air travel passengers flew on "flying boats" that took off and landed on waterways, simply because a system of runways for aircraft had not yet been developed. After World War II, the many runways built for military use could now be used for landplanes and many immigrants have simply flown to their new home. Cars, buses, and trains serve people within the American continent. While the ordeal of getting to North America may have stopped many potential immigrants in past centuries, today the obstacle is documentation. In 1940 Congress passed the Alien Registration Act, which required all noncitizens in the United States to register with the government. Today, if people desire to immigrate to the United States, they must start by applying for an immigrant visa from the U.S. consulate in their country, or they can apply for permanent residence in this country. If successful, the person will receive an alien residence card, commonly known as a green card. This gives the immigrant the right to live and work in the United States.

All documented noncitizens, or aliens, who live in the United States are called either nonquota or quota immigrants. Nonquota immigrants are the spouses, children, and parents of U.S. citizens. Other people who apply to live in the United States are called quota immigrants. Every year there is a limit as to how many immigrants can be admitted, and each country has its own quota. Most quota immigrants are family members, but not immediate family members, of U.S. citizens, or have a persuasive employment reason for coming here. Those prospective immigrants who do not have relatives or job prospects in the United States can try their luck in the annual U.S. Diversity Immigrant Visa Lottery program, or Green Card Lottery. The lottery makes available fifty-five thousand permanent residence visas, or green cards, through a computer-generated lottery drawing.

Undocumented immigration

Until the 1920s, there were no attempts in the United States to stop undocumented immigration across the border with Mexico to the south or the border with Canada to the north. The only border authorities were a force of fewer than forty mounted inspectors who rode the borders looking for Chinese migrants attempting to enter the country in violation of the 1882 Chinese Exclusion Act. Mexican workers were so valuable to the economy of the American Southwest that little effort was made to prevent them from crossing the Rio Grande (a river that forms the border between the United States and Mexico) to work for cotton and sugar beet growers and as farm laborers. A literacy test, used to ensure that someone could read, passed in 1917 and made it more difficult for many farm hands to enter the country. Many avoided the test

Border Patrol agents taking illegal immigrants into custody along the border of the United States and Mexico in 1993. *Reproduced by permission of © David Turnley/Corbis.*

by sneaking into the country at night, and enforcement was careless because few were concerned about these crossings. When the quota systems were put in place in the early 1920s, no restrictions were placed on the peoples of the Americas largely because farmers were dependent on a supply of migrant workers coming in across the Mexican border.

In 1924 a new anti-Mexican movement arose in the U.S. Congress. Politicians, using racist arguments, raised alarms about Mexicans in the United States. Mexicans made up the largest portion of immigrants from the New World. Almost 100,000 Mexicans entered the country legally in 1924. Thousands more had crossed the border illegally to escape paying the eighteen-dollar visa fee required of all immigrants under the new law. (The flow of Central and South Americans coming into the country numbered fewer than five thousand that year and was not perceived as a threat.) Labor unions argued that Mexicans were taking away American jobs and working for starvation wages. The unions began a campaign to include Latin Americans under the quota system that applied to the Eastern Hemisphere. But they had strong opposition from farmers and business owners, who argued that Mexican labor was far too valuable to the economy to exclude them. They also pointed out that Mexicans did the jobs other Americans simply would not do, for wages Americans would not accept. They would not become permanent residents, and they offered no political threat since they generally were not able to vote.

The debate continued and the federal government decided to take action. The United States Border Patrol was established on May 8, 1924, under the Immigration Act. The 1924 act mandated a ten-dollar visa fee and a six-dollar head tax for each applicant. Few Mexicans could afford these fees. For a small sum paid to smugglers, Mexican peasants could enter the country illegally. In its first year of operation, the small Border Patrol staff reported turning back fifteen thousand aliens seeking illegal entry, although an estimated one hundred thousand farm workers successfully evaded the border guards. In 1926 Congress doubled the size of the Patrol and made it a permanent part of the Bureau of Immigration and Naturalization. In 1929 Congress voted to double the size of the Border Patrol once again and demanded a crackdown on illegal entry. The creation of the Border Patrol made illegal entry into the United States much more difficult than it had ever been.

Most modern immigrants have come with papers and some prospect of a job or a family to help them. However, an estimated seven to nine million people in the United States in the first years of the twenty-first century came into the country without documentation. Approximately 70 percent of those undocumented immigrants are from Mexico. Many illegal immigrants are people who originally came to the United States with a visa—for example, a student visa allowing them to study at an American college. When the visa expires, the person just stays in the country. Other illegal immigrants cross the border illegally on foot or by car. Most do not intend to stay on a permanent basis, but come to work for a season, send money to their families at home, and then go back to join them.

During the 1990s the United States stepped up its border security, making it far more difficult to cross the Mexican–United States border undetected. Because of this, people who do cross are forced to enter the country at particularly dangerous spots. One of these crossings is a 260-mile stretch of the Sonora Desert in southern Arizona. Hundreds of immigrants die each year making the crossing in the rough terrain and in tremendous heat. Sometimes parents make it to the United States and then send for their children in Mexico. To get them across the border they hire a "coyote," or people smuggler, who charges excessively high fees. Coyotes have been known to leave people to die in the desert or to lock up people once they arrive in the United States until they get money for their passage. Smuggling brought in such profits in the early twenty-first century that former drug traffickers turned to dealing in human traffic. It is a very dangerous business for the migrants.

Tens of thousands of Mexicans still secretly cross the border each year. Some come because they cannot afford to feed their families on what they make in Mexico; for others with job skills, there seems no hope for a prosperous future for them in Mexico. Many are very unhappy here and return at the first chance, while others enroll their children in public schools and find a way to live in relative comfort without papers.

Mexicans are only one group, albeit the largest, of undocumented immigrants in the United States. Many Latin American countries are highly represented in this population. Thousands of Irish people, plagued by a depressed economy during the early 1980s, also came to America illegally. Failing to qualify under the preference system or as refugees, they arrived as tourists and stayed in the United States when their visas expired. An estimated five hundred thousand illegal Chinese immigrants entered the United States between 1984 and 1994. In 2000, the top fifteen countries from which undocumented immigrants arrived, besides Mexico, were El Salvador, Guatemala, Colombia, Honduras, China, Ecuador, Dominican Republic, Philippines, Brazil, Haiti, India, Peru, Korea, and Canada.

Amnesty, terrorism, and the debate about undocumented immigration

In 1986 President Ronald Reagan (1911–) signed the Immigration Reform and Control Act (IRCA). The act provided amnesty (pardon to a group of people) for undocumented

immigrants who could prove they had entered the United States before 1982. Three million undocumented aliens who had been living in the country obtained U.S. citizenship through this act. The measure also outlawed the knowing employment of undocumented immigrants and made it more difficult for undocumented immigrants to receive public assistance. Since that time, measures to protect the nation's borders from illegal entries have intensified. However, the U.S. economy was very strong and undocumented workers continued to find ways to enter the country, where work was easily obtained.

Debate in the United States about undocumented workers remains strong and unresolved. Clearly, a nation must have some control over who enters its borders. At the same time, since the country profits from the labors of millions of undocumented workers, and large corporations and farming interests are directly involved in bringing them into the country, there is a real contradiction involved in federal

Cuban immigrants trying to enter the United States illegally in April 1980.
Reproduced by permission of © Bettmann/Corbis.

policies that do not acknowledge the place of foreign workers in the United States. The debate about what to do about illegal aliens does not follow traditional political lines. Numerous big business interests depend on illegal workers; they would prefer to see some form of amnesty or guest-worker programs or at least relaxed immigration measures. Normally financially conservative, these interests are generally allied with the Republican Party. However, another large group of conservative Republicans is strongly in favor of taking drastic measures to further control illegal entry to the country, viewing the immigrants as an unwanted burden on the U.S. taxpayers. Some trade unions, usually allied with liberal interests and the Democrats, tend to side with the conservative Republicans in wanting to prevent illegal entries to the country. Their interest is to protect American workers from the competition and lower wages brought about by illegal workers. Even many documented immigrants fight to keep undocumented immigrants out of the country. For them, too, the competition is unwanted and some have expressed dismay that illegal behavior might be awarded by an amnesty program.

In the week before terrorists attacked the World Trade Center in New York City and the Pentagon in Washington, D.C., on September 11, 2001, Mexican president Vicente Fox (1942–) and U.S. president George W. Bush (1946–) were in the process of negotiating another possible amnesty program for the millions of Mexicans living in the United States illegally. The two presidents agreed on the premise that both countries gain economically from the exchange of labor that occurs between the borders. Bush had ruled out a blanket amnesty for illegal immigrants, but he brought up the idea of a program in which some "guest workers" could obtain green cards and gain legal residency in the United States. However, these negotiations abruptly ended with the terrorist attacks of September 11. After these attacks, new security measures were put in place to further protect the United States from illegal immigrants entering its borders. Within weeks of the attacks, federal agents arrested thousands of people on immigration-related charges.

The government's antiterrorist measures since the terrorist attacks of September 11, 2001, have made things more difficult for many documented immigrants as well as undocumented immigrants. In 2002 the new Homeland Security

Department began to require the annual registration of temporary male immigrants from twenty-four predominantly Arab or Muslim countries as well as North Korea. The countries are as follows: Afghanistan, Algeria, Bahrain, Eritrea, Iran, Iraq, Lebanon, Libya, Morocco, North Korea, Oman, Pakistan, Qatar, Saudi Arabia, Somalia, Sudan, Syria, Tunisia, United Arab Emirates, and Yemen. In 2003 Bangladesh, Egypt, Indonesia, Jordan, and Kuwait were added to the list. Of the 83,519 people who registered in 2002, 13,799 were put in deportation (being sent back to one's home country) proceedings. Others reported humiliating interrogations and harsh conditions during their registration process. Immigrant and civil liberties groups have been protesting the policy.

For More Information

Books

Daniels, Roger. *Coming to America: A History of Immigration and Ethnicity in American Life.* New York: HarperCollins, 1990.

Kraut, Alan M. *The Immigrant in American Society, 1880–1921,* 2nd ed. Wheeling, IL: Harlan Davidson, 2001.

Portes, Alejandro, and Rubén G. Rumbaut. *Immigrant America: A Portrait,* 2nd ed. Berkeley, CA: University of California Press, 1996.

Schmidley, A. Dianne. *U.S. Census Bureau, Current Population Reports, Series P23-206, Profile of the Foreign-Born Population in the United States: 2000.* Washington, DC: U.S. Government Printing Office, 2001.

Web Sites

"Coming to America Two Years after 9-11." *Migration Policy Institute.* http://www.ilw.com/lawyers/immigdaily/letters/2003,0911-mpi.pdf (accessed on February 26, 2004).

"Immigration." *Library of Congress: American Memory.* http://lcweb2.loc.gov/ammem/ndlpedu/features/immig/introduction.html (accessed on February 26, 2004).

Simkin, John. "Immigration." *Spartacus Educational.* http://www.spartacus.schoolnet.co.uk/USAimmigration.htm (accessed on February 26, 2004).

Immigrants in Motion: Getting There and Getting Started

2

Moving to a new home in a faraway place in the early twenty-first century can be complex, difficult, and expensive. Like immigrants of the past, twenty-first-century families who are thinking about immigrating need to plan ahead. They have to take care of things like shipping their belongings, finding a new home in a suitable neighborhood, and finding schools and health care facilities. Anyone migrating to a different country has a mountain of paperwork to do. If they move to a country in which they do not already know the language, there is much more to think about.

The act of moving has evolved greatly over the years. Today's immigrants are following in the footsteps of the earlier immigrants who overcame obstacles that are difficult for us to imagine. The hardships they endured in the process of immigrating (traveling to a country of which one is not a native with the intention of settling there as a permanent resident), migrating (moving from one place to another, not necessarily across national borders), and settling into their new homes brought about rapid changes in the systems of transportation, governmental administration, and education.

One of the remarkable and defining stories in the history of the United States is the process of hundreds of thousands of people—speaking different languages, practicing many religions, and offering a wide variety of skills and ideas—moving to new homes in a new nation.

Colonial immigration

During the era in which Europe was establishing colonies (groups of people living as a political community in a land away from their home country but ruled by the home country) in the Americas, the decision to immigrate always involved joining up with a colonizing expedition (a group of people making a journey together for a common purpose). It was nearly impossible to embark on the process of immigrating to the North American continent alone. Generally either the national government or a joint stock company (a group that organizes an enterprise and then sells shares of this enterprise to investors) organized the colonizing expeditions. In both cases, the purpose of establishing colonies was to provide long-term profit for the mother country. It was often difficult, however, to find people willing to risk their lives and part with everything they knew to go live in the New World.

The first European nation to colonize regions of the New World, Spain, had little trouble finding eager young men once gold had been discovered in the Caribbean and Mexico. Besides the lure of precious metals, Spain awarded *encomiendas* to the settlers—large parcels of land and the authority to rule over the Native Americans who lived there. In England and Holland, large trading companies organized the colonizing expeditions. They published propaganda (information spread to further a cause) to persuade people to go. The Dutch, desperately short of qualified settlers, tried a *patroon* system, promising large amounts of land to powerful aristocrats with authority to rule over the farm laborers who lived there as in an old European feudal estate (a system in which a local lord who had received his land from the king owned all the land and ruled over the people in his area.) Most Dutch people were still not interested in emigration. Both the French and the Dutch were very short of colonists and may have lost their New World empires partly because of it.

Fact Focus

- By the mid-nineteenth century, "America fever" swept through nation after nation in Europe, when thousands of people who were discouraged with their lot in life began to dream of going to America.

- With the mass migrations from Europe to the United States beginning in the 1850s, shipping companies were suddenly faced with hundreds of thousands of people trying to cross the Atlantic. They hastily created spaces in every nook of each ship, overcrowding their steerage-class passengers terribly. This overcrowding created conditions that were dangerous, unhealthy, and nearly unbearable for the passage to America.

- In 1855 New York created an immigration reception station called Castle Garden, located on the southwest tip of Manhattan in Battery Park. There, for the first time, people were processed as they entered the country.

- Ellis Island, a tiny three-acre island situated in New York Harbor, became the official U.S. immigrant screening station in 1892. From 1892 to 1924 Ellis Island processed thousands of immigrants each day.

- In 1910 the Angel Island Immigration Station in San Francisco Bay became the point of entry for most of the 175,000 Chinese immigrants who came to the United States between 1910 and 1940.

- When the United States was still a new nation in 1790, about 95 percent of the total population resided east of the Appalachian Mountains. By 1840, about 33 percent, or one-third, of the nation's population lived between the Appalachians and the Mississippi River.

- By 1840 overland roads were crowded from early spring to late fall with settlers moving westward.

- During the latter half of the nineteenth century, bilingual education programs thrived in the United States. In 1900, an estimated six hundred thousand elementary students in the United States were being taught many of their standard subjects by teachers speaking in the German language.

The European colonists who decided to make the journey were in for a very difficult and dangerous trip. The voyage across the Atlantic could take from one to three months on sailing ships. If the voyage went on too long, due to uncooperative winds or poor navigation (setting the course of the ship), there was a chance that the food and water supplies would run out. Navigation to the New World

Antique compasses lie atop a map of the New World and the Atlantic Ocean that dates to the seventeenth or eighteenth century. Navigation to the New World was new and very dangerous during those times. *Reproduced by permission of © Richard T. Nowitz/Corbis.*

was still in its infancy. Even if the voyage went smoothly, arriving in the New World was very dangerous. The early colonists had urgent work to do once they arrived. They needed to quickly build rough homes to keep them warm in their first winter and prepare food to get them through their first season. To create a farm, it was first necessary to clear forests, a daunting task that could take years of hard labor. The colonists needed to have with them all the manufactured supplies they needed to build homes, prepare farms, and lead their daily lives, because getting more supplies was a very long ordeal. Planning ahead was vital, and many of the first colonists in Jamestown died because they were not prepared for their first winter. In the early colonial days, the colonies had a difficult time maintaining a population because so many people died. Many colonists gave up and returned to their original country. By the end of the seventeenth century, however, the population in the colonies soared. This was largely due to the high rate of births in the

Words to Know

Assimilation: The way that someone who comes from a foreign land or culture becomes absorbed into a culture and learns to blend into the ways of its predominant, or main, society.

Bilingual education: A system of education in which students who speak languages other than the nation's primary language are instructed at least partly in their native language.

Colony: A group of people living as a political community in a land away from their home country but ruled by the home country.

Emigration: Leaving one's country to go to another country with the intention of living there. Loosely, "emigrate" is used to describe departing *from* one's country—for example, "she emigrated from Ireland." "Immigrate" is used to describe coming *to* a new country—for example, "she immigrated to the United States."

Encomienda system: A system in which the Spanish nobles, in return for taking part in a war, were granted a large section of land and the right to rule as lord over the nonreligious people on that land.

Expedition: A group of people making a journey together for a common purpose.

Immigration: To travel to a country of which one is not a native with the intention of settling there as a permanent resident.

Industrialization: The historic change from a farm-based economy to an economic system based on the manufacturing of goods and distribution of services on an organized and mass-produced basis.

Joint stock company: A group that organizes an enterprise, such as trading in a certain overseas market, and then sells shares of this enterprise to investors.

Mass migration: Times in history when thousands, or even millions, of people from one country or area have immigrated to a new country or area within a short period of time.

Migration: To move from one place to another, not necessarily across national borders.

Navigation: Setting the course for ship travel.

New World: The western hemisphere, including North and South America.

Old World: The regions of the world that were known to Europeans before they discovered the Americas, including all of the eastern hemisphere—Europe, Asia, and Africa—except Australia.

Steerage: An area below the ship's deck. For a period of time in the mid-nineteenth century to the early twentieth century, steerage compartments of ships were overcrowded with immigrants and conditions in steerage were notoriously bad.

Transatlantic: Crossing the Atlantic Ocean.

New World. With more colonists already here to provide advice and aid, the new colonists had an easier time and the death rates rapidly decreased.

Despite the hardship and death toll of the colonial expeditions, their journey to the New World was generally voluntary, with the exception of some prisoners who were sent to labor in the New World as punishment. Whether the colonists emigrated to make money, practice their religion freely, or to escape the social or economic limitations of their home country, they generally looked to the New World with the hope of a better future. Not so for Africans, who were captured and sold to slave traders. Bound together and marched to the African coast where European slave vessels awaited, these people never chose to leave their homes or to provide lifetimes of labor for strangers across the sea. On the miserable journey from Africa to the Americas, men, women, and children were bound hand and foot and crammed into tiny spaces to make room for the maximum cargo. They remained in that space for much of the voyage, which in the sixteenth century could last from twelve to twenty weeks. The sanitation needs of the captives were largely ignored. Seasickness and dysentery (severe diarrhea) created appalling conditions. Infectious diseases quickly spread in the close quarters. Many tried to jump overboard or to starve themselves, and there were some rebellions at sea. When the Africans arrived in the New World, most were immediately sold at auction. About five hundred thousand new Americans arrived in the country under these nightmarish circumstances.

First and second wave, 1800–1921

After the United States was formed at the end of the eighteenth century, the initial reluctance of Europeans to immigrate turned gradually into an overwhelming rush to go, as the early immigrants sent news about the New World to their family and friends in the Old World. By the mid-nineteenth century, nation after nation suddenly was filled with what has been called "America fever," when thousands of people who were discouraged with their lot in life in Europe began to dream of going to America. There, they heard, there were plenty of jobs, open land to farm, political and religious freedom, and no structured social ranks. News of the United States reached even the tiniest villages in remote areas of Russia, Finland, and Greece. Newspapers reported on it; people received letters from former neighbors who had already gone. Shipping companies, eager for the business of transporting the swarms of immigrants, published books and pamphlets intended to encourage anyone entertaining the idea of going into doing it.

By the nineteenth century, European people tended to make the decision to emigrate on an individual or a family basis. For such a huge decision, family, friends, and even distant relatives were often consulted. Having decided to go, a family of immigrants would frequently have to sell almost everything they owned and perhaps borrow money as well to get enough money to pay for ship passage, food and necessities for the voyage, and, once there, to reach a destination within the United States and get started in the new country. Many immigrants from Europe and Asia during the eighteenth and nineteenth century joined a friend or a relative who had already immigrated. In fact, from 1900 to 1910, it is estimated that 95 percent of the people who checked in at Ellis Island were meeting friends or family in the United States. Most families opted to send one member ahead to the United States to settle in and find work. The whole family might work to earn passage for the father or the oldest son to immigrate first. When that first person was able to send home money for passage, one or two other members or the rest of the family would follow. Toward the turn of the twentieth century, around half of the immigrants to the United States had received their passage from a relative already in the country.

Buying a ticket on a ship heading for the United States was relatively easy because there were ticket agents throughout most European countries. Tickets could be bought in one of three categories: first class, second class, and steerage (the enclosed lower deck space of a ship). Steerage tickets cost about thirty-dollars. After 1900 it was also necessary to get a passport and a visa, an official document permitting a person to enter the country. Before railroads connected the European ports (harbors from which ships embarked to the New World) to the countryside, traveling to the port city with one's possessions was a great ordeal. As emigration picked up, it was common in Europe to see heavy traffic on the roads heading to ports as people with all their belongings packed into a pushcart or a small wagon made their way to find a ship. The port cities were often full of petty criminals who took advantage of inexperienced travelers. If the ship was not ready to go, or there was difficulty in getting a passport or a visa, an immigrant might have to wait in the port for weeks before setting sail.

Transportation across the Atlantic

Many American writers have noted the miserable condition of the immigrants who crowded the docks upon arriving in the United States in the nineteenth century. Some of the writers looked on with contempt, probably unable to imagine the conditions aboard many of the immigrant ships. Anyone disembarking from the steerage section of a ship from Europe was almost certain to be filthy, exhausted, sick, and terrified. Thousands died on these transatlantic journeys (journeys across the Atlantic Ocean).

The earliest sailing ships that took immigrants from Europe to the New World were generally cargo vessels whose primary function was to transport livestock, produce, cotton, manufactured products, and in some cases, slaves. They were not built to carry passengers. Prior to the mid-nineteenth century, these cargo ships would usually take on several passengers in addition to their cargo. But as the mass migrations of the Irish and the Germans got underway, the shipping lines were suddenly faced with hundreds of thousands of people trying to cross the Atlantic. (Mass migrations are times in history when thousands, or even millions, of people from one country in the Old World have immigrated to the New World within a short period of time.) Shipping companies became extremely competitive for this huge new business, rapidly creating spaces in every nook of each ship for passengers, and often relying on old, rickety boats that were ready for the scrap heap to keep up with the overwhelming demand. Enterprising shipping agents often paid the shipping company for the entire steerage area of a ship. Then the agents sold tickets to prospective immigrants, crowding as many as humanly possible into a limited space and charging enough to double or triple their investment. A large ship, for example, could squeeze from fifteen hundred to two thousand people into its steerage decks. At thirty dollars a head, it was highly profitable to do so.

Although some ships were better than others, by almost any account the transatlantic voyages of the eighteenth and nineteenth centuries were terrible, and on some ships, the experience was dangerous and deadly. On the decks, tiny berths (living areas) were hastily erected for second-class passengers. They were generally about six feet square and there were two levels, one on top of the other. Each square was to hold a family and all its belongings. The families on the deck shared their space with the ship's livestock. Tickets for the steerage section below were cheaper and the conditions much worse. The dark steerage decks were deep inside the ship, usually allowing no exit into fresh air during the journey. They were usually wedged in between the ship's machinery, which emitted dirty smoke. There were not enough toilet facilities for all the passengers and no place to clean up. People who became sick had no way to get outside. The smell in the steerage area was often unbearable. People were crowded in close—each in an area no more than a few square feet—

Andre Basset's hand-colored etching "La Nouvelle Yorck" depicts the Manhattan waterfront around the eighteenth century. *Reproduced by permission of © Corbis.*

An arriving immigrant family on Ellis Island looks across the harbor to New York. *Reproduced by permission of © Bettmann/Corbis.*

for the entire trip, which would probably last about five weeks. There was no privacy.

Infectious diseases spread quickly on many ships, and the dead were buried at sea with a short ceremony. In 1847, as hundreds of thousands of Irish fled the potato famine, an outbreak of typhus (an infectious disease transmitted by fleas and lice) on the ships carrying them to the New World caused an estimated seventeen thousand deaths. In 1853 Asiatic cholera (an infectious, often fatal disease) killed thousands, often as many as 15 percent of the passengers on an affected ship.

Provisions (food and drink) onboard were generally very basic—flour, tea, salted fish, potatoes, grains, and drinking water. In many cases the passengers were responsible for their own food. When weather or other disasters caused delay in the ship's arrival in the United States, there were cases of starvation. As if these horrors were not enough, there was also the constant fear involved in being at sea, where a small fire could rapidly engulf the ship or a storm could sink it. Like the ships that carried the slaves over from Africa, many of these overcrowded ships were called "coffin ships" because so many of their passengers died.

Sometime around the 1850s, new shipping lines began to use ships that were built to handle passenger business. England and the United States tried to enforce shipping regulations that would protect passengers from the worst abuses of corrupt companies. In some cases the shipping lines were fined for each passenger who died while aboard their ships. By the end of the 1860s and early 1870s, steamships (large vessels propelled by one or more steam-powered propellers or paddles) had replaced many of the old sailing vessels. The steamships cut the time of travel down to about ten to fourteen days. Although diseases still spread on board, these ships improved the voyage. Steamships opened the way for even more immigration, as many people who had been unwilling to risk a month or more on an old sailing ship could handle ten days on a steamship. However, through the 1920s, there were still many reports of horrible conditions in steerage compartments of ships.

In 1891 the United States government required the steamship companies transporting passengers from overseas to give the passengers a physical examination and to vaccinate and disinfect them prior to setting off to sea. The U.S. immigration agents inspected the arriving passengers. People with infectious diseases were quarantined and often sent back to their home country at the steamship company's expense. By the turn of the twentieth century, some shipping companies had done away with steerage accommodations and replaced them with third-class quarters. Although the third-class accommodations were far from luxurious, they were more comfortable than steerage.

In his book *The Huddled Masses: The Immigrant in American Society, 1880–1921,* Alan M. Kraut summarizes the impact of the transatlantic experiences of nineteenth- and early twentieth-century immigrants: "The details of the journey's hardships suggest that even before reaching America, the migrants began a readjustment in their lives. They learned to live in close proximity to those from different countries practicing different customs and worshipping God in ways unlike themselves. Many began the slow and painful process of compromising some of their own values and customs to the demands of the environment. And finally, most newcomers in the steerage mastered the art of survival under the severe stresses and strains of daily life in a strange environment, far from the support of family and friends. Immigrants were weaning themselves from the Old World even before they landed in the New World."

Arriving

New York City was the port of entry of the vast majority of immigrants before 1855. About two-thirds of all immigrants passed through the city. Before state or federal regulations for arrival were in place, landing there was a confusing event. An army of fast-talking swindlers came aboard the incoming ships to relieve unsuspecting immigrants of their money. Peddlers, tavern owners, and boarding-house agents all attempted to sell the immigrants things they did not want or need, usually at outrageous prices. The people who did not speak English were particularly vulnerable.

In the 1850s the federal government did not have a policy for regulating incoming immigrants. With so many people passing through its port in New York City, the State of New York established an immigration commission in 1855 to regulate the landing procedures and license the agents and vendors who sold goods and services to the newcomers. New York also created a reception station called Castle Garden (called Castle Clinton National Monument today), located on the southwest tip of Manhattan in Battery Park. There, for the first time, people were processed as they came into the country. The station's purpose was to prohibit entrance to the United States to people who had infectious diseases. It also regulated the vendors at the port. Castle Garden operated as an immigrant-landing depot for thirty-five years, processing over eight million immigrants. By the end of the 1880s, it was apparent that Castle Garden could not accommodate the masses of immigrants pouring through its halls.

Around that time, the era of unrestricted immigration into the United States was coming to an end. The federal government began to legislate who could enter the United States, notably through the Chinese Exclusion Act of 1882,

which prohibited Chinese people from entering the country and barred them from citizenship. In order to enforce these restrictions, the government established the House Committee of Immigration in the 1880s. The committee took over the processing and regulation of incoming immigrants, choosing Ellis Island, a tiny three-acre island situated in New York Harbor about one mile from the southern tip of Manhattan Island, to be the official U.S. immigrant screening station. The government had purchased Ellis Island from the State of New York in 1808, initially using it as a fort and later an ammunitions arsenal (storage area). Construction on the immigration station began in 1890, but first, the island was made several acres larger by using landfill (alternate layers of trash and earth). The huge twelve-building depot opened for business in 1892.

The original buildings at Ellis Island featured a shower facility capable of bathing eight thousand people each day. The famous registry room, or Great Hall, was two hundred

A view of the immigration station at Ellis Island in New York. *Courtesy of the Library of Congress.*

feet long and fifty-six feet high. A "line inspection" by a physician included a test in which the unsuspecting immigrants were made to haul their luggage up a staircase so the inspector could judge their strength. The inspector then marked the immigrants with infirmities with a chalk letter, such as L for lameness, G for goiter (swelling of the thyroid gland in the front of the neck), or X for mental illness. Those who failed the exam were detained; some, after a few days of rest and nourishment, were able to pass. Of the average three to four thousand people who passed through Ellis Island each day, about 80 percent were admitted without delay.

Those denied admission to the United States were given free return passage by the shipping companies, because the government held these companies responsible for delivering sick immigrants. If a child over the age of twelve was too ill to be admitted to the country, he or she was sent back to the home country alone. If the child was under age twelve, however, it was required that an adult accompany the child back to the home country. Sometimes families had to make a very emotional decision about who was to go back with the child.

The original building at Ellis Island burned to the ground in 1897 and another was built with many more buildings and facilities. Meantime, two more islands were created by loading tons of landfill in the harbor next to the first island. The new islands made room for the masses of immigrants passing through the island. From 1892 to 1924 Ellis Island processed thousands of immigrants each day. In 1907, one of the peak immigration years, Ellis Island processed well over one million immigrants.

Immigration was temporarily halted during World War I (1914–18). The hostilities of the war provoked a strong anti-immigrant attitude within the American public. In the 1920s Congress passed restrictive legislation as to which nationalities, and how many members of each nationality, could enter the United States. The admission of immigrants to the country fell drastically below the prewar level. Since the reduced numbers of immigrants could be screened onboard the ships on which they arrived, Ellis Island lost its importance as an inspection center by the 1930s. By World War II (1939–45), the island handled only new arrivals being detained and aliens being deported. In 1954 it closed down altogether.

Angel Island

The first major restriction of immigration to the United States was the Chinese Exclusion Act of 1882. Under this act the only Chinese immigrants allowed to enter the United States were government officials, merchants, students, teachers, visitors, and those claiming U.S. citizenship. All potential immigrants of Chinese descent, both new arrivals and returning U.S. residents, if admitted, were subjected to medical scrutiny and an elaborate questioning process before being released.

In 1910 the Angel Island Immigration Station in San Francisco Bay became the point of entry for most of the 175,000 Chinese immigrants who came to the United States between 1910 and 1940. The site held hundreds of people at a time, many of them women and children, for up to two years while they proved their eligibility for residence. In an attempt to bypass the exclusion laws and enter the country,

One of the barracks at the Angel Island immigration station. *Photograph by Hope Cahill. Reproduced by permission of Connie Young Yu.*

Famous Quotations about Immigration

- "Here is not merely a nation, but a teeming nation of nations." From Walt Whitman's poem, *Leaves of Grass*, Book XXIII.

- "Since 1607, when the first English settlers reached the New World, over forty-two million people have migrated to the United States. This represents the largest migration of people in all recorded history. The importance of immigration to America is that every American who ever lived, with the exception of one group, was either an immigrant himself or a descendant of immigrants. We can only speak of people whose roots in America are older or newer. Yet each wave of immigration left its own imprint on American society; each made its distinctive contribution to the building of the nation and evolution of American life." John F. Kennedy. *A Nation of Immigrants*. New York: Harper & Row, 1967.

- "We must also lift by legislation the bars of discrimination against those who seek entry into our country, particularly those who have much needed skills and those joining their families. In establishing preferences, a nation that was built by the immigrants of all lands can ask those who now seek admission: 'What can you do for our country?' But we should not be asking: 'In what country were you born?' For our ultimate goal is a world without war, a world made safe for diversity, in which all men, goods, and ideas can freely move across every border and every boundary." Lyndon B. Johnson, State of the Union Address, 1964.

- "Remember, remember always, that all of us, and you and I especially, are descended from immigrants and revolutionists." Franklin D. Roosevelt.

- "Remember that when you say 'I will have none of this exile and this stranger for his face is not like my face and his speech is strange,' you have denied America with that word." Stephen Vincent Benet.

- "My ancestors didn't come over on the Mayflower, but they were there to meet the boat." Will Rogers.

many young immigrants procured false papers, claiming to be related to resident Chinese. To trap these "paper sons and daughters," new arrivals were asked hundreds of questions before an inquiry panel. Witnesses were called to corroborate their testimony, and each side's answers had to be identical. Anyone who failed the interrogation was held for deportation. The long detentions of those awaiting deportation often led to despair and sometimes even to suicide. People confined to the barracks at Angel Island carved poems in the walls that remain to this day. These poems expressed the immigrants' impressions of their voyage to the United States, their longing for families back home, and the outrage and humiliation they felt at the unjust treatment they endured. In 1924, a smuggling ring was exposed on Angel Island. Immigration authorities were charged with taking bribes from immigrants for allowing them to enter the country illegally. In 1940, when a fire destroyed the administration building, the government abandoned the immigration station.

Westward expansion

The American Revolution (1775–83) ended in 1783 with the Treaty of Paris, in which Great Britain ceded, or turned over, to the new United States all the territory between the Atlantic Ocean and the Mississippi River except New Orleans and Spanish Florida. The new country stretched for more than one thousand miles in every direction. However, most Americans lived along a tiny ribbon of settlement along the Atlantic seaboard at the close of the eighteenth century. The grand new maps rolling off American printing presses, showing the huge realm of the United States, failed to account for the fact that much of that territory was occupied and governed by the tens of thousands of Indians who had traditionally lived there. Most of the European American settlers did not venture very far West. In fact, about 95 percent of the population of non-Indians resided east of the Appalachian Mountains.

In the early decades of the nineteenth century, the population of the United States increased dramatically, with a high birth rate and millions of people arriving in the United States from other lands. The growing population needed food and other goods to sustain itself, and the country sought farmlands and farmers to move westward to farm them. Thus, the federal government promoted westward expansion. But it first had to deal with the people who already lived on the land in the West. After the United States fought the two-year War of 1812 with Great Britain, the British agreed not to give any more aid to the Native Americans. It was a devastating blow. Without supplies to help in their fight against the United States, the Indian nations east of the Mississippi River fell entirely under the control of the U.S. government. By the

1830s the government adopted a policy of forced removal of Indians to territory west of the Mississippi.

With less threat of attack, pioneers began to set out for the West. The government did what it could to facilitate their migration, offering free land to those who would farm it and subsidizing the building of roads, railroads, canals, even mail systems. Between 1830 and 1850 an estimated four million people migrated to the West.

The Old Northwest, the region northwest of the Ohio River that became the states of Ohio, Indiana, Illinois, Michigan, and Wisconsin, drew the first westward mass migrations, resulting in the creation of the states of Indiana (1816) and Illinois (1818). So many settlers poured into the Old Southwest region that Mississippi and Alabama were admitted as states into the Union by 1819. By 1830 there were probably twenty thousand Americans in Texas, which still belonged to Mexico. During the 1830s the movement to Michigan and Arkansas reached such large proportions that they, too, were admitted as states to the Union. Illinois nearly tripled in population, and two new territories, Wisconsin and Iowa, were created. By 1840 fully one-third of the nation's thirteen million people lived between the Appalachian Mountains and the Mississippi River.

During the 1840s frontier expansion continued into Wisconsin and Iowa, and thriving American settlements appeared on the Pacific Coast. Prior to the 1840s, people traveling to the West Coast either arrived on ships from Asia or took a ship down around Cape Horn at the southernmost tip of South America and then up the Pacific Coast—a journey that often took a year to complete. Only a few hardy explorers had crossed the rugged paths across the North American continent. But in the 1840s, pioneers began to traverse the 2,000-mile-long Oregon Trail from Independence, Missouri, to the Pacific Northwest. In 1846 and 1847 the Mormons (members of the Church of Jesus Christ of Latter-Day Saints) were forced to leave Missouri because their religious beliefs and their strong style of government clashed with the beliefs of their neighbors. Tens of thousands of Mormons made a mass migration, creating their own trail across part of the nation to get to their new home in Utah. At the close of the decade came the mad rush of thousands of people of every

Map of the Northwest Territory as it appeared after the spread of the Northwest Ordinance of 1787. *Reproduced by permission of the Granger Collection, Ltd.*

description to the newly discovered gold fields in California. During the decade of the 1850s, migration to Oregon, California, and Texas continued unabated. New converts swelled the population of the Mormon colony in Utah, and the Territory of New Mexico attracted thousands of settlers.

Modes of travel

The pioneers determined to settle in the West faced a difficult journey. As obstacles to overland travel arose, however, new solutions were found. Stagecoaches expanded their established routes and—despite thick dust and turbulent shaking inside the stagecoaches—carried people to destinations across the continent. Steamboats traveled up inland rivers and through the canals that were being built. Roads were laid, and bridges opened routes across waterways. By 1870, the railroads had connected the United States from the Atlantic Ocean to the Pacific Ocean.

Fulton's Steamboat

In 1807, the first practical, reliable steamboat began its trials on the Hudson River. Built by American engineer and inventor Robert Fulton (1765–1815), the 150-foot *Clermont* steamed from New York City to Albany in thirty-two hours. A sailing sloop took four days for the same trip. Soon, steam-powered river craft were carrying people and goods along many of the nation's waterways. In 1815 a steamboat left New Orleans and ascended the Mississippi River to Louisville, Kentucky, providing long-distance transportation into the new territories. The success of these new steam-powered crafts led to the disappearance of the slower keelboats, but flatboats, another familiar form of river transportation, continued to carry people and goods down river. The Ohio and Mississippi River systems bore seventy steamboats by the early 1820s and five hundred by 1840.

Smaller roads had connected the colonies prior to the formation of the new republic, but the roads West were primarily built in the nineteenth century. The Santa Fe Trail, the first of the pioneer roads, was created in 1822 and stretched between the Mississippi River and the Far West. The National Road, initially funded by the federal government, stretched from Cumberland, Maryland, to Columbus, Ohio, by 1833. The first pioneers intending to settle in the Pacific Northwest set out on the Oregon Trail in 1834. The Oregon Trail started at Independence, Missouri, and ran along the Platte River in the Midwest, over the Rocky Mountains to Utah, Wyoming, and Idaho, and down the Columbia River to the fertile Willamette Valley, Oregon, the destination of many of the pioneers. Once the gold rush started in California in 1849, many took a southern fork off the Oregon Trail to reach California.

In 1843 about one thousand people set off on the Oregon Trail to settle in the West. This migration was continual for the next quarter of a century, creating hundreds of American settlements in Oregon and California. The Oregon Trail was so rough that many died in their travels. In fact, an estimated 10 percent of all who set out on the trek died before reaching their goal. Most died of diseases, exposure to harsh weather, and accidents—drowning, accidental gunfire, or falling under wagons, among many others.

By 1840 overland roads were crowded from early spring to late fall with settlers moving westward. The typical migrating unit was the family, moving to a new home in the West with their belongings in a single covered wagon, with perhaps a cow or two. For most, migrating from the Midwest to the West was a four- to six-month journey. Some migrating farmers or plantation owners were wealthy enough to put together a large caravan of well-supplied wagons, but the more common sight was a family with a two-wheeled cart, pulled by a horse or an ox. Many made the journey to a new home in the West on horseback or by foot. Generally speaking, only the driver of the animals rode in the wagon. The rest of the family walked—in fact, many made the long trip with no shoes. The wagons were full, packed with furniture and other supplies that desperately would be needed to set up housekeeping on the frontier.

By 1869 the railroads had traversed the entire continent, giving pioneers an alternative route to the West. With railroad connections, it was no longer necessary to situate towns and cities on waterways, and new communities began to appear throughout the Great Plains and the Pacific Northwest. By the 1890s, the frontier was considered settled, and when Arizona was annexed as a state in 1912, it was the last of the forty-eight contiguous states (connecting or bordering states, meaning all the states except Alaska and Hawaii) to join the Union.

Canals

On October 26, 1825, the Erie Canal officially opened. The canal stretched more than 350 miles from Buffalo, New York, on Lake Erie to the Hudson River at Albany, New York. The canal had taken eight years to build and had cost about $7 million. New York's accomplishment became a huge and immediate success for the state. For two decades the United States went through an upsurge in canal construction. State governments rushed to connect cities and regions with rivers and lakes. Other canals appeared throughout the Northeast and Midwest, but no other man-made American water channel ever witnessed more transportation of goods than the Erie Canal, which carried more than one million tons of cargo in 1845.

Learning the ropes

By 1850 industrialization had greatly changed the nation's major cities. (Industrialization was the historic change from a farm-based economy to an economic system based on the manufacturing of goods and distribution of services on an organized and mass-produced basis.) Although most Americans continued to live in rural areas, nearly one out of every five people lived in cities. By 1880 that proportion would double to 40 percent. From only six cities that had populations of one hundred thousand or more in 1850, there

Immigrants on the Lower East Side of New York around 1890. *Reproduced by permission of © Bettmann/ Corbis.*

would be nineteen in 1880, including one—New York—with over one million inhabitants.

With rapid industrialization, the social roles and economic outlook of the city's social classes became more firmly set: the wealthy became very rich and powerful and the poor became locked into a cycle of poverty. With the arrival of millions of immigrants, by the end of the century the cities were overcrowded beyond their capacity. With steep competition among laborers, newly arrived immigrants faced a struggle just to earn a living wage. The urban neighborhoods in which these immigrants lived were filled with overcrowded tenements that lacked kitchens and bathrooms. Tenants drew water at a sink or pump in the hallway and used unsanitary bathroom facilities in the basement.

Shaped in large measure by the need for cheap housing, ethnic neighborhoods also reflected the desire of many first-generation immigrants to maintain connections to their country of origin. They were knit together by bonds of language, religion, and ethnic identity that were often also regional. Although it was rare for an ethnic group to monopolize an entire neighborhood, each group occupied particular blocks or streets. There, immigrants could buy familiar food, speak their native language, and find that their customs and traditions still had relevance. Mutual-aid societies, such as the Sons of Italy, provided basic services such as life insurance. Churches were crucial anchors in ethnic neighborhoods, with the parish priest functioning as spiritual leader, social worker, and mediator between old customs and the demands of what was for many newcomers a bewildering urban world. Most ethnic groups had their own newspapers that preserved their language and published news from the old country. Saloonkeepers and ethnic politicians helped immigrant workers find jobs and resolve disputes. Those immigrants who came with some money in their pockets, or with valuable skills, opened small grocery stores, butcher shops, boardinghouses, and other institutions that knit ethnic communities together.

As the economy (in which the rich did well and workers earned barely enough to survive) and overcrowding made settling in the new country more and more difficult, the settlement-house movement was established to help immigrants and the working poor. Settlement houses helped newcomers adapt to American life and customs by providing job placement and training, citizenship classes, legal aid, health services, childcare, public kitchens, cultural programs, and classes on subjects such as nutrition and parenting. Created in most major cities, settlement houses were staffed mainly by educated middle-class white women who "settled" among the people they helped. The movement was not financed by government funds and depended solely on the labor of charitable women and men. The first settlement house in the United States was Hull-House, founded in Chicago in 1889 by Jane Addams (1860–1935). Many others quickly followed. In 1893 Lillian Wald opened the Henry Street Settlement in New York City, and graduates of Wellesley College opened Denison House in Boston. By 1900 there were some one hundred settlement houses nationwide, through which immigrants received much-needed assistance in learning to become self-sufficient in the new country.

Public schools

By the 1850s American educational reformers, led by politician and educator Horace Mann (1796–1859), had established publicly supported "common schools." Most wealthy citizens of the time disliked the idea of public education. Their children went to private schools, and the privileged classes did not wish to be taxed to finance the education of poor immigrant children. The argument that convinced them of the need for public schools was that these schools could "Americanize" the immigrants, who were often distrusted or looked down upon by the well-to-do. Public schools were to teach immigrant children to speak English and to make good citizens of them.

Many immigrants did not immediately see much value in the school system. Italians and Poles arriving in the country distrusted the public schools that taught their children values that were foreign to them. Irish Catholics fought hard to eliminate the anti-Catholic teachings that had become commonplace in the schools. They also established parochial, or religious, schools to educate their children in the way they saw fit. Many immigrant families did not send their children to school because they needed their children to work and bring in an income to help support the family. As a result, immigrant children frequently dropped out of school at an early age; before World War I, only a small minority completed high school. On the other hand, some groups of immigrants, like the Jews and the Japanese, for example, favored education and urged their children to attend school.

One of the problems faced by public-school educators in the mid-nineteenth century was the high absentee rate among immigrant children. During this period the first compulsory school attendance laws (laws that required all children under a certain age to go to school) began to be passed by state and local legislatures. Prior to the 1850s, lawmakers tended to avoid any measure that might be viewed as interfering with parents' rights with respect to child rearing. By mid-century, however, the flood of immigration led to a sense of an impending social crisis. Educators reported that they could not Americanize immigrant children in the schools if the children did not attend. Corps of truant officers could be seen in the major cities, making sure that school-aged children were off the streets.

Adult immigrants were also recipients of educational reform aimed at rushing them through some assimilation processes, the processes through which someone who comes from a foreign land or culture becomes absorbed into a culture and learns to blend into the ways of its predominant, or main, society. In 1921, the National Education Association (NEA) established the Department of Immigrant Education. This voluntary association for public-school educators organized "Americanization" classes for adult immigrants. Later the term "Americanization" was replaced with the term "adult education."

Languages

During colonial times in the Americas, many languages could be heard throughout the continent. Besides English and the numerous Native American languages, German, Spanish, Dutch, French, Swedish, and Welsh were regularly spoken. English was not the only language to be considered as the primary language for the new nation. Many of the founding documents were prepared in French and German.

After the first and second waves of immigration in the nineteenth century, a wide range of different languages— German, Scandinavian, Chinese, Italian, and Polish, to name but a few—could be heard spoken on the streets of American cities and in country villages as well. The United States sometimes tolerated the language differences comfortably and sometimes reacted against them.

In the first half of the nineteenth century, the most prevalent language next to English was German. Many German Americans found it very important to maintain their native language and took political action to make sure their children could be educated in the German language. By 1850, bilingual schools (schools in which two languages were taught; in this case, German and English) were operating in Baltimore, Cincinnati, Cleveland, Indianapolis, Milwaukee, and St. Louis. In Ohio and Missouri, German American parents succeeded in their efforts to get laws passed that mandated that teachers speak in German when teaching the standard subjects when a quota of parents in the community wanted it.

Similarly, Louisiana, with its large French-speaking population, passed a law allowing bilingual instruction in its schools. When Mexico ceded California, New Mexico, Arizona, and other parts of the Southwest to the United States after the Mexican-American War (1846–48; a war fought between the United States and Mexico over possession of Texas and other lands now in the southwest United States), the Treaty of Hidalgo gave the citizens of those areas the right to speak their native tongue—Spanish. The constitution of the state of California, drawn up in 1849, required that all of the state's laws be published in both Spanish and English. In 1900, an estimated six hundred thousand elementary students in the United States were being taught in the German language. Around that time, however, several states began to legislate against teaching in other languages, particularly German. In 1906 the United States enacted an English-speaking requirement to become a citizen of the country.

In 1914 the outbreak of World War I pitted the German armies—leagued with Austria-Hungary and Turkey—against the United Kingdom, France, Russia, and eventually the United States. In the United States, German Americans suddenly became the faces of the enemy and they were subjected to violent harassment. Anything remotely "German" was attacked and destroyed. Books were burned, street names changed, and German businesses boycotted. Music by German composers like Ludwig van Beethoven (1770–1827) was removed from public performances. Hamburgers, sauerkraut, and dachshunds were renamed "liberty burgers," "liberty cabbage," and "liberty hounds." German Americans were physically attacked, tarred and feathered, and even killed. Many German Americans went underground, hiding their ethnicity and attempting to blend in as much as possible with mainstream American society to avoid attack. Many changed their names to sound more American. New immigrants made efforts to lose their German-ness as quickly as possible. In the years during and after World War I, repeated legislation prohibited German instruction in the schools, public or private. Even teaching German as a foreign language was generally prohibited for a time.

The backlash against German Americans began during wartime, but lasted long after the war was over. The ill will extended to most non-English-speaking immigrants. Somehow, speaking the English language became associated with loyalty and "being American," which had not been true in earlier times. By the 1920s, American schools no longer allowed bilingual education, and several states had enacted "English only" policies in their schools. Many educators believed that they were helping non-English speaking students by placing them in English-only schools where they were to learn by "immersion." Statistics show, however, that the immigrant children forced into classes in a language they did not understand were not well served. In 1908 only 13 percent of the twelve-year-old immigrant children who were enrolled in New York City schools would go on to high school, as opposed to 32 percent of the native born. This trend was mirrored across the country, as non-English-speaking immigrant children, not understanding the language of instruction, fell further and further behind their native-born classmates. One of the methods educators applied to some of the

non-English-speaking children was to tag them as mentally retarded or learning impaired. Once so characterized, these children were placed in remedial (corrective) instruction programs, where they were constantly reminded how different they were from their native, English-speaking classmates.

After World War I the United States changed from a multilingual nation (many languages) to a monolingual nation (one language). It remained a one-language country until the 1950s, when the Spanish language started to become prevalent in many parts of the country. Mexicans were migrating into California and Texas in large numbers. Many of the people of New Mexico had retained their Spanish language. In New York, Spanish-speaking Puerto Ricans were arriving in large numbers. After the Cuban Revolution of 1959, thousands of Cubans fled to Florida. There, a new bilingual-education program evolved. In 1968, Congress passed the Bilingual Education Act, which funded states with bilingual-education programs. Many states then put together programs.

In 1974 the Supreme Court ruled on a class-action suit bought to it by eight-year-old Kenny Lau on behalf of eighteen hundred students in the San Francisco School District. There, a school with a majority of its students speaking only Chinese was teaching under the English-only system. The Court ruled that the school was not providing equal education to all its students because it did not have special provisions for the language-minority students. After this ruling, the government funded more bilingual-education programs nationwide. During this period, test scores repeatedly showed that students exiting from well-designed bilingual programs consistently performed at or above grade level and thus were on a par with their native English-speaking classmates.

By the 1980s, the number of immigrants in the United States who did not speak English as their first language rose sharply. Some Americans began to question bilingual programs in the schools. They argued that the aim of bilingual education was not to speed immigrants into the mainstream but rather to help them maintain their culture through state-sponsored programs. The government began cutting back in its sponsorship of bilingual education. In California, with its large population of foreign-born residents, public attitudes grew increasingly hostile to immigrants. In 1998 California voted to eliminate all state bilingual-education programs, adopting an English-only requirement for instruction in its schools. Arizona followed with similar legislation two years later.

For More Information

Books

Kraut, Alan M. *The Huddled Masses: The Immigrant in American Society, 1880–1921,* 2nd ed. Wheeling, IL: Harlan Davidson, 2001.

Web Sites

"American West: Transportation." *World-Wide Web Virtual Library's History Index.* http://www.ku.edu/kansas/west/trans.htm (accessed on February 26, 2004).

Hogan, Róseann Reinemuthe. "Examining the Transatlantic Voyage," Parts I and II. *Ancestry Magazine,* March 1, 2001. http://www.ancestry.com/library/view/ancmag/4130.asp (accessed on February 26, 2004).

Pre-Columbian Migrations: The First American Immigrants

3

The earliest immigrants to the Americas arrived thousands of years ago. There are no written records of their migrations or of the migrations of the later generations that settled throughout the Americas. (Migration differs from immigration in that it can take place within one country, while immigration involves moving across national borders.) From the bone remains and the artifacts (products made by the people of earlier periods) that the earliest Americans left behind, some facts are known about them, but in many important ways, these early Americans remain a mystery. Science shows that human beings did not originate on the American continents—no remains of early forms of humans have ever been found there as they have been found in Africa, Europe, and Asia. Thus, according to most scientific studies, the first Americans were immigrants to the land who traveled to North and South America by boat or walked across long-vanished land bridges over the sea. Who these people were, where they came from, and when they came is still very much in question. In contrast, many Native Americans believe their ancestors originated on the American continents

Much of what we know about the pre-Columbian people comes from ruins, artifacts, and remains. Archaeologists and anthropologists, the people who recover and examine these relics, are pictured here as they work in a small Chacoan Culture archaeological site in New Mexico. *Reproduced by permission of © Dewitt Jones/Corbis.*

and did not immigrate there at all. Oral traditions (history, mythology, folklore, and other foundations of a culture that have been passed by spoken word, often in the form of stories, from generation to generation within a culture group) strongly link tribal origins to the land on which the tribes traditionally lived.

In this chapter, most of the information about the arrival of the first immigrants and their migrations through the American continents—North and South America—comes from the evidence uncovered by archaeologists (scientists who study past human activity by uncovering and examining fossils, artifacts, and buildings from earlier eras). They have pieced together some proven facts and then made some theories (assumptions based on careful analysis of the available information) about what the evidence means. The result is a tale of immigration not unlike later tales: The earliest Americans were pioneers who faced danger and extreme conditions in a new and strange environment, probably to make

Fact Focus

- The last full ice age, the Pleistocene, began about 1.8 million years ago and ended about 10,000 years ago.

- Around 10,000 years ago, many large mammals—such as the mammoth, the mastodon, the American lion, the western horse, the western camel, the stagmoose, and the giant beaver—became extinct within just a few hundred years.

- One of the great seats of the mound-building Mississippian culture was Cahokia, in present-day western Illinois. An estimated thirty thousand people lived in and around Cahokia at any given time during the period from 1050 to 1150 C.E. About five square miles wide, Ca-hokia contained more than one hundred mounds situated around central plazas.

- The Anasazi, who thrived from about 400 C.E. until the thirteenth century in the Southwest, built remarkable communities in the walls of canyons. Pueblo Bonito was a very influential Anasazi religious and trading center in Chaco Canyon, New Mexico. More than four hundred miles of roadways led out to surrounding villages.

- In 1000 C.E. Norse explorer Leif Eriksson set out from Greenland and apparently sailed to Vinland, in present-day Newfoundland, Canada. Leif's settlement in Vinland lasted between three and ten years.

better opportunities for themselves and their families or to avoid danger or hunger in their current location. After many generations of traveling to new regions, groups of these first Americans began to settle, and they adapted to the specific environments in which they settled. Their societies were built around using the local resources—fishing, farming, hunting, gathering, or trading. As they settled, they populated the Americas with a wide variety of lifestyles, political systems, art styles, languages, and social traditions.

Ice ages and the Great Ice Age

Before the first humans arrived, the North American continent was a very different place than it is today, and not simply because the human influence was missing. Perhaps the most overwhelming difference was the climate. Throughout its history, Earth has experienced long periods in which the weather was very cold. During these periods, called ice ages, large masses of ice, or glaciers, have built up from snow accumulations. These glaciers moved slowly across the land, growing larger and then shrinking back as the weather cooled and warmed. In extremely cold periods within an ice age, glaciers will grow to cover vast areas. Those frigid periods within an ice age when the glaciers are at their largest are called "glacial" periods.

The last full ice age, the Pleistocene, began about 1.8 million years ago and ended about ten thousand years ago. The Pleistocene reached its maximum glacial period about twenty thousand years ago, with ice sheets covering nearly one-third of Earth. That last glacial period has come to be known as the "Great Ice Age" (with capital letters to set it apart from the term "ice age," referring to the longer eras). During the height of the Great Ice Age twenty thousand years ago, two huge ice sheets covered northern North America from Greenland to British Columbia. By about fifteen thousand years ago, the ice sheets had begun to shrink, but parts held on, particularly in Canada and down the West Coast of what is now the northern United States.

A time of giant mammals

A second difference between present-day North America and how it was fifteen thousand years ago is the assortment of animals that lived there. Extremely large and often very dangerous animals roamed through the land in large numbers. There were beavers as large as today's brown bears; massive, tusked elephantlike creatures called mammoths and mastodons; huge stag-moose; giant armadillos the size of cars; giant ground sloths (mammals that live in trees and hang upside down from the branches) that could grow as large as present-day elephants; ferocious saber-toothed tigers; and gigantic and deadly short-faced bears. There were also ice-age variations of horses and camels (the western horse and western camel, for example), giant tortoises, and many other animals that later became extinct (no longer existed) on the continent. (Europeans would bring horses back to the Americas in the sixteenth century). Animals had been migrating to the North American continent from Asia and South America for millions of years. They were able to do so

Words to Know

Anthropologist: A scientist who studies human beings in terms of their relations with one another, race and ethnicity, populations, migrations, and culture.

Archaeologist: A scientist who studies past human activity by uncovering and examining fossil relics, artifacts, and monuments from earlier eras.

Arctic: The northernmost region of North America, with its shores on the Arctic Ocean. It includes parts of Alaska, Canada, and much of Greenland.

Artifact: A product made by humans of an earlier period.

Band: A social and economic group of nomadic hunting people.

Chiefdom: A society in which a person's rank and prestige is assigned by how closely he or she is related to the chief.

Culture: A way of life shared by a group of people who have things such as art, religion, and customs in common with each other.

Ecosystem: A natural community of plants, animals, and microorganisms living in relation to each other in a particular habitat.

Hereditary: Passed on from generation to generation along family lines.

Longhouses: Long buildings that housed many families, usually associated with the Iroquois.

Maize: A variety of corn initially cultivated in Mexico that became an important food source for many Native Americans.

Mesoamericans: People from the cultural area located in present-day Mexico and most of Central America where civilizations such as the Mayans and the Aztecs lived before European contact.

Migration: To move from one place to another, not necessarily across national borders.

Nomads: People who travel and relocate often, usually in search of food and other resources or a better climate.

Oral traditions: History, mythology, folklore, and other foundations of a culture that have been passed by spoken word, often in the form of stories, from generation to generation within a culture group.

Pre-Columbian era: Before the arrival of Spanish explorer Christopher Columbus in 1492.

Ritualistic: Performing ceremonial acts in about the same way each time.

Theory: An assumption based on careful analysis of the available information.

Tundra: Bitterly cold plains consisting of a layer of mud and vegetation covering permanently frozen soil.

because land bridges between continents had formed during the peak glacial periods.

The Bering land bridge, or Beringia

When glaciers form, they freeze up vast quantities of water that would otherwise return to the oceans. Because of this, the water levels of the oceans go down. As the water level lowers, it exposes higher lands usually covered by the sea. Scientists believe that glacial periods beginning about one hundred thousand years ago lowered the sea level by 300 to 400 feet from where it stands today, exposing a vast land bridge between Siberia in northern Russia and North America, at present-day Alaska near the Bering Strait. This link between Asia and North America probably remained exposed until about twelve thousand years ago, when it once more vanished under the rising ocean as the Great Ice Age ended.

Beringia, or the Bering Land Bridge, would not have appeared to be a bridge at all. It was a 1,000-mile-wide prairie covered in grasses and brush, with rivers flowing through it and swamps forming in its flooded areas in the warmer seasons. This vast territory, above the sea for tens of thousands of years, became home to many large mammals. Scientists believe that humans followed the routes of big game (large animals) from Siberia out into Beringia. Until the end of the twentieth century, many scientists thought these people were the first immigrants to the Americas.

It is likely that immigrants crossing the Bering land bridge to North America came from northeastern Asian areas such as China, Siberia, and Mongolia. It is also quite likely that they traveled back and forth across Beringia over many generations in their search for big game and other food. They were able to protect themselves from the frigid weather with protective clothing and they were armed to kill the giant mammals, such as the mammoth and mastodon, many of which were dangerous killers. There could not have been many of these early people in one area at any one time because the very limited food supply could only feed a small number. Many historians believe that at some point, probably between twelve and fifteen thousand years ago, humans began to travel from Beringia onto the North American conti-

Bronze Age cave paintings with hunting scenes found in Norway. These cave paintings probably date as far back as 4500 B.C.E. *Reproduced by permission of © Archivo Iconografico, S.A./Corbis.*

nent, which was still covered by ice sheets in the north. From there, they migrated throughout North and South America.

New evidence, new mysteries

For almost a half century most scientists have believed that the people who crossed from northeastern Asia to Beringia were the first immigrants to the Americas, but new evidence has brought this into doubt. By the early twenty-first century, archaeologists have proved that at least a few of the first migrations to the Americas were earlier than had been widely believed. There is also evidence that they may have come from different populations than the later migrations. Skeletons found in South America that are more than eight thousand years old belonged to a group of people that are now being called Paleoamericans. The skeletons appear to have quite different types of skulls, as a group, than the type of skull that modern Native Americans and their ancestors have. These very old skulls feature long, narrow brain cases and short, thin faces. The skulls are similar to the ancient skulls of populations from places like southeast Asia and the southern Pacific, like those of aboriginal (native) Australians. The more broad-cheeked skulls of modern Native Americans in both North America and South America and the remains of skulls of their ancestors, who are called Paleo-Indians, are very similar to the skulls of the people of northeastern Asia.

Some anthropologists (people who study human beings in terms of their culture and society, physical characteristics, and origins) and archaeologists think the Paleoamerican people may have already been in the Americas before the Paleo-Indians arrived from northeastern Asia. A skeleton, the famous Kennewick Man, was found in Washington State in 1996. Dating back 9,200 years, the remains of Kennewick Man had different skull characteristics altogether, more like skulls from Europe or India. It may be that instead of one great first migration to the Americas, there were actually many migrations over the years. Recently, examinations of some two-thousand-year-old skulls in Baja, Mexico, showed them to be of the Paleoamerican type rather than the Paleo-Indian type. This finding might mean that the Native American ancestors lived on the American continents with people of different origins who have since disappeared. Many Native Americans are offended by this kind of speculation, since they do not believe their ancestors were immigrants at all. Perhaps the one clear point to be made about this investigation into American roots is that there are many things that are simply not known at this time.

The early Americans

Wherever they came from, evidence shows that the earliest immigrants to the Americas were nomads, people who traveled and relocated often, usually in search of food and other resources or a better climate. They survived by gathering roots and vegetables and by hunting with very simple stone tools and weapons. They traveled in small groups and lived in tents, caves, or temporary shelters so they could easily move on to a new home. They dressed in animal skins and clothing made of plant fibers. These early Americans hunted the giant mammals—the wooly mammoth and mastodons and the plentiful bison. They probably

Kennewick Man

In July 1996, two men watching a boating race on the Columbia River near the eastern Washington town of Kennewick found part of a human skull in the river. When most of the rest of the skeleton was found, the local coroner (a public official who investigates the circumstances of deaths not due to natural causes) and an anthropologist found the remains to be more than nine thousand years old, making the Kennewick Man one of the oldest and most complete skeletons ever to be found in the United States. The anthropologist described the remains as "Caucasoid," a term that generally refers to people of the white race, from European, North African, or southwest Asian origins.

In 1990, the United States passed a law to protect the rights of Native American groups to bury the remains of their dead. The law, called the Native American Graves Protection and Repatriation Act (NAGPRA), was created in response to disrespectful handling of Native American remains in the past. It was an important step in forcing museums and government agencies to return the remains and cultural objects of Native American groups to them. The law requires that any new remains be reported to the related Native American tribal group for burial. In order to claim the remains for burial by the tribal group under NAGPRA, a specific tribe must prove that the remains are in some way related to their tribal group. In the past, any remains over five hundred years old have been considered to be Native American.

Several tribal groups—the Umatilla, Nez Perce, Yakama, Colville, and Wanapum—claimed Kennewick Man as an ancestor they call "the ancient one," and made plans to bury the skeleton. The government agreed and was about to give the skeleton to the Native American groups, when eight anthropologists sued to stop the government. The anthropologists, who wished to study Kennewick Man and believed that he could provide a great deal of information about the first American peoples, argued in court that there was no proof that Kennewick Man was related to the Native Americans who claimed him. The case, which remained in the courts in 2003, placed a new emphasis on some old questions: Who were the first Americans? Where did they come from? Were they all ancestors to the Native American tribal groups that live in the Americas today?

hunted the big game by herding them into gullies (ditches or channels cut in the earth by running water) and then killing them. Smaller animals were bludgeoned to death. When the animals they hunted or the plants they gathered for food became scarce, the group moved on to new territory, sometimes a few miles away, but often farther.

Clovis arrowheads. Clovis points—sharpened rocks that were attached to lances or spears for hunting—are identifiable because they are grooved at the base and show remarkable craftsmanship. *Reproduced by permission of © Warren Morgan/Corbis.*

Clovis culture and the extinction of the great mammals

By about 11,500 years ago, a group of Indians known as the Clovis culture had spread throughout most of North America and parts of Central America. A culture is a way of life shared by a group of people who have art, language, religion, and customs in common with each other. Archaeologists have been able to easily identify the Clovis culture by its artifacts, particularly its stone points. Clovis points—sharpened rocks that were attached to lances or spears for hunting—are identifiable because they are fluted, or grooved, at the base and show remarkable craftsmanship. The points were often made from stone that came from hundreds of miles away, showing that Clovis people were accustomed to traveling long distances. The Clovis people used their stone weapons to hunt the giant mammals. They also carried stone tool kits that included blades and scrapers for cutting the meat and cleaning the hides of their game.

The Clovis era, which coincided with the end of the Great Ice Age, was a time of tremendous change in the Americas. In many places, extreme shifts in weather brought about major alterations to ecosystems (the natural communities of plants, animals, and microorganisms living in relation to each other in a particular habitat). Less rainfall in some areas meant that once-green valleys became desert areas. Receding glaciers in the north formed new lakes and canyons. Forests disappeared in some places, or appeared in others. Even plants moved to places where the weather was favorable—dying out in one area and then arising in another and, over time, another. Archaeologist J. M. Adovasio, in his book *The First Americans: In Pursuit of Archaeology's Greatest Mystery*, explains that during the Clovis era: "the living things of North America were undergoing what was one of the more traumatic times in the history of the earth. For people living here at the time, the world may well have seemed an unstable place. Familiar animals might suddenly disappear, seeking their favored food, which had also gone somewhere else. What might have been a good place for your parents might change into something that would not support you. People would have been on the move."

Around the time of the Clovis culture, between twelve and eight thousand years ago, many large animals became extinct. For example, the mammoth, the mastodon, the American lion, the western horse, the western camel, the stag-moose, and the giant beaver all disappeared between 10,500 and 10,200 years ago, and those are just a few of the many disappearing species. The extinctions occurred when two unique events were taking place on the continent. The Ice Age was ending, causing many climate and landscape changes, and human beings—the Clovis era hunters and their followers—had arrived. The extinctions were probably due to the dramatic change in the climate. Some researchers believe that the Clovis people were so good at hunting that they helped bring about the extinction of their prey, but evidence for this theory is lacking.

Cultural development in North America before agriculture

The Clovis culture was probably in existence for only a few hundred years. By the time it disappeared—that is, when the special stone points that identified the culture were no longer being made—the American continents had experienced a large increase in human population. By the end of the Clovis era there were hundreds of human settlements throughout both American continents. Responding to the climate changes, people had moved about the land, finding places where life was more stable. In these places, small groups developed their own habits and tools as was best suited to their particular region. As the population in North America increased, groups of people began to live in smaller areas. There was less interaction among the different groups of people, and differences in lifestyles became apparent.

For example, in about 6000 B.C.E. in what is now southwest Texas, the Coahuiltecan (pronounced koe-uh-WHEEL-teh-cahn) people formed a distinct culture that lasted until the Europeans arrived in the sixteenth century. Coahuiltecan people lived in small bands (social and economic groups of nomadic hunting people). They fished in the Pecos and Rio Grande Rivers, hunted rabbits with throwing sticks, and gathered plants.

In about 5500 B.C.E. a group of cultures emerged in southern California that based their economy on coastal resources such as shellfish. These cultures remained in existence until about 1000 C.E.

In about 5000 B.C.E. hunting and gathering groups began to live in small camps in the Arctic. (The Arctic is the northernmost region of North America, with its shores on the Arctic Ocean. It includes parts of Alaska, Canada, and much of Greenland.) The hardy groups that inhabited the Arctic hunted caribou, elk, deer, and moose in bitterly cold plains called the tundra, which consisted of a layer of mud covering permanently frozen soil. Only certain plant life, such as moss and some shrubs, can survive in the tundra. The people who lived in this region had to develop very special tools and techniques in order to survive.

From 4500 to 2500 B.C.E. people in northeastern California were the first known groups in North America to build sturdy earth lodges in permanent villages. In the later part of this period, however, the climate became dry, and many groups were forced to leave their homes.

In 2000 B.C.E. groups of hunters and fishers became the first humans to live in the eastern Arctic, one of the world's harshest environments. These people were the ancestors of the modern Inuit (IH-noo-wet; formerly called Eskimos). They developed remarkable technology such as special harpoons for hunting seals, walrus, and whales.

The rise of agriculture, communities, and trade

In around 2500 B.C.E the rise of agriculture in North America changed the social patterns of Native American groups. Hunters and gatherers had tended to live in small bands that moved frequently and therefore did not form complex social and cultural patterns. But when care was taken to plant a crop, a band would usually stay in one place to reap the harvest. As farming methods and tools developed, permanent communities with some form of government often followed.

An illustration depicting the migration of the Aztecs as they traveled into the Valley of Mexico.
Reproduced by permission of © Gianni Dagli Orti/Corbis.

Farming came to different areas of North America at different times. It was well established in parts of South America and central Mexico before it emerged in what is now the United States. Sometime around 2000 B.C.E. people in the East began farming native plants such as squash, sunflowers, marsh elder, and may grass. By 500 B.C.E. agricultural practices among southeastern groups brought about a change from nomadic lifestyles to community life in small, permanent villages. Newly developed pottery skills allowed storage of foods. In about 350 B.C.E. beans and squash were introduced in the Southwest. By about 1 C.E., societies in what is now Kansas seem to have been regularly growing maize, a variety of corn initially cultivated in Mexico that became an important food source for many Native Americans. By 100 C.E. maize had become a major crop there.

Mississippian cultures in eastern North America

In eastern North America in around 1500 B.C.E. a series of complex societies known as the "moundbuilders" arose. They had advanced farming skills and the ability to store their grains with pottery. The moundbuilders practiced ritualistic (performing ceremonial acts in the same way each time) burial practices that involved building large earthen mounds. Over the centuries they built thousands of these large, intricate mounds throughout the Southeast and Mississippi River Valley. Some of the mounds were shaped like animals and some like pyramids. In fact, in the Ohio River Valley alone, ten thousand mounds have been found. Poverty Point, the Adena Culture, and the Hopewell Societies were moundbuilder cultures that thrived from about 1500 B.C.E. to 700 C.E. The moundbuilder societies gave rise to the Mississippian cultural tradition around 700 C.E., which lasted there until the Europeans arrived, continued in places for around a century, and disappeared completely in about 1750.

The Mississippian people built farming communities along the banks of rivers, where irrigation occurred naturally through seasonal flooding and long-distance traders could bring goods in and out in their canoes. Many of the Mississippian groups formed elaborate social and political systems. Leadership was hereditary (passed on along family lines) and the villages developed into chiefdoms, societies in which a person's rank and prestige is assigned by how closely he or she is related to the chief. Mississippians built hundreds and perhaps even thousands of awe-inspiring conical burial mounds and some of the first flat-top mounds in North America. The flat-top mounds were probably built beneath temples or homes of important people in the village. As the culture developed, the houses in a village were often grouped formally around the plazas (public squares) and the earthen mounds. The city or village was enclosed by palisades (fences made out of stakes for protection against enemies). Inside were elaborate gardens.

One of the most spectacular Mississippian centers was Cahokia. Cahokia was about five square miles wide, and contained about a hundred mounds situated around central plazas. Some of the mounds were huge. Monk's Mound, for instance, at sixteen acres wide, was the largest known earthen mound or

building known in the pre-Columbian era (before the arrival of Spanish explorer Christopher Columbus in 1492) of North America. An estimated thirty thousand people lived in and around Cahokia at any given time during the period from 1050 to 1150 C.E. Sometime after 1200 the city began to decline.

In 1540 Spanish explorer Hernando de Soto (c. 1500–1542) and his army of six hundred men explored some of the vast Mississippian territory in what is now Florida, Georgia, Alabama, North and South Carolina, Tennessee, Mississippi, Louisiana, Arkansas, and Texas. They were amazed at the elaborate Mississippian cities they found. But by that time most of the Mississippian tribes were in decline, and the infectious diseases spread by de Soto's army probably caused many deaths among the people, who had no immunity (resistance) to the diseases carried by the Europeans. Twenty years later, when explorers returned to the area, the tribes de Soto's teams had encountered were gone. Those who had survived had probably gone to live with other Native American groups.

The Southwest

In the Southwest (of the present-day United States) about two thousand years ago, the Mogollon (meaning "mountain people") were the first to develop agriculture in the high-desert region. They disappeared in about 1400 C.E. and were probably the ancestors of the Hopi and Zuñi, present-day Indians of the Southwest.

The Hohokam (pronounced huh-HOE-kum, meaning "vanished ones") lived in central and southern Arizona from about 150 B.C.E. to about 1450 C.E. Because the Hohokam were highly skilled in many of the arts and techniques of the Mesoamericans (people from the cultural area that lies in present-day Mexico and most of Central America where the Mayans, Aztecs, and others developed complex civilizations), many historians and archaeologists believe the Hohokam migrated to the Southwest from central Mexico in about 300 B.C.E. It is also possible that they picked up the strong Mesoamerican influence on their culture through regular trading with Mexico. Like the Mesoamericans, the Hohokam built elaborate irrigation systems to maintain their maize, bean, squash, and cotton crops. Their irrigation canals stretched out hundreds of miles, and some individual canals were up to 10 miles long. Irrigation made it possible to farm in the desert, and the Hohokam were very successful, producing an abundance of food.

The Hohokam lived in earthen rectangular pit houses within small farming villages. They had many trading and religious relationships with other groups in the Southwest as well as with people from northern Mexico. They played a ball court game similar to one played in Mesoamerica and built pyramid-like mounds. With influences from all around, they created a very unique and complex culture. The Hohokam were the ancestors of the modern-day Pima-Papago Indians. No one knows why they disappeared in the middle of the fifteenth century.

The Anasazi emerged in about 400 C.E. in the Four Corners region of present-day Arizona, New Mexico, Utah, and Colorado. They, too, had been hunter-gatherers with a nomadic way of life. But during the first century C.E. they took up a settled way of life, raising crops such as maize, beans, and squash. They also became highly skilled artists, making beautiful baskets and pottery with distinctive black-on-white geometric patterns.

Later, they built remarkable communities in the walls of canyons with large multiroomed "apartment" buildings. One of these buildings had more than twelve hundred rooms. The Anasazi also built Pueblo Bonito, a very influential religious and trading center in Chaco Canyon, New Mexico. There were more than four hundred miles of roadways from Chaco Canyon leading out to villages near and far, and many of the roads were thirty feet wide. The Anasazi were the ancestors of the modern-day Pueblo Indians. The Anasazi disappeared in about the thirteenth century and the reason is unclear.

A section of an Anasazi house, the Cliff Palace, located at present-day Mesa Verde National Park in Colorado. *Photograph by Ansel Adams. Reproduced by permission of the National Archives and Records Administration.*

The Great Plains

Various cultures developed in the river valleys of the Great Plains, a vast area in the central United States and Canada bordered by the Mississippi River on the east and the Rocky Mountains on the west. The Indians on the Great

First Migrations to Hawaii

About five thousand years ago, a group of seafaring people, probably starting from a home base in Southeast Asia and New Guinea, began what would be centuries of migrations across the waters of the Pacific Ocean in their large canoes. At first their ocean migrations took them short distances to nearby islands. Eventually, though, their navigational and boat-building skills had become so advanced that they could make voyages thousands of miles long. They sailed into, and colonized, the islands and archipelagoes (groups of islands) of Indonesia, Micronesia, and Fiji and then moved on to the Polynesian islands of Tahiti and Samoa. (Polynesia is comprised of volcanic and coral islands in a large area of the Pacific, including the Hawaiian Islands, Samoa, Cook Island, French Polynesia, Tuvalu, Easter Island, and the large islands of New Zealand).

These ancestors of the Polynesians were far ahead of Europeans in their navigational and colonizing skills. They were masters of observational techniques, using the stars, the ocean currents, the flight patterns of birds, and other natural signs to guide them thousands of miles through the open oceans. Their typical sea craft was a double canoe with two hulls (frames) that provided stability and carrying capacity. The canoes were powered by sails and by long paddles. With a central platform for living and working space, a normal-sized canoe could carry twenty to twenty-five people along with the supplies needed for a long ocean voyage and for colonizing a new island. The Polynesians, understanding what was involved in settling an uninhabited island, brought with them plants and animals so they could establish small farms to sustain themselves in their new habitat.

The remote islands of Hawaii had been uninhabited for thousands of years when the first settlers arrived in about 400 C.E., probably coming from the Marquesas Islands in what is now French Polynesia. All of the Hawaiian Islands had been settled by ongoing migrations by about 900. From what can be gathered through the oral traditions of the Native Hawaiian people and from archaeological finds, the early Polynesians led a peaceful existence on the islands until about 1200, when another migration occurred, this time from Tahiti. The new settlers overpowered the people already living there, imposing their religion and customs on them, and perhaps even enslaving them. Many scholars believe that the original group of Hawaiians was somewhat smaller in size than the later immigrants. Hawaiian legends featuring the *menehunes,* or local elves, may be based on the newcomers' impressions of Hawaii's first inhabitants.

When English sea captain James Cook (1728–1779) arrived in Hawaii in 1778, the population there was probably between half a million to a million people. Although the islands had no metals and the people were limited to stone utensils, their methods of agriculture and social organization were advanced.

Plains spoke a wide variety of languages, including the Algonquian, Siouan, Caddoan, Uto-Aztecan, Athabascan, and Kowan-Tanoan languages. Because bison were so plentiful, most of the Plains Indians had a nomadic lifestyle as hunters. The bison, or buffalo, gave them food from its meat, shelter and clothing from its hide, and tools constructed from its bones. Several groups in the Plains developed farming communities along the major rivers and built earth-covered, multifamily houses.

The Northeast

From 1000 to 1300, people along the Saint Lawrence River Valley in New York and Ontario began to build small villages and to farm maize, beans, and squash for the first time in this area. By the end of the period they were constructing multifamily longhouses (long buildings, usually associated with the Iroquois, that housed many families). Some of the longhouses were more than two hundred feet long. The villages were surrounded by walls and other fortifications suggesting that warfare was probably an important part of life. These people were the ancestors of the Iroquois.

The Vikings: Visitors from Europe

Could there have been other migrations to North America over the thousands of years of unrecorded human history? It is likely that, over the centuries, ships from very distant lands lost their course and landed on American shores. Many scholars have expressed doubt that there were ships seaworthy enough in pre-Columbian times to enable large numbers of people to travel by sea to the Americas. There is a notable exception to this theory. The Scandinavian Peninsula, which in modern times is the home of Norway and Sweden, was home to some of the most skilled boat builders of the Old World: the Vikings. They did travel by boat to the New World.

The term "Viking" arose in England and seems originally to have applied to the Scandinavian pirates who were famous for their attacks on coastal regions during what is called the Viking Age, the eighth to the thirteenth century C.E. In that

The Vinland Sagas

A great deal of what is known of Erik the Red and later stories of the Viking's North Atlantic adventures was told in the *The Vinland Sagas,* which includes the *Greenlanders' Saga* and *Erik the Red's Saga.* These stories were written down in the thirteenth century C.E. by someone who was attempting to transcribe (write down) the oral traditions that accounted for the voyages in the North Atlantic. The stories are said to document the first European encounters in the New World and early meetings with the Native American people. However, the sagas were written down centuries after the events took place, and stories tend to change—to become more heroic and adventurous, usually—over the course of time and many tellings. Still, these are remarkable documents that have provided great insight into the historical events.

time Scandinavian vessels raided a wide variety of places in England and the rest of Europe and even Russia and North Africa. In the following years, the Norse settled down in a variety of the countries they had raided. The word Viking has come to be used to refer to the Scandinavian explorers, traders, and colonizers of later eras, and it should be noted that these were not the seafaring warriors whose raids instilled fear in coastal towns. Modern United States culture often inaccurately portrays all Vikings as stereotypical barbaric warriors.

In about 870 C.E. a group of Norwegian farmers migrated to Iceland, an island about 570 miles west of Norway lying between the North Atlantic and the Arctic Oceans. Under a Scandinavian process called *landnám,* or "land-taking," any settler who went there was given a parcel of farmland. By 930 there were approximately thirty thousand people in Iceland, and a parliamentary government (a government made up of members of the country's aristocracy [or upper classes], clergy, and common people) was established.

Erik the Red and Leif Eriksson

In 982 the Iceland parliament banished a troublemaker from Iceland for a period of three years. His name was Erik the Red. After his banishment, Erik the Red (950–1005) headed west and found Greenland, a huge island in the Arctic Circle in northeastern North America. He then returned to Iceland and organized a group of people to colonize Greenland. The island was uninhabited in the south, and the new colonists instituted *landnám* in several areas.

Sailors returning to Greenland from a storm-tossed voyage in the late tenth century told tales of new lands they

had seen to the west. There were three different areas that the Greenlanders named and described: Helluland, Markland, and Vinland. (Helluland is now thought to be southeastern Baffin Island, in the eastern part of the present-day Northwest Territories in Canada; Markland is now thought to be Labrador, Canada; and Vinland is thought to be Newfoundland, Canada, and part of the Gulf of Saint Lawrence). Erik the Red's son, Leif Eriksson (c. 971–1015), set out to explore the new lands with other family members and explorers. In 1000 C.E. the party first set foot in the New World. Although investigators do not know for certain how far into North America their travels led them, new evidence of the Leif Eriksson party's stay on the continent emerged in 1961 when archaeologists found L'Anse aux Meadows—the Meadow Cove site—in Newfoundland, which dates to 1000 and is thought by many to be the settlement from which the party carried out its explorations. Leif's settlement in Vinland lasted between three and ten years. According to the sagas,

Sod Houses at L'Anse aux Meadows in Newfoundland, Canada, a Viking settlement dating back to 1000 that was discovered in the 1960s.
Reproduced by permission of © Wolfgang Kaehler/Corbis.

the Norse were eventually driven out by constant attacks of the Skraelings, the Norse word for native peoples.

Excavations (digs) at the Meadow Cove site turned up evidence of three timber-and-sod longhouses (long buildings in which several families live together, usually found among northeastern tribes) and some smaller buildings that probably served as a charcoal kiln and a small iron smithy. There were hundreds of eleventh-century Norse artifacts at the site. Although it is the only settlement that has been found in North America to date, archaeologists have found many artifacts that suggest a strong Norse influence on some of the Native American groups in the area.

Old World and New World meet

The lands that the Viking explorers encountered were by no means uninhabited in 1000. The people of the Dorset culture had been living in Helluland, northern Greenland and the eastern Canadian Arctic, since about 300 B.C.E. Although there is only a little evidence of contact between the Vikings and the Dorset people, many historians and archaeologists speculate that there was some trade between the two groups. The Dorset had walrus skins and ivory to trade for the iron the Vikings may have brought with them. The Thule people had lived in northern Alaska until about 1000 C.E., when they migrated into the western Canadian Arctic, where the Dorset people lived. Over the next few centuries, the Dorset culture disappeared and the Thule prospered. Like the Dorset people, the Thule desired iron and likely would have traded with the Norse for it. It is also possible that they attacked the Vikings to rob them of their goods. Many Norse materials were found in one Thule village, although there are a variety of ways they could have gotten there.

In Markland and Vinland, the Vikings probably encountered the ancestors of today's Innu. (The Algonkin-speaking Innu were formerly known as the Montagnais/Naskapi and were enemies of the Inuit.) When the Viking ships sailed into the shores of Newfoundland, where they established the Meadow Cove settlement, they were entering the home of the ancestors of the Beothuk group of Native Americans. If the Vikings had traveled south from there, they would have found the land more highly populated and the villages bigger, encountering the ancestors of the Micmac, the Maliseet, and the Eastern Abenaki tribes. Some scholars have speculated that the Vikings may even have traveled west and encountered the Iroquois tribes, who were at that time forming the powerful Iroquois confederacy among the Mohawk, Oneida, Onondaga, Cayuga, and Seneca nations.

There has been only one undisputed Viking artifact dating back to the eleventh century found in the United States: a Norwegian penny that dates back to 1065–1080. It was found on the coast of Maine at the site of a fourteenth-century Indian settlement. The coin was most likely introduced in Maine as the result of trading among Indians rather than being brought by the Vikings.

The Norse colony at Greenland disbanded in the mid-fifteenth century. Throughout the centuries the Norse inhabited Greenland, there were probably frequent excursions to the North American continent in search of wood and other resources. The Norse do not seem to have established any enduring colonies on the continent.

Settling in

By the time of the second and more permanent European contact in the New World, the Native Americans had settled and resettled throughout the two American continents. Because the Europeans of the sixteenth century brought with them deadly viruses that killed a huge part of the population, no one knows for sure how many American Indians there were at the time of contact, but a middle-of-the-road estimate is about fifty-four million people. At the time Columbus arrived, there were about one thousand languages in the Americas. There were large cities, villages, extensive trade and long-distance interaction, farming technology, fine arts, religions, astounding architecture, and hundreds of unique traditions. Native Americans had migrated throughout the nation to find the best resources and most accommodating climates and to fulfill the human need to explore and conquer new frontiers. Along with the advances, there were wars among the native groups that compelled migrations. Changes in climate and overuse of resources compelled others. The arrival of the European colonizers in the sixteenth century would drastically alter the nature of life for the people who had settled it first. (See chapter 13 for more information on some of the later migrations of Native Americans.)

For More Information

Books

Adovasio, J. M., with Jake Page. *The First Americans: In Pursuit of Archaeology's Greatest Mystery.* New York: Random House, 2002.

Fagan, Brian M. *Kingdoms of Gold, Kingdoms of Jade: The Americas Before Columbus.* London: Thames and Hudson, 1991.

Fitzhugh, William W. "Puffins, Ringed Pins, and Runestones: The Viking Passage to America." In *Vikings: The North Atlantic Saga,* edited by William W. Fitzhugh and Elisabeth I. Ward. Washington, D.C., and London: Smithsonian Institution Press in association with National Museum of Natural History, 2000.

Odess, Daniel, Stephen Loring, and William W. Fitzhugh. "Skraeling: First Peoples of Helluland, Markland, and Vinland." In *Vikings: The North Atlantic Saga,* edited by William W. Fitzhugh and Elisabeth I. Ward. Washington, D.C., and London: Smithsonian Institution Press in association with National Museum of Natural History, 2000.

Periodicals

Lovgren, Stefan. "Who Were the First Americans?" *National Geographic,* September 3, 2003. *NationalGeographic.com.* http://news.national geographic.com/news/2003/09/0903_030903_bajaskull.html (accessed on February 26, 2004).

McIlroy, Anne. "Skulls Enliven Debate on Earliest Americans." *Globe and Mail,* September 4, 2003, p. A3.

Wade, Nicholas, and John Noble Wilford. "New World Ancestors Lose 12,000 Years." *New York Times,* July 25, 2003.

Spanish Colonization and Immigration

4

The European movement to colonize the New World was a response to a new age. In the fifteenth century Europe was just emerging from the Middle Ages (c. 500–c. 1500 C.E.). Most people of that age lived in a feudal system, in which a local lord who had received his land from the king owned all the land and ruled over the people in his area. The workers, or peasants, farmed the lord's land and worked for him in exchange for his protection. Over the centuries, the lords became more and more powerful while the power of the heads of state weakened. Because of the constant violence of wars, people tended to focus on religion and safety more than on learning or venturing out into unknown territory. It was not until the end of the Middle Ages that many heads of states in the countries of Western Europe began to bring their nations together, uniting under a central monarch or ruler. Then, in 1347 Europe was hit by an outbreak of the deadly bubonic plague (a highly infectious and fatal disease) that killed an estimated twenty-five million people in just a few years.

Fact Focus

- Spain was responsible for the early colonization of the present-day states of New Mexico, Arizona, Texas, and California.

- An estimated two hundred thousand Spaniards migrated to the New World between 1492 and 1592. They were the first Europeans to immigrate to the Americas.

- Between 1500 and 1650, Spain mined more than ten times the amount of gold in the New World than was mined by the rest of the world together.

- The Spanish set up their New World capital, Mexico City, on the site of the former Aztec capital, Tenochtitlán, in 1536. Many expeditions into the New World set out from Mexico City.

- Catholic missions were the foundation of all Spanish settlements in North America. When a community was to be settled in the New World, expeditions were sent to the area that included priests to form the mission and soldiers to put up the presidios, military posts and forts. The settlers would follow.

- Santa Fe, New Mexico, established in 1610, is the oldest capital city in North America.

An age of exploration and discovery

The horror of the "Black Plague," as this outbreak of the bubonic plague is commonly referred to, ushered in widespread change in the fifteenth century. Profitable trade increased and a larger middle class developed, with many more people living in towns than in farming villages. The Roman Catholic Church lost some of the strong political power it had held during the Middle Ages as the state rulers—the kings of England and France and other nations—acquired more power. A new era was starting, called the Renaissance (a revival of classical art, literature, and learning in Europe in the fourteen through the sixteenth centuries). The Renaissance was a movement in Europe from about 1450 to 1600 in which scholars returned to the study of the ancient Greek and Roman classics, and people, in general, began to educate themselves in science, art, and philosophy. An era of exploration and discovery lay ahead.

The Renaissance began in Italy, which grew to be a center of international trade. The Italians had trading relations

Words to Know

Colony: A group of people living as a political community in a land away from their home country but ruled by the home country.

Confederacy: A joining together of different groups of people for a common purpose.

Encomienda system: A reward system in which the Spanish nobles, in return for taking part in a war, were granted a large section of land and the right to rule as lord over the infidels (non-Christians) on that land.

Hacienda: A large country estate or ranch.

Indigenous: Native to an area.

Infidel: Non-Christian.

Mestizo: A person of mixed Spanish and Indian descent.

Middle East: The part of the world that encompasses Southwest Asia and North Africa, extending from Turkey to North Africa and east to Iran.

Mission: An organized effort by a religious group to spread its beliefs in other parts of the world. The word *mission* refers either to the project itself, or to the buildings built in a new area in order to spread the religious beliefs.

Mulatto: A person of mixed European and African descent.

Navigator: A person who sets the course for ship travel.

Presidio: A military post or fort.

Treaty: An agreement between two parties or two nations, signed by both, usually defining the benefits to both parties that will result from one side giving up title to a territory of land.

Vaquero: Cowboy.

Viceroyalty: A state in which the viceroy governs as the representative of the king.

West Indies: Islands in the Caribbean Sea on which explorer Christopher Columbus first landed in 1492, including Hispaniola (now Haiti and the Dominican Republic), Cuba, Jamaica, Puerto Rico, and others.

with people from the Middle East who brought them goods from Asia. (The Middle East is the part of the world that encompasses Southwest Asia and North Africa, extending from Turkey to North Africa and east to Iran.) Seeing the wealth the trade with Asia brought to Italy, other European nations wanted to form their own links with Asia. They began to finance navigators (people who set the courses for ships) for expeditions into unknown parts of the world. The Portuguese were the first Europeans to find routes around the Horn of

Africa (a peninsula in northeastern Africa) to India. In addition, by the mid-fifteenth century, the Portuguese had begun the African slave trade that would later extend to the New World.

Spain in the fifteenth century

During the Middle Ages, Spain had become divided into many smaller realms like the rest of western Europe. Its history differed, though, because, in 711, North African Muslims, called Moors, had taken power in Spain, expelling the various Germanic tribes who had been in control. The Moors had led Spain in rapid advancements in the arts, math and science, farming, philosophy, and architecture. The Christians who remained in Spain never stopped fighting for control of the government. In 1469 the two largest Christian kingdoms united when Isabella of Castile (1451–1504) and Ferdinand of Aragon (1452–1516) married. They soon took the throne as the Catholic king and queen of all of Spain. In January 1492 Isabella and Ferdinand defeated the last of the Moors, driving them all out of the country. A few months later they drove all Jews from Spain. They brought the local lords under their political control and united Spain under one government and the Roman Catholic Church.

Christopher Columbus sets the stage

In April 1492 Isabella and Ferdinand, having completed their goal of expelling non-Christians from Spain, entered into an agreement with a very determined ocean navigator from Genoa, Italy, named Christopher Columbus (1451–1506). Columbus believed that he could find a new ocean route to Asia by sailing west rather than east. Isabella and Ferdinand needed money after years of warfare. They were eager for profitable trade on foreign shores and agreed to finance the trip. Columbus's now-famous three ships—the Niña, the Pinta, and the Santa María—set sail. After five weeks, on October 12, 1492, they landed on a small island in the Caribbean Sea. Columbus then sailed to another island that he named La Española (Hispaniola, which is today shared by Haiti and the Dominican Republic). In the islands, the expedition encountered an Arawak-speaking tribe of in-

NORTH AMERICA
ATLANTIC OCEAN
Gulf of Mexico
Bahamas
Watling Island
Rum Cay
Samana Cay
Crooked Cay
Long Island
Ragged Island
Bahia Bariay
Cuba
Cap Haïtien
La Navidad
Samana Bay
Windward Passage
Hispaniola
Santo Domingo
Puerto Rico
Virgin Islands
Jamaica
Guadeloupe
Marie Galante
Dominica
Martinique
Caribbean Sea
Margarita Island
Ensenada Yacua
Trinidad
Gulf of Paria
Serpent's Mouth
VENEZUELA
Orinoco River
Panama
Veragua
SOUTH AMERICA
PACIFIC OCEAN
0 150 300 mi
0 150 300 km
N

digenous, native, people. Columbus thought he had found Asia and mistakenly called these people "Indians" ("the Indies" was Europe's name for India, China, and Southeast Asia). He described the Arawak as a loving and gentle people.

When Isabella and Ferdinand learned of the success of Columbus's expedition, they asked the pope to recognize Spain's authority over the new lands, still thinking the expedi-

A map of the Caribbean region showing the route taken by explorer Christopher Columbus in 1492 from Europe to the Bahamas, Cuba, Hispaniola, and back northeast toward Europe. *Reproduced by permission of the Gale Group.*

An illustration of explorer Christopher Columbus pointing to the eclipse of the Moon, surrounded by frightened Native Americans. *Reproduced by permission of Hulton Archive/Getty Images.*

tion had landed in Asia. At around the same time Portugal asked Pope Alexander VI (c. 1431–1503) to recognize its authority over its African discoveries. The pope drew a line of demarcation—an imaginary line running north and south, dividing the globe in half. In an act called the Treaty of Tordesillas, Portugal was given authority to all non-Christian lands to the east of the line and Spain was given authority over the land to the west. They did not know about the New World yet and so could not have guessed that Spain had just been given colonial powers over most of the two American continents. (Brazil runs east of the line and so was colonized by Portugal. It is the only country in South America that is not Spanish-speaking.)

Settlement begins

Columbus returned to the New World in 1493 with seventeen ships, twelve hundred men, and a large shipment

Some Spanish Explorers and Conquistadors of the Americas: 1492–1542

1492–1504: Christopher Columbus (1451–1506), Italian navigator financed by the Spanish crown, locates, explores, and begins to colonize the New World. He is thought to be the first European, after the Viking explorer Leif Eriksson, to have set foot on the American continents.

1513: Vasco Núñez de Balboa (1475–1519) becomes the first European to find the eastern shores of the Pacific Ocean which he calls the South Sea and claims for Spain.

1513: Juan Ponce de León (c. 1460–1521) leads the first European expedition to Florida, which he claims for Spain.

1519–21: Ferdinand Magellan, or Fernño de Magalhães (1480–1521), a Portuguese navigator financed by the Spanish king, becomes the first to circumnavigate (go all the way around) the world. He names the Pacific Ocean for waters that seem calmer, more peaceful, than those of the Atlantic Ocean.

1519–21: Hernán Cortés (1485–1547) explores and conquers central Mexico.

1527–36: Alvar Núñez Cabeza de Vaca (c. 1490–c. 1557) survives a shipwreck and then wanders through Texas and Mexico for eight years. He trades with Native Americans and writes popular stories about the New World.

1527–28: Pánfilo de Narváez (c. 1470–1528) leads a disastrous expedition to Florida and places on the Texas shoreline of the Gulf of Mexico.

1532–33: Francisco Pizarro (c. 1478–1541) conquers the Incas in present-day Peru, opening much of South America to Spanish settlement.

1539–42: Hernando de Soto (c. 1496–1542) leads a gold-seeking expedition through Florida, Alabama, Tennessee, Mississippi, Arkansas, Oklahoma, and Louisiana; first European to encounter the Mississippi River.

1540–42: Francisco Vásquez de Coronado (c. 1510–1554), seeking the legendary Seven Cities of Cíbola, explores present-day New Mexico, Colorado, Texas, Oklahoma, and Kansas.

1541–42: Juan Rodríguez Cabrillo, or João Rodrigues Cabrilho (c. 1520– 1543), a Portuguese explorer in service of the Spanish, becomes the first European explorer of the California coast, including San Diego and Monterey Bays.

of cattle and horses. He landed on the Virgin Islands and Puerto Rico before returning to Hispaniola. There, he founded the first permanent European settlement in the New World, La Isabela. Putting his brother in charge of the colony, he continued his travels around the New World. The leadership of his colony on Hispaniola was poor and the settlers were very abusive to the Arawak people. Demanding food and labor of the people, the settlers delivered terrible punishments for those who failed to meet their requirements. The Arawak rose in rebellion and were brutally defeated by the settlers.

Although the early treatment of the Native Americans by the Spanish was not usually called slavery, it had most of the characteristics of a slave system. In fact, in 1495 five hundred captured Arawaks were sent to England as slaves. More were kept as slaves in the New World. Tribute (periodic payments of one nation to another for protection or to acknowledge superior strength) was demanded of the defeated tribes. When they could no longer find the gold dust (particles of gold found around gold mines, usually by pouring water over rocks and dirt until the gold separates out) required of them, Columbus, his brother, and their followers put the Indians to labor in the newly discovered gold mines, where thousands perished from the miserable working conditions. Neither Columbus nor his brother fulfilled the instructions from the queen to use kindness in converting the native people to Christianity. To many in Europe, the Columbus brothers' behavior toward the Indians did not seem unusual. Others did object, and although Queen Isabella sponsored him through four expeditions to the New World, Columbus's standing in the royal court and elsewhere in England continued to sink. He died in poverty, still believing that he had found a route to Asia.

Columbus was the first of many in the age of exploration in the New World for Spain. The explorers soon found gold in the Caribbean, After the first settlement in Hispaniola, Spanish settlers spread to Puerto Rico in 1508, to Jamaica in 1509, and to Cuba in 1511. When word spread in Spain that gold and silver had been found, especially when it was found in large quantities in Mexico, hundreds of Spanish *hidalgos* (pronounced ee-DAHL-goes; meaning noblemen) or *conquistadors* (pronounced cone-kees-tuh-DOORS; meaning conquerors) rushed to join the expeditions heading for the Americas. The spirit that guided most of these first Spanish immigrants was their tremendous desire for gold and silver. None of them immigrated to the New World with the intention of laboring, and the forcible use of Native Americans in the mines continued.

The government of Spain profited greatly from the gold fever that prompted so many men to sail to the Americas. Between 1500 and 1650, historians estimate that Spain carried more than 180 tons of gold and 16,000 tons of silver from the New World to Europe. The extraction of gold during this period was about ten times more than that of all of the rest of the world together. Spain, which took a hefty tax on all gold mined, became one of the wealthiest and most powerful nations in the world during the sixteenth century.

Encomienda system

During the first century of Spanish settlement in the Americas, an estimated two hundred thousand Spaniards migrated to the New World. The Spanish royalty, beginning with Isabella and Ferdinand, sponsored (paid for) the expeditions. These first European immigrants to the Americas were acting as agents of the Spanish crown. They were, for the most part, minor nobles and military officers fresh from the battlefields of Spain's war to expel the Moors. They were all men, and they were an ambitious group.

Besides the gold mines, the Spanish decided to extract wealth from their new colonies by planting sugar in large plantations (farms). They needed labor to operate the plantations. During the wars against the Moors in Spain, many of the hidalgos had grown accustomed to the *encomienda* system, a system of reward for their valor on the battlefield. Under this system, the warriors had laid claim to the land owned by the infidels (non-Christians) that they had defeated. They became the lords of their own feudal estates and were appointed a certain number of defeated infidels for their use as laborers and servants. When the hidalgos settled in Hispaniola, they expected the king to grant them the same kind of rewards.

Spanish explorer Hernán Cortés. *Reproduced by permission of the Granger Collection, Ltd.*

To encourage people to colonize, Spain offered land grants (gifts of the title to large parcels of land as a reward for service) in the New World. It also gave the settlers authority over the Indians within the assigned land grants under the encomienda system. In return, the settlers were directed to convert the Indians to Christianity and to ensure that their needs were met. In effect, it enslaved the Indians. In Mexico, the encomiendas were vast estates. Within one encomienda there could be several whole Indian villages, and all were subject to the rule of one owner. The Spanish explorer Hernán Cortés, for example, held a huge encomienda in which he ruled over twenty-three thousand Indians.

Upon arriving on Indian lands, explorers from Spain, beginning with Christopher Columbus, were compelled to read aloud the king's summons (an order to do something) to the Indians, which was called the *Requierimento,* or Requirement. The Requierimento stated that the explorers were taking possession of the Indians' land for the Spanish monarchy and informing them of the truth of Christianity. The Spanish took this exercise seriously, even though the Indians could not understand the Spanish language.

In about 1523 Dominican friar Bartolomé de las Casas (1474–1566), a former plantation owner who had freed his Indian slaves and taken up the priesthood, began a fight against the cruel practices of the Spanish colonists against the Indians. After about twenty years of pushing for the human rights of the American Indians, las Casas succeeded in getting the Spanish laws changed. In the early 1600s the king ended the encomienda system. Despite changes in laws, the cruel practices continued.

The result of the Spanish migrations to the New World was devastation for the Native Americans. The Spanish settlers in the Caribbean forced the Arawak to labor in the mines and on plantations. While thousands died of the diseases introduced by the Spanish—smallpox and measles—others were worked to death in the gold mines and many died of starvation. Entire Arawak villages disappeared as a result.

African slavery under the Spanish

In order to continue to profit from the colonies, vast sources of labor were required. It soon became apparent to the Spanish that they could not rely solely on the Native Americans, who were dying in large numbers and escaping from labor whenever possible. The colonists in the West Indies (islands in the Caribbean Sea on which explorer Christopher Columbus first landed in 1492, including Hispaniola, Cuba, Jamaica, Puerto Rico, and others) asked the permission of the king of Spain to import African slaves to labor in their mines and on their plantations. The king consented to the import of four thousand Africans as slaves, the first of whom arrived in the West Indies in 1518. The Spanish brought slaves to Guatemala as early as 1524. By the end of the century at least sixty thousand Africans had been brought to Mexico alone and an estimated three hundred sixty-seven thousand African slaves had been brought to North and South America. (See chapter 8 on African American immigration for more information.)

Development of New Spain

In order to continue its successes in the New World, Spain continued to conquer vast areas. Spain defeated the Aztec in Mexico in a brutal war in 1519 and 1520 and then conquered the Incas in Peru from 1532 to 1535. After leveling the Aztec capital city of Tenochtitlán (pronounced tay-noach-teet-LAHN), Spain set up its first province, New Spain, in Mexico. The capital, Mexico City, was built right on the site of the former Aztec capital in 1536. The recently strong, wealthy, and highly sophisticated Aztec government became a model for the Spanish rule. The Aztec society had been based on different social-class levels. The chief was a powerful ruler chosen from a royal family. Under the chief ruler were viceroys (people who govern as representatives of the chief ruler) to attend to specific functions within the city. Councils were appointed to rule over other regions. Foreign tribes had long been paying tribute to the powerful Aztecs. When the Spanish took over, they continued to take the tribute money for themselves, as rulers. The Spanish left most of the Aztec power structure intact, but placed Spanish rulers and viceroys in charge of the whole system. Mexico City became the power center from which many expeditions into the New World originated. Most of the people who settled in the north had lived in Mexico first.

The mission system

When the Spanish set out to establish a town or a settlement in the New World, they often started by building a presidio and a Catholic mission. A presidio was a military post or fort. Some presidios were small, staffed by only a few soldiers of the Spanish army, while others were staffed by hundreds of soldiers. The presidios mainly served to protect the settlers in the new community from attacks by Native Americans.

A mission is an organized effort by a religious group to spread its beliefs in other parts of the world. The word *mission* refers either to the project itself, or to the buildings erected in a new area in order to spread the religious beliefs. Starting with Columbus's second voyage, Catholic missionaries came in large numbers to America for the purpose of converting the native population to Christianity. The most important mission orders (different groups of persons living according to a religious rule) were the Franciscans, Dominicans, Augustinians, and Jesuits. These orders established missions throughout Florida, Mexico, and the American Southwest.

Since the Catholic Church was so closely affiliated with the Spanish government, the missionaries in America served dual roles as representatives of the church and the Spanish crown. They converted the Indians to Christianity, but they also strove to convince Native Americans to adopt what they felt was the superior civilization of Catholic Spain. Spain's aim in settling its huge new empire was al-

ways twofold: to acquire money and resources and to create an empire guided by Christianity and the Catholic Church. Some of the monks who came to the New World hoped to find a more innocent kind of human life in the New World. They leaped at the chance to leave Spain and begin a new order in the Americas in keeping with their religious beliefs.

Despite the intentions of some dedicated missionaries, the Spanish missions subjected Indians to hard labor, separating families and denying them of their basic human rights. Once they entered the missions, most Native Americans were not allowed to practice their traditional cultures. Both Spain and the Catholic Church profited from their practice of forcing Mission Indians to labor. As they developed, the missions became powerful estates in their own right, with prosperous farming and industry, and vast amounts of land. For a number of years, Catholic missions were the foundation of all Spanish settlement in North America. The mis-

Mission San Xavier de Bac, founded in 1700, in present-day Tucson, Arizona. *Reproduced by permission of © David G. Houser/Corbis.*

A painting of a vaquero riding a horse in early California. *Reproduced by permission of the Bancroft Library, University of California.*

sions became the centers of military defense, political control, and economic gain as well as religious teachings.

Life in New Spain

Spain's colonizing expeditions to the Americas were made up strictly of males, unlike the later English colonizing groups, which usually consisted of families. Most expeditions included a priest, who quickly baptized the native peoples in an area. Because they had no women with them, the Spanish settlers often took partners from among the baptized Indian females. Sometimes they married the Native American women, but more often they entered into "consensual unions," in which both partners agreed to have a sexual relationship but there was no legal or religious marriage. In Latin America, there were more consensual unions than had ever occurred in any European society, with the number of illegitimate births (births out of wedlock) making up about half of the total number of births. A person of mixed Spanish and Indian descent was called a mestizo.

A class system began to take shape in New Spain. The earliest settlers, the conquistadors, had received the largest land grants in the New World and they were the new upper class. Much of the class division was along racial lines. Born in Spain, the conquistadors were considered "pure" Spaniards. People of Spanish descent who had been born in the New World were the next level from the top in the social structure of New Spain. Next came the people who were a mix of Spanish and Indian descent, called mestizos and the people who were of Spanish, or other European, and African descent, called mulattoes. Indians and Africans were generally at the bottom of the social system.

A system of inheritance (passing wealth or power from one generation to the next) known as *mayorazgo* was practiced throughout the Spanish provinces. Under this system, a family's lands and real estate could never be divided and could only be inherited by the oldest son. Thus, no one could ever sell any portion of the land. When one aristocrat married into another aristocrat's family, the end result was the merger of two huge estates. These holdings, often the large ranches or haciendas associated with the Spanish settlers, were usually worked by the Indians under the encomienda system. After a few generations, the upper class in Spanish America had become very small and its holdings and power were very large. The provinces of New Spain were set up as viceroyalties, states in which the viceroy governs as the representative of the king. Spanish viceroys were to rule their New World colonies in Spain's interest, but this policy was not always followed. The viceroys eventually became extremely powerful in their own right. With a small group enjoying great privileges and power, most of the population of New Spain had become laborers.

The Spanish settlements in present-day United States

Florida

Spain was jealous of its claims in the north (in what is now the southern United States). When France built a

Vaqueros and Cattle Ranching in America

When the first Europeans arrived, there were no cattle or horses in the New World. The Spanish began bringing livestock as early as Christopher Columbus's second expedition in 1493. In Mexico the livestock was allowed to wander freely. Soon huge herds of wild horses and cattle roamed the plains.

Many of the encomiendas awarded to the early Spanish settlers—and to Spanish missionaries and priests—became cattle ranches. The free-roaming cattle needed to be rounded up at least once a year for branding, slaughter, and counting. The Spanish had a horse culture, but the *charros,* or the gentlemen riders, and the encomenderos, or ranch owners, did not want to undertake such a strenuous and dirty job as the roundup. Although it was illegal in Mexico for Indians to ride horses because horses were viewed as equipment for war, missionaries trained the Indians on the mission encomiendas to ride and hunt cattle anyway. This use of the Indian laborers as vaqueros, or cowboys (*vaca* means "cow" in Spanish), spread quickly to all encomiendas. The Spanish skills at horsemanship were quickly passed on to the Indians and the mestizos who followed them.

In a cattle roundup, vaqueros rode horses to chase down and herd the wild cattle on the plains. In his book *In the Days of Vaqueros: America's First True Cowboys,* Russell Freedman describes the roundup: "Each ranch sent a team of riders, who often came from a great distance. A really big roundup might cover hundreds of square miles, last for weeks, and involve three or four hundred vaqueros along with tens of thousands of head of cattle." Working together, the vaqueros flushed out (chased out of their hiding places) and drove the cattle into one group, until they stampeded and ran furiously into the

colony in Florida in 1564, a Spanish fleet arrived there quickly thereafter to drive the French out of the area. After they had defeated the French, the Spanish established Saint Augustine, the oldest permanent European settlement in the United States, taking possession of the territory for the king of Spain in 1565. The colony had been carefully planned: The settlers had ample supplies and among them were farmers and carpenters who could build shelter and feed the new settlement. Still, the first winter brought disease and starvation to the colonists in Saint Augustine. Saint Augustine grew slowly. Its three hundred or so inhabitants included soldiers,

grounds where the vaqueros were rounding them up. There the vaqueros began branding calves and slaughtering steer. The vaquero was highly skilled in riding, throwing *la reata* (the lariat or lasso), wrestling down bulls, breaking (making them tame enough to ride) horses, and many other dangerous and athletic feats.

After the encomienda system was outlawed in the mid-sixteenth century, the ranchers began to pay vaqueros small wages for their work. American Indians, mestizos, and freed blacks were the most common vaqueros. They generally lived on the large haciendas (ah-see-END-as; huge cattle ranches) of Spanish America. There the ranch owner lived in an elaborate house or mansion, with many servants tending to his family's needs, while most vaqueros slept in bunks in the stables. The vaqueros generally never saw their salary. Under a system called *debt peonage,* most vaqueros ended up borrowing from their future wages in order to make ends meet. They were never able to pay back the money. Children were often born into their father's debts, and might never see their own wages either.

There was little prestige attached to being a vaquero, as there would later be for the cowboys in the United States. Nevertheless, the vaqueros took great pride in their uniquely perfected skills. Vaqueros dressed in a certain way, sang certain songs, and held to strong traditions. When Anglo-Americans in the Southwest began to work cattle, many learned the trade from the vaqueros. The Anglo-Americans mispronounced the Spanish word "vaquero," calling them "bukera." The word finally evolved into "buckaroo," which remained the word for cattle workers until about 1860, when the word "cowboy" came into use.

craftsmen, traders, Native Americans, and an occasional Frenchman or Portuguese. Notably, Saint Augustine was the earliest example of an established colony on the North American mainland to use African slaves.

In 1573 the Franciscan monks arrived in Florida to build a mission. Over the next century, the Franciscans would build several missions from St. Augustine north to South Carolina, before moving westward. These missions set the pattern for Spanish settlement in the New World, but they were not long-lived. Spain was at war in Europe, fighting Austria, Britain, France, and other countries. One result of the European wars was that Spain ceded, or turned over, Florida to France in 1763. Most of its Florida missions were soon destroyed.

New Mexico

In 1595 Spanish explorer Juan de Oñate (1550–1630) obtained permission from Spain to establish a province in New Mexico. In February 1598 Oñate's expedition set out from Mexico. It consisted of four hundred men, many with their wives and children, and ten Franciscan friars. They brought with them seven thousand head of livestock and eighty-three carts. Traveling across the Rio Grande River, they passed into what is now New Mexico, where they built the settlement of San Juan de los Caballeros (meaning knights, or gentlemen) and San Gabriel, the first two Spanish towns in New Mexico. Settling in New Mexico was difficult. Food quickly became scarce. Relations with the nearby Pueblo Indians became hostile when the settlers tried to force the Indians to provide them with food.

Oñate was a cruel man in his dealings with his own settlement and especially with the Pueblo people. He hanged several deserters and stormed the Indian pueblo (town) of Acoma with his army after the Indians had killed some of his settlers. Oñate condemned the survivors of Acoma to twenty years' servitude, ordering that the right feet of all males over twenty-five years of age be cut off. Two Hopi Indians had been captured at Acoma. Oñate had their right hands cut off and sent them home as a warning to other tribes in the area. When he forced a group of fleeing settlers to return to his colony in 1601, some of the settlers appealed to the viceroy of Mexico for help. The viceroy recommended that Oñate be replaced as governor and Oñate resigned his post.

The group of Franciscan friars who had accompanied Oñate to New Mexico had quickly set about building churches and missions. Moving slowly up the Rio Grande River and working peacefully with Native Americans, the missionaries met with relatively little resistance. The Franciscans did not insist that the converts master the new religion. With the priests' help, the Pueblo Indians learned how to raise sheep

The San Miguel Mission in Santa Fe, New Mexico, is the oldest church in the United States. *Reproduced by permission of Mr. James Blank.*

and cultivate new crops such as wheat, peach trees, and watermelon. Many Native Americans converted to Christianity because of the Franciscans' efforts.

After Oñate's resignation, the king of Spain was ready to abandon the province of New Mexico because it was so difficult to sustain colonies there. The Catholic Church, worried about the fate of the Christianized Indians, demanded that the king continue the colonization of the area. The crown agreed. New Mexico became a province of New Spain in 1608. The king dispatched colonial official Pedro de Peralta (c. 1585–1666) to govern, ordering him to establish a new village right away. This new town, built in 1610, was named San Francisco de la Santa Fe. Santa Fe is the oldest capital city in North America.

New Mexico, like most Spanish settlements, became dependent on the forced labor of the native population, including herding, farm labor, blacksmithing, silversmithing, and domestic labor. In 1680 the Pueblo Indians formed a confederacy (a joining together of different groups of people for a common purpose) and drove out the Spanish in what is known as the Pueblo Revolt, killing hundreds of Spanish settlers and clergy. The remaining settlers fled to El Paso. The Spanish gradually gained back control of the pueblos and in 1693 set about resettling Santa Fe, making it a presidio (fort) with one hundred soldiers.

In 1695 a group of families from Santa Fe established New Mexico's second town, Santa Cruz de la Cañada; eleven years later Albuquerque was founded. Twenty-one missions were also reestablished. By 1749 New Mexico's Spanish population had risen to about forty-three hundred. Meanwhile, the Indian population declined drastically from an estimated seventeen thousand Native Americans in 1679 to about nine thousand in 1693. Pueblo populations would continue to decline for the next two centuries, mainly due to the infectious diseases spread by the Europeans.

Arizona

In 1687 Jesuit missionary Eusebio Kino (1645–1711) took over the mission effort in an area of northern New Spain that included present-day Sonora, Mexico, and southern Arizona. Over a period of twenty-four years, Kino rode on horseback throughout the region, founding twenty missions and teaching European farming and livestock techniques to the Indians, introducing both wheat and beef cattle to the region.

There was not a large Spanish population in Arizona until the late eighteenth century because the Apaches in the

area were successful at defending the area from invaders. Around 1790 the Spanish military stopped the deadly attacks of the Apaches. Spanish colonists entered into treaties (an agreement between two parties or two nations, signed by both, as in reference to terms of peace or trade) with the Native Americans of the area. At that time more than one thousand Spanish settlers moved into Arizona's Santa Cruz Valley.

The Mission Concepcion, built from 1733 through 1755 in San Antonio, Texas. *Reproduced by permission of © Sandy Felsenthal/Corbis.*

Texas

The colonization of Texas by the Spanish was a slow process. In 1685 the French founded Fort Saint Louis on the Gulf Coast of present-day Texas. Four years later, the governor of the Mexican province Coahuila (pronounced coe-aw-WHEE-la) sent out an expedition to drive out the French. In the early eighteenth century, the French had begun to settle in large numbers in the Louisiana area, and the Spanish wished to establish a colonial presence in Texas to protect their claim there. In 1718 they began to build a mission, San Antonio de Valero, and a fort, San Antonio de Bexar, at the site of the present-day city of San Antonio. As a halfway post between Mexico and the Louisiana border, San Antonio grew to be Texas's most important city of that period.

The Spanish found it very hard to settle Texas. The local Comanche tribes attacked settlers, destroyed forts, and raided ranches for livestock. Most of the Spanish settlers gathered in villages along the lower Rio Grande Valley, at what is now the border between Texas and Mexico. In 1749 Spanish commander José de Escandón brought thousands of settlers into the new province of Nuevo Santander (lying on what is now the Mexican state of Tamaulipas, as well as a part of Nuevo León and a part of South Texas). Escandón and his colonizing expeditions established more than twenty towns in the area. Nuevo Santander included Laredo on the north bank of the Rio Grande River and the towns of Mier, Camargo, and Reynosa on the south bank. By 1776 Reynosa was larger than the city of Philadelphia at the time. After these towns were established, settlers began to push another hundred miles north to the Nueces River Valley in South Texas. By 1835 large South Texas ranches had become home to five thousand people and about three million head of livestock.

California

At the end of the eighteenth century, Spain was concerned about the movements of other nations—particularly Russia and Britain—on the West Coast of North America, north of Baja (lower) California. Spain made the decision to put more effort into settling Alta (upper) California, an area that had been very slow to colonize. In 1769 two expeditions, one by land and one by sea, left Mexico to colonize Alta California, the present-day state of California. On July 3, the chaplain of the expedition, Father Junípero Serra (1713–1784), founded a Franciscan mission at San Diego. The next year, he founded a mission supported by a presidio at Monterey. These two missions would serve as the seats of government for Spanish Alta California.

In 1775 Captain Juan Bautista de Anza (1736–1788) led an expedition of 240 Spanish settlers, 700 horses, and 350 cattle out of northern Mexico into Alta California. Almost all the expedition members had been born in the Americas and came from mixed European, African, and Indian descent. De Anza was carrying out orders from the government of New Spain to build a presidio in northern California. The presidio of San Francisco was founded in 1776.

At about the same time, California's new governor, Felip de Neve (1727–1784), received orders from the Spanish king to create a town at a site that had been recommended by a group of missionaries. The governor set to work planning the layout of the new town, its fields, and its irrigation system. The town that would become Los Angeles had a population problem right from the start—there were not enough people. The problem was finding settlers who would migrate to such a remote place. After a long period of recruiting, a group was organized in Sonora, Mexico, consisting of eleven men, eleven women, and twenty-two children. The company of settlers was called *Los Pobladores* (the settlers). In this group, three of the men were of mostly Spanish blood, two were of African descent, two were mulattoes, and four were Native American. They named the town "El Pueblo de Nuestra Señora la Reina de los Angeles de Porciuncula" ("the town of our lady the queen of the angels of Porciuncula"). Life was not easy for these first settlers of Los Angeles. They built and lived in very small adobe (baked clay brick) houses, using rawhide for doors. Rain was either nonexistent or came in sudden downpours that would wash out the narrow streets. Getting supplies was difficult, but slowly the town grew. In 1800 there was a population of 315 settlers in the city of Los Angeles.

Most of California's coastal populations of Native Americans lived in small hunting and fishing villages. The Spanish missionaries created a chain of twenty-three missions, each a day's horseback ride from the next. These institutions were much more than churches, resembling, in many ways, Caribbean plantations. Under Spanish law, once baptized, the Indians were compelled to move from their own villages into quarters within the mission, where they were tutored in Christianity, separated from their families, and forced into hard labor for the mission.

Most of the labor done by the Mission Indians was farming in the missions' vast lands. Ranching, too, was introduced. The missionaries trained hundreds of Indian vaqueros, or cowboys, in the skills of cattle ranching. Cattle ranching, under the missions, was California's biggest industry, and the missions prospered.

Between 1769 and 1836, about eighty thousand California Indians were baptized and subjected to labor in a system that amounted to slavery. The result was terrible loss for the Native Americans: of their human rights, ways of life, and culture. Mostly owing to the infectious diseases brought to California by the Spanish, an estimated one hundred thousand Indians died during the mission era. Then, in 1821, Spain lost the Mexican war for independence, a bloody revolution that had been ongoing since September 1810. At that time in California there were about 3,720 people with some Spanish blood and about 30,000 Mission Indians.

Mexico and other Spanish colonies win independence

By the end of the mission era, Spain had lost its Mexican colonies in the Mexican war for independence (1810–21). In fact, by 1825 Spain had lost its entire empire in the New World, including the colonies in the Caribbean and Central and South America. As of 1823 New Mexico, Arizona, Texas, and California were governed by, and part of, Mexico. Texas won its independence from Mexico in 1836 and became the Republic of Texas. In 1846 it became a state in the United States. New Mexico, California, and Arizona, along with parts of Nevada, Utah, and Colorado, were ceded by Mexico to the United States after the Mexican-American War ended in 1848. The people in these former Mexican provinces were suddenly U.S. citizens.

The legacies of the Spanish immigrants to the United States—the Spanish language, the arts, the history of exploration and settling, ranching, and the culture and lifestyles—have had a tremendous impact on the nation. In the years to come, large waves of immigrants from the populations of the former Spanish colonies would come to live in the United States. They were no longer identified as Spanish, African, or Native American. They were Mexican, Chilean, Salvadoran, Cuban, or any number of other nationalities. For more information on these later immigrants who were to bring with them more of the Spanish legacy, see chapters 21 and 22 on Mexican and Other Latino and Caribbean immigration.

For More Information

Books

Freedman, Russell. *In the Days of the Vaqueros: The First True Cowboys.* New York: Clarion Books, 2001.

Gonzalez, Juan. *Harvest of Empire: A History of Latinos in America.* New York: Viking, 2000.

Jackson, Robert H., and Edward Castillo. *Indians, Franciscans, and Spanish Colonization: The Impact of the Mission System on California Indians.* Albuquerque: University of New Mexico Press, 1995.

Loewen, James W. *Lies My Teacher Told Me: Everything Your American History Textbook Got Wrong.* New York: Touchstone Books, 1996.

Middleton, Richard. *Colonial America: A History, 1565–1776,* 3rd ed. Oxford, UK: Blackwell, 2002.

Web Sites

Brown, Maria A. "Spain's Colonial Enterprise." *Journey Through the American Past: Online Multimedia History.* http://online.elcamino.edu/hist1a/spain.htm (accessed on February 26, 2004).

English Immigration

5

At the turn of the seventeenth century, few could have foreseen that England was going to be the great colonizer of North America. Wealthy Spain began colonizing in the New World almost immediately after explorer Christopher Columbus (1451–1506) set foot on the Caribbean islands. England was not rich enough to pay for colonizing expeditions (sending ships with settlers and supplies to establish a community ruled by, and part of, England) from its national treasury. England and Spain had been engaged in sea conflicts periodically during the second half of the sixteenth century and, as the weaker nation, England could not afford to exhaust its naval or military strength on colonizing. Nonetheless, the spirit of the age of exploration gripped the nation. Swift English sea vessels crossed the Atlantic regularly. Unable to mine for gold and silver themselves, as the Spanish had been doing since the early 1500s, the "sea dogs," or English pirates, looted the Spanish ships as they carted home their riches. Back home, the English people were drawn to the tales of adventure coming from the New World. Many looked to America as a key to a better future.

Fact Focus

- The English government could not afford to sponsor colonization in the Americas, so it fell to the hands of big business. In 1606 two charter companies, the Plymouth Company and the London Company, formed for the purpose of creating colonies in North America.

- The Jamestown immigrants in the colony's first half century were, for the most part, single, male tradesmen and laborers from the cities of England. Many planned to return to England and thus had little community spirit.

- About 40 percent of the immigrants to the Chesapeake Bay area in the seventeenth century were indentured servants.

- Between 1630 and 1640 about twenty thousand English men, women, and children came to New England in what is known as the Great Migration.

- The Puritans in Massachusetts believed that only certain people were "God's elect," or "saints." They developed an examination to determine which ones among them were saints.

- Seventy thousand English "war brides" immigrated to the United States in the 1940s. They were English women who met American servicemen stationed in England during World War II and married them.

Financing the colonies

The first English colonizing expeditions in the New World were financed by Walter Raleigh (1552–1618; also spelled Ralegh), the daring and adventurous navigator (a person who sets the course of a ship), poet, explorer, and special favorite of Queen Elizabeth I (1533–1603), who ruled from 1558 to 1603. Raleigh claimed for England a stretch along the Atlantic Coast that lies approximately between North Carolina and Maine today. He named it Virginia for the Virgin Queen Elizabeth. (Raleigh, like most European explorers of his time, did not acknowledge the native inhabitants' right to the land.) In 1585 he put together the first of two expeditions of colonists to attempt to establish a permanent settlement on Roanoke Island off the coast of what is now North Carolina. Raleigh's attempts to settle Roanoke failed. The first group of settlers did not have enough supplies and the survivors returned to England. The settlers on the second Roanoke expedition had vanished by the time a long-delayed

Words to Know

Aristocracy: Government by the elite or a small class of the privileged.

Colony: A group of people living as a political community in a land away from their home country but ruled by the home country.

Dissent: To disagree with, and not conform to, the practices of a particular religion.

Indentured servants: Servants who agreed to work for a colonist for a set period of time in exchange for payment of their passage from Europe to the New World. At the end of the service term (usually seven years), the indentured servant was given a small piece of land or goods to help set up a new life in the colony.

Inheritance: The passing of one's wealth from one generation to the next.

Investors: People who buy shares of a company in order to share in its profits, while also sharing in its risks.

Joint stock company: A group that organizes an enterprise, such as trading in a certain overseas market, and then sells shares of this enterprise to investors.

Palisade: A defensive fence or wall made of stakes.

Primogeniture: A system of inheritance under which all of the wealth from one family is passed to the oldest son upon the father's death, ensuring that the estates of the wealthy did not get divided into small pieces, but rather remained in the hands of a few.

shipment of supplies could reach them. Raleigh lost a great deal of money. After that, it was clear that no single individual could sponsor the colonizing expeditions.

It also became clear that the Spanish experience of discovering vast wealth in the gold and silver mines was probably not going to repeat itself. The kinds of economic opportunities that presented themselves in North America—farming, logging timber, fishing, and obtaining a variety of other natural resources—were going to take more time, planning, and, above all, labor. In order to succeed, the colonies would need a good supply of people to work in them. The colonists needed to be prepared to work hard and to stay there for the long run, probably for the rest of their lives.

In 1589 Richard Hakluyt (pronounced HAK-loot; c. 1551–1616), a geographer, clergyman, and friend of Raleigh, published his first edition of *Principle Navigations, Voyages, and Discoveries of the English Nation*. This widely read book was very persuasive in promoting the colonization of North America. It particularly championed the idea of turning to farming to establish strong, profitable, and permanent colonies. Hakluyt argued that permanent colonies would keep Spain out of North America, secure a new source of badly needed raw materials for England's industries, and create a new market for English exports. He also saw the New World as the ideal place to send England's poor, unemployed, and criminal elements. His book was well received and inspired a new look at the prospects of colonizing North America at the turn of the century.

English merchants at that time were exploring every possible avenue for trading opportunities. They had developed what is known as the joint stock company, a group that organized an enterprise, such as trading in a certain overseas market, and then sold shares of this enterprise to investors—people who bought shares of the venture in order to share in its profits (but also shared in the risks). In 1600 the East India Company was formed for trade with India and the Far East. English merchants were eager for the creation of English colonies in North America for the trading potential they would provide.

England won a decisive naval campaign against Spain in 1588 when it defeated the Spanish Armada, a fleet of Spanish war ships trying to attack England. The two nations then signed a peace treaty. Spain had claimed the right to colonize all of the Americas under the 1495 Treaty of Tordesillas, under which Spain and Portugal had divided up the trading rights to the globe under the direction of the Catholic pope. But after the defeat of its Armada, Spain was ready to allow England to colonize some areas of North America.

The way was cleared for colonization, but the English crown still did not have the money to finance it. Thus, building the British Empire fell to the hands of big business. In 1605 two charter companies formed for the purpose of creating colonies in North America: the Plymouth Company, or the North Virginia group, and the London Company, or the South Virginia group. In 1606 the Virginia companies received a colonial charter (a grant from the king) from King

James I (1566–1625), who had succeeded Elizabeth in 1603. With this colonial charter the king gave the companies the power to found and govern a colony. The charter companies were to be overseen by a council of fourteen people chosen by the king. Thus, the new colonies would be run by a business corporation but overseen by the English government.

Once the charter companies had found investors to back the colonization efforts, the only task that remained was to find the colonizers themselves. They needed people who would risk their lives and forsake their friends and family and the comforts of home. These first immigrants would have to take a long, difficult, and dangerous voyage to an unknown land. They would have to work very hard in miserable conditions—and for this they would receive only a small salary.

Why go to America?

Opportunity

The English people's urge to colonize North America continued to grow despite the disasters the Roanoke colonists had encountered. The main motivation was certainly economic. The rich may have been looking for a good investment, but some of the poorer English people were looking to escape bad circumstances at home. The great quantities of gold and silver Spain had brought home from Mexico and South America had driven up prices throughout Europe. Wages for workers in England lagged far behind price increases. At the same time, England experienced a population explosion, increasing from three million people in 1500 to over five million by 1650. From 25 to 50 percent of the population lived in poverty. Plagues (deadly epidemic diseases) and famine were common. Some of the rural, or country, poor migrated to England's cities seeking jobs. London's population grew from about 200,000 in 1600 to 575,000 in 1700.

There were many things that were unlikely to change in England. The nobles, or "gentlemen," already owned all the large spreads of land. The roles people played within the social world were already set. If a person was born to a low position, it was highly likely that he or she would maintain the lowly status. In England, inheritance (the passing of one's

Advertising the Colonizing Business, 1609

The colonizing of Jamestown and New England was almost entirely a commercial endeavor, organized and carried out by the Virginia Company. The company had hoped to get rich quick, but it was apparent after the first couple of years in Jamestown—with the first immigrants dying in great numbers and no return on investment—that much more money and more labor would be required to make good on the initial investment. In a bind, the Virginia Company did what companies today would do: It put together an advertising campaign.

Most advertising played on the English working person's longing for land. In *The Longman History of the United States of America*, Hugh Brogan cites the prevalent slogan of the times: "In Virginia land free and labour scarce; in England land scarce and labour plenty."

One persuasive instrument of propaganda, *Nova Britannia: Offering Most Ex-*cellent *Fruites by Planting in Virginia,* a pamphlet published by the London Company in 1609, made a long and well-developed argument for colonizing the Americas. The anonymous author embellished the truth when he wrote of a virtual paradise inhabited by generous people waiting only for the instruction of the good English people:

> *The country it selfe is large and great ... [and] also commendable and hopefull every way, the ayre [air] and clymate most sweete and wholsome, much warmer then [than]* England, *and very agreeable to our Natures: It is inhabited with wild and savage people.... They are generally very loving and gentle, and doe entertaine and relieve our people with great kindnesse: they are easy to be brought to good, and would fayne [like to] embrace a better condition: the land yeeldeth naturallie [provides naturally] for the sustentation [sustenance, or necessities] of man.... But of this that I have said, if bare nature be so amiable in its naked kind, what may we hope, when Arte and Nature both shall*

wealth from one generation to the next) was ruled by a system called primogeniture, under which all of a family's wealth passed to the oldest son upon the father's death. This system ensured that the estates of the wealthy did not get divided into small pieces, but rather remained in the hands of a few, leaving the aristocracy (government by the elite or a small class of the privileged) intact. For the excluded younger members of some families, the prospect of sailing to unknown shores to make one's fortune had strong appeal.

America held the promise of a future that was not already set in stone. In England, there was a shortage of trees

joyne, and strive together, to give best content to man and beast?

Captain John Smith (c. 1580–1631), upon returning from Jamestown, also became a champion marketer of the American colonizing expeditions. In 1609 he wrote *A Map of Virginia: With a Description of the Countrey, the Commodities, People, Government, and Religion,* in which he described at length the almost endless variety of nature's bounty in the New World, also promoting its suitability for commercialization and industry:

> *The mildnesse of the aire, the fertilitie of the soile, and the situation of the rivers are so propitious to the nature and use of man as no place is more convenient for pleasure, profit, and mans sustenance. Under that latitude or climat, here will live any beasts, as horses, goats, sheep, asses, hens, &c. as appeared by them that were carried thither. The waters, Isles, and shoales, are full of safe harbours for ships of warre or merchandize, for boats of all sortes, for transportation or fishing, &c. The Bay and rivers have much marchandable [sellable] fish and places fit for Salt coats, building of ships, making of iron, &c.*

Many other propaganda pieces of these years attempted to recruit settlers or investors by overstating the virtues of the New World and its inhabitants. While there was truth in the descriptions, like all advertisers the recruiters presented only one side of the picture. Disease and harsh weather would claim thousands of lives in Jamestown. At the very time these pieces were published, the people at Jamestown were experiencing the devastating "starving time" during the winter of 1609–10. Although land was plentiful, clearing the forests and establishing farms was backbreaking, dangerous, and long-term work that had been reaping few gains in those first years. While the advertising drew many potential settlers and investors, none were well prepared by this propaganda for the difficult times that lay ahead in the colonies.

and other necessary resources. There was no land available for the taking, as there seemed to be in the Americas. English people heard about the beauty of the new territory: the trees and the lakes and rivers. For some of the discontented and adventurous, the New World provided new hope.

Religion

The upheavals in the religion of England played a large role in the settlement of the New World, particularly New England. Before the sixteenth century, England had been a Roman Catholic state. Starting in 1529, King Henry

VIII (1491–1547) broke the English Church from Rome and the pope (the head of the Roman Catholic Church). Henry had been married to Catherine of Aragon (1485–1536), the daughter of the Spanish King Ferdinand (1452–1516) and Queen Isabella (1451–1504). When Catherine failed to give birth to a male heir to the throne, the king asked the pope to annul the marriage so he could marry his new favorite, Ann Boleyn (c.1504–1536), who was pregnant. The pope refused his request. King Henry then broke with Rome and placed himself at the head of the English Church. His third marriage to Jane Seymour (1509–1537) produced a son, Edward (1537–1553). In reality, little changed in the church during Henry's reign. The English Church continued its Catholic practices as before, but without the sanction of the pope.

When Henry VIII died, there followed two short but fairly extreme reigns. In the reign of Henry's young son, Edward VI, who ruled from 1547 to 1553, England's national church was made over into a truly Protestant church, a Christian church that denies the pope's authority and accepts the Bible as the only source of revealed truth. When Edward died, Mary (1516–1558), Henry's daughter by Catherine of Aragon, took the throne and proclaimed all of England to be Roman Catholic once again. When the Protestant leaders rebelled, Mary had many of them executed.

Mary died in 1558 and was succeeded by Elizabeth I, who reigned until 1603. Elizabeth strove to unify England under one religion that would be accepted by all. She created a state church—its beliefs and its leaders were chosen by her—with a Protestant basis but retaining many Roman Catholic practices. The religion was called the Church of England, or the Anglican religion. The compromise worked well for most of the people of England, but there were dissenters. The Protestant nature of the church displeased a portion of the many Catholics in the country and there were Protestants who wished to "purify" the Church of England of the remnants of Roman Catholicism. This group of Protestants, called the Puritans, arose in England in the 1560s. Elizabeth invited Puritans to participate in England's political system and to form their own places of worship as long as they recognized her as the head of the Church of England. As a whole, the Puritans did not wish to separate from the Church of England, only to wait for its reform. Elizabeth was skillful in bringing the country together, and it was only after her death that the great migrations of religious dissenters (nonconformers) would begin.

Jamestown

In 1606 the Plymouth Company sent out its first expedition to find a place for a colony. The first vessel never made it to the New World, but a second expedition landed in what is now Maine and returned with glorious accounts. The company sent out two more ships in 1607, and a settlement was begun near the mouth of the Sagadahoc (now Kennebec) River. This colony quickly failed for lack of supplies and discipline.

The London Company, in the meantime, had bought three ships and recruited 144 men and boys to volunteer for its South Virginia project. The group included forty soldiers, thirty-five "gentlemen," a doctor and a minister, and the rest artisans and laborers. The expedition sailed on December 20, 1606. On board was John Smith, an ex-soldier and adventurer with a very strong and daring (and sometimes irritating) personality. During the passage, Smith insulted one of the ships' captains and was arrested and held prisoner for the duration. The four-month journey was long and difficult, and only 105 passengers survived. They landed near the Chesapeake in April 1607 and then traveled about fifty miles up the James River, where the colonists decided to build their settlement. Though well suited for defense and travel, the site was located near a swamp that was home to mosquitoes and a deadly disease called malaria. The deaths due to disease among early settlers were staggeringly high.

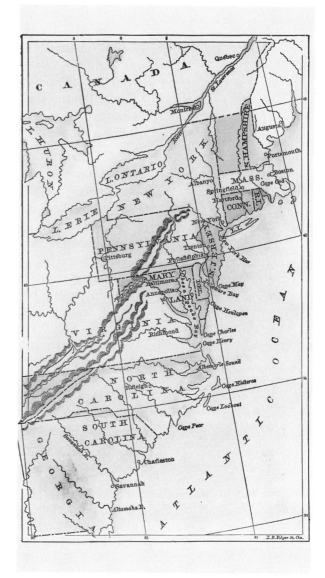

A map showing the original thirteen English colonies in America. *Reproduced by permission of © Bettmann/Corbis.*

According to plan, the surviving colonists built their settlement—some small wooden thatched-roof cottages set inside a palisade, a large fence or wall set up for protection. The London Company had sent a sealed box on the trip with them, to be opened only when they had arrived at their new home. It contained a document appointing the new colony's council, or local governing board of fourteen men. Smith was among those appointed.

The settlers badly needed to get crops planted quickly in order to set a store of food away for the next winter. Unfortunately, many of them, hoping to get rich quick, went out in search of gold instead of farming. It was a deadly mistake, for they found no gold and suffered terribly from shortages throughout the winter that followed. Supplies from home were never enough—ships from England reached Jamestown only four times between 1607 and 1609. When autumn came, two-thirds of the settlers had already died, and it was clear that the rest of them did not have enough food to survive the winter. Smith, seeing that the situation was desperate, stepped in and took power over the colony. Refusing to allow the settlers to give up and sail off for England, he made a deal with the neighboring Powhatan Indians to obtain food. He forced the colonists to get to work. Because of his leadership, the colony had a corn crop the next year (which was, unfortunately, eaten by rats). Smith was named president of Jamestown by the other colonists in 1608. Hurt in a gunpowder explosion, he returned to England in 1609.

Death in the colony

Even with the help of the Powhatan, Jamestown colonists suffered terribly. The London Company sent another expedition to Jamestown in 1609 with eight hundred more settlers—this time, sending families rather than just men. They arrived to a terrible situation. The winter of 1609 to 1610 was called the "starving time" in Jamestown colony. There were 838 settlers as winter approached, and only 60 of them survived. The London Company, nevertheless, sent along more settlers and more supplies and the deadly pattern continued. According to Roger Daniels in *Coming to America: A History of Immigration and Ethnicity in American Life*, be-

The Powhatan and the Jamestown Settlers

Before the Jamestown settlers arrived, the Powhatan Indians had met with other Europeans. The Spanish had landed on the coast of Virginia in 1525 and hostilities and violence had resulted. The Powhatan also had contact with the English settlers at Roanoke, but no one knows the extent. By the time of Jamestown, the European diseases had taken their toll on the Indians in the area, but they were again prospering. By the end of the sixteenth century, the shrewd and powerful Chief Powhatan (c.1550–1618) had built up a large empire, controlling over thirty-six tribes in the area. The estimated population of his Powhatan Confederacy was about eight or nine thousand people living in 128 to 200 villages. The confederacy was advanced in trading and had a skilled military.

Chief Powhatan was peaceful with but suspicious of the Jamestown settlers when they arrived. Their numbers were not great and they posed little threat, so they were tolerated. According to the accounts of John Smith, during his first year in the colony the Powhatan captured him and threatened to execute him. Powhatan's daughter, Pocahontas (1595–1617), Smith claimed, saved him from being slain and then begged her father to help the settlers. This story is strongly questioned by most historians, but the Powhatan did save the settlers that first year from almost certain starvation.

Pocahontas continued to serve as a go-between for the two groups. After Smith went back to England in 1609, some of the Englishmen kidnapped Pocahontas and held her hostage. Her father did not pay the full ransom they asked and so they kept her, though after a while she was allowed to move about freely. She met and married colonist John Rolfe (1585–1622) in 1614. In 1616 Rolfe brought Pocahontas and their infant son to England, where she was introduced to the royal family and other notables. Pocahontas caused great excitement in England and probably did much to help the London Company recruit settlers and investors. But while she was in England, she caught an infectious disease, and died just as they were preparing to return to Virginia in 1617. Her father died the next year, and the Powhatan would pass into the hands of less skillful rulers. In 1622 the Powhatan attacked the Jamestown colony and killed many of the colonists, beginning a war that lasted ten years. The war weakened the Powhatan. By 1675 the Confederacy had crumbled and the remaining Indian population was forced to live by Virginia law.

tween 1619 and 1622 the London Company sent about 3,750 people to Virginia, adding to the population of about 700 that was already living there. An estimated 3,000 of those settlers died, leaving only about 1,200 in 1625.

Social life in early Jamestown

The early community of Jamestown had nothing in common with the aristocratic society that would later arise in the South. In fact, the social life in Virginia lacked most of the manners and morality found in any English community. Despite attempts to create a family base in the colony, Jamestown remained predominantly male for nearly half a century. Of the 1,200 survivors in the colony in 1625, only an estimated 244 were women. Most of the gentlemen who had immigrated either died or went back to England, where life was easier. The immigrants, for the most part, were single tradesmen and laborers from the cities of England, who were in search of quick wealth. Many planned to return to England and had little community spirit. Disorder, drunkenness, and lawlessness were common among these restless residents. To add to the lawless atmosphere, Britain began sending its convicted criminals to the colonies.

Motivation to work hard within the colony was lacking as well. Thus, in 1619 the London Company began to give parcels of land outright to its shareholders. It also issued a new charter, under which the colony of Jamestown was to have its own governing assembly. The assembly did give the colonists the right to express their views to their rulers. By 1622, though, when the Powhatan attacked the settlement, it was a last straw for the Virginia Company, which disbanded. Jamestown became a royal colony.

The tobacco plantations

After the attack, the Jamestown colonists began a period of brutal retaliation against the Powhatan. Another war took place in 1644, in which the colonists defeated the Native Americans. By 1646 Indians were banned completely from the Jamestown peninsula and the settlers took over the Indians' land to start tobacco farms.

In 1612 tobacco had been introduced in Virginia by colonist John Rolfe (1585–1622; famous for having married

Pocahontas, the Powhatan chief's daughter). The king, believing smoking to be immoral, had been against the growing of tobacco, but the tobacco market in the New World boomed, making easy profits for Jamestown. By 1640, tobacco farming had become the main attraction for potential immigrants and a center of life in Virginia. The main thing required to profit from tobacco was plenty of land. Tobacco crops spread up and down the James River throughout the territory. As the production of tobacco went up, the price went down, and so more tobacco was produced. With the promise of tobacco-crop profits, the population of Jamestown grew rapidly. In 1640 Virginia had become the largest English settlement with ten thousand people.

By about 1650, the terrible death rate in the Virginia settlement was steadily decreasing. Some wealthy families began to emigrate from England to establish tobacco plantations. Although they could finance their own venture, they desperately needed laborers. The solution throughout the

The ruins of the Ambler Mansion, in Jamestown, Virginia, built in 1750. The Amblers were one of the wealthy and powerful families in eighteenth-century Jamestown.
Reproduced by permission of © Lee Snider/Corbis.

1600s lay in bringing in indentured servants. In fact, the English crown granted the farm owners a small parcel of land for each immigrant whose passage they financed. The farm owners paid for the indentured servant's passage from England to Virginia, for which the indentured servant agreed to work for the farmer for a set number of years, usually seven. At the end of the service term, the indentured servant was supposed to be given either a small piece of land and some tools or other goods to help him or her set up in a new life in the colony. Under this system, there was a constant turnover of people on the tobacco farms, as the indentured servants filled out their terms and moved on.

About 40 percent of the immigrants to the Chesapeake area in the seventeenth century were indentured servants. Most came from England's working class and three-quarters of them were young, single males. There were laws in place to protect them from the worst abuses by their employers and to ensure that they were paid for their service. But in reality much depended upon their individual masters. Many indentured servants died in service and stories of abuse were widespread. At the end of their terms, some employers did not fulfill their contracts and the indentured servant, without means of support, had little choice but to remain in servitude.

Among the indentured servants in the Virginia colony were a small number of Africans. In the early years the African servants were treated more or less like other indentured servants, and some went on to own and farm their own lands when their term of servitude was over. By the last quarter of the seventeenth century, however, when an aristocracy had developed around the tobacco plantations, a new system was forming. Slave labor was instituted to meet the needs of the large plantations.

Between 1603 and 1660, fifty thousand English men and women had immigrated to Virginia and Maryland, most coming after 1624.

Pilgrims

Around the turn of the seventeenth century, a small group of English Puritans, many living in the town of Scrooby in Yorkshire, decided to break away from the Church

of England in order to remain faithful to their beliefs. This group was initially called the Separatists, but much later came to be known as the Pilgrims, a word that means "travelers." Apart from the leaders, most of the Pilgrims were poorly educated farmers. In the beginning of the seventeenth century, after King James succeeded Elizabeth to the throne, the authorities in the Church of England had arrested and otherwise persecuted some of the Separatists for their refusal to conform to the church. A group of the Pilgrims migrated to Holland, where they lived in the community of Leyden for about ten years.

Not happy living in Holland, the Pilgrims applied to immigrate to the new English colony in Virginia. Virginia, though, only accepted Anglicans, members of the Church of England. Fortunately, another London Company project was just getting organized for the purpose of colonizing New England. The Pilgrims and the investors of this project set up a joint stock company. On September 16, 1620, 102 men,

An engraving of the Pilgrims at prayer before embarking on the *Mayflower,* on their voyage to the New World.
Reproduced by permission of © Bettmann/Corbis.

women, and children boarded the *Mayflower,* a ship heading
for the new colony. Of this group, only 41 were actually from
the Leyden Separatists. The remainder were hired men, paid
servants, or "strangers," non-Pilgrims who wanted to make a
new life in America. During their two-month sail to America,
the Pilgrims created the Mayflower Compact, a document
that set forth the method of government of their new colony.

The Pilgrims came ashore in Plymouth Harbor on the
western side of Cape Cod Bay on December 21, 1620. They
had chosen a much more healthful place to live than had the
settlers at Jamestown. The cold weather of New England kept
the disease level low. The Pilgrims had also come equipped to
feed themselves. Even so, during that first winter nearly half
of them died. In the spring they planted corn, with help
from the neighboring Pokanoket band of the Wampanoag
nation of Indians. Through good fortune, an Indian named
Squanto, who spoke English, lived nearby. Squanto, a
Wampanoag of the Patuxet band, had been kidnapped by an

English explorer and sold into slavery to the Spanish. A Spanish friar had secured Squanto's release and he had then lived in England for some time before returning to the New World with another English explorer. When he returned home, Squanto found that his band of the Wampanoag had abandoned its village and disappeared, and the Pokanet Wampanoag soon captured him. He was still among them when the Pilgrims arrived.

Relations between the Wampanoag and the Pilgrims were quite good at first. The Pilgrims made a meal of thanksgiving in 1621 and shared it with some of the Wampanoag. This is often considered as the first Thanksgiving, although it would not become a yearly tradition for many years to come.

The Pilgrims built a very small community within protective palisades at Plymouth. Each family built its own simple house. From the start, the financial situation was not promising for the company. The Pilgrims created small, self-sustaining farms in the New World, fighting rocky soil and a harsh climate. They were a hardworking group and were able to feed themselves, but their labor did not result in profits for the investors. The company eventually gave up on the project and sold the Pilgrims their shares.

Among the Pilgrims there was a common goal of leading a simple and pious life. This led to harmonious relations among them. However, they were not very welcoming to new settlers—the non-separatists who were arriving steadily from England. For the most part, those newcomers moved on and founded their own towns in surrounding areas. By the 1630s, only one decade after they had arrived, the tiny town of Plymouth was well-established and its population was stable at about three hundred people. The Pilgrims, by their own desire, remained separate from the growing population around them.

Massachusetts, 1630–40

Immigration to Massachusetts, like the Plymouth colony, was stimulated by religious dissenters: the Puritans. The Puritans were the disciples of the French theologian John Calvin (1509–1564). Puritans believed that the world had been a corrupt place since the time of the original sin, when Adam and Eve fell from grace in Eden. In their view, only a few elite persons, through the grace of God, could be saved. The Church of England, on the other hand, held that human beings could bring about their own salvation through repentance of their sins and doing good works. The Church of England continued to employ bishops in the church and use other Catholic rituals and symbols, to which the Puritans objected. Although the Puritans believed in a more simple worship based on the Bible, they were not separatists. They believed the Church of England could be reformed.

England's King Charles I (1600–1649), who took the throne in 1625, was married to the Catholic daughter of the French king. He quickly grew tired of the Puritan activism, which consisted mainly of petitioning the British Parliament for the reform of the Church of England. In 1629 Charles dissolved Parliament, thereby denying the Puritans their public forum. In a surprising move, he then turned around and granted a royal charter to the Puritan-controlled Massachusetts Bay Company. These acts had the effect of pushing the Puritans to leave England and at the same time providing them a place to go. Massachusetts was settled remarkably quickly.

The Great Migration

The first Massachusetts Bay Company settlers landed in Massachusetts in 1630. During the next ten years, the migration to the New World was the largest England would experience. The reasons for the rapid migration from England were numerous. The harassment of Puritans in England was certainly one cause. The economic problems in England were another. The lure of land that was ripe for the taking (the English did not believe that Indians were proper owners) was great, as was the idea of creating a new moral order and a new society. There was some talk of converting the Indians to Christian beliefs, but this was a less important motivation for the Puritans than it had been for many Spanish settlers.

In just ten years, about twenty thousand English people came to New England in what is known as the Great Migration. In fact, approximately sixty thousand people left England during those years, two-thirds heading in other directions. Many of the American immigrants in New England were Puritans and developed their communities according to Puritan principles.

The leader of the Massachusetts migration was John Winthrop (1588–1649), a wealthy country lawyer. Winthrop sailed with the first fleet of seven hundred people who arrived in Massachusetts in 1630 in June—early enough to begin planting crops. Two hundred settlers died the first year, and another hundred returned to England. But others continued to arrive.

The Puritan immigrants

The Puritan immigrants, like the Plymouth settlers, intended to settle permanently in America. This meant that they often came as families or, if single, were placed in family groups. They were older than the Virginia settlers, with average ages in the thirties and forties. The New Englanders settled in an orderly fashion, forming themselves into small groups that bought land from the Indians, petitioned the legislature for the right to become a town, and then moved to the town site and set up. Husbands, wives, and their children set up housekeeping immediately. Those men and women who were as yet unmarried boarded in the houses of those who were married. The towns that the first immigrants established filled quickly, and those who came on later ships spread out and created new towns.

New England towns came in many sizes and shapes. Some had individually owned farms and others had community fields where all the townspeople worked together and split up the crops. In settling, though, the colonists usually followed a basic pattern. The site for the town was chosen by the colony's government and was generally given to a group of about thirty or forty families. The people in the group had generally known one another back in England, but they might take in a "stranger" if he or she had the right skills and good standing in the community. The typical New England village had a town green with a meetinghouse (church); the

A portrait of the first Massachusetts governor, John Winthrop. *Courtesy of the Library of Congress.*

A painting of the Puritans going to church. *Reproduced by permission of © Bettmann/Corbis.*

homes were arranged near the meetinghouse and close to one another. Most of the government work was done at the local level by the town officials. New England towns had their own militias, groups of citizens organized for military service.

The Puritans believed that only certain people were "God's elect," or in their terminology, "saints." They developed a form of examination to determine who among them were the saints. To keep their commonwealth pure, they ruled that only saints could govern or vote. (A commonwealth is a form of government based on the common good of the citizens rather than the rule of a monarch.)

Dissenters

Freedom of religion was not supported in Massachusetts and it wasn't long before some colonists began to question some of the Puritans' ideas. In 1631 Puritan clergyman Roger Williams (1603–1683) arrived in Massachusetts, taking a

The First Colonial Houses

When a family first arrived in one of the early British colonies, they needed immediate shelter. Some were lucky enough to find homes that had been abandoned by Native Americans. The answer for many in both Virginia and New England was to quickly build a sod house (sod is turf, or a piece of soil with grass growing at its surface). The settlers dug a six- to seven-foot hole, lined it with wood, and then covered it with sod or a thatch (straw or grasslike material used as covering) roof. Sometimes they continued to live in these sod houses for several years because there was so much other work to do in clearing land and establishing a farm that they did not have the time to build a house.

When the time came to build, the first real house in the New World was generally a very simple hut. Most of these huts were one big square room, and some had a sleeping loft above that was accessible by ladder. The floors were dirt. Windows were tiny and covered by shutters to keep out the elements. Like the sod houses, the door opening was very low, making it difficult for large animals or unfriendly humans to enter. The roof was usually thatched or made of sod. Generally in the first house a family built, there was just one big hall, without separate rooms or closets.

The fireplace was an important feature in every house. With spaces between boards so big that the light came through, these early houses were very cold and drafty. The fireplace provided the heat as well as light and a place for cooking. Fireplaces were so heavily used that people had to spend a lot of time cutting down firewood year-round. There was very little furniture in the early settlers' homes. Most settlers did not own beds, but slept instead in bedrolls, which could be put away during the day. They often ate their meals off of a board while sitting on chests or stools. The privy, or outhouse, was located outside. The early colonial houses were very dark inside. Candles were rare and difficult to make. People usually went to bed when the sun went down, but when necessary, kindling was thrown on the fire to flare up and make useful light.

Over the years, the colonists could add more rooms onto the house. Variations on the basic shelter grew in different regions and in accordance with the family's needs. But most settlers, out of necessity, started out with the basic one-room hut.

post as a minister in the church at Salem. Williams questioned the Puritans' failure to break off completely with the Church of England and urged his Salem church to break with the other Puritan churches in the commonwealth. He also argued

that the Massachusetts Bay charter did not give the Puritans the right to take land away from the American Indians. This was taken as a direct challenge, and the Puritan general court banished Williams from Massachusetts in 1635.

Anne Hutchinson (1591–1643), a highly respected Puritan who had arrived in Boston in 1634, expressed her own dissent. Hutchinson believed that long ago, in the beginning of time, God had decided who would find salvation and who would not. She argued that nothing individuals could do would change their status. She did not believe that all the Puritan ministers were necessarily "saints." She argued that each individual should obey the voice of God rather than the commands of either church or state. Hutchinson did not hold a position in the church, but she was known for her sharp intellect and had many powerful friends in the community. The general court banished her in 1637.

A portrait of Roger Williams, founder of Rhode Island. *Reproduced by permission of Hulton Archive/Getty Images.*

Rhode Island

After being banished from Massachusetts, Roger Williams took refuge among the Indians. A few other dissenters joined him and they moved on to establish a new settlement, which they called Providence, in what is now Rhode Island. Williams purchased the land from the Indians and welcomed other outcasts. He provided each new settler with a home lot and a farm. Providence grew very slowly. It was a simple farm community with no financial help from outside. The heads of families participated in a "town meeting" type of government. The governing officials were not given authority over any church matters. Williams firmly believed in the separation of the church and the state (the idea that religion should not influence government and government should not interfere with matters of religion).

Anne Hutchinson and some of her supporters started another settlement in Rhode Island called Portsmouth. Another settlement was established at Newport, and then another at Warwick. All of these settlements, although not yet joined together in a confederation (an alliance or union), had been created by dissenters.

The New England Confederation

In 1639, three small towns, Wethersfield, Windsor, and Hartford, that had been settled by migrants from Massachusetts, joined together as the colony of Connecticut. Another settlement, New Haven, was established nearby. Connecticut, without a major harbor, could not grow as Massachusetts had. Its population relied mainly on farming and raising livestock. Most of its population came from Massachusetts and so shared its English orientation. The few African slaves who helped work the farms of the wealthy were the exception. In 1774 the white population numbered 191,000; nonwhites, including Indians, totaled 6,450.

As the Puritans spread out in their territory, they came into conflict with the Pequot Indians. An English trader was killed in 1634 and another in 1636. Although it was never clear who killed the traders, the Massachusetts authorities demanded that the Pequot hand over the murderers. The Pequot refused. As the colonists prepared for war, the Pequot attacked the town of Wethersfield in 1637, killing nine settlers. A joint attack by the colonists of Massachusetts, Plymouth, and Connecticut was launched in response, and the Pequot fort was burned to the ground, with five hundred men, women, and children trapped inside to burn to death.

After the Pequot War, the colonies decided to join in a confederacy (a joining together of people or states for a common purpose). The United Colonies of New England, or the New England Confederation, was founded on May 19, 1643, in Boston. It consisted of the four colonies of Massachusetts, Plymouth, Connecticut, and New Haven. Meanwhile, Roger Williams, convinced that the four settlements of Rhode Island had to cooperate with each other in order to prevent its neighbors from seizing control of them, also worked for a federation, or union. In September 1644 the

English crown authorized the union of Providence, Portsmouth, and Newport as "The Incorporation of Providence Plantations." Warwick was included later.

New England continued to thrive and grow after the Great Migration, even without new settlers arriving. In 1650 there were about twenty-two thousand people of European descent in New England. Fifty years later there were about ninety thousand people of European descent; most of them second-generation Americans of English descent. As late as the American Revolution (1775–83), 98 percent of the New England colonies' population was of English descent. All of the signers of the Declaration of Independence, with one exception, were of English descent.

Maryland

Like the Puritans, some Catholics wished to practice their religion in a purer way. One such Catholic was George Calvert, Lord Baltimore (c. 1580–1632), whose 1625 conversion to Catholicism had cost him his royal positions. He was, however, granted a petition for land in Mary's Land, or Maryland, in the New World. Calvert died in 1632, and Maryland's charter was not signed until a month after his death. It awarded a proprietary grant to Calvert's son and heir, Cecilius Calvert (1606–1675), second Baron of Baltimore. (A proprietary grant awards full ownership of a colony to an individual, with the authority to govern and distribute land.)

Hoping to create a European-style aristocracy, Cecilius Calvert sought wealthy families to buy his land, but he found few. Under King Charles I, most Catholics were content to stay in England. Although Calvert welcomed Christians of all denominations, most non-Catholics hesitated to place themselves in a Catholic's power. In the end about twenty-five Catholic gentlemen investors joined the expedition, along with about one hundred servants, yeoman farmers (farmers who work their own land), and artisans. Some of the members of the expedition were Protestants, and a few were women.

The settlers bought land from the Native American inhabitants on the northern bank of the Potomac River and created the settlement of St. Mary's. The suitability of Maryland's land for tobacco set it on a course much like Virginia's. Those with some capital or connections amassed large land-holdings. Those without came to work for them, often as indentured servants. Their life was very hard, with long, grueling hours of labor and miserable living conditions. Most of these settlers were young men.

By 1648 the population of Maryland was low, at 350 people. There were not enough women to provide wives for the men. The death rate was very high. But immigration and natural reproduction helped the colony's population grow. By 1660 the colony had an estimated 2,500 people; in 1675, 13,000; and in 1701, when an official census was undertaken, 32,000. By 1760 population estimates had reached 162,000. In 1692 the Church of England was established in Maryland and three years later the capital of the colony was moved to the Protestant city of Annapolis.

Pennsylvania

Pennsylvania's founder, William Penn (1644–1718), was a member of the Society of Friends (the Quakers), a radical Protestant sect in England founded by George Fox (1624–1691) in the late 1640s. The British king awarded Penn a proprietorship in the American colonies as payment of a debt owed to his deceased father. Like the proprietary charter Lord Baltimore received for Maryland, it made Penn the owner and grantor of all land in the province and gave him authority to establish the form of government and make the laws.

Penn intended Pennsylvania to be a holy commonwealth (a land with a government based on the common good of the citizens), characterized by peace, brotherly love, and religious toleration. As a member of the Society of Friends, he rejected formal creeds and worship. Quakers believe that the Holy Spirit dwells within each person, and that a person who yields completely to the prompting of this divine presence, or "inner light," will be saved, or regenerated. Like other proprietors in the New World, Penn hoped to profit from the sale or rent of land in his colony, but his primary aim in setting up a colony was a religious one.

Most of the first immigrants to Pennsylvania were from the British Isles and Germany. From 1681 to 1710 numerous English and Welsh Quaker migrants populated the Philadelphia area. By 1750 most German immigrants had settled in a ring around them, just outside the Philadelphia area. In 1717 the Scotch-Irish began to populate the land in a ring just beyond that of the Germans. By 1776 each of the major groups—which remained quite distinct—constituted roughly one-third of the three hundred thousand Pennsylvanians. Minorities included about ten thousand Scots, ten thousand Irish Catholics, eight thousand French Huguenots, eight thousand African slaves (despite Quaker hostility to slavery), and one thousand Jews.

Georgia

As the colonies began to flourish, economic depression and unemployment in England had filled the prisons with debtors. A committee led by James Edward Oglethorpe (1696–1785) succeeded in freeing thousands of debtors from the prisons, but they had no place to go. Finally, Oglethorpe's group petitioned the crown for a tract of land south and west of the Carolinas with the intention of establishing a settlement especially for debtors. In 1732 England gave the twenty-one-member group of trustees a charter authorizing them to found and to manage the colony that was to be Georgia.

The trustees considered the project the greatest social experiment of their age and went to work eliciting contributions from churches, organizations, and individuals. Since the settlers were to participate in a social experiment, they were individually selected. Each would receive free passage to Georgia, fifty acres of land, and tools, seeds, and provisions. By the fall of 1732, more than one hundred settlers had been chosen. Oglethorpe led the expedition to America. Landing at Charleston, South Carolina, he soon chose a site for the town of Savannah and reached an agreement with the chief of the Yamacraw Indians who resided there. In February 1733 the colonists arrived in small boats.

Oglethorpe arranged the settlement in an orderly fashion. To make sure they did not spread out so far that all sense of community would be lost, no one was allowed more than fifty acres. Each family owned a town lot with a garden and a piece of farmland nearby. Settlers held their land for

life, and only eldest sons could inherit land. The prohibition against sale or rental of property eliminated the possibility of unselected immigrants becoming part of the community.

In addition to the debtors, the trustees also admitted approved "adventurers," persons who paid their own passage to the colony. Persecuted Protestants from Europe were also welcomed. The social experiment was halted, though, because the English government failed to send many debtors to the new colony. After a few years, the adventurers and foreigners far outnumbered the debtor element in the population.

The English colonies grow

By 1733 the settlement of the Atlantic seaboard from Maine to South Carolina by English colonies was completed. All thirteen colonies were established, including New York, which had been seized from the Dutch (under whom it had been known as New Netherland) in 1664.

James Oglethorpe, standing on left with sword touching the ground, in council with several Indians. *Courtesy of the Library of Congress.*

As the colonies grew, five cities developed as centers of trade and commerce: Boston in 1700 was the largest with 6,700 people; followed by Philadelphia and New York, each with 5,000; Newport, Rhode Island, with 2,600; and Charles Town, South Carolina, with 2,000. The cities and surrounding areas were growing in wealth and population. Having survived the early stages of colonization, the colonies were surpassing all expectations.

Although the initial numbers of settlers had been small, immigration increased steadily throughout the colonial period. The population of Massachusetts Bay Colony grew from two thousand to sixteen thousand in just thirteen years (1630–43). Georgia's population increased from a mere one hundred in 1733 to as many as nine thousand in 1760. Between the years of 1717 and 1760, the number of settlers in North Carolina jumped from nine thousand to ninety-three thousand. South Carolina in the same period, jumped from nineteen thousand to one hundred thousand.

Overall, the total population of the thirteen original colonies went from 220,000 in 1690 to 1,500,000 in 1760, then soared to 2,750,000 by 1790. Between 80 and 85 percent of the population was English. English customs, clothing, architecture, language, literature, law, and religion dominated in the colonies and shaped early U.S. culture precisely because the English population was the largest in the early stages of the nation's history. (On the other hand, of course, the American culture has always had a variety of ethnic communities and many Americans speak other languages along with English.) As immigrants from other countries arrived in the United States thereafter, their cultures would add to the American identity.

English immigration after the colonial period

Once the American Revolution (1775–83) began, English immigration to America virtually ceased until about 1790. Then, a shortage of land in England caused a number of farmers to take advantage of the new lands being cleared in the United States. Beginning in the late 1790s, thousands of textile workers began flocking to the United States from England, settling in the mill towns of New England and New Jersey. Im-

English Industry Immigrates to the United States

At the age of fourteen, Samuel Slater (1768–1835) became an apprentice in a cotton mill in his hometown in England. He worked there for eight years, getting to know the textile machinery and the industry in general very well. At the end of that time, he decided to immigrate to the United States, but there was a problem. England had the most advanced textile machinery in the world and wanted to keep its technology secret. It had therefore forbidden the export from England of anything related to the machinery, including the textile engineers themselves. Slater managed to emigrate in disguise, not even telling his family he was going.

Once settled in the United States, Slater went to Pawtucket, Rhode Island, where work was already in place in the attempt to industrialize the textile industry. Slater recreated the most important of the British water-powered spinning machines based on the designs of English inventor Richard Arkwright (1732–1792). Since Slater had been a manager in the mills in England, he also provided many of the successful business techniques and training for a textile factory. In 1793 the first successful water-powered U.S. cotton mill—Old Slater Mill—was in operation. Slater is credited with founding the American cotton-textile industry in Pawtucket.

migration was brought to a halt again when England and France went to war in 1803, and all ships were commandeered (seized) for military use. When the war ended in 1815, English immigration to the United States resumed with force, bringing 750,000 English people to the shores of the United States between 1815 and 1860. Most settled in the northeast.

The American Civil War (1861–65) once again halted immigration, but as soon as the war ended, the largest wave of English immigration to the United States began. (The American Civil War was a war in the United States between the Union [North], who was opposed to slavery, and the Confederacy [South], who was in favor of slavery.) A series of crop failures in England, plus a tremendous increase in opportunities available in the United States because of industrialization and westward expansion, created a high motivation for immigration. From 1865 to 1895, some 2.3 million English people moved to the United States. Some took industrial jobs in the East, while others became farmers or ranchers in the Midwest and West.

One interesting group of English immigrants to the United States were the gentlemen ranchers who set up huge cattle operations in the West in the late nineteenth century. Most were young aristocrats who had been educated at elite schools in England. They played tennis and chess, drank tea, and rode with the cowboys during round-up time. The English gentlemen were drawn to the romance of the "Wild West." As the open range became overcrowded, harsh winters killed off the cattle, and Native Americans fought for their dwindling lands, most of these gentlemen packed up and moved back to England, leaving behind new cattle breeds to blend with the American stock.

Since the late nineteenth century, most English immigration to the United States has been made up of individuals and individual families. Immigration from England to America steadily dropped off during the twentieth century, with the exception of the seventy thousand English "war brides" who came to the United States in the 1940s. War brides were English women who met and married American servicemen stationed in England during World War II (1939–45). English war brides were the largest group of female immigrants to the United States in the 1940s. Because there were so many of them, the U.S. Congress passed the War Brides Act of 1945 and the Alien Fiancées and Fiancés Act of 1946 to allow qualified women, and men, to immigrate more easily. The U.S. Army set up embarkation camps in England to process applicants, then provided free overseas transportation on army ships. The war brides comprised the last significant wave of English immigration so far in U.S. history.

English Americans today

The 2000 U.S. Census reports 28.3 million people in the United States who are of English ancestry. Approximately 13 percent of the nation is of English descent. Fewer than 1 percent of English Americans are foreign born (many of whom are likely to be war brides).

The official church of England is the Church of England, or the Anglican Church. Anglican immigrants to the United States created the Episcopal Church in America. Other early English immigrants were Puritans and Anabaptists: the Mennonites and the Amish, the German Brethren, or Dunkards, and the Society of Friends, or the Quakers, Congregationalist, Unitarian, and American Baptist.

Because the original thirteen states were former English colonies, the language, religion, architecture, customs, and legal, economic, and governmental systems of those English colonists set many of the standards for the United States. For centuries to come, other immigrants were expected to conform in major and minor ways to the English norm. Although English immigration to the United States has been minimal since the beginning of the twentieth century, there remains a pervasive English American foundation to U.S. culture, despite the fact that people who claim English descent are now only the third largest ethnic group in America.

For More Information

Books

Barrett, Tracy. *Growing Up in Colonial America*. Brookfield, CT: Millbrook Press, 1995.

Brogan, Hug. *The Longman History of the United States of America,* 2nd ed. London and New York: Addison Wesley Longman, 1999.

Daniels, Roger. *Coming to America: A History of Immigration and Ethnicity in American Life*. New York: HarperCollins, 1990.

Hawke, David Freeman. *Everyday Life in Early America*. New York: Harper & Row, 1988.

Middleton, Richard. *Colonial America, a History: 1565–1776,* 3rd ed. Oxford, UK: Blackwell Publishers, 2002.

Scott, John Anthony. *Settlers on the Eastern Shore: The British Colonies in North America, 1607–1750*. New York: Facts on File, 1991.

Web Sites

Virtual Jamestown: First-Hand Accounts of Virginia, 1575–1705. http://jefferson.village.virginia.edu/vcdh/jamestown/page2.html (accessed on February 26, 2004).

Scots and Scotch-Irish Immigration

6

In the 2000 U.S. Census, 4,319,232 people claimed Scottish heritage and 4,890,581 people claimed Scotch-Irish heritage. The two groups represent just over 3 percent of the U.S. population. In their early history in America, a good number of Scottish and Scotch-Irish Americans preferred to be far away from interfering neighbors and governments. Already skilled at dealing with difficult conditions in their homelands of Scotland and Northern Ireland, the Scots and Scotch-Irish gained the reputation of being rugged frontiersmen. Although they were initially looked down upon by the English and German colonists, both Scots and Scotch-Irish assimilated (blended) into the American mainstream easily and did not retain separate social customs.

Historical background

The Scottish belonged to two distinct groups, Highlanders and Lowlanders. Highlanders came from the north of Scotland, where the land is rugged and remote and the people were less influenced by England. Lowlanders came from

- The first Scottish immigrants to America were prisoners of war, sent (or transported) to the colonies by English ruler Oliver Cromwell (1599–1658) after he defeated Scotland in 1650.

- After the Battle of Culloden in 1746, the British placed the Act of Proscription upon the Highland Scots, which prohibited them from almost every aspect of practicing their traditions: wearing their tartan kilts, bearing arms, and even playing their traditional pipe music. The act completely destroyed the Highlands clan system.

- In the early 1600s British King James I (1566–1625) decided he wanted a Protestant population in Northern Ireland. From 1608 to 1697, about 200,000 Presbyterian Scots from the Lowlands immigrated to Ulster in Northern Ireland. Later, when these immigrants relocated once again to North America, they would come to be known as the Scotch-Irish.

- In the American Revolution (1775–83), Scotch-Irish Americans generally joined the rebel cause while Scottish Americans tended to side with the British crown.

- Golf was invented in Scotland and brought to America by Scottish and Scotch-Irish immigrants.

southern Scotland, which had been much more influenced by English language and culture. The Highlanders wore tartan kilts (colorfully patterned knee-length skirts) and spoke the Gaelic language. Social and political life in the northern Highland area of Scotland was, from ancient times, organized around clans, communities of people with strong family ties. The powerful clan leaders demanded loyalty and service in exchange for protecting the people from invasion.

Scotland had been dominated by English monarchs up to the fourteenth century, but by the sixteenth century, it was an independent nation. At that time Scotland became embroiled in the religious divisions between Roman Catholicism and the new Protestantism that had swept through much of Europe. Protestantism had been introduced in 1517, when German monk and scholar Martin Luther (1483–1546) nailed to the church door in Wittenberg his list of ninety-five theses, or statements, questioning the practices of the Roman Catholic Church. Luther believed that people should live their lives by following the Bible, not the pope. His call for reform brought about the rise of Protestant churches throughout Europe.

In the mid-1500s John Knox (1505–1572), a Catholic priest in Scotland, converted to Protestantism. He took several trips to Geneva, Switzerland, to study with John Calvin (1509–1564), the founder of the Puritan movement. Puritans believed that the world had been a corrupt place since the time of the original sin (when Adam and Eve fell from grace in Eden). In their view, churches,

Words to Know

Assimilation: The process for an outsider of being absorbed, or blending, into the mainstream culture.

Celtic: pronounced KEL-tick; Relating to an ancient race of European people—the Celts whose descendants live today in the Scottish Highlands, Ireland, Wales, and Brittany, a part of France. *Celtic* also refers to the language spoken by these people.

Gael: A Gaelic-speaking person from the Scottish Highlands, Ireland, or the Isle of Man.

Gaelic: The language spoken in the Celtic Scottish Highlands; forms of Gaelic are also spoken in Ireland and on the Isle of Man.

Haggis: A kind of sausage made from a combination of boiled sheep organs (heart, lungs, and liver), beef or sheep suet (raw fat), and oatmeal placed inside a sheep's stomach, which is sewn up and then boiled.

Indentured servants: People who contracted to work for an agreed-upon term with someone in the New World in exchange for payment for their passage.

Presbytery: A group of ministers and lay people who lead a Protestant church, as opposed to the bishops who head the Episcopalian churches, or the congregations, or members of the local church, who led the Puritan churches.

with their rituals and bishops, could not bring about religious enlightenment. They believed that only elite persons, through the grace of God, could be saved. Knox returned to Scotland from Geneva to form a Protestant denomination that he called the Church of Scotland. Knox had a fiery hatred for the Catholic Church, even declaring that the Scottish people had the right to violently overthrow a government headed by Catholics. By 1560 a new Scottish Parliament, backed by the English, led the Protestant reformation in Scotland. Knox persuaded Parliament to abolish Roman Catholicism as the official church in Scotland and to create a Scottish Presbyterian church. This church differed from other forms of Protestant churches mainly in that the church was led by a presbytery, a group of ministers and lay people (members of the church who are not ministers), rather than by bishops as in Episcopalian churches, or by congregations (the members of the local church) as in the Puritan churches. The Church of Scotland remains Presbyterian in the early twenty-first century.

Oliver Cromwell, the head of the English Parliament, who appointed himself Lord Protector of England, Scotland, Wales, and Ireland. The first Scottish immigrants to America were prisoners of war, forcibly sent to the colonies by Cromwell.

Scotland's history is strongly connected with England's. Although Scotland had its own royal family, the royal families of England and Scotland merged in 1603 when King James VI (1566–1625) of Scotland became the successor to the English throne upon the death of Elizabeth I (1533–1603). Becoming King James I of England, James united England and Scotland under one crown for the first time and started the Stuart line of English monarchs. Throughout his reign, Scotland remained torn by religious conflicts between the Catholics, who sought an alliance with France, and the Protestants, who were allied to the British. James's son Charles I (1600–1649) succeeded him to the English/Scottish throne in 1626. Charles married the daughter of the French king, a Catholic. Charles was Protestant, but he favored high Anglicanism (the Church of England, based on Roman Catholicism) with its rituals and bishops. Charles believed in his own divine right (God-given powers) as king to dictate religious matters, and everything else as well, to the people in his realm. Early in his reign, Charles imposed upon the Scottish church a bishop system. Scotland reluctantly went along with this action. Religion was the center of all political and social life in Scotland, but the small nation did not have the strength to rush to battle against a powerful king.

When Charles tried to impose a prayer book on Scotland, he drew firm opposition in the country. In 1638 the Scottish nobility drew up the Scottish National Covenant, which described the king's authority as being secondary to that of the Scottish Church, or *kirk,* as they called it. Charles, convinced of his divine right, declared war upon Scotland, and the Bishops' Wars (1639–40) ensued. During the wars, Charles ran out of money and had to ask Parliament for the funds to renew his forces in Scotland. He had offended the English Parliament too many times. They had had enough of the willful king and would not agree to fund the war. When the infuriated Charles had some members of Parliament arrested, the English Civil War (1642–51) began, pitting Parliament, with Oliver Cromwell (1599–1658) at its head, against the king and his supporters. Charles was defeated in Scotland. Because the English Parliament had promised religious reform in Scotland, the Scots handed Charles over to the British, even though he was a Stuart—a Scottish monarch. The British executed Charles for treason.

The troubles were not over for Scotland. Cromwell appointed himself Lord Protector of England, Scotland, Wales, and Ireland. Although Cromwell was a Protestant, the Scots did not align themselves with him. Charles's son, Charles II (1660–1685), signed the Scottish National Covenant, agreeing to the demands of the Scots. The Scots, in an attempt to restore Charles and the Stuart monarchs to the throne, fought a war against the forces of Oliver Cromwell and were defeated.

The first Scottish immigrants

The first Scottish immigrants to America were prisoners of war, forcibly sent to the colonies by Cromwell after he defeated Scotland in 1650. The Scottish prisoners of war served out their sentences by laboring in the English colonies of North America. There were also two failed Scottish colonies: one, in what is now New Jersey, was settled by a group of Quaker refugees in 1683, and the other, in South Carolina, was settled by a group of Presbyterians in 1684. More than a thousand prisoners were sent by Cromwell during his years at England's head. Because Scots were legally barred from emigrating from Scotland to America until 1707, there was not significant voluntary immigration until then.

In 1707 the Act of Union made Scotland, together with England and Wales, part of the United Kingdom, sharing a single parliament. Scots were given the same freedoms as English citizens. After the 1707 Union of the Parliaments, trade between Scotland and America increased. Scottish emigration at that time was mostly to Virginia, where tobacco was high in production and financially rewarding business.

In the early eighteenth century, more Scots were transported to America as political prisoners of England. Be-

A small house in Scotland. In order to prevent Scottish uprisings, many Highlanders were forced out of their homes by their landlords. *Reproduced by permission of © Bjorn Backe; Papilio/Corbis.*

tween 1715 and 1745, more than fourteen hundred defeated Jacobite rebels (Scots who wanted to return a Stuart monarch to the throne of Britain) were sent to America. They were forced to become indentured servants—people who contracted to work for an agreed-upon term with someone in the New World in exchange for payment for their passage. Another large group of involuntary immigrants were Scottish soldiers who had been brought to America by the British to fight in the French and Indian War (1754–63). (The French and Indian War was a war over territory in America between France and England where Indians fought as allies to the French.) In fact, when the soldiers of the famous Scottish Highlands Black Watch regiment marched out of Philadelphia in 1758, it was the first time a Scottish tartan kilt had ever appeared in Pennsylvania. At the end of the war, when the soldiers were discharged, the majority of Scottish soldiers elected to remain in America. The British offered them land in western Pennsylvania as an alternative to being shipped

The Highland Clan System

In Gaelic, the word "clan" means children or family. In Gaelic tribal culture, clans were communities made up of people descended from a common ancestor (the "children" or "family" of that ancestor). The whole community viewed themselves as family. Every clan had a powerful male clan chief to whom everyone in the group remained loyal. Groups that branched off from the main community but continued to owe allegiance to the clan chief were known as septs. Clans did not believe in individual land ownership. Land belonged to all members of the clan in common. Highland clans supported themselves by farming and raising cattle and also sometimes by stealing cattle in order to survive. Feuds among clans were common and often very bloody, but the Highlands culture was also developed in its arts and some of its social institutions.

Because of their distinct language and traditions, the clans of Highland Scotland were completely separate from the *Sassenach,* or southerners—a word the Highlanders used for both the English and the Lowland Scots. The Highlands was the home of the colorful tartan kilts that have become a symbol to many Americans of Scottish roots. The colorful tartan existed in the Highlands for many years. Tartan cloth had check patterns, usually repeated in two or three different colors. By about 1700 the patterns of the tartans came to be distinguished from each other, and each was associated with a particular clan. By that time kilts (knee-length tartan skirts worn by men) were also part of customary Highland dress.

England's last battle on its own soil was the Battle of Culloden of 1746. Although the battle had little to do with the Highlanders, it would end their way of life forever. In this battle the Jacobites, people who wished to restore the British crown to the Catholic monarchs, fought with the British troops and were quickly defeated. After the battle, the British government weighed down the Highland Scots with the Act of Proscription. This act prohibited Highlanders from nearly every aspect of practicing their traditions: wearing their tartan kilts, bearing arms, and even playing their traditional pipe music were all strictly forbidden. It is estimated that there were about thirty-six Highland clans in existence before the Battle of Culloden. The clan system was completely destroyed by the harsh oppression of the British after the battle.

home. Of the twelve thousand Scottish soldiers discharged, only seventy-six returned to Scotland.

Voluntary Scottish immigration to America picked up in the years between the union with England (1707) and the

American Revolution (1776–83). Conditions were already difficult for Highland Scottish farmers with a cold, rainy climate, short growing season, and rocky ground. In the Highlands, one method of earning a living had been armed raiding of the more prosperous Lowlands. In the mid-eighteenth century the British prohibited the Highlanders from bearing arms. Without being able to raid, there was not enough work to support the clans.

Making matters worse for the Highlanders, landlords began to raise the rents for Scotland's tenant farmers (farmers who rented their land), also seizing grazing grounds and evicting tenants in order to squash Scottish uprisings. Wealthy landowners in America advertised for indentured servants, immigrants who would work for a period of years in exchange for passage to America. A number of Scots jumped at the opportunity and hired on. Others sold their farms and livestock to pay for their own passage. Some Highland clan leaders organized mass migrations to the New World. When this happened it was not unusual for a whole community to pack up and emigrate. In 1738, following a series of failed rebellions, eighty-three families from a neighborhood in Argyllshire, Scotland, immigrated to the Lake George area of New York. Some of the mass migrations included thousands of people from the same town or area. Scots settled in all of the thirteen colonies, with an especially strong concentration of Highlanders in North Carolina.

The Scotch-Irish

From 1608 to 1697, about two hundred thousand Scots immigrated to Ulster in Northern Ireland. King James I had decided he wanted a Protestant population in the area and soon began evicting the Irish Catholics who lived there. The immigrants were from Scotland's Lowlands and were almost entirely Presbyterian. They settled in communities and cities in Northern Ireland with some English immigrants as well. The Protestants in Northern Ireland built up a thriving textile (cloth-making) industry and successfully farmed the land, but they were forced to live in constant fear of attack by the Irish, who had been driven off their own land. If the wrath of their neighbors was not enough, the Scotch-Irish were infuriated when British King Charles I tried to impose elements of the Church of England upon their Presbyterian church in 1632. Then, in 1639, Charles demanded that the Scots swear loyalty to the crown and particularly to reject the National Covenant. The king's required oath against the popular covenant became known as the "Black Oath." The penalties for not taking the oath were harsh. When the Scotch-Irish resisted his demands, the king sent in troops to evict them from their farms.

The Ulster Scots began to leave Ireland in large numbers in the early eighteenth century, seeking self-government and religious freedom. They were disappointed in the English government and tired of being attacked by the Catholics in Ireland for being Protestant and by the Anglicans (the official church of England, also Protestant) for being Presbyterian. Like the Scots at home and their Irish neighbors, the Ulster Scots had been the victims of English landlords who charged outrageously high rents. They sought a new place to live where they could own their own land and practice their religion freely. Pennsylvania encouraged religious freedom for all, and in the early eighteenth century it was still largely unsettled frontier, so it was very attractive to the Scotch-Irish. By 1749, about 25 percent of the total population of Pennsylvania was Scotch-Irish. Many of their descendants still live in towns such as Gettysburg, Chambersburg, Carlisle, and York.

Scots and Scotch-Irish in America

As the American Revolution got underway, the Scots and Scotch-Irish had to take sides. Scotch-Irish Americans, with their anti-English stance, were quite ready to join the rebel cause in the American Revolution. Scottish Americans tended to side with the British crown. But, fearing that the Scots would side with the rebels, the English prohibited Scottish emigration to America beginning in 1775. The damage was already done, however, and the Scotch-Irish (and some Scottish) Americans contributed significantly to the downfall of the British. Scottish and Scotch-Irish American Revolution leaders include Patrick Henry (1736–1799), John Stark (1728–1822), and Henry Knox (1750–1806), who led the rebel troops at the Battle of Bunker Hill (1775); naval commander John Paul Jones (1747–1792); and General "Mad"

Frontiersman Davy Crockett, center with rifle above his head, fighting along with Texans to defend the Alamo. Crockett, a man of Scottish descent, played a major role in the opening of the American frontier. *Reproduced by permission of Hulton Archive/Getty Images.*

Anthony Wayne (1745–1796). After the Revolution, many Scottish emigrants who had remained loyal to Britain chose to go to British-friendly Canada.

Although many Scottish Americans remained in the South, other Scots would go on to play a major role in the opening of the American frontier. During the frontier days, Scottish and Scotch-Irish Americans tended to be the first to clear an area, making it easier to settle on and farm. Then they would sell it to other settlers who would improve it while the Scots moved on. The Scots were such fierce fighters and defenders of their territory that eventually the U.S. government had to step in to protect friendly Native Americans from Scottish American attacks. Some of the best-known frontiersmen were of Scottish descent, including Daniel Boone (1734–1820), Christopher "Kit" Carson (1809–1868), and Davy Crockett (1786–1836). Scottish American Sam Houston (1793–1863) led the Texans to independence and became the first president of the Republic of Texas.

Not all Scottish American contributions to American society in the nineteenth century were positive. In the Whiskey Rebellion of 1792 to 1794, Scotch-Irish farmers in the Pittsburgh area of Pennsylvania who had distilled whiskey from their surplus corn refused to pay required local and federal taxes. The federal government had to send in troops to force payment. The farmers almost set fire to Pittsburgh in retaliation but were discouraged from doing so at the last minute by members of the clergy. The Ku Klux Klan, a secret society advocating white supremacy that frequently resorted to violence and terrorism, was founded in the South after the American Civil War (1861–65) by a group of Scotch-Irish Americans.

After its post–American Revolution decline, Scottish immigration to the United States picked up again in the nineteenth century. In Scotland, the spread of sheep-raisers in the Highlands had had a devastating impact. The vast amounts of land used for the sheep displaced thousands of tenant farmers who had leased tiny lots and squeezed out a living from them. Many of these people made their way to the United States. Perhaps the largest wave occurred after World War I (1914–18), when Britain descended into an economic depression with high unemployment. (World War I was a war between Germany and many other countries, mainly Britain, causing severe economic hardship on both sides after the war.) Over three hundred thousand Scots immigrated to the United States between 1921 and 1930 in search of better opportunities. When the Great Depression hit the United States in 1929 and 1930, however, conditions became just as bad there as in Scotland, and Scottish immigration virtually ceased. Since then, small numbers of Scots have moved to the United States.

Scottish American culture

There are three Gaelic languages: Irish Gaelic, Manx Gaelic, and the Scottish Gaelic that was spoken by the Highlanders. Although Scottish Highlanders spoke Gaelic when they first arrived in America, they shifted to English to avoid harassment, and fluency in Gaelic was lost rapidly. Today, few Scottish Americans speak Gaelic. Although Lowlanders in Scot-

President Andrew Jackson was one of the many American presidents of Scotch-Irish descent.
Engraving by Alexander Hay Ritchie after a painting by Dennis Malone Carter. Courtesy of the Library of Congress.

land spoke the Gaelic language at one time, by the seventeenth century Lowlanders and Scotch-Irish spoke standard English or a Scottish dialect of English.

With no language barrier, Scottish and Scotch-Irish assimilation was generally quick and uneventful after the early migrations. Like other groups, Scots married people of other national ancestry and many lost touch with their roots for generations. Individual Scottish Americans have made far too many contributions to U.S. culture and society to be described here.

In the last few decades there has been a surge of interest in family ancestry and national roots. People of Scottish descent have led the way in forming associations and organizing events that celebrate their heritage. There are many large and powerful Scottish American societies, such as the St. Andrews Societies and the Caledonian Groups. Scottish American events are held all over the country with enthusiastic and ever-growing participation. Although clans that immigrated to the United States quickly lost the clan system, "clan gatherings" are being organized in the United States in modern times as glorified family reunions. Most Scottish and Scotch-Irish Americans are several generations removed from Scotland and Northern Ireland, so their ethnic identity is largely symbolic, yet often fiercely defended.

Music in ancient Scotland was often associated with battle. The harp has a long-honored spot in Scottish history, going back to the seventeenth-century court of King James I. In the Highlands, harpists went to battle with the clan chiefs and also performed for celebrations. Bagpipes later replaced harps on the battlefield. Bagpipes became the national instrument of Scotland and are very popular today in the United States, particularly in parades and celebrations.

Scotland is also famous for fiddle music, Gaelic songs and ballads, and Celtic bands that combine fiddles, bagpipes,

Did You Know?

- The terms for the Scots are often confused. The Scottish people are called Scots, and things from Scotland are called Scottish. The word "Scotch" refers to the alcoholic drink or, in the United States, to someone who is Scotch-Irish.

- A large portion of Scottish immigrants to the United States were Scotch-Irish, who were from Scotland's Lowlands. When Americans try to represent their Scottish ancestry, many who have descended from the Lowlanders mistakenly use Highlander articles of dress, such as tartans and kilts. Their Lowlander ancestors would never have worn such Highlander gear.

- Haggis, a kind of sausage, is a popular food in Scotland. It is made from a combination of boiled sheep organs (heart, lungs, and liver), beef or sheep suet (raw fat), and oatmeal placed inside a sheep's stomach, which is sewn up and then boiled. Scotland's national dish is haggis, neeps (turnips), and tatties (potatoes).

- At the time of the American Civil War (1861–65), it has been estimated that about three-quarters of the population of the South was Scotch-Irish, Scottish, or Irish. In fact, the flag for the Confederate States of America was called "the bonnie blue flag," in good Scottish terminology ("bonnie" being a Scottish word used to mean fine or beautiful).

- Scottish fiddle music, brought by the Scots to the southern regions of the New World, developed into the type of American music called bluegrass.

- In 1860 the Reformed Presbyterian Church, made up mostly of Scotch-Irish Americans, declared that it would not serve Holy Communion to slaveholders. It was the first church in America to take a stand against slavery.

- There have been many U.S. presidents of Scotch-Irish descent: Andrew Jackson (1767–1845), James Polk (1795–1849), James Buchanan (1791–1868), Andrew Johnson (1808–1875), Ulysses Grant (1822–1885), Chester Arthur (1830–1886), Grover Cleveland (1837–1908), Benjamin Harrison (1833–1901), William McKinley (1843–1901), Woodrow Wilson (1856–1924), Richard Nixon (1913–1994), and Jimmy Carter (1924–).

whistles, and guitars. Traditional Scottish music is very popular in the United States today. Artists such as world-renowned Scottish American fiddle virtuoso Bonnie Rideout (1963–) have gone back to the old country to learn the traditions of the Scottish fiddle. The traditional Scottish singer Jean Red-

path (1937–) has a large and enthusiastic following in the United States. Recognized worldwide for her interpretations of traditional Scottish songs and ballads, Redpath has drawn from Scotland's ancient oral tradition to portray the Scottish national character in her music. She is particularly known for her extensive work on the songs of Scotland's national poet, Robert Burns (1759–1796).

One indication of the renewed interest in Scottish history within the popular culture of the United States are two hit movies of 1995: *Braveheart* and *Rob Roy.* In *Braveheart* Mel Gibson (1956–) plays thirteenth-century Scottish hero William Wallace (c. 1270–1305), who led the resistance when England took control of Scotland in 1296. Under Wallace, Scotland's commoners and knights united to begin the fight for Scottish independence, which would eventually free them of English rule. *Braveheart* won several awards, including the Academy Awards for Best Picture and Best Director. *Rob Roy* is based on a swashbuckling novel by Scottish novelist Sir Walter Scott (1771–1832). Liam Neeson (1952–) plays the title role of Rob Roy (1671–1734), an eighteenth-century Jacobite (Catholic Scots) Highlands clan leader who finds himself at odds with the Protestant English elite. Both films reflect the spirit and history of the Scots and their age-old fight against the dominating British.

The great contribution Scots have made to American sports is the game of golf, which was invented in Scotland and brought to America by Scottish and Scotch-Irish immigrants. Scots also brought the sport of curling, known better to Canadians than Americans, though there are American teams. Curling began as a cold-weather sport. Two four-person teams compete by taking turns sliding heavy stones over a long stretch of ice toward a circular target.

Scottish American holidays and events

National Tartan Day

In 1998, April 6 was designated National Tartan Day by the U.S. Senate, commemorating Scottish Americans and their contributions to the nation. The date commemorates the April 6, 1320, signing of the Declaration of Arbroath, which created an independent Scotland. The document is considered to be one of the inspirations behind the American Declaration of Independence. In 2004 New York City celebrated its Sixth National Tartan Day Parade with three thousand bagpipers and drummers marching along 6th Avenue. In 2002 the event drew the largest group of bagpipe players ever to assemble in the United States with somewhere between seven thousand and eight thousand bagpipes. The parade was led by the kilt-clad Scottish actor Sean Connery (1930–). Tartan Day parades take place in cities throughout the United States.

Highland Games

Scotland has an ancient tradition of holding an annual competitive athletic event called the Highland Games. For nearly a thousand years the Highlands clans assembled from all over Scotland to compete against one another. The earliest gatherings were probably war games organized for

Contest winners carrying their trophies at the Cowal Highland Games.
Reproduced by permission of © Peter Turnley/Corbis.

the purpose of testing the warriors in each clan. Races and other competitions soon became an essential part of the games. The 1746 Act of Proscription following the Battle of Culloden put a stop to all Highlander traditions, including the Highland Games. Thirty-five years later, in 1781, the Highland Games began again at Falkirk, Scotland. Soon many other Scottish cities and towns sponsored the traditional games. Scots immigrating to the United States brought this tradition with them. In the United States the first Highland Games were organized by the Highland Society of New York in the mid-1800s. The first games on the West Coast were held in San Francisco in 1865.

There are hundreds of annual Highland Games held throughout the United States in the twenty-first century. The athletic competitions include the Sheaf Toss, using a pitchfork to throw a large bag of hay over a bar; Heavy Athletics, including Turning the Caber, or Tossing the Caber, which involves picking up a 100-pound, 16- to 20-foot log and flipping it end over end, as well as the throwing of heavy weights and stones; the Farmer's Walk, which involves holding very heavy weights and walking a course; the Tug-of-War; the Kilted Mile (run in a kilt); Kilted Golf (played in a kilt); the Fell Race, which is run over rough terrain; sheep dog competitions; and fly casting. There are many other clan-related events, with musical and dancing competitions and celebrations of the Scottish culture.

Burns Supper

Scotland's national poet, Robert Burns, has attained a mythical stature not only in his native land but also around the world. Revered as the poet of the common man, in his short life Burns expressed the soul of his people in his poems. His work made acceptable for the first time the use of Scottish dialect in serious poetry, and his depiction of rural Scottish life and manners marked a radical departure from the stateliness of eighteenth-century verse. For more than two hundred years since his death, on January 25 each year, Burns fans worldwide have held Burns Suppers, celebrations of the life and work of the beloved poet. In recent times Burns Suppers have become increasingly popular in the United States. The suppers can be large literary affairs or informal gatherings of a few friends. While some may be serious intellectual gatherings, many tend more toward the spirit of the poet, whose humor and taste for Scotch whiskey and "the ladies" were legendary. During the course of an evening, the participants at a Burns Supper eat a meal of haggis, mashed neeps (turnips), and tatties (potatoes) and drink Scotch whiskey. (Haggis is a kind of sausage made from a combination of boiled sheep organs [heart, lungs, and liver], beef or sheep suet [raw fat], and oatmeal placed inside a sheep's stomach, which is sewn up and then boiled.) There are tributes to the poet, recitations of his poems, and singing of his songs. One such recitation might be his poem "Address to a Haggis," in which Burns praises Scotland's national food. The first lines of the poem are:

> Fair fa' [fall] your honest, sonsie [cheerful] face,
> Great chieftain o the puddin'-race!
> Aboon [above] them a' [all] ye tak [take] your place,
> Painch [paunch or stomach], tripe, or thairm [guts]:
> Weel [well] are ye wordy [worthy] of a grace
> As lang's [long as] my arm.

For More Information

Books

Daniels, Roger. *Coming to America: A History of Immigration and Ethnicity in American Life.* New York: HarperCollins, 1990.

Hook, Andrew. *From Gooseneck to Gandercleugh: Studies in Scottish-American Literary and Cultural History.* East Linton, Scotland: Tuckwell Press, 1999.

Web Sites

The Scottish History Pages. http://www.scotshistoryonline.co.uk/scothist. html (accessed on February 26, 2004).

French and Dutch Immigration

7

Like Spain and England, France and the Netherlands sought to expand their empires in the seventeenth century. Both nations established important colonies, and each stood a good chance of building an enduring empire in North America. But the competition was becoming fierce among the European nations. No nation could hold onto territorial claims in the New World without populating the land with its people. Populating the early colonies meant a tremendous commitment: tens of thousands of people, many of whom might die; long-term financial investment that was extremely risky; and well-planned government and security systems in the New World that could hold the new settlements together. Although their methods of colonizing and their situations in the homelands differed greatly, both France and the Netherlands failed in some or all of these commitments and ultimately lost their North American colonies.

French colonization in the New World

In the first century after European contact with the New World, a series of conflicts hindered France's ability to

Fact Focus

- During the sixteenth century, persecution of French Protestants called Huguenots began in France. The height of the violence was the Saint Bartholomew's Day Massacre on August 24, 1572, in which an estimated thirty thousand Huguenots were killed.

- In 1682 French explorer Robert Cavelier (1643–1687), Sieur de La Salle, descended the Mississippi River from the Illinois River all the way to the Mississippi's mouth in the Gulf of Mexico. He laid claim to virtually all of the interior of North America for France and named the land Louisiana.

- When the United States bought the Louisiana Territory in 1802, it comprised 828,000 square miles of land, which nearly doubled the size of the nation.

- France ceded, or turned over, its American colonies in 1763.

- The third governor of the Dutch colony New Netherland, Peter Minuit (1580–1638), purchased Manhattan Island from the Canarsee Indians for sixty guilders, or about twenty-four dollars, in trinkets. Minuit later also bought the island from the Manhattan tribe, who had a better claim to it than the Canarsee.

- The bad management of the West Indies Company made the prospect of immigrating to New Netherland very unappealing to the Dutch people and the population of Dutch in the colony remained very low.

- The Dutch only ruled their American colony for fifty years before the English seized it.

- Between 1820 and 1914, about two hundred thousand Dutch people immigrated to the United States. The majority of them were farming families

settle overseas colonies. Wars with Spain and England drained vital resources in military, shipping, and finances. Perhaps the deepest trauma to the nation was the religious division within. The Protestant Reformation had begun in about 1517, when a German theologian (one who studies religion) named Martin Luther (1483–1546) challenged the practices of the Roman Catholic Church and launched his ideas about reforming it in a new Christian church. Although France's national church was the Roman Catholic Church, Luther's Protestant reforms spread rapidly.

Words to Know

Artisan: Craftsman.

Assimilation: The process for an outsider of being absorbed, or blending, into the mainstream culture.

Calvinism: The belief system of theologian John Calvin, which asserted that the human world was basically corrupt and only the Bible—not the church—could reveal the true religion.

Chain migration: A pattern of immigration in which an individual (or group of individuals) immigrates to a new country. Once the first immigrant is settled and communicates to people back home about the new country, he or she is followed by family members and friends, who settle nearby in the new community. They are then followed by their family and friends, and soon there is a small community from a particular village or neighborhood in the homeland within the new community.

Coureurs de bois: pronounced KOO-ruhr deh bwah; The French term for "travelers in the woods," or fur trappers and traders.

Extermination: Killing an entire group or population.

Huguenots: French Calvinists.

Missionary: A member of an organized effort by a religious group to spread its beliefs in other parts of the world.

Northwest Passage: A mythical water route through the American continent that the early Europeans hoped would lead to the Pacific Ocean.

Patroonship: A system developed by the Dutch West Indies Company to promote emigration in which the company granted large parcels of land to any person of wealth who would commit to bring over a certain number of colonizers and house them on his land (usually fifty settlers within four years). In turn, the patroons owned the land and had great authority over their tenants.

Persecution: Causing to suffer, especially for a difference of religious views.

Theologian: One who studies religion.

Walloons: French-speaking people from the southern and eastern parts of Belgium.

Religious division in France

Over time, French Protestants became strongly influenced by Calvinism, the name given to the belief system of French theologian John Calvin (1509–1564). Calvinists believed that the symbols and rituals of the Roman Catholic practice were useless in finding salvation (being saved from eternal damnation). In their view the only instrument necessary to achieve grace (God's help or mercy) was the Bible, newly available to them in their own languages—unlike the Catholic practice of presenting the Bible in Latin. Calvinists viewed deep faith in God as very important for the soul, but even with faith, salvation and grace were not available to all. They believed that God had already chosen "the elect"—the people predestined to receive divine favor and to be saved from damnation.

The French Calvinists, who came to be called Huguenots, were never a majority in France. In fact, with their population at its highest, their churches made up only about 10 percent of all of French churches. But a fairly large portion of the Huguenots were from France's nobility and the upper middle classes. Many were very outspoken about their beliefs, working tirelessly for the spread of Protestantism throughout France. Although the French royalty was not closely tied to Rome, French kings feared the Huguenots. They believed the nobility should be aligned with the king and that, by threatening the national church, the Huguenots diminished the power of the monarch. The persecution (causing to suffer, especially for a difference of religious views) of Huguenots in France varied over the years. Some monarchs were very hostile, while several other French kings established good relations with them.

The Huguenots: the first French colonists in the New World

Hostility toward the Protestants was strong in 1536, when the French government issued a general order urging the extermination (the killing of an entire population) of the Huguenots. Even under the threat of death, Protestantism continued to spread. As the number of Huguenots grew, the hostility between them and the Catholics increased as well. By 1550 Huguenots who refused to convert to Catholicism were being burned at the stake. Then, in 1562, about twelve hundred Huguenots were slain at Vassey, France. The Huguenots had the determination, the numbers, and the resources to fight back, and the war that followed, called the French Wars of Religion, devastated France for the next thirty-five years.

The height of the violence against the Huguenots was the Saint Bartholomew's Day Massacre on August 24, 1572. Starting as a three-day massacre of three thousand Huguenots in Paris, the killing spread throughout France. When it was over, an estimated thirty thousand Huguenots had been killed, and some say it was many more.

Just before the Vassey slayings in 1562, the French king had decided to establish a French colony in Florida. The purpose of settling this first colony was both financial—the French were looking for the riches the New World seemed to offer—and political. France wished to keep the Spanish out of the north and felt a French settlement would do that. The first attempt at settlement was to be a Huguenot expedition. Despite some opposition, Protestant leader Jean Ribault (pronounced jawn ree-BOE; c. 1520–1565) was chosen by the navy's admiral to go to the New World with ships carrying about 150 Huguenot sailors, soldiers, and a few noblemen. The group eventually settled in a place that they called

An illustration by Roger Viollett depicting the Saint Bartholmew's Day Massacre of 1572, in which an estimated thirty thousand Huguenots were killed because of their religious views. *Reproduced by permission of Roger Viollett/Getty Images.*

Charlesfort, on what is now Parris Island, South Carolina. They were sorely lacking in supplies. Because the massacre at Vassey occurred soon after they left, they did not receive the expected help from France. The settlers in Charlesfort had to abandon their settlement and return home.

A second expedition of 304 Huguenot colonists, anxious to escape religious persecution in France, left for the New World. The expedition included several families who had equipped themselves with livestock, tools, and the supplies they would need in the New World. The group was made up of gentlemen, common laborers, artisans (craftsmen), a few women, and a few free Africans. They settled in Fort Caroline, a site near what is now Jacksonville, Florida. After a time, hunger set in and soon some of the colonists stole boats and left, while others rebelled within the colony. A Spanish force led by Pedro Menéndez de Avilés (1519–1574) sailed to the area to drive the French out of Florida to keep the territory clear for Spanish colonization. In late 1565 Avilés's troops killed the Huguenots and destroyed Fort Caroline.

In April 1598, the new French king, Henry IV (1553–1610), signed the Edict of Nantes, which ended the Wars of Religion and allowed the Huguenots some religious freedoms, including free exercise of their religion in twenty specified towns of France. Nevertheless, in 1623 significant numbers of Huguenots settled in the Dutch colony in America, in the city of New Amsterdam, which later became New York City. Others went to Fort Orange (Albany), Kingston, and New Paltz in New York. Between two and three hundred Huguenot families migrated to Boston.

The period of relatively peaceful existence between the Huguenots and the Catholics in France ended in October 1685 when King Louis XIV (1638–1715) signed the Revocation of the Edict of Nantes, renewing the persecution of the Huguenots. This time the Huguenots fled France to other countries by the hundreds of thousands. Since the Huguenots of France were in large part artisans and professional people, they were usually well received in the countries to which they fled. Between 1618 and 1725 about five to seven thousand Huguenot refugees reached the shores of America. The largest concentrations were in New England, New York, Pennsylvania, Virginia, and South Carolina.

In France, the Promulgation of the Edict of Toleration in November 1787 partially restored the civil and religious rights of Huguenots, and the number of Protestants flowing out of the country gradually decreased. The largest population of Huguenots, in the United States had settled in Charleston, South Carolina. Like most immigrants, within a few generations they began to speak English rather than French. The Huguenots in the United States generally joined Protestant churches, particularly the Presbyterian Church. Many adapted to the prevailing culture around them, while others maintained the strict Calvinism of their past.

The Jesuit missionaries in the New World

France's missionaries, like the missionaries of other colonizing European countries, felt a duty to spread the Christian religion in the New World. A missionary is a member of an organized effort by a religious group to spread its beliefs in other parts of the world. Among the missionaries in colonial times, some of the French missionaries distinguished themselves. While their efforts often angered Native Americans, who had their own beliefs, some of the French missionaries showed respect and made the effort to try to understand the native traditions in the territories they were settling. The bulk of the mission of converting (persuading to believe in Christianity) the Native people fell to the Catholic order of the Jesuits, who lived and worked closely with the American Indians. (Jesuits were members of the Society of Jesus, a Roman Catholic religious order for men.) France came to rely on the Jesuits to

A Huguenot church and French settlers' graveyard in New Paltz, New York.
Reproduced by permission of © Lee Snider/Corbis.

cultivate friendly relations with the Indians so that settlers and traders could follow.

The French Jesuit priests came to the settlements in New France (now Canada) in the early 1600s. They tried to convert many Indian nations, such as the Naskapi, the Montagnais, the Malicite, the Huron (later called Wyandotte), and the Iroquois. Many of the French Jesuits were from peasant families in France. The Jesuits put great emphasis on study, and some of these missionaries came to appreciate the differences among cultures. The Jesuits taught Christianity by drawing comparisons between Christian religious beliefs and Native American beliefs. Sometimes they tolerated traditional Native American beliefs to be practiced with Christian beliefs among their converts.

Between 1639 and 1663, the Jesuits created the St. Joseph de Sillary Mission near Montreal, which was designed to settle the Indians into a monasterylike lifestyle and to teach them farming as well as the Catholic faith. The mission failed for a number of reasons, but mainly because the Indians were not willing to take up either the mission lifestyle or the Catholic faith. After the failure of the Sillary Mission, the Jesuits decided to spend most of their time living among the Indian nations seeking converts. They set up many missions among the Great Lakes Indians and were responsible for settling much of the region. In 1760, the Jesuits were recalled to France because of political difficulties at home. By that time they had made many lasting converts among the Indian nations. The letters they left behind provide modern-day readers the opportunity to share many of their experiences. The Jesuit documents give some of the most detailed material about the traditions of the Indian nations of North America at the time of European contact.

New France

Unlike England and the Netherlands, France did not turn over the establishment of New World colonies to joint stock companies, preferring to keep colonization in the hands of the monarchy. Most of France's early dealings with North America involved the fur trade. French fur traders established alliances with many North American native tribal groups, who supplied them with furs, guides, and transportation in return for European goods. In 1603 French King Henry IV (1553–1610), intrigued with the commercial possibilities in the New World but especially fur trading, sent explorer Samuel de Champlain (c. 1567–1635) to investigate. After his first trip Champlain convinced the king that the French claims in North America had the potential for settlement and commercial development. He received financial backing in his lifelong efforts to explore and colonize New France.

In all, Champlain would make twelve journeys to New France, what is now Canada. He settled in an area called Acadia in 1604, which consisted approximately of the present-day Maritime Provinces of Canada: Nova Scotia, New Brunswick, and Prince Edward Island; and also founded a permanent settlement at Quebec City in 1608. Within a few years Quebec would become the center of French fur trading in the New World. But despite Champlain's efforts at colonizing, New France grew very slowly in the first decades.

Recruiting French settlers

In 1629, a development system was instituted in New France called the seigneurial system. The French government gave a large parcel of land to an individual. That person, called a seigneur, was required to populate and farm the area. To do so, the seigneur recruited immigrants to work in his house and on his farms on a wage basis. He was also responsible for helping the settlers adapt to the new country. The recruits were committed to stay for at least three years. If they chose to stay beyond that time, they were granted a small piece of their own land. Champlain awarded some of the first settlers in the Saint Lawrence Valley immense parcels of land under the seigneurial system, encouraging them to recruit emigrants from France. The seigneurs of the Saint Lawrence Valley, in the present-day northern United States and southern Canada, were responsible for bringing in the first immigrants from France to settle in the area.

The French king awarded grants of fur-trading rights to large companies with the understanding that they would recruit and help settle emigrants from France. The companies provided few settlers. The men they hired were often young, the so-called *coureurs de bois* (pronounced KOO-ruhr duh

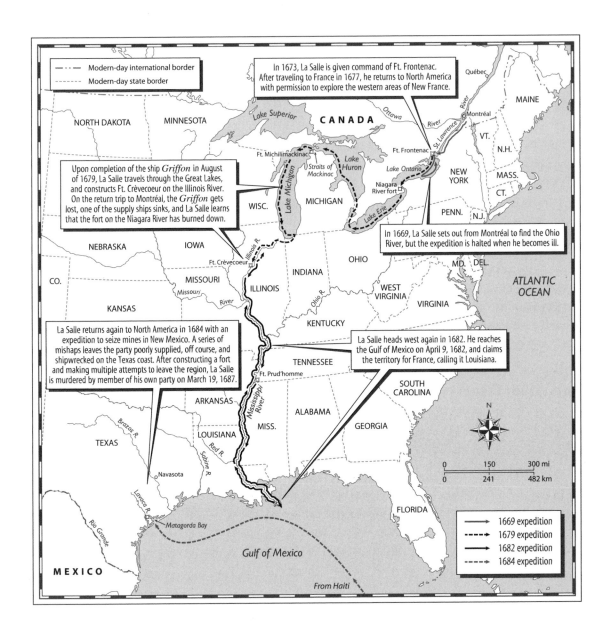

Modern-day international border
Modern-day state border

In 1673, La Salle is given command of Ft. Frontenac. After traveling to France in 1677, he returns to North America with permission to explore the western areas of New France.

Upon completion of the ship *Griffon* in August of 1679, La Salle travels through the Great Lakes, and constructs Ft. Crèvecoeur on the Illinois River. On the return trip to Montréal, the *Griffon* gets lost, one of the supply ships sinks, and La Salle learns that the fort on the Niagara River has burned down.

In 1669, La Salle sets out from Montréal to find the Ohio River, but the expedition is halted when he becomes ill.

La Salle returns again to North America in 1684 with an expedition to seize mines in New Mexico. A series of mishaps leaves the party poorly supplied, off course, and shipwrecked on the Texas coast. After constructing a fort and making multiple attempts to leave the region, La Salle is murdered by member of his own party on March 19, 1687.

La Salle heads west again in 1682. He reaches the Gulf of Mexico on April 9, 1682, and claims the territory for France, calling it Louisiana.

	1669 expedition
	1679 expedition
	1682 expedition
	1684 expedition

A map of French explorer Rene-Robert Cavelier, Sieur de La Salle's explorations of the western areas of New France. *Reproduced by permission of the Gale Group.*

bwa) or "travelers in the woods," trappers and traders. They usually made good money by making a few fur-trading trips and then settled down in another business that was less rugged, dangerous, and lonely.

For the century and a half of French colonization, three-quarters of the emigrants were men, although from time to time the French government sent women to the colonies to marry these workers. In 1665 France sent one thousand soldiers to help fight the Iroquois and of those, four hundred chose to stay when offered land of their own. But these numbers never mounted up to a mass migration, and France's holdings were never well populated.

Down the Mississippi

The fur trade was by far the most profitable endeavor in New France. Thus, early in the seventeenth century, a plan was devised to gain a route down to the Gulf of Mexico through the interior of the states and to establish fur-trading posts along the route. In 1682 the bold French explorer Robert Cavelier (1643–1687), Sieur [pronounced syor] de La Salle, navigated the Mississippi River all the way to its mouth in the Gulf of Mexico. La Salle laid claim to virtually all the interior of North America for his country, naming the land Louisiana, after the French king Louis XIV (1638–1715).

While the English were hemmed in on the Atlantic coast by the Allegheny Mountains (western part of the Appalachian Mountains and extends from northern Pennsylvania to southwest Virginia), the French found easy access to the heart of the North American continent from Canada. French explorers and woodsmen overran the Great Lakes and the Mississippi Valley, establishing key forts: Fort Cataraqui, now Kingston, Ontario, in 1673; Fort Miami, now Saint Joseph, Michigan, in 1679; and Fort Saint Louis and Fort Crévecoeur in Illinois from 1680 to 1682. In the South, Fort Biloxi, in present-day Mississippi, was founded in 1699; Mobile, in present-day Alabama, in 1702; and New Orleans, Louisiana, in 1717. By then the colony of New France extended from the Gulf of Saint Lawrence in Canada to the Gulf of Mexico.

Le pays des Illinois

The French presence in what would become the United States was mainly confined to villages along the Mississippi River in what became known as the *pays des Illinois,* or Illinois country, and in Louisiana. The villages of Kaskaskia, Cahokia, Fort de Chartres, Saint Philippe, Prairie de Rocher, and

Daily Life in New France

In the cold climates of the Saint Lawrence Valley in New France, the early settlers who had been recruited under the seigneurship system developed their yearly routines by the necessities of living in a harsh climate. Most had built huts to keep them warm on the small piece of land provided to them by the seigneur when they arrived; they would add on to their homes later.

During the winter, members of the family spent much of their time taking care of the livestock and cutting firewood. They learned how to dress for the cold climate from the Native Americans, adopting moose-leather mittens and boots lined with beaver fur, and fur-lined coats. In the spring, the family ploughed their fields, planted vegetables and grains, and put the livestock out to pasture. In summer, they put up hay for the livestock and then harvested and ground the grains. Autumn was the time to prepare for winter by storing the ground grains and other provisions, bringing the animals in from pasture, and butchering those animals needed for food. The colonists ate the foods their own animals and garden provided—eggs, milk, meats, and the vegetables and grains they had grown—but they also supplemented their diet by fishing and hunting small animals, with the seigneur's permission. Their efforts at farming and raising meat were not always enough to keep them well fed throughout the winter. Hunger was a very real threat.

Family life and the Catholic religion were very important to the French Americans in the Saint Lawrence Valley. Even those who were single often socialized in a neighboring family home. Large families with lots of children became very common among the settlers who stayed. Education was scattered because of the great distances between settlements. Much of the children's education, at home or school, focused on religion. Families in New France also found time for socializing and recreation. The settlers relied on neighbors for social gatherings—evenings spent playing cards or parlor games or singing and dancing. Those new settlers who were able to develop good relations with their neighbors in New France often agreed to stay beyond their three-year commitment.

Sainte Genevieve along the Mississippi began to attract a few Frenchmen from Canada, especially the *coureurs de bois,* who spent much of their time living among the Native Americans. At Cahokia they began to settle down, often with Indian wives, away from the government of New France in Canada and most other authority. These settlements never had large populations.

By 1752 some 58 percent of the white settlers in Illinois country came from Canada, 38 percent from France, and the small remainder from Switzerland, Italy, and Louisiana. There was also a considerable black slave population, brought in by whites from the different territories of the Americas and from the Caribbean. By the mid 1760s there were an estimated eleven hundred whites, five hundred black slaves, and also a few Indian slaves living in the Illinois country.

Louisiana

Louisiana Territory was vast but vaguely defined. When the United States bought it in 1802, it comprised 828,000 square miles of land, which nearly doubled the size of the nation. Louisiana stretched west from the Mississippi River to the Rocky Mountains and north from the Gulf of Mexico to the Canadian border. For France, the settlement of this enormous territory began and ended slowly.

In 1684 the French government financed La Salle in a disastrous expedition in which he brought four ships, with about two hundred soldiers and three hundred settlers, to the New World. The ships got lost, missing the mouth of the Mississippi River, and then experienced a string of disasters. The crew eventually rebelled and murdered La Salle. A second expedition settled in Biloxi Bay, in present-day Mississippi. The settlers struggled to survive in the sweltering tropical climate; most later moved north to the upper Mississippi and Illinois. The first census of Biloxi, Mississippi, in 1699, listed only eighty-two persons, all male. By 1708 there were 278 persons in Louisiana. In 1718, when Louisiana became a province (a division of the French nation, like a state), the colony had four hundred Europeans. During the next few years the high mortality rates kept the population low, despite new arrivals.

The colony of Louisiana was governed by several directors and then fell into the hands of the Company of the Indies in 1717. The company believed a surge in population was their only hope of making the colony a financial success. Consequently between October 1717 and May 1721, 7,020 colonists were sent to Louisiana from France; only 5,420 survived the crossing. Two thousand African slaves were also sent to the colony. By 1726 a census showed that the population was only 1,952 people—thousands of people had been lost, mainly to diseases that prevailed in the hot, humid climate. The Company of the Indies lost control of the colony in 1731, and slave imports ceased. By 1763, when France surrendered Louisiana to the Spanish, the population stood at some 3,654 whites and 4,598 slaves. The colony had experienced terrible human suffering with little to show for it. This was largely due to France's neglect. The lack of private investment in the endeavor and the lack of French people willing to emigrate were also key factors in the hardships.

The French takeover of the Mississippi Valley in the interior section of the New World settlements led directly to the clash with Great Britain in the French and Indian War (1754–63; a war between England and France with some Indians fighting as allies to the French), which cost France its entire American empire. New France ceased to exist after the final surrender to England in 1763, with the exception of Louisiana, which was ceded (given) to Spain the same year.

France was in the process of regaining Louisiana from Spain at the beginning of the nineteenth century when a slave revolt on the West Indian island of St. Dominique erupted. The uprising doomed France's hopes for profit from its Caribbean sugar plantations. Without the sugar trade, France had no interest in Louisiana. The United States wanted the land, and France quickly sold it to the U.S. government for fifteen million dollars. The inhabitants of Louisiana were suddenly U.S. citizens. At the time the United States purchased the Louisiana Territory from France, the population of the whole area was about 97,000. In 2002, the population from the same area was 36.1 million.

Despite the slow start and abrupt ending of French colonization in Louisiana, the French population there created one of the most distinctive cultures in the United States. The character of Louisiana was established first by the French and French-speaking people, who continued to arrive long after France lost its empire. The Spanish era from 1763 to 1800 also influenced the territory. One of the most profound influences in Louisiana was the large population of both free and enslaved Africans and Caribbean Africans there, whose social world merged with that of the French and the Spanish to make a truly unique and enduring culture. (For more information on Louisiana, see chapter 8 on African American immigration, sections on Louisiana and the Creoles; and chapter 13 on forced migrations, section on Cajuns.)

French Americans

During the entire century and a half of French colonization in North America, only about ten thousand people actually migrated from France to the New World. But French immigrants continued to arrive long after France's colonial role in America ended. During the 1790s, a number of French aristocrats fled to the United States to escape persecution or even death in the French Revolution (1789–93; a war in which the monarchy was overthrown and a republic was established). At the same time, a revolution in the French colony of St. Dominique in the Caribbean drove out the French aristocrats there, most of whom also came to the United States. A shift in French politics in 1815 led to another French migration. Between the 1790s and 1850s, between ten and twenty-five thousand French immigrated to America. Between 1840 and 1860 it is estimated that about one hundred thousand French people immigrated to the United States, forming the largest French immigration wave.

French immigration to the United States has never been substantial. For the most part, conditions in France have been good enough that few French citizens have wished to leave. Those who do immigrate tend to adapt quickly to their new surroundings, assimilating (blending) into mainstream American culture. In the United States, only Louisiana and, to a lesser extent, New England, have cultures that are distinctly French. The state of Louisiana continues to base its legal system on the Code Napoléon (a code of laws written by French Emperor Napoleon Bonaparte [1769–1861]), the only state to do so; other states use English common law. Louisiana's population retains a mixture of people of original French descent and Cajuns. Cajuns were people who were exiled from French-speaking Acadia, in present-day Nova Scotia, Canada. There is also a French-speaking culture in New England, made up of immigrants from Quebec.

During the late 1800s, there was a mass migration of French Canadians, many from the Quebec area, to the indus-

The annual Mardi Gras Parade in New Orleans, Louisiana. Although the French ceded Louisiana in 1763, French traditions and customs remain distinctive in the state. *Photograph by Drew Story. Reproduced by permission of Hulton Archive/Getty Images.*

trializing towns of New England, and a second wave began in the 1910s, peaking in 1920. Thousands arrived in northeastern cities and towns, such as Manchester and Nashua, New Hampshire; and Lowell, Fall River, New Bedford, Holyoke, Salem, and Southbridge, Massachusetts. The logging mills in Lewiston, Maine, also drew many French Canadians. Many retained the French language and French Canadian customs in their new home for several generations. Later French Canadian migrations were often to places closer to the Canadian border, especially focusing on Michigan, Minnesota, and Wisconsin.

French Americans, often called Franco Americans, trace their ancestry to France or to other French-speaking countries. The 2000 U.S. Census listed 8,309,908 persons of French ancestry, and an additional 2,349,684 with French Canadian ancestry. The biggest population of people of French Canadian descent can be found in New England and the Great Lakes states. The remainder are scattered throughout the country. The percentage of foreign-born French Americans is just slightly over 1 percent of the total French American population. Although many early French immigrants were Huguenots, most French Americans today are Catholic.

In the twenty-first century, about 1.3 million U.S. students learned French in school; after Spanish it is the second most commonly studied foreign language in the nation. In the United States, French place-names abound, including New Orleans, St. Louis, Detroit, New Rochelles, Duluth, Sault Ste. Marie, Boise, and many others. Many French words have become common in American usage, such as boulevard, avenue, coup, potpourri, r.s.v.p. (répondez, s'il vous plait, or "respond, please"), chic, déjá vu, á la carte, and cuisine. In the realm of cuisine, Americans have adopted not only a number of French foods but also their names and terms for their preparation: omelet, mayonnaise, hors d'oeuvres, bouillon, café au lait, croissant, hollandaise, parfait, purée, á la mode, and au gratin, to name just a few.

The Statue of Liberty

Perhaps the most famous French contribution to American culture is the Statue of Liberty, designed by French sculptor Frédéric-Auguste Bartholdi. (1834–1904). The statue was presented to the United States by France in 1884 to commemorate the French-American alliance begun in the American Revolution (1775–83) and continuing through the French Revolution (1789–93) and beyond. The site chosen for the statue was Bedloe's Island in New York Harbor, where Huguenot immigrant Isaac Bedloe had pastured his cows in the 1650s. The island was renamed Liberty Island.

The Dutch colonizers and immigrants

The Netherlands was enjoying a golden age as the century began. It was successful in international trade, with its Dutch East Indies Company charting profitable trade routes and coming home laden with riches from Africa and Asia. The Netherlands had some of the finest ships and best-trained sea captains in the world. Its industries were thriving, and its people had a higher standard of living than most Europeans.

The Netherlands' interest in colonizing was mainly a commercial one. There were looming hostilities between the Dutch and the Spanish, and the Dutch wanted a base in the New World to compete with Spain. Besides, there was great interest in the possibility of finding the legendary Northwest Passage—a mythical water route through the American continent that the early Europeans hoped would lead to the Pacific Ocean and new trading with Asia. In 1609 the Dutch East India Company engaged British explorer Henry Hudson (1565–1611) to explore the American continent for the Northwest Passage. He and his men found instead the Hudson River, with Native Americans along its shores with plentiful supplies of fur. Hudson laid claim to the river for the Dutch. The furs the Dutch obtained from trade with the natives there were in great demand in Europe. In fact, just one shipload of furs could make its owners wealthy. By 1614 traders began setting up temporary forts along the Hudson.

The Netherlands chartered the Dutch West Indies Company for the purpose of creating a permanent trading post in the New World. The post would need people to live in it, and this proved to be a problem. In the Netherlands the standard of living was good. The government was fair and there was freedom of religion. Motivating people who were comfortable at home to move to America, with all the risks and hardships involved in setting up a colony, was difficult.

The Dutch West Indies Company resolved the dilemma as best they could by paying people to make the trip. The first wave of immigrants to New Netherland was composed of thirty Walloon families (French-speaking people from the southern and eastern parts of Belgium), who arrived in New Netherland in 1624. A few of the immigrants remained at the mouth of the Hudson River but most settled up the river at Fort Orange, where the city of Albany now stands. A fort was also built on Nut Island (now Governors Island). In 1625 the thinly settled colony was reinforced by the coming of forty-two new immigrants. In addition, one of the directors of the company sent 103 head of livestock, including horses, cows, hogs, and sheep.

New Netherland constituted some of the most choice real estate in North America, then and now. It encompassed Manhattan Island and the New York Harbor, part of Long Island, the area from the Hudson River east to the Connecticut River and west far out into the fur-trading region, and included most of present-day New Jersey and Delaware and part of Pennsylvania. The port on the Atlantic Ocean (now New York City) was excellent for trade, and the Hudson afforded excellent transportation. The surrounding land was fertile, and the climate was healthful. For the first settlers, there was

t' Fort nieúw Amsterdam op de Manhatans

A drawing of the earliest view of New Amsterdam.
Courtesy of the Library of Congress.

no devastation from disease or hunger as there had been for the British in Virginia and Massachusetts or the French in Canada and Louisiana.

The colony was governed by directors-general appointed by the Dutch West Indies Company, who were under orders to purchase any lands they wished to settle from the Native inhabitants. The third governor of New Netherland, Peter Minuit (1580–1638), decided to create a new capital on Manhattan Island in 1626. At the time of the purchase, it was a beautiful island covered with a great forest and abounding with game and wild fruits. Minuit, who was described as a shrewd and somewhat dishonest man, became a legend for making one of history's greatest bargains when he purchased the land rights to the Manhattan Island from the Canarsee Indians for sixty guilders, or about twenty-four dollars, in trinkets, such as beads and metal ware that was valuable in trading. Since the Manhattan tribe, for whom it was named, had a better claim to the island than did the Canarsee, Minuit later also bought the island from them. Through this, their first major land purchase from the Indians, the Dutch secured a legal title of sorts to Manhattan. (The traditional Native American relationship to the land differed drastically from the Europeans'. They generally did not believe that humans "owned" land and therefore could not give it away permanently.)

The patroon system

The West Indies Company decided to try a system called "patroonship" to get people to emigrate in larger numbers. The company would give a very large grant of land to any person of wealth who committed to bringing over a certain number of colonizers and housing them on his land (usually fifty settlers within four years). In turn, the patroons were given the power of a feudal lord on their land. Feudalism was the political system prevailing in most of Europe during the Middle Ages (c. 500–c. 1500) in which a lord owned the land and had great authority over his tenants. The patroons in New Netherland were entitled to an oath of loyalty from their tenants and were the officials of justice and government on their huge estates. The tenants paid the lord rent and gave to him a portion of their crops and livestock each year. Since the Dutch in their homeland had been free of feudalism for centuries, when the West Indian Company instituted it in the New World, this system was not very appealing.

The patroon system was not successful, with one exception. Dutch diamond and pearl merchant Kiliaen Van Rensselaer (c. 1580–1644), one of the founders of the Dutch West India Company, was one of the first patroons in New Netherland, although he never lived there. Rensselaer had his deputies pay the Mohican nation for a vast tract of land for which he received a charter from the company. His enormous estate, called Rensselaerswyck, comprised a large part of the present-day counties of Albany, Rensselaer, and Columbia, in New York. Kiliaen Van Rensselaer found it nearly impossible, however, to attract farmers to work his lands—it took him nearly ten years to fulfill the numbers specified in his contract. But the estate remained in his family for many years after the Dutch had lost the colony to England, and the power of the Rensselaer patroonship system continued.

Life in New Netherland

As might be expected, the first settlers in New Netherland were most often poor and illiterate. The mix of people also lacked in farming and artisan skills that were badly needed. Most of the people who went to the New World were hoping to find quick wealth but instead found only hard work, mainly on farms. In their early days, the Dutch colonists built very rough log huts thatched with straw. The people developed a reputation for rowdiness and heavy drinking. In the 1660s, New Amsterdam (now New York City) was a community of about thirteen hundred people. It was very dirty, with animals running loose and sewage running down its streets. Gradually the rude huts in the colony became houses and the tiny, scattered dwellings grew into villages and then towns.

As they settled in, the Dutch colonists tried to make their new home more like the Netherlands. They put together the funds to build a school and established the Dutch Reformed Church, a Protestant Calvinist denomination. Founded

Dutchmen arriving in Jamestown, Virginia, in the 1600s with slaves.
Reproduced by permission of Getty Images.

in 1628, it is one of the oldest denominations in the United States. True to their background, the Dutch settlers welcomed people of most religions, including Jews. (They were initially hesitant about Quakers [Christians opposed to war, oathtaking, and rituals].) African slaves were brought into the colony. The Dutch were generally a little kinder than were their British neighbors. They permitted manumission (formally freeing a slave) and approximately one-fifth of Africans in the colony were free. Finally, the people began to speak out against the governors who ruled the colony without letting them have a voice in the government. In this endeavor, they were unable to prevail against the West Indies Company.

The company was interested in profits and not the welfare of the population, and their ineffective management of the colony and poor planning kept emigration from the Netherlands very low. The attractive land and waterways brought immigrants from England, France, and Sweden into New Netherland. Then, in the early 1660s, the British decided to begin a military campaign to take control of the colony, which lay between its New England and Chesapeake colonies. In 1664 four British ships arrived off New Amsterdam and demanded the surrender of the colony. In return for surrendering, they offered guarantees to the Dutch inhabitants: all the rights of Englishmen, trading privileges, freedom of religion, the continuance of Dutch customs and inheritance laws, and up to eighteen months for the settlers to decide whether to leave or not. At first, the governor of New Netherland, Peter Stuyvesant (c. 1610–1672), refused to surrender and began to make preparations for the defense of his colony. But Stuyvesant had angered his people with his high-handed rule. The residents of New Amsterdam would not help him defend the colony, sensing they would be no worse off under the British. Stuyvesant was forced to surrender the town. A week later, the remainder of the colony fell into British hands.

Dutch immigration after the colonial era

The Dutch had lost their chance at an empire in the New World, but the Dutch people's emigration had barely begun. Between 1820 and 1914, about two hundred thousand Dutch peasants and rural artisans immigrated to the United States in several major waves of migration. The first wave lasted from 1847 to 1857 and consisted largely of Catholics and conservative Dutch Reformed Protestants searching for greater religious freedom after the Dutch government cracked down on nonconformists in religion. Most settled in the New York area, while others scattered throughout the East Coast.

After the American Civil War ended in 1865, a second wave of Dutch immigrants flocked to the United States. This migration was made up largely of farm laborers and headed West, to the West Coast and to the Great Plains. The United States wanted to expand its territory westward and recruited immigrants through programs such as the 1862 Homestead Act, under which parcels of land were given for free to those who agreed to farm them for a certain number of years. Available land was dwindling in the Netherlands, and with fewer opportunities at home, landless peasants were motivated to make the move.

The third wave from 1880 to 1893 was prompted by a farming crisis in the Netherlands. Bad weather and overworked land caused low crop yields for several years in a row, beginning in 1878. Even farm owners chose to leave their homes and search for better opportunities elsewhere, particularly in the American Midwest and West, where land was still available at fairly cheap rates. The fourth major wave of Dutch immigration to the United States occurred from 1903 to 1913, spurred by an economic slump in the Netherlands. This time the immigrants were mostly urban (city-oriented), and they settled in major industrial centers in America, such as New York City and Chicago. Some craftspeople and merchants had also immigrated with the farmers of the previous three waves, escaping high taxes and fees in the Netherlands, but the majority of Dutch immigrants from 1847 to 1913 were farming families.

In the years immediately following World War II (1939–45), another wave of Dutch immigrants came to the United States to escape the conditions left in the aftermath of the German occupation of their homeland during the war, which had brought about persecution, starvation, and immense suffering. About eighty thousand Dutch entered the United States during this last major wave of immigration. Some were Jews who had survived the Holocaust.

Many of the early Dutch immigrants strongly resisted Americanization (changing or abandoning their own culture

Washington Irving's Dutch American works

More than a century after the Dutch lost New Netherland to England, Washington Irving (1783–1859) was born to English-Scottish American parents in New York in 1783. He became the United States' first professional fiction writer and created some of America's favorite stories. Because of Irving's writings, most Americans have a sense, fictional though it is, of the long-faded Dutch American culture in the Hudson River Valley.

As a child growing up in New York, Irving was surrounded by the Dutch character, manners, and mythology left imprinted on the land and people from the colonial days of New Netherland. This would be the most successful focus of his fiction. Irving first gained fame through his humorous two-volume book, *A History of New York, from the Beginning of the World to the End of the Dutch Dynasty: Containing Among Many Surprising and Curious Matters, the Unutterable Ponderings of Walter* *the Doubter, the Disastrous Projects of William the Testy, and the Chivalric Achievements of Peter the Headstrong, the Three Dutch Governors of New Amsterdam; Being the Only Authentic History of the Times that Ever Hath Been, or Ever Will Be Published* (1809), published under the fictitious name Diedrich Knickerbocker. His alias and narrator, Knickerbocker, presented himself as an absent-minded old caretaker of the Dutch history of New York. The book sets out the life of Manhattan's early Dutch settlers, with a focus on the disastrous rule of three of the original Dutch governors: Wouter Van Twiller (1580–1656), Willem Kieft (1597–1647), and Peter Stuyvesant (c. 1610–1672). But this "history" is a blend of fiction, local folklore, and, above all, humor at the expense of the bumbling Dutch settlers and all human beings. The work was so popular in New York that the word "Knickerbocker," taken from Irving's pseudonym, came to mean a person from New York, and in fact was the origin of the

to become more American), especially in their church life. The Dutch Reformed Church carried out its sermons in the Dutch language and taught that the Dutch way was the true way. Nearly a century later, in 1762, the Dutch Reformed Church conceded to Americanization and began holding some services in English to maintain its membership. By the end of the American Revolution (1775–83), all Dutch Reformed Church services were in English.

Dutch Catholics who immigrated to America usually assimilated more quickly into mainstream American life. They tended to be wealthier and more urban than Dutch

Washington Irving often wrote about the Dutch American culture that surrounded him in New York. *Reproduced by permission of the National Portrait Gallery, Smithsonian Institution.*

name of the New York Knickerbockers, which later became the New York Knicks.

In 1819 and 1820, Irving published his most treasured work, *The Sketch Book.* Among its stories are two American classics: "Rip Van Winkle" and "The Legend of Sleepy Hollow." Both stories, which are presented as having been found among the papers of Dietrich Knickerbocker after his death, are loosely based on local history and Irving's own Hudson River Valley experience, but they come directly from folklore. "Rip Van Winkle," adapted from a German myth, tells of a farmer in the British colony of New York's Catskill Mountains who falls asleep for twenty years and wakes up after the American Revolution (1775–83). In "The Legend of Sleepy Hollow," a Yankee schoolmaster, Ichabod Crane, tries to settle the mystery of the headless horseman in a Dutch American community. Although Irving had no Dutch roots himself, his affectionate depiction of the Dutch American society in the Hudson River Valley became the best-known portrait of the culture in American literature.

Protestants, who were mostly farmers, so more Catholics had the resources to establish themselves quickly in industrialized U.S. society. Dutch Catholic, and later Jewish, immigrants also came to the United States, but by far the majority of Dutch Americans were and are members of the Dutch Reformed Church.

Although the earliest Dutch settlers lived in what became New York State, the first wave of later immigrants settled almost entirely within a fifty-mile radius of the southern shoreline of Lake Michigan. Later, they spread throughout the country.

Most Dutch Americans immigrated in entire family units and settled in communities with others from the same province of the Netherlands. This process occurred in a pattern called chain migration. After immigrants of the first wave (1847–57) established themselves in the United States, relatives and friends of the original immigrants followed them to America. These newcomers settled near their kin, creating tightly knit communities of Dutch Americans. Surrounded by compatriots, they were slow to assimilate and kept the Dutch culture wholly intact for a number of generations.

According to the 2000 U.S. Census, 5,203,974 Americans claim Dutch descent. About one-third live in the Midwest. A significant number continue to live in the Hudson River Valley area of New York.

Some Dutch words that have been adopted into common American usage are cookie, waffle, spook, and perhaps Yankee (which may have been a Dutch nickname for Dutch sailors). The American name for Santa Claus also comes from the Dutch: Sinterklaas is their word for St. Nicholas.

Dutch foods have also had their impact. In the United States we owe such fare as pancakes, waffles, doughnuts, cookies, coleslaw, and pretzels (though pretzels are also credited to German Americans) to the people who came here from the Netherlands.

There are many famous Dutch Americans. Film director Cecil B. DeMille's (1881–1959) family was of Dutch ancestry and had been in America since 1658. Starting his career in the days of silent pictures, he made the transition to "talkies" with his epic dramas, including *The Ten Commandments* (1923, remade 1956), *Samson and Delilah* (1949), and *The Greatest Show on Earth* (1952). Herman Melville (1819–1891), the author of *Moby Dick* and other top American fiction, was the grandson of Revolutionary War general Peter Gansevoort (1749–1812) of Albany. The family descended from Gansevoorts of early colonial days in the Americas. The great inventor Thomas Alva Edison (1847–1931) was the great-great-grandson of John Edison, who came to the United States from the Netherlands in 1730. Walter Percy Chrysler (1875–1940), who introduced the Chrysler automobile and became a leading automobile manufacturer, could trace his descent through his mother from Tuenis Van Dalsen, a Netherlander born on Manhattan Island before the settlement of New Amsterdam. President Theodore Roosevelt (1858–1919; served 1901–08), and President Franklin Delano Roosevelt (1882–1945; served 1932–45) both traced their heritage back to Klaes Martensen van Roosevelt, who immigrated to the United States in 1644.

For More Information

Books

Middleton, Richard. *Colonial America: A History, 1565–1776,* 3rd ed. Oxford, UK: 2002.

Mulder, Arnold. *Americans from Holland.* Philadelphia and New York: J.B. Lippincott, 1947.

Swierenga, Robert P. *Faith and Family: Dutch Immigration and Settlement in the United States, 1820–1920.* New York: Holmes and Meier, 2000.

Web Sites

"Virtual Museum of New France." *Civilization.ca.* http://www.civilization.ca/vmnf/boucher/3.5/3.5.5.htm (accessed on February 26, 2004).

African American Immigration

8

One of the earliest groups of immigrants to colonial North America was the Africans, the majority of whom had no choice but to immigrate. Forcibly taken from their homelands and loaded into slave ships that crossed the Atlantic, the African captives were deprived of the most basic human rights. While willing immigrants came to the United States with hopes of new opportunities and increased freedom, these forced immigrants could only look forward to hard labor for someone else's profit.

The stories of the hundreds of thousands of people brought as slaves from the Old World (the areas of the world that were known to Europeans before they knew of the Americas) to the New World (the part of the world that includes North and South America) are varied. Their experiences depended on when they came and which part of the country they came to, on their slave owners and managers, and of course, on their own individual outlook. Africans brought a strong sense of their Old World cultural heritage to the New World. Through shared or private memories, prayers, song, and oral traditions (telling stories of earlier times), they

Fact Focus

- The Portuguese were the first Europeans to travel to Africa and enslave its people, beginning in the early fifteenth century.

- The stretch of the western coast of Africa that provided most of the slaves for the Americas was more than 3,000 miles long. The regions most heavily involved in the slave trade were West Africa and West Central Africa.

- The average age range for an African purchased in the Atlantic slave trade was between ten and twenty-four years old.

- When the first Africans arrived in British and Dutch North America, no laws had established the institution of slavery, and the Africans were often treated as indentured servants. A few were able to serve their term, gain their freedom, and acquire some property.

- Between ten and twelve million Africans were brought into the New World by slave traders between 1500 and 1900. Of those, between eight and ten million went to the West Indies and Brazil. What became the United States imported about five hundred thousand slaves.

- Vermont was the first to abolish slavery in its constitution in 1777, but it was not yet a state. Massachusetts was the first state to abolish slavery in 1783.

- The cotton gin was invented by Eli Whitney (1765–1825) in 1793. With its use, southern plantations were able to increase cotton production from 3,000 bales in 1793 to 178,000 bales just seven years later. With the increase in production and potential profits, more crops were planted and there was a large increase of labor to be done on the plantations. Reliance on slaves in the South increased dramatically.

- In French Louisiana in the years before the American Civil War (1861–65), there were more people of mixed race and more free blacks than in other parts of the South.

- Recent African immigrants to the United States are among the most educated groups of American immigrants, with 49 percent of adults holding bachelor's degrees.

passed along some key elements of their various African pasts from generation to generation, even though they were often separated from others from their homeland. At the same time, African Americans were some of the first settlers in the nation and they helped to build its foundations. Like other immigrants, their ties to the Old World weakened through the generations as they became Americans.

Long after slavery had been abolished, racial discrimination pervaded the legal system, public institutions, and social structures of the United States. African American people were prohibited, or greatly hindered, from assimilating (blending in) to the mainstream culture. Despite, or maybe even because of, all the adversity, African American culture developed and flourished, producing some of the country's most notable art forms, political movements, and social reformers.

Africans arrive with the Spanish

The first Africans who came to the Americas did not arrive on slave ships. In fact, some historians believe that as far back as the seventh century B.C.E., African traders made their way by sea to Mexico, where they traded with the Olmecs, an ancient American civilization. Evidence in the artifacts found in Olmec sites raises this theory, but it has not been proven to be true.

Africans arrived in the New World a century before the Pilgrims (a group of British Protestant colonists, the first colonists to settle in New England) arrived. In 1526 a fleet of six Spanish ships arrived in present-day South Carolina with five hundred settlers, including African slaves, to establish a settlement there. When the leader of the expedition died, there was an uprising over who would lead the colony. The African slaves reportedly took advantage of the disturbance to escape and may have gone to live with the Indians. If so, these Africans may well have been the first non-native immigrants to settle in what would become the United States. Throughout the next century, hundreds of African slaves arrived with the Spanish explorers, and others slipped off to live with the Native Americans as well.

There were many Africans and people of mixed heritage who took part in the Spanish settling of what would become the southwestern portion of the United States. Africans arrived in significant numbers to settle Santa Fe and, later, Texas and California. Some served in the Spanish military; others lived with Indians. As in Mexico and South America, these Africans frequently had children with, and sometimes married, both the Spanish and the Native Americans.

Words to Know

Animism: The belief that all the world's natural matter is endowed with a soul—that trees, rocks, and rivers are spiritual beings.

Civil disobedience: An act of protest against a questionable law through nonviolent acts of breaking that law.

Constitution: The written document that sets out a political body's laws. The Constitution describes how power and duties are distributed within its government and guarantees the rights of its people.

Ethnic group: A group of people who have a distinctive identity and cultural heritage.

Great Depression (1929–41): The period, following the stock market crash in 1929, of depressed world economies and high unemployment.

Indentured servant: A person who, in exchange for his or her passage to the New World, was bound by contract to labor for a period of years (usually seven). After their term of service, indentured servants were generally provided with land and goods to help them get settled.

Islam: The religion of the Muslims, who believe in Allah as the one supreme god and Muhammad as the prophet, or the interpreter of the will of Allah; the religion is based on the Muslim holy book, the Koran.

Middle passage: The journey by slave ship from Africa to the Americas, the middle leg in the European traders' triangular system—the first leg was the trip from Europe to Africa, and the last was the trip from the Americas to Europe.

The Old World: Africa

For many centuries before the Europeans began to colonize the Americas, the vast continent of Africa was home to a wide variety of societies, ranging from simple farming villages to sophisticated empires with large cities, intricate trade networks, and a wealth of culture. Egypt, a highly advanced civilization by 3000 B.C.E., had a profound impact on the rest of the world. Ghana and Mali also had very advanced cultures in early history.

Africa is a huge continent. In fact, at 12 million square miles, the continent is so vast you could fit all of the land of the countries of China, India, Europe, Argentina, New Zealand, and the United States into it, according to the Natural History Museum of Los Angeles' *Africa: One Continent, Many Worlds*

Moor: An African person of Arab and Berber descent, generally a member of the religion of Islam.

New England: The northern colonies (later the states) of Massachusetts, Rhode Island, Connecticut, and New Hampshire.

Pidgin language: A simple speech created to make trade possible between two groups that speak different languages.

Pilgrim: A member of the group of British Protestant colonists, who sailed on the *Mayflower* and founded the colony of Plymouth in 1626.

Quaker: A member of the Society of Friends, a Christian group, dedicated to social reform, that rejects the rituals and preachers of formal churches, and instead holds open meetings at which all are free to speak.

Racism: A system of belief based on an assumption that important characteristics, such as intelligence, morality, or sophistication, of the different races are passed along from generation to generation and are determined by the ethnic group or race. This allows some people to assert that one race is superior to another.

West Indies: Islands in the Caribbean Sea on which explorer Christopher Columbus first landed in 1492, including Hispaniola (now Haiti and the Dominican Republic), Cuba, Jamaica, Puerto Rico, the Virgin Islands, Windward Islands, Leeward Islands, and the islands in the S. Caribbean Sea north of Venezuela, usually including Trinidad and Tobago.

Web site. Until fairly recently, most African people did not identify themselves as Africans or by nationality. Rather, they identified with their ethnic group (a group of people who have a distinctive identity and cultural heritage) or tribe, such as the Mandingo, Ibo, or Ashante. The many ethnic groups of Africa had different kinds of governments and economies, spoke different languages, and produced different kinds of art.

Religious practices among the ethnic groups varied, but most African societies were very devout. Many practiced some form of animism, a belief that all the natural world is invested with spirits, but they also worshipped a supreme god. In the eighth century the Islam religion gained a large following in northern Africa. (Islam is the religion of the Muslims, who believe in Allah as the one supreme god and

Muhammad as the prophet, or the person who was able to interpret the will of Allah; the religion is based on the Muslim holy book, the Koran.) Muslim traders from the north spread the religion, and different ethnic groups and tribes throughout the continent began to practice it.

In physical appearance, the African people were as varied as their cultures. The tribes differed in the color of their complexion as well as in height, build, and facial bone structure. The idea that the people of Africa could all be described by the one word "black" would have made little sense to them.

Before European ships reached its shores, Africa had been in contact with other parts of the world for thousands of years. Egypt had dealings with the people of the Mediterranean Sea area. East Africans traveled to Asia. Ethiopians had contact with Greece, and other Africans had traveled in Europe. So when the Portuguese began exploring the African coast in the 1420s, most of the coastal leaders welcomed them, hoping for profitable trade. Along with their trade, the Portuguese began a side business of kidnapping people from Africa and bringing them back to Portugal as slaves. By 1450, they were transporting one thousand to two thousand Africans from the western coastal region to Europe each year to be sold as slaves.

The Atlantic slave trade begins

In 1502, Spanish colonists asked their king for African slaves to provide the labor they needed for their large farms, or plantations, in the West Indies (islands in the Caribbean Sea on which explorer Christopher Columbus [1451–1506] first landed in 1492, including Hispaniola (now Haiti and the Dominican Republic), Cuba, Jamaica, Puerto Rico). The Native Americans they had initially enlisted to do the labor were dying in large numbers from the infectious diseases brought to the New World by the Spanish. They were also being killed by overwork and poor conditions. When the Spanish king agreed that African slaves could be transported to the New World, the Atlantic slave trade began.

The coast of Africa from which slaves were taken stretched from the Sénégal River in the north (at the present-day border between Sénégal and Mauritania) to the Congo

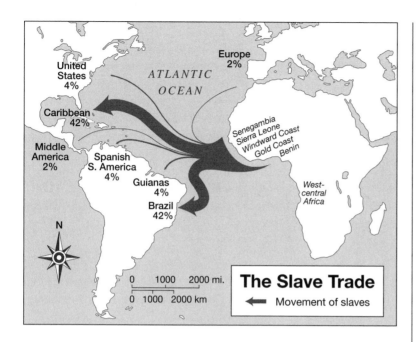

A map showing the movement of slaves from Africa to the Western Hemisphere as part of the slave trade. The coast of western Africa from which slaves were taken by Europeans stretched 3,000 miles. *Reproduced by permission of The Gale Group.*

River in the south (at the present-day border between Democratic Republic of the Congo and Angola). This area was more than 3,000 miles long—a distance greater than that between New York and California. The regions that were involved most heavily in the slave trade were West Africa and West Central Africa. Senegambia, the region between the Sénégal and Gambia Rivers south of the Sahara Desert, was the region from which most of the first slaves were taken. The early Portuguese traders encountered two groups on the coast with whom they traded: the Mandingo and the Wolof (also called Jolof).

Most of the people in the Senegambian region were farmers, but others were livestock herders, potters, blacksmiths, and other skilled craftspeople. Among the groups in Senegambia, farmwork was typically considered women's work, and women also did the domestic chores, food preparation, and child-rearing. Some of them were highly skilled at spinning cotton and were famous in the region for the beautiful blue robes that they made and colored with dye made from the indigo plant. Along with other crafts, men of the Senegambian region were boatbuilders, traders, hunters, trappers, and fishermen. They were also warriors, when necessary.

Slavery within Africa

Slavery had existed in Africa long before Europeans arrived on its West Coast. Individuals who were captured as prisoners of war made up the largest proportion of slaves, but others were sentenced to slavery as punishment for crimes or chose slavery over starvation when food was scarce. Although most African societies deprived slaves of their freedom, they treated slaves as human beings, and sooner or later the slaves would assimilate, or blend, into the master's society as a free person or be freed by their owner. Slaves often served in high positions, as city officials or as soldiers, and they could own businesses. They often married the free men or women of the community.

Europeans took advantage of the existing practice of slavery in West and West Central Africa by giving African traders merchandise in exchange for their enslaved captives. Africans rarely, if ever, traded slaves from among their own people. The coastal tribes obtained slaves in wars with tribes located further inland. The inland tribes then looked to tribes even further inland for more slaves. Africans who sold slaves for guns and ammunition were able to use the guns to capture even more slaves from groups that were not as well armed. Those groups, in turn, felt compelled to capture and sell slaves so they could purchase guns to protect themselves. Warfare along the coast of western Africa increased greatly as the slave trade took hold.

The trade in human beings

Most new slaves destined for the Americas were young people. In his book, *From Africa to America: African American History from the Colonial Era to the Early Republic: 1526–1790,* William D. Piersen provides some statistics about slaves: 14 percent were children; 30 percent were women; 56 percent were men. The average age range was between ten and twenty-four years old. Few people over the age of thirty were sent to the New World because they had less chance of surviving the trip and were not as fit for the hard labor ahead. Slaves taken in war were often people of distinction, sometimes princes, priests, or nobility.

During the 1500s the Portuguese obtained slaves from the Wolof and the Serer from present-day Sénégal; from the Mandingo from present-day Gambia; from the Bram, Banyun, and Biafada from present-day Guinea-Bissau; from the Baga, Temne, and Landuma peoples from present-day Sierra Leone; and in West Central Africa, from the Bakongo, Teke, and Ambundu people of present-day Congo/Angola. As the 1600s began, slaves were obtained from the Akan from the Gold Coast (modern-day Ghana), from the Fon from Benin, and from the Ibo from Nigeria.

Middle passage

By 1500, the Portuguese were taking about three thousand African slaves per year through direct trade with African traders. It is terrible to imagine what the ordeal for the captives must have been. Slaves captured in raids or warfare were bound together and marched to the coast from inland, heavily burdened with goods for trade. Along Africa's west coast, the Portuguese traders had built some sixty forts or trading posts on land they had rented from the African rulers. Many captives were brought to these stations, at the time called "factories," where they were confined in hot, dungeonlike cellars. Others were simply brought to the shore, where European ships bearing guns, rum, and other goods had come to exchange their wares for human beings. British or Dutch sailors then brought the men, women, and children to the slave boats.

The slave vessels, known as slavers, anchored off the coast until they had a full cargo of people, and then set a course west to the Americas. The miserable journey from Africa to the Americas was called the "middle passage" because it was the middle leg in the European traders' triangular system—the first leg was the trip from Europe to Africa, and the last was the trip from the Americas back to Europe. Aboard these slavers, men, women, and children were bound hand and foot and crammed into narrow spaces no more than 4 feet high, and often half that, in order to make room for the maximum cargo. They remained in that space for much of the voyage, which in the sixteenth century could last from twelve to twenty weeks. The sanitation needs of the captives were largely ignored. Seasickness and dysentery (severe diarrhea) created appalling conditions. Infectious diseases quickly spread in the close quarters. Many tried to jump overboard or to starve themselves, and there were rebellions at sea. The sailors whose job it was to oversee the captives were generally a rough lot; despite the goal of keeping as many slaves alive as possible, their treatment of the people was often inhumane. The rate of death among the captives aboard the slavers was high, particularly in the early days of the trade—about 24 percent, or one out of every four people, died in the middle passage in the 1680s.

It is estimated that somewhere between ten and twelve million Africans were brought into the New World by slave traders between 1500 and 1900. Of those, between eight and ten million went to the West Indies and Brazil. By comparison, what became the United States imported relatively few slaves, about five hundred thousand people. Anywhere from 8 to 23 percent of those captured in Africa died before they reached the Americas.

The first slaves to be imported to the American colonies in the seventeenth century came mainly by way of the West Indies. In the islands, first large tobacco plantations, and later even larger sugar plantations, were established. These plantations demanded a tremendous supply of physical labor. In Haiti and Cuba, the numbers of Africans imported as slaves rose drastically to meet the labor demands during the eighteenth century. Unfortunately for the slaves, the profits on the Caribbean plantations were so high that many of them were worked to death within a year or two of arriving. With the profits of less than one year's slave labor, the plantation owners were able to purchase another slave to replace one who died. Some of those who survived several years of hard labor in the West Indies were sold in the American colonies as "seasoned" (or experienced) slaves, worth more because they needed less training.

Slavery in the early North American colonies

Before the end of the seventeenth century, people of African origin who were brought to the North American colonies were often viewed by the colonists as servants rather than as slaves. Few settlers in the British and French colonies of North America had any experience with slavery. Farming in colonial North America was on a much smaller scale than in the plantations of the Caribbean, and so were the profits. The purchase of a slave was a major investment for a farmer—one to

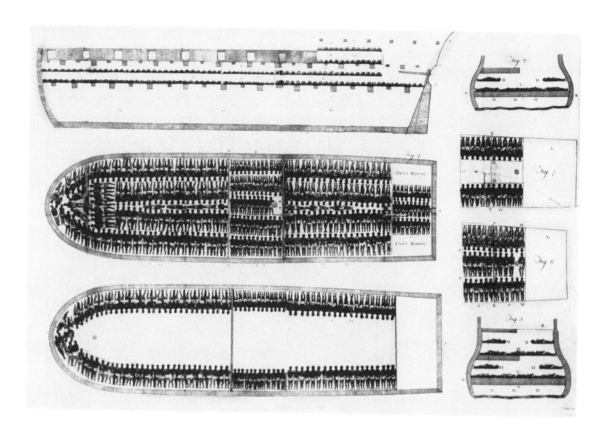

take care of and preserve, perhaps for a lifetime. In the British North American colonies, unlike on the Caribbean plantations, the life expectancy of a slave was about the same as the life expectancy of a British settler. Slaves had a good birth rate (that is, they produced enough children to replace themselves and more), so the need to import more slaves was low.

In 1625 there were only twenty-three Africans in Virginia, and most of them were probably servants, not slaves. It is estimated that in 1640 Virginia had about three hundred slaves and, in 1670, about two thousand out of a total population of forty thousand. But in 1700, as farming in the South became large scale, Virginia's population ratios changed dramatically, with a rise to twelve thousand blacks and a decrease in the white population to eighteen thousand. In the Carolinas in 1700 the black population was about equal to the white population, whereas in New England blacks numbered only about one thousand out of a total population of ninety thousand. Slavery, rather than servitude, became the rule in

This set of diagrams of the decks of the slaver *Brookes* illustrates how the captives were packed into tiny slots aboard ship. The quarters were so cramped that some slaves were crippled for life by the time they arrived in the New World. *Courtesy of the Library of Congress.*

TO BE SOLD on board the Ship *Bance-Iſland*, on tueſday the 6th of *May* next, at *Aſhley-Ferry*; a choice cargo of about 250 fine healthy

NEGROES,

juſt arrived from the Windward & Rice Coaſt. —The utmoſt care has already been taken, and ſhall be continued, to keep them free from the leaſt danger of being infected with the SMALL-POX, no boat having been on board, and all other communication with people from *Charles-Town* prevented.

Auſtin, Laurens, & Appleby.

N. B. Full one Half of the above Negroes have had the SMALL-POX in their own Country.

most colonies over time: Of more than 750,000 Americans of African descent in 1790, all but 60,000 were enslaved.

Africans in Virginia

In 1619 a Dutch warship carrying twenty Africans landed at Jamestown, Virginia. The Africans, who had probably been stolen by the Dutch from Spanish slave traders, were the first to arrive in the British colonies. Since neither British laws nor the charter of the colony established the institution of slavery, the first African slaves to arrive were treated as indentured servants. Indentured servants in colonial America were people who, in exchange for their passage to the New World, were bound by contract to labor for a period of years (usually seven). Most of the colonies had laws about the treatment of Africans. It was commonly required that after their term of service, indentured servants were provided with small tracts of land and a few goods with which to settle. Indentured servants outnumbered slaves in the southern colonies during the seventeenth century and always far outnumbered the slaves in the other colonies.

African servants in early Virginia were not treated on equal terms with European indentured servants. They were forced to serve longer terms and they were the object of special prohibitions, but in the early seventeenth century at least some servants from Africa managed to serve their term of indenture, gain their freedom, and acquire some property. Such cases had become rare by mid-century. As early as the 1640s some African servants were serving for life, and their numbers increased throughout the decade. In a 1640 court case, for example, three servants faced punishment for running away. Two of them, who were white, were sentenced to four years of service beyond the time they already owed, while the other, a man of African descent, was ordered to serve his master for life. In the 1650s some African servants were being sold for life with the bills of sale indicating that their offspring would inherit the slave status. Thus slavery developed according to custom before it was legally established in Virginia. By the 1660s Virginia law dictated that the children born to slaves were slaves for life as well. Before the end of the seventeenth century, Virginia slave codes had reduced slaves to the legal status of property. Slaves could not bear arms, own property, or leave a plantation without written permission from the master. Capital punishment was provided for murder and rape; lesser crimes were punished by maiming, whipping, or branding.

Virginia was not alone in adopting slavery. The system existed early both in Maryland and in the Carolinas. Georgia at-

A slave auction in the Dutch city of New Amsterdam, in New Netherland.
Reproduced by permission of © Bettmann/Corbis.

tempted to prevent slavery at the time of its settlement, but the prohibition was repealed in 1750. The Dutch brought slavery to New Netherland early in the seventeenth century. When the British took command of the colony in 1664, the institution of slavery was recognized in New York and New Jersey, but in Pennsylvania and Delaware the religious objections of the Quakers delayed legal recognition until the early eighteenth century. (Quakers are members of the Society of Friends, a Christian group that rejects the rituals and preachers of formal churches and instead holds meetings at which all are free to speak.)

Slavery in New England

In 1638 a ship named *Desire* unloaded New England's first shipment of African slaves at Boston Harbor. (As a group, the northern colonies of Massachusetts, Rhode Island, Connecticut, and New Hampshire were known as New England.) The *Desire* was the first of many ships to sail into New England's harbors carrying slaves and goods from Africa and the West Indies. Nevertheless, there were few slaves in New England because the cold climate and rocky soil did not accommodate large farms. Most New Englanders who could afford servants only had one or two. If they purchased a slave, they would most likely house him or her in close quarters with their family. Slaves often ate with a family, slept in the house with them, and worked with them in their fields. They often took second positions outside the household, as blacksmiths or seamstresses or laundry washers, to earn extra income for the household. In general, there was a stronger family relationship between slaves and owner-families in New England than elsewhere in the New World. The slave laws that developed there were less severe than in the South and marriage between blacks was honored. In fact, in New England marriage was required of black couples wishing to live together. However, because the households were small, many slaves in New England were isolated from other people from their homelands. Like all slaves, they were denied the most basic human freedoms.

Elsewhere in the North

Up to about 1750 there had not been many slaves in the North, but at that time they came to be employed in a

The Roots of Alex Haley's *Roots*

Alex Haley (1921–1992) was a freelance writer known for his interviews with famous people when he had a lucky break in the early 1960s: Civil rights activist Malcolm X (1925–1965) asked him to help him write his autobiography. *The Autobiography of Malcolm X* (1965) became a bestseller. Haley took this success as an opportunity to follow up on a passionate interest—his ethnic roots as an African.

As a child Haley had spent summers with his maternal grandparents in Tennessee. His grandmother and great aunts had often spoken of their African ancestor named Kin-tay, captured and sold into slavery in America during the late 1700s. Wishing to know more, Haley obtained advances from publishers to research his family history. He consulted libraries, archives, and other research centers. A linguist (someone who studies languages) helped him to link the many "k" sounds his ancestor Kin-tay used with that of the Mandingo people of Gambia in West Africa.

In 1967 Haley traveled to Gambia to meet with a griot, or oral historian, of the Kinte clan in the Mandingo village of Juffure. Working with an interpreter, Haley learned the story of the Kinte clan, including marriages, births, deaths, and other events. Eventually he heard the story of a young man named Kunta Kinte, who left his village to chop wood and was never seen again.

The story of Kunta Kinte paralleled the tale he had heard from his grandmother and great aunts. Kunta Kinte and his ancestor Kin-tay were probably the same person. Haley conducted more research and discovered records that supported the story that Kunta Kinte was kidnapped and sent to America on a British slave ship. When he sailed home to the United States from Liberia, Haley lay in the ship's hold on a rough board between bales of raw rubber, wearing only his underwear, in an attempt to understand the filth, death, and deprivation that slaves had endured on their passage across the Atlantic.

After struggling to understand the experiences of his ancestor, Haley went on to write a book about them. In 1976 *Roots: The Saga of an American Family* was published, and it quickly rose to the top of the bestseller list. The fictionalized account of seven generations of Haley's family from their ancestral home in Africa to slavery in America was made into a television movie that aired for one week on consecutive nights in 1977, drawing a record-breaking 130 million American viewers. Although Haley's book drew criticism and is regarded more as a piece of fiction than for its historical value, *Roots* created an unprecedented interest in black history and genealogy and effectively changed the way mainstream America thought about its history and people.

variety of roles. In the 1760s blacks made up more than three-quarters of Philadelphia's servant population. Slaves worked in distilleries (plants that make alcoholic drink), shipyards, factories, farms, lumber camps, and ropewalks (places where rope is made). Slaves in the cities were often apprentices (trainees) and helpers in shops. Most lived alone or in groups of two or three in a home or workshop. New York had an unusually high proportion of skilled slaves—masons (builders with stone), shipwrights, goldsmiths, and glaziers (people who install glass), among others. New York did not free all its slaves until 1827. In New Jersey, which had a gradual abolition law (a law eliminating the institution slowly over time), there were still a handful of slaves on the eve of the American Civil War (1861–65).

After winning independence from Britain in the American Revolution (1775–83), the newly formed United States adopted its Constitution in 1787. (A constitution is the written document that sets out a political body's laws, describes how power and duties are distributed within its government, and guarantees the rights of its people.) Neither the nation nor any of the states had yet abolished slavery. Vermont, not yet part of the United States, was opposed to the institution and did abolish slavery at the time. Within a few years, Delaware and Virginia prohibited the importation of slaves and Pennsylvania provided for the gradual abolition of slavery. In 1783 Massachusetts abolished slavery. It was the first state of the United States to do so.

The rise of southern plantations

About three hundred thousand slaves arrived in the North American colonies between 1675 and 1775. At the time, land in the South was being cleared for the large farms that came to be called plantations. Tobacco, rice, grains, indigo (plants to produce a dark blue dye), and a variety of other crops were grown on a large scale in the long warm seasons. These large-scale farms could bring in huge profits, but only if there was enough inexpensive labor to power them.

In the eighteenth-century South, the majority of slaveholders owned only a few slaves and small farms; most people did not own slaves at all. Most of the South's slaves

were owned by a small elite group of planters who ran large plantations. The word "plantation," which originally meant an area that had been planted with some kind of vegetation, in the South came to mean a large farm that employed more than twenty slaves. The planter class made up only about 10 percent of the South's population but controlled 90 percent of its wealth in the form of land and slaves.

Life for slaves on the plantations was, at best, very difficult. Plantation managers or overseers were often in charge of punishing rebellious slaves—the lash, or cowhide whip. was one method of discipline. There are many historical examples of terrible cruelty, and the extent of the brutality experienced by people who never had a chance to tell their stories will never be known. Laws and enforcement were in place to ensure slaves did not run away. Certainly not every slave was treated harshly. There was a tendency among wealthy southern plantation owners to view themselves almost as father figures for their slaves. People who owned smaller farms and worked alongside the slaves tended to be less brutal. Even in the better circumstances, however, there was a tendency to treat slaves like children, and self-determination, or the ability to choose one's own path in life, was always denied them.

On plantations, slaves generally received a bare minimum of the necessities of life. Their food was rationed. Shoes were only provided for winter months. Slaves in southern plantations usually lived in tiny cabins with no floors or windows and very little furniture. To save space and costs, the slave owners often crammed as many slaves into a cabin as possible. Sleep was kept to a minimum; work was kept at a maximum.

Slaves struggled to keep stable family relations against terrible conditions. Members of a slave family could be sold to a faraway owner at any time. Slave owners often raped slave women and, in such cases, children born to them might be biological children of the owner. Still, most slaves placed a high value on their marriages, which were not recognized by the white society. Family and community ties were surprisingly strong under the extraordinary circumstances.

Religion had been a crucial part of daily life in Africa and continued to be so in America. The Christian religion spread rapidly and was often practiced alongside African religions. Slaves conducted their own religious services whenever possible, but as more and more slaves were brought into the South, the slave owners became concerned about uprisings. In 1835 it became illegal for black preachers to conduct religious services for black people without a white minister present. Slaves continued to hold religious meetings in secret. Together, they found comfort in songs, folk stories, old ways of worship, and the stories of the Bible.

On the plantations, when the slaves were able to find places to hold secret church meetings outside the view of the white population, they prayed together in a blend of African tradition and Christian concepts. Their prayers often broke into song and dance, intermixed with preaching, shouting, and storytelling in a rhythmic call-and-response pattern. The person expressing a spiritual experience would call out words and melody, and the rest of the group would answer in a repeated refrain. While many of the words of these spirituals came from the Bible, the call-and-response pattern had its

Recrossing the Atlantic

The modern nation of Liberia was founded in 1822 by the American Colonization Society (ACS). The society, a private organization of white people, purchased a large area in West Africa with the purpose of creating a colony where slaves, once they had been emancipated (freed) from slavery, could settle. Many of the society's members were slaveholders who supported a gradual abolition of slavery. Some of them did not want to see free African Americans living in the same community with whites or competing with them for jobs. Their offer was simple: If a slaveholder freed a slave on the condition that the slave would then migrate to Liberia, the ACS would pay for the ocean voyage and help the freed slave to settle. Between 1822 and 1846 between thirteen and fourteen thousand freed slaves immigrated to Africa under this plan.

Abolitionists and the black community opposed the obvious racism of the ACS's activities. Southern plantation owners, concerned about losing their work force, did not like the plan either. The plan was not appealing to the indigenous (original) people of Liberia, who considered the newcomers arrogant. The Liberians rebelled, repeatedly attacking the Americans. The ACS went bankrupt and in 1847, under order of the company, the American Liberians founded the Republic of Liberia. Liberia's state seal shows a ship at anchor in a tropical harbor, and bears the inscription, "The Love of Liberty Brought Us Here." The American Liberians, seizing power, dominated over the sixteen native ethnic groups within Liberia's borders for more than a century.

roots in West Africa and West Central Africa. To replace the drums that had been used for rhythm in Africa, many worshipers stomped and danced.

The cotton gin and a one-crop South

In 1793 Eli Whitney (1765–1825) invented the cotton gin, a machine that separated cottonseed from cotton fiber. With its use, southern plantations were able to increase cotton production from 3,000 bales in 1793 to 178,000 bales just seven years later. Production amounts and profits from cotton would continue to soar. At first the Carolinas and Georgia grew most of the cotton, but cotton cultivation pushed westward to Alabama, Mississippi, and Louisiana.

The tremendous increase in cotton farming meant an immediate increase in the number of African slaves imported into the South. In 1790 there were fewer than seven hundred thousand slaves in the United States. By 1830 there were more than two million slaves and only about three thousand of them lived in the North. At the time of the American Civil War, there were four million slaves in the United States and about 3.5 million of them lived and worked on the plantations in the South. Although the United States abolished the importation of slaves after 1807, the trade continued to flourish right up to the American Civil War. An interstate slave trade developed as well. In the states of Maryland, Virginia, and Kentucky, slaveholders began to breed slaves to sell. In 1832 an estimated six thousand slaves were exported from Virginia. The slaves were sold down into the Deep South and west—Georgia, Alabama, Mississippi, Louisiana, and Texas. The economy of the South became thoroughly dependent on cotton—and on the slave labor that made the plantations possible.

Abolition and escape

By the 1830s antislavery societies had arisen in both the North and the South. The press was the primary weapon of the antislavery movement. In 1827 African American journalists Samuel Cornish (1795–1858) and John Russwurm (1799–1851) launched *Freedom's Journal*, the first African American newspaper. In 1831 white abolitionist and editor William Lloyd Garrison (1805–1879) published the first issue of the *Liberator*. Other antislavery papers followed, including the *North Star*, launched by black abolitionist leader Frederick Douglass (1817–1895). While many of the antislavery organizations were dominated by whites, African Americans such as Douglass played an important role in the abolition movement. Other notable black abolition leaders were scholar and Episcopalian minister Alexander Crummell (1819–1898), educator Charlotte Forten (1837–1914), activist and Presbyterian minister Henry Highland Garnet (1815–1882), orator and activist Sojourner Truth (c. 1797–1883), and David Walker (1785–1830), who advocated the violent overthrow of slavery.

A vast network of individuals and groups developed to help African Americans escape from slavery on what became known as the Underground Railroad. Abolitionists provided "stations" where food, shelter, and financial assistance were available. Experienced "conductors" (often themselves runaway slaves) led thousands of "passengers" to freedom in the northern United States, Canada, and the Caribbean. Most of the movement occurred at night, with passengers hiding in barns and homes during the day. Two of the most famous conductors were Josiah Henson (1789–1883) and Harriet Tubman (c. 1826–1913). Henson's memoirs, published in 1849, inspired writer Harriet Beecher Stowe to write *Uncle Tom's Cabin*. Tubman made at least fifteen trips from the North into Southern slave states, leading over two hundred slaves into free Northern states.

In the 1850s Sojourner Truth, a former slave, traveled about the country on foot, winning over her mostly white audiences on the issue of abolition by relating her own experiences as a slave. *Reproduced by permission of Getty Images.*

Louisiana

The huge territory known as Louisiana remained in French hands until 1763, when it was ceded to Spain. Spain returned it to France in 1800, but in 1803 the United States bought it in the Louisiana Purchase. The culture in Louisiana was significantly different from the rest of the South. French Louisiana imported a relatively large share of African slaves in the 1700s—there were seven thousand by 1735. The white population in early years remained low owing to a high death rate and low immigration. In many parts of the vast territory, African Americans outnumbered European Americans. Marriages or sexual unions between Africans and the French, Spanish, or Indians were common.

Because of the high ratio of blacks to whites in southern Louisiana and the liberal French and Spanish attitudes toward the intermingling of the races, African influence on the culture was very strong. A relatively high degree of racial tolerance prevailed, and laws allowed slaves, in certain circumstances, to gain their freedom. As a result, a greater num-

Who's Creole in Louisiana?

In early colonial days, the word "Creole" was used to distinguish people who were born in the Americas to European parents as opposed to the Europeans who had been born in Europe and then migrated to the New World. The term was originally used in French Louisiana to refer to white descendants of the French settlers in the area. Because these people had a special culture of their own, Creole began to take on a slightly broader cultural meaning. Creoles, for example, were distinct from the Cajuns, a group of French descent that had been exiled from Canada and made its way to Louisiana. (For more information on the Cajuns, see chapter 13 on forced migrations.)

By the nineteenth century, the term "Creole" was used by white, African American, and mixed-race Louisianians to set themselves apart from foreign-born Europeans and American settlers of British descent. Before the Civil War, the term *Creoles of Color* came to be applied to mixed-race Louisianians. People of a more pure African descent began to call themselves "black Creoles." For many years after the war, white people also continued to call themselves Creoles. In modern times, though, the term is usually used to refer to Louisianians of African or mixed descent. Creoles are renowned around the world for their popular style of music called *zydeco*. This dance music of Southwest Louisiana is characterized by the sound of accordion playing and the scraping of a percussion instrument called a rubboard that is worn like a metal vest.

ber of slaves were freed in southern Louisiana before the Civil War than in other parts of the South. Called *gens libres de couleur* (pronounced zhahn LEE-breh duh koo-LEHR) or "free people of color," these blacks worked in occupations ranging from laborer and craftsman to merchant and planter. The most privileged members of this group formed an elite population. Some owned slaves themselves. A number sent their children to school in Europe.

After slavery

The Thirteenth Amendment to the Constitution, passed in December 1865, abolished all slavery in the United States. The forced migration of Africans to the United States finally stopped. Few Africans chose to immigrate to

the United States over the century that followed. At the close of the Civil War, African Americans accounted for 14 percent of the U.S. population. Slavery was over, but turbulent years lay ahead.

In 1867 the U.S. government placed the defeated southern states under military control under its Reconstruction policy. For a time, protections on the voting rights of blacks in the state governments were enforced. African Americans held political offices and made advances in several areas, especially in education. At the end of this decade, in 1877, a new era of repression began, marked by lynchings (hangings and other killings by mobs) and other forms of persecution. White Southerners who had resisted Reconstruction once again dominated the state governments. Racism and white supremacy took on an ugly new form with the rise of the Ku Klux Klan, which was organized in 1866 to resist the integration of African Americans into politics, schools, and neighborhoods and to prevent them from claiming their

A sharecropper's family at Pettway Plantation, Gee's Bend, Alabama, in 1939. *Courtesy of the Rare Books and Special Collections Division, The Library of Congress.*

Martin Luther King Jr. delivers his landmark "I Have a Dream" speech in 1963, inspiring African Americans to continue the struggle for equality and civil rights.
Reproduced by permission of AP/Wide World Photos.

rights as citizens. By 1868, the organization had grown from a social club into an armed group engaging in terrorist activities.

After the war many of the freed people had little choice but to return to the farms of their ex-masters to work under conditions not much better than before. Some worked for wages, which were very low. Others worked on a sharecropping basis, in which they farmed land owned by someone else in exchange for a share of the crop. Their expenses were sometimes higher than the value of their crops, and after paying the owner his share, many sharecroppers ended up in debt.

In 1909 the National Association for the Advancement of Colored People (NAACP) was formed. The following two decades saw the migration of about 1.6 million southern blacks to northern cities in search of newly available industrial jobs (see chapter 18 on industrialization and urbanization). Weathering the hardships of the Great Depression (1929–41; a period, following a stock market crash in 1929, of depressed world economies and high unemployment), blacks continued their northward migration. Unfortunately, racism and segregation were not limited to the South.

During the civil rights movement of the 1950s and 1960s, some of the country's worst forms of racism were eliminated, as blacks joined forces to demand their legal and human rights through civil disobedience (protesting questionable laws through nonviolent acts of breaking the law) and other forms of protest and social activism. The 1954 Supreme Court ruling in *Brown v. Board of Education* declared

The Gullah

The Gullah are a group of African Americans who have lived on the Sea Islands off the coast of South Carolina and Georgia since the 1700s. During the 1750s, plantation owners brought African slaves to the islands to work the rice and indigo crops; fifty years later many more slaves were brought in to work the new cotton plantations. The Sea Islands were so isolated from the mainland and plagued by disease that few whites lived there. Because of this, the slaves preserved many native African cultural traditions and language patterns.

After the Civil War ended in 1865, many white landowners abandoned the area, leaving the Gullah even more isolated than before. The Gullah managed to scrape out a living in largely independent communities on the island well into the twentieth century. Researchers who arrived on the islands in the early twentieth century found a wealth of African-based arts and customs there.

The distinctiveness of the Gullah community is perhaps best reflected in its language, which is based on the pidgin English that developed along the African coast during the peak of the slave trade. Pidgin English—a blend of English and native languages—served as a means of communication among Africans and British slave traders. Many of the slaves who were brought to South Carolina used the pidgin language to communicate with one another in the New World. Over time, the pidgin mixed with the language spoken by the South Carolina planters and took on new form, called Gullah.

school segregation (separating schools or classrooms along racial lines) illegal. Progress was also made in the area of voting rights as well as in the desegregation of public facilities, especially in the South. The advances of the century were made at great cost to African Americans, who were often barred from the opportunities available to others in the nation and were consequently poorer and, on the whole, lived in worse conditions than the national average.

During the years of strife, from the Reconstruction Era to the 1960s, some of the nation's great reformers and thinkers emerged, from educator and writer Booker T. Washington (1856–1915) to sociologist, educator, and writer W. E. B. Du Bois (1868–1963), and from clergyman, orator, and reformer Martin Luther King Jr. (1929–1968) to religious leader and orator Malcolm X (1925–1965).

African immigrants today

Few Africans immigrated to the United States in the century after the Civil War. Those who have come to this country in the twentieth century have very different lifestyles and cultures than African Americans. In 1960, fewer than thirty thousand foreign-born African immigrants lived in the country. According to the 2000 U.S. census, about one million African immigrants were living in the United States, representing about 3 percent of the foreign-born population in 2000. About half of those immigrants had arrived since 1990. The sharpest rise in African immigration to the United States began in 1995, with increased political turmoil on the African continent.

Many of the new African immigrants are professionals. In fact, they are one of the most educated groups of American immigrants today, with 49 percent of African adult immigrants holding bachelor's degrees. An estimated 90 percent of African-born U.S. residents had a high school education or higher, compared with 76 percent of Asian-born and 46 percent of Central American–born immigrants. The incomes of African immigrants are also higher than those of other groups. A large percentage of the new immigrants hope to return to their own countries in the future. Many came to the United States to gain experience in high-tech industries so they can bring the skills back to their countries.

The borough of New York City known as Harlem is now home to a large African immigrant population that has been developing since the 1980s. In one neighborhood in Harlem, most of the residents are people from the African nations of Sénégal, Somalia, Yemen, Nigeria, Ethiopia, Ivory Coast, Guinea, and Mali. Senegalese natives make up the majority of Africans in this area, but there are many other people from the French-speaking nations of West Africa.

In Chicago, the number of immigrants from sub-Saharan Africa rose from 7,230 to 21,828 between 1990 and 2000. Nigeria, Ghana, and Ethiopia are the largest sources of African immigrants in the Chicago area. The United States has the largest population, at about 17,000 in 2000, of southern Sudanese outside Sudan. The Sudanese live mainly in the Midwest. Many fled the brutal civil war in their native country. About 100,000 Ethiopians, the largest population outside

Africa, lived in Washington, D.C., in 2003. Washington, D.C., and the surrounding region have the highest proportion of African immigrants compared with other U.S. cities.

African Americans today

In the 2000 census, 36.4 million people said they were either African American or African American combined with some other race, making up 12.9 percent of the total U.S. population. Fifty-four percent of African Americans lived in the South. The annual per capita income (the average income per person) for African Americans is $14,953, and the poverty rate is 22.7 percent. Although the poverty rate for African Americans was lower in 2000 than ever before, it was still three times higher than the poverty rate for non-Hispanic white people. Among African Americans age twenty-five and over, 72 percent have a high school diploma or more. This shows a significant increase in educational achievements over the past couple of decades: In the 1990 census the figure was 63 percent and in the 1980 census it was 51 percent. Similarly, among African Americans age twenty-five and older, 14 percent have a bachelor's degree or higher, another increase over the past couple of decades. Among the same age range, 954,000 African Americans have a graduate or professional degree.

A few highlights from African American culture

Literature

Education was generally not open to slaves and neither was publishing, so it is little wonder that only a few African American writers became widely known prior to the nineteenth century. Among these was Phillis Wheatley (c. 1753–1784), whose first poem was printed in 1770. Wheatley, born in Sénégal, was sold into slavery at the age of seven. The Wheatleys, who purchased her to serve as a maid-servant, soon adopted her into the family and educated her. Wheatley proved to be an extraordinary student, mastering Greek and Latin and creating her first poem at the age of thirteen. Trained to write in British poetic forms, her first book of poetry was published in London. She was the first African American to publish a book.

Slave narratives, autobiographies by former slaves that described the conditions of slavery, set a basis for African American literature. Probably the most notable slave-narrative writer was Frederick Douglass (c. 1817–1895). The brilliant abolitionist speaker, journalist, and statesman was also the author of the most popular slave account in American history, the *Narrative of the Life of Frederick Douglass, an American Slave, Written by Himself,* published in 1845. Harriet Jacobs (1813–1897; author of *Incidents in the Life of a Slave Girl, Written by Herself*) was another slave-narrative writer among the many who put their experiences into written form. William Wells Brown (1814–1884) published a slave narrative in 1842 and went on to write what is considered the first African American novel, *Clotel, or the President's Daughter,* as well as a play and several other noteworthy works.

During the half century after the end of slavery many African American writers struggled to find their place between existing European-based literary forms and forms that were more meaningful to them. These writers paved the way for the Harlem Renaissance, which began around the time of World War I (1914–18) and extended into the early 1930s. During that time, African American writers and artists poured into Harlem with a mission to define, create, and celebrate black art and culture. Important writers of this era include Langston Hughes (1902–1967), Countee Cullen (1903–1946), Claude McKay (1890–1948), Nella Larsen (1893–1964), and Zora Neale Hurston (1891–1960).

Since the Harlem Renaissance, African American writing has been highly visible within American literature. Themes have varied from highly charged and political to private and introspective. During the 1960s and 1970s African American writers were the focus of the new African American studies departments at universities around the country. African American writers have been working in every style of writing, from scriptwriting to poetry. Among the great writers since the Harlem Renaissance are: poets Gwendolyn Brooks (1917–2000) and Maya Angelou (1928–); novelists Ralph Ellison (1914–1994), James Baldwin (1924–1987), Richard Wright (1908–1960), Toni Morrison (1931–), Ishmael

Reed (1938–), and Alice Walker (1944–); playwrights Amiri Baraka (1934–), Lorraine Hansberry (1930–1965), Ntozake Shange (1948–), and August Wilson (1945–); and screenwriter and filmmaker Spike Lee (1957–).

Music

African American music forms are everywhere in the American music scene. They are performed not only by African American artists but by musicians of all backgrounds. African American music includes spirituals, gospel, rhythm and blues ("R&B"), ragtime, swing, boogie-woogie, jazz, soul, Motown, disco, funk, rock, hip-hop, and rap music.

Spiritual music, developed by the slaves, was the forerunner of gospel music, which reached great popularity by the end of the 1800s. One of the earliest gospel songwriters was Charles Albert Tindley (1851–1933), a Methodist preacher. His song "I'll Overcome Someday" resurfaced more than a half century later as "We Shall Overcome," the anthem of the 1960s civil rights movement. Thomas A. Dorsey (1899–1993), a religious songwriter, accompanist, and choir director, became known as "the father of gospel music" after he combined gospel and blues into a unique and passionate form of gospel. Other great gospel singers include Sallie Martin (1896–1988) and Mahalia Jackson (1912–1972).

By the late nineteenth century, a dance music called ragtime became very popular. Its heavily syncopated rhythms and sprightly melodies had a distinctly African American flavor. Scott Joplin (1868–1917) was one of the great ragtime artists. About the same time, a form of African American folk music called the blues emerged. Some blues greats were T-Bone Walker (1910–1975), Muddy Waters (1915–1983), and B. B. King (1925–). The blues had an impact later on such styles as rock and soul music. Jazz was born when the styles of ragtime (primarily instrumental) and blues (at first primarily vocal) came together. New Orleans was one of the first places to bring the experimental music to popularity. New Orleanian Louis Armstrong (1901–1971) would have a huge impact on the future of jazz and American music. Jazz quickly spread in a variety of forms. Among the many brilliant jazz composers and musicians were Duke Ellington (1899–1974) and Miles Davis (1926–1991).

Two of the most renowned jazz musicians and composers of all times, Duke Ellington (1899–1974) at the piano and Louis Armstrong (1901–1971) on the trumpet, rehearse in 1946.
Reproduced by permission of AP/Wide World Photos.

In the 1940s an exciting blues style called jump blues was being played by small combos, or small groups of musicians. With its roots in boogie-woogie and the blues-swing arrangements of artists like Count Basie (1904–1984) and Cab Calloway (1907–1994), this new blues style acquired an enormous following in black urban communities across the country. Soon many jump blues ensembles began to feature singers versed in a smooth gospel-influenced vocal style. Just as blues, religious spirituals, and hymns formed gospel, rhythm and blues drew upon gospel, electric urban blues, and swing jazz.

From these bases, a host of other African American music styles was spun. In the 1950s several rhythm and blues musicians made a shift to rock and roll, including Antoine "Fats" Domino (1928–), "Little" Richard Penniman (1932–), and Chuck Berry (1926–). In the 1960s a powerful gospel-influenced rhythm and blues style emerged called soul. Because it paralleled the 1960s civil rights and black power movements, soul embodied a sense of racial pride and independence. After soul, popular African American music continued to shape and reshape American music through dynamic and innovative forms such as Motown, funk, and rap.

The holiday: Kwanzaa

The African American holiday of Kwanzaa (also spelled Kwanza) is celebrated from December 26 to January 1. Kwanzaa was created by the philosopher Maulana Karenga (1941–) in 1966 to celebrate traditional African values. Each of the seven days of the week of Kwanzaa is dedicated to one of the Ngozo Saba, or seven principles, which are: Umoja (pronounced oo-MOE-jah): unity, or sticking together; Kujichagulia (pronounced koo-jee-cha-GOO-lee-yah): self determination, or finding one's own path and identity; Ujima (pronounced oo-JEE-muh): collective work and responsibility, or sharing work, resources, and duties; Ujamaa (pronounced oo-JAH-mah): cooperative economics, or being connected; Nia (pronounced NEE-yuh): purpose, or taking charge; Kuumba (pronounced (koo-OOM-bah): creativity; Imani (pronounced ee-MAH-nee): faith.

On each evening of the week of Kwanzaa a candle is lit in the kinara, a special Kwanzaa candelabra, and the value of that day is discussed among the family or gathering. On the sixth day, December 31, a feast called Karamu is held for family and friends. The discussion and celebration at the feast is focused on African roots and the unity of the African American community. Gifts, called zawadi, are traditionally given on Imani, the last day of Kwanzaa. They are often made rather than bought because Kwanzaa emphasizes creativity.

Religion

The National Baptist Convention of the U.S.A., Inc., with 8.2 million members in 1992, is the largest black religious denomination, followed by the Church of God in Christ, a Pentecostal sect, with an estimated membership in 2000 of 8 million. The African Methodist Episcopal Church (AME; with a 1991 membership of 3.5 million), Roman Catholicism (with a black membership of about 2 million), and the Nation of Islam (with a black population in 2000 of 2.8 million) both claim large black followings as well. Other religious affiliations include the African Orthodox Church, Judaism, and Rastafarianism.

For More Information

Books

Palmer, Colin A. *The First Passage: Blacks in the Americas, 1502–1617*. New York: Oxford University Press, 1995.

Piersen, William D. *From Africa to America: African American History from the Colonial Era to the Early Republic, 1526–1790*. New York: Twayne, 1996.

Wood, Peter H. *Strange New Land: African Americans 1617–1776*. New York: Oxford University Press, 1996.

Web Sites

"Africa: One Continent, Many Worlds." *Natural History Museum of Los Angeles*. http://www.nhm.org/africa/facts/ (accessed on February 26, 2004).

"The Story of Africa: Slavery." *BBC*. http://www.bbc.co.uk/worldservice/africa/features/storyofafrica/9chapter9.shtml (accessed on February 26, 2004).

German Immigration

9

In 2000, people of German descent comprised the largest nationality or ethnic group (group of people who are not from the majority culture in the country in which they live and who keep some part of their former culture, language, and institutions) in the United States. According to the 2000 U.S. Census, 46.5 million people, or 15.2 percent of the population, claimed German ancestry. About seven million Germans have immigrated to North America since the eighteenth century. Some left the Old World in response to the many historical events in Europe over the last two centuries. Most Germans came to the United States seeking economic opportunities or religious or political freedom. There were many different motivations behind the mass migrations (the movement of thousands, or even millions, of people from one country to another within a relatively short period of time) from Germany that took place between 1800 and 1920.

Diversity (difference) among the people called German Americans is great. When many of them left the Old World, there was no nation called Germany. They came from nation-states in the large German-speaking area of Western

Fact Focus

- German Americans in Pennsylvania have come to be known as the Pennsylvania Dutch, although they are not from the Netherlands. In the German language, the word for "German" is "Deutsch" (pronounced doytch). It is likely that other settlers mistook the word for the English "Dutch."

- A form of Protestantism that arose in Germany was called the "plain" churches, or Anabaptists. Among them were the Mennonites and the Amish, the German Brethren, or Dunkards, and the Society of Friends, or Quakers. All these groups believed in nonviolence and simple worship. Anabaptists differed from most Protestant groups in their belief that an individual should be baptized as an adult rather than in infancy.

- In 1848 German rebels who wanted the German states to unify under a democratic, constitutional government set off a series of uprisings. The movement did not succeed. Afterward, facing arrest and persecution at the hands of the German princes, between four and ten thousand "forty-eighters" immigrated to the United States.

- German American craftspeople brought their guild system to the United States. These craft guilds evolved into trade unions, giving rise to the general labor-union movement.

- Until World War I (1914–18), millions of German Americans continued to speak the German language. Many lived in German-speaking enclaves, and even those who did not tried to maintain their native language. German Americans even took political action to make sure their children could be educated in the German language.

Europe. German immigrants came from three religious backgrounds: Protestant, Catholic, and Jewish. They moved to many parts of the United States, some becoming farmers and others entering trades in the cities and towns. Some lived in German American communities in which the German language was spoken and German customs prevailed; others assimilated (blended) quickly into the American mainstream. German immigrants had a high rate of returning to the old country. Though the German states of the eighteenth and nineteenth centuries experienced political and economic turmoil, many Germans came from far better circumstances than the Irish Catholics who were migrating to the United States in large numbers at the same time because of famine and oppression in Ireland. Unlike the Irish Catholics, many Germans had professional skills and capital with which to get started in America.

Historical background

Until 1871, Germany as a nation did not exist. At the time of the voyage to the New World in 1492 by explorer Christopher Columbus (1451–1506), the cities and states where Germanic-speaking people lived were part of the Holy Roman Empire. In earlier centuries, an emperor had ruled over the entire empire with the approval of the Roman Catholic pope. The empire's territory roughly included present-day Germany, Austria, Bohemia, Moravia, and parts of northern Italy, Belgium, Switzerland, and the Netherlands. But in the thirteenth century the central rule of the emperor weakened, and local rulers became powerful in their districts. One royal family line, the House of Habsburg, took over and then held onto the crown, but the princes of the large towns and districts had more control of their people than the central monarch. At that time, many of the German nation-states were flourishing, becoming major European centers of finance and the arts. The people of the empire were Roman Catholics, but a time of reform of the church was at hand.

On October 31, 1517, German priest and scholar Martin Luther (1483–1546) nailed to the church door in Wittenberg, a city in the state of Saxony in eastern Germany, his list of ninety-five theses, or statements, questioning the practices of the Roman Catholic Church. Luther believed that people should live their lives by following the Bible, not the pope. Pointing to the corruption he had witnessed in the church, he urged people to find their own salvation through faith; they did not need the Catholic church. His call for reform brought about the rise of Protestant churches throughout Europe. As it would in other European countries, the era of reformation and Protestantism brought about widespread religious dissension (disagreement and conflict) and led to war in the German states of the Holy Roman Empire. From 1517 to 1555, the Roman Catholics warred against the Lutherans. In the peace accord that ended these wars, Lutheranism (a Protestant church following the teachings of

Words to Know

Anabaptist: A category of radical Protestants, including the Mennonites and the Amish; the German Brethren, or Dunkards, so called for how they baptized adults; and the Society of Friends, or the Quakers, who believe in nonviolence and in simple worship based on readings of the Bible. Anabaptists believe that knowledge of God must come from within oneself and that the rituals and politics of existing churches are a hindrance to true faith and worship. The Anabaptists believe that an individual should decide to be baptized as an adult, when he or she fully understands what it means, rather than in infancy.

Anarchist: Believing that governments are unnecessary and should be eliminated, and that the social world should be organized through the cooperative efforts of the people within it. Some anarchists have encouraged violence to overthrow the government.

Anti-Semitic: Hostile toward Jews.

Assimilation: The way that someone who comes from a foreign land or culture becomes absorbed into a culture and learns to blend into the ways of its predominant, or main, society.

Colony: A group of people living as a political community in a land away from their home country but ruled by the home country.

Discrimination: Unfair treatment based on racism or other prejudices.

Emigration: Leaving one's country to go to another country with the intention of living there. "Emigrant" is used to describe *departing from* one's country—for example, "she emigrated from Ireland." "Immigrant" is used to describe *coming to* a new country—for example, "she immigrated to the United States."

Enclave: pronounced AHN-klave; A distinct cultural or nationality unit within a foreign territory.

Ethnic: Relating to a group of people who are not from the majority culture in the country in which they live, and who keep their own culture, language, and institutions.

Exiles: People who have been sent away from their homeland.

Immigration: To travel to a country of which one is not a native with the intention of settling there as a permanent resident. "Immigrant" is used to describe *coming to* a new country—for example, "she immigrated to the United States." "Emigrant" is used to describe *departing from* one's country—for example, "she emigrated from Ireland."

Indentured servants: Servants who agreed to work for a colonist for a set period of time in exchange for payment of their passage from Europe to the New World. At the end of the service term (usually seven years), the indentured servant was given goods or a small piece of land to help set up a new life in the colony.

Industrialization: The historic change from a farm-based economy to an economic system based on the manufacturing of goods and distribution of services on an organized and mass-produced basis.

Labor unions: Organizations that bring workers together to advance their interests in terms of getting better wages and working conditions.

Mass migration: The movement of thousands—or even millions—of people from one country to another within a relatively short period of time.

Migration: To move from one place to another, not necessarily across national borders.

Multiculturalism: A view of the social world that embraces, or takes into account, the diversity of people and their cultures within the society.

Nativism: A set of beliefs that centers around favoring the interests of people who are native-born to a country (though generally not concerning Native Americans) as opposed to its immigrants.

New World: The Western Hemisphere, including North and South America.

Old World: The regions of the world that were known to Europeans before they discovered the Americas, including all of the Eastern Hemisphere—Europe, Asia, and Africa—except Australia.

Persecution: Abusive and oppressive treatment.

Quaker: A member of the Society of Friends, a radical Protestant sect in England founded by George Fox (1624–1691) in the late 1640s.

Reparations: Payments to the other side for damages and expenses attributed to the war.

Socialist: Believing in a society in which no one owns private property, but rather, the government or public owns all goods and the means of distributing them among the people.

Martin Luther) was finally accepted, and each German state was allowed to choose its own religion.

After the peace of Augsburg in 1555, the biggest German nation-states grew very powerful, wealthy, and militaristic. The states of Bavaria, Brandenburg (later known as Prussia), Saxony, and Hanover all formed their own governments and economies. Austria acquired Hungary and parts of the Balkan countries. Later Prussia and Austria would become fierce rivals for power.

After these wars, other forms of Protestantism arose, many of which were not accepted. One of the largest was Calvinism. Established by John Calvin (1509–1564) in Geneva, Switzerland, Calvinism applied more rigid "puritanical" interpretations to Luther's Reformation. Calvin felt that the purpose of life was to know or understand God as well as possible and then to follow God's will. Calvinism demanded that all people strive to live a moral lifestyle. The church was to be an instrument of strict moral discipline. Calvinism also believed that the world had been a corrupt place since the time of the original sin (when Adam and Eve fell from grace in Eden). In the Calvinists' view, churches, with their rituals and bishops, could not bring about religious enlightenment. They believed that only elite persons, through the grace of God, could be saved. Calvinism spread quickly among the German peoples, as did several other forms of Protestantism, including the "plain" churches, called the Anabaptists, the Mennonites and the Amish, the German Brethren, or Dunkards, so called for the way they baptized members by dunking them, most likely in a stream; and the Society of Friends, or the Quakers. All these groups believed in nonviolence and in simple worship based on readings of the Bible. They believed that knowledge of God must come from within oneself and that the rituals and politics of existing churches were a hindrance to true faith and worship. The Anabaptists believed that an individual should decide to be baptized as an adult, when he or she fully understood what baptism meant, rather than in infancy as was the custom in the Roman Catholic Church. These beliefs brought persecution upon the Anabaptists, particularly the Mennonites, especially those living near the shores of the Rhine River in a region known as the Rhineland.

With more Protestants taking control in their countries in the late sixteenth century, Catholic rulers armed themselves for war. The complicated, long, and terrible Thirty

William Penn receiving the charter of Pennsylvania from Charles II. *Reproduced by permission of Mary Evans Picture Library.*

Years' War began in 1618, with the German states forming opposing alliances. It is estimated that one-third of the population of the German states died during and after these wars. When the Peace of Westphalia ended the fighting, there were three hundred independent German states, many only the size of a small city. Unfortunately, the small states were often unable to defend themselves against neighbors and were vulnerable to armed attacks. Fearing the ongoing violence and uncertainty, some Germans began to emigrate.

Colonial immigration and the Pennsylvania Dutch

From sixty-five thousand to one hundred thousand German-speaking people made their way to the United States during the colonial era (before 1776). One of the first points of settlement was Germantown in the British colony of Pennsylvania. Pennsylvania's founder, William Penn (1644–1718), was a member of the Quakers, a radical Protestant sect in England founded by George Fox (1624–1691) in the late 1640s. The British king had awarded Penn a proprietorship in the American colonies. The proprietorship made him the owner of a large tract of land and gave him the authority to create the government and make the laws. Penn set out to establish a holy commonwealth, characterized by peace, brotherly love, and religious toleration. (A commonwealth is a form of government based on the common good of the citizens rather than the rule of a monarch.) As a member of the Society of Friends, he rejected formal creeds and worship. Like other proprietors in the New World, Penn hoped to profit from the sale or rent of land in his colony, but his primary aim in setting up a colony was a religious one. His search for settlers started among English people, especially Quakers. Before long, he was recruiting among the Mennonites (an Anabaptist group founded by Menno Simons [1496–1561], a Dutch priest) in the Rhineland, where Anabaptists were experiencing persecution.

The founding of Germantown

In 1683 thirteen families from Krefeld, Rhineland, boarded the ship *Concord* and sailed for Philadelphia, arriving in October. Most were Mennonites who wished to participate in Penn's noble experiment. An agent for a German land investment company, Francis Daniel Pastorius (1651–1720), though not a Mennonite, became their leader. He obtained from Penn a large tract of land close to Philadelphia, which he split, giving half to the Krefelders and keeping half for the land investors. This was the settlement of Germantown.

The settlers in Germantown quickly built stone houses and a church. Most of these early German settlers were farmers or craftspeople. Besides selling their farm produce in Philadelphia, the Mennonites in Germantown also established a successful linen-weaving business. They were the first known group to formally protest the institution of slavery in the American colonies. More and more families came to join the original settlers, and by 1790 the Germantown population had grown to three thousand.

Pennsylvania Dutch

Germantown was just the beginning of the settlement of large portions of Pennsylvania by German-speaking people. The

Germans in Pennsylvania have come to be known as the Pennsylvania Dutch. Despite the name, they are not from the Netherlands. In the German language, the word for "German" is "Deutsch" (pronounced doytch), and it is likely that other settlers mistook the German word for the English "Dutch." Although many people associate the Pennsylvania Dutch with the Amish (another Anabaptist sect), the term "Pennsylvania Dutch" includes all German-speaking immigrants who settled in Pennsylvania and areas immediately surrounding. Many of the Pennsylvania Dutch came from the Rhineland states, especially the Palatinate (Pfalz).

Immigrants from the Palatinate started arriving in larger numbers after 1710. The first settlers sent home flattering reports of the new colony, leading to more people making the journey and settling in the increasingly German areas. Pennsylvania's population was one-third German by the time of the American Revolution (1775–83). Living in a dense concentration of German-speaking people, the Pennsylvania Dutch maintained old-world language and customs. Their language was, and in some places still is today, the same basic language used in the Palatinate in Germany, with a little standard German and English mixed in. Many of the new German Americans successfully resisted assimilating into American culture for many years. Since many of the Anabaptist settlers had come to the new country to lead a simpler life according to their religion, they often isolated themselves and their children from American culture and society, even rejecting public schooling. The Amish and the Mennonites were pacifists, meaning they favored peace and would not fight in wars. The Amish were especially separatist (wanting to live apart from other people) and strict about how they dressed, what kinds of tools and machines they could use, the language they spoke, and their methods of worship. The Amish in areas like Lancaster, Pennsylvania, who make up a

Present-day Amish in Lancaster, Pennsylvania. The Amish are a portion of the Pennsylvania Dutch and have maintained a culture apart from mainstream American society.
Reproduced by permission of Mr. James Blank.

The Hessians

In the American Revolution (1775–83), British King George III (1738–1820) did not have enough soldiers to fight the rebels in his American colonies, so he purchased the services of approximately thirty thousand soldiers from the German states and shipped them to America to fight. Quite a few of the states provided him with soldiers, but the majority of them came from the state of Hesse-Kassel. Because there were so many soldiers from Hesse-Kassel, all the Germans fighting on the British side came to be called Hessians by the Americans. The prince of Hesse-Kassel sold at least twelve thousand soldiers to King George, receiving a significant sum per head. The prince did not pay the soldiers, however, and many of them had been forced into the service against their will. About six thousand Hessians deserted the British army and fought on the side of the colonists. After the war was over, as many as twelve thousand of these soldiers stayed in the new country and became U.S. citizens. This was made easier for them because there was already a fairly substantial German American population that they could join.

very small portion of the Pennsylvania Dutch, have maintained a culture apart from mainstream Americans right up to modern times. They are well known for not using electricity or driving cars and living a simple, rural life.

Germans who were not Anabaptists were arriving in the British colonies as well. The shipping companies hired recruiters to travel through the German states. They would arrive in a village or a town in brightly colored wagons with a fanfare of trumpets and drums. When a crowd had assembled, the recruiters would describe the wonders of the New World and urge the people to migrate. Their advertising campaign was successful. Many Germans, seeking better opportunities, contracted themselves out as indentured servants, people who agreed to work for a colonist for a set period of time in exchange for payment of their passage from Europe to the New World. At the end of the service term (usually seven years), the indentured servant was given a small piece of land or goods to help set up a new life in the colony. By 1790 the German American population in the American colonies had reached about 360,000.

Passage to America

Although political turbulence and religious repression in Europe triggered small waves of German migration to the United States, most historians note that the mass migrations were mainly motivated by the desire for economic opportunity and prosperity. For many years rural Germans had lived on small family farms. As the German states faced industrialization (the change from a farm-based economy to an economic system based on the manufacturing of goods and distribution of services on an organized and mass-produced basis), the old way of rural life was quickly disappearing. Many were forced to move into cities and learn new skills. Yet, with unemployment in Germany rising, the cities did not always hold much hope. Among those who emigrated, some had few options left in Germany and sought more opportunity. Steady migrations were ongoing starting in the early nineteenth century.

It was a dangerous and difficult trip across the Atlantic. Germans began the journey by making their way to a port city. During the high peaks of emigration there was a steady flow of traffic on the roads to the ports made up of families pushing carts loaded with their belongings. In Germany, most emigrants left from Bremerhaven or Hamburg. Some made their way to Britain in the early eighteenth century, hoping to find passage to North America from there. Others went to Rotterdam, Holland, or Le Havre, France, and sought a ship there. They were often robbed or swindled when they arrived in ports.

The conditions on the sailing ships that took the German immigrants across the Atlantic were terrible. Many people could not afford to purchase a first- or second-class ticket, and so they traveled in steerage, in the lower decks of the ship that were designed to carry cargo. Aside from being miserably overcrowded, the accommodations often lacked clean drinking water and adequate toilet and washing facilities. Rats, head lice, and bedbugs were common, and infectious diseases spread quickly. In the years after, steamships would shorten the voyage and regulations on ships would correct some of the worst abuses of travelers. Even so, throughout the eighteenth and nineteenth centuries, many immigrants faced misery and even death to get to the United States. Despite the hard trip, for over a century Germans immigrated by the hundreds of thousands to the United States.

Mass immigration begins

Immigration from Europe to the United States overwhelmingly increased in the mid-1800s. The U.S. population recorded in the census of 1860 was 31,500,000; of that population, 4,736,000, or 15 percent, were of foreign birth. The greater part of these immigrants had come from two countries: 1,611,000 from Ireland, and 1,301,000 from Germany (principally from the southwestern states of Württemberg, Baden, and Bavaria). The mass migration from Germany had begun in the 1830s, but the peak decades were the 1850s, with more than 950,000 immigrants, and the 1880s, with nearly 1.5 million.

By the 1850s, New York had become the principal port of arrival for German immigrants. Many chose to stay in the East, while others moved westward along the Erie Canal through Buffalo and out to Ohio. By the 1840s large numbers of German immigrants went to New Orleans on cotton ships from Le Havre, France. The majority moved to the valleys of the upper Ohio and Mississippi Rivers. By 1880, Wisconsin had more German Americans than any other state. Here, as in the East, those who settled in urban centers brought a range of crafts and professional skills, while others setting up farms brought their farming skills from Germany. In the years between 1860 and 1890, three-fifths of German immigrants moved to rural areas, while two-fifths moved to the cities. When they settled, they often established German-speaking communities, setting up their own churches, schools, newspapers, and other institutions, and keeping their cultural traditions alive in the New World.

Religious backgrounds

Most of the German immigrants were Protestants, and among them Lutherans were the majority. About one-third of German immigrants were Catholics. A substantial segment—about 250,000—of the German immigrants were Jews. Jews had lived in Germany since the fourth century, many having settled in the Rhine area. Jews had long been assimilated in German cultures when suddenly, from the 1830s into the 1880s, several German states began to pass anti-Semitic laws (laws hostile toward Jews). In southern Germany, these laws prohibited young Jews from marrying or starting a family in their communities. Some decided to immigrate to the United States. The first Jews from Bohemia, Bavaria, Baden, Württemberg, and Alsace-Lorraine came in the 1820s. Many of these immigrants were young, aspiring, and middle class, skilled at a trade or a profession. Often they were equipped with savings to get themselves started in a trade in the new country. A significant portion were well educated. Many of the Jewish immigrants settled in New York, Baltimore, and Philadelphia, but other cities, including San Francisco, Chicago, and New Orleans, had large Jewish communities as well. (For more information, see chapter 15 on Jewish immigration to the United States.)

Political dissidents: the forty-eighters

In the early 1800s many people hoped that the German states would unify under a democratic, constitutional government. Some organized into groups of resistance to fight against the tyrannical princes of the various German states. In 1848 the rebels, or the "forty-eighters," so nicknamed because of the year of their uprising, set off a series of uprisings in Vienna, Berlin, Baden, and southwest Germany. For a time after the uprisings, the princes of the states worked with the rebels toward establishing a constitutional government for a united Germany. Within months, though, the process had fallen apart. The rebels faced arrest and persecution at the hands of the German princes. Between four and ten thousand bitterly disappointed forty-eighters immigrated to the United States at that time. The forty-eighters were an elite group; many had been educated at the finest European universities and had highly prestigious careers ahead of them.

The forty-eighters had little in common with the farmers and craftspeople who had preceded them to America. German American farmers had tended to live quietly in German-speaking communities. The forty-eighters came from a world of radical politics, idealism, debate, and activism. Conflicts arose between the old immigrants, called the "Grays,"

A Leading Couple: Carl Schurz and Margarethe Meyer Schurz

Carl Schurz (1829–1906) was a forty-eighter who led the German American community in the late nineteenth century. Of humble origin, he was reared a Roman Catholic, but as an adult he considered himself a freethinker. Schurz attended university at Bonn and there began to make a name for himself in politically liberal circles. Then came the revolutionary fervor that led to the uprisings of 1848. Schurz eagerly joined in the fight to establish a unified German state with a democratic constitution. When the revolutionaries were forced to surrender, Schurz fled into exile, barely escaping with his life. In 1850 he decided to leave the Old World for America. If he could not be a citizen of a free Germany, he concluded, he would become a free citizen of the United States. Before leaving, he married Margarethe Meyer (1833–1876).

Meyer came from a prominent family and had received a distinguished education. She and her sister both became involved in the teachings of Friedrich Froebel (1782–1852), the founder of kindergartens (in German, the word means "garden of children") in Germany. Meyer's sister had opened several kindergartens and Margarethe taught in one of them before marrying Shurz.

Schurz and his wife arrived in the United States in 1852, eventually settling in Watertown, Wisconsin, in 1855. They were quite well off financially. Margarethe's dowry (the money a woman brings into a marriage) alone was enough to set Schurz up in business. His fame as a daring fighter for freedom in Germany, his solid education, his gifts as a writer and speaker, and his political ambition combined to make him a well-known figure almost immediately. Although he rarely stood for election himself, his persuasiveness with German American voters made him a force to be reckoned. His wife, too, was active in bringing new ideas in education to the United States. In 1856 Margarethe Schurz founded what many consider the first kindergarten in the United States in Watertown. Like many German schools in the United States, the kindergarten was conducted in the German language until World War I (1914–18).

Schurz was antislavery and became an avid supporter of Abraham Lincoln (1809–1865) in the presidential campaign of 1860. He is said to have traveled more than twenty-one thousand miles campaigning for Lincoln, speaking in both English and German. He was credited with swinging much of the German American vote. After

and the new immigrants, known as the "Greens." However, the intellectuals' presence gave a new depth and vitality to the German American community and gave them a more powerful voice in national politics.

Influential German Carl Schurz. *Courtesy of the Library of Congress.*

the American Civil War (1861–65), in which he served as a general, Schurz settled in St. Louis, Missouri, and became a U.S. senator. In Washington, D.C., he turned to issues of corruption. Because of his criticisms of U.S. politicians, some alleged that he was not a patriotic American. He responded with a phrase that has become famous: "My country right or wrong: if right, to be kept right; and if wrong, to be set right."

In 1876, Margarethe Schurz died, but by that time she had passed on her knowledge to others who established more

kindergartens and set a standard for preschools in the nation. Schurz was made Secretary of the Interior that year. He attempted to initiate environmental controls, particularly over forestlands, and to follow a humanitarian (promoting human welfare) policy with respect to the Indians, but stronger powers within the nation overpowered his liberal idealism. Schurz left government office for good in 1881 and began a second successful career as a journalist, author, and lecturer. He made New York his home, where he became editor-in-chief of the *Evening Post* and eventually *Harper's Weekly*.

Schurz saw himself as a mediator between German and American culture. He continued to be equally fluent in German and English, writing his widely read memoirs in both languages. He traveled back and forth many times between the United States and Germany, filled with pride for both. When accused of mixed loyalties, he responded that he loved equally his "old mother" and his "new bride."

Anti-immigrant reactions

In the 1840s, nativist groups (organizations that promoted the rights of the native-born as opposed to immi-

Know-Nothing Party 1844 campaign ribbon.
Reproduced by permission of © David J. & Janice L. Frent Collection/Corbis.

grants) took up an anti-immigrant, particularly anti-Catholic, campaign. One of the primary nativist organizations was the American Party, which promoted "traditional American ideals" and claimed that immigrants were threatening to destroy American values and democracy. The party, originally called the Know-Nothing Party (because when asked what their political agenda was, members of the secretive party would say they knew nothing about it), mounted very successful political campaigns across the nation. Nativist politicians called for restricting the rights of aliens (who live and work legally in the country but are not citizens) and foreign-born citizens, especially with respect to voting and holding political office. Their primary target was the Irish Americans who were immigrating in great numbers at the same time as the Germans. German Americans probably became the targets of the nativists because of their large numbers. With a different language, customs, and in some cases, a different set of religious or political beliefs, Germans were viewed by some as foreign and therefore dangerous. Many German Americans were Catholics, another target of the Know-Nothings, who claimed that the pope was conspiring to get political control in the United States. Some Americans, too, were beginning to feel the intense competition from German American tradesmen and merchants.

Among the Germans who immigrated after the 1848 revolutions, there were quite a few politically radical intellectuals who continued to pursue their ideals in the United States. Some of these people had come from socialist or anarchist groups in the old country. (Socialists believe in a society in which no one owns private property, but rather, the government or public owns all goods and the means of distributing them among the people. Anarchists believe that governments are unnecessary and should be eliminated, and that the social world should be organized through the cooperative efforts of the people.) Although their goals were usually right in line with the American values of equality, justice, and personal freedom, the political reformers were viewed as radical extremists. The Know-Nothings seized some of the radical political beliefs to stir up the public against German Americans.

By the mid-1850s, the Know-Nothing Party was so popular that its candidates had been elected to important political offices throughout the United States. German Americans, who were typically divided amongst themselves, united in their efforts to fight back against the discrimination directed at them. They were greatly aided by mounting tensions over the issue of slavery in the United States, which divided the Know-Nothing supporters and weakened them as a political group.

German Americans in the labor movement

German Americans were instrumental in the labor-union movement of the late 1880s. (Labor unions are organizations that bring workers together to advance their interests in areas such as work benefits, wages, and working conditions.) German American craftspeople had brought their guild system (associations of craftspeople or merchants) along with them to America. These craft guilds evolved into trade unions, giving rise to the general labor-union movement. Some of the German Americans in the labor movement were influenced by German political philosopher Karl Marx (1818–1883), whose theories of socialism had swept through European intellectual and working-class circles. The more radical German Americans in the labor movement drew criticism from the American public, but in later years their demands would not seem radical. Into the twentieth century, the labor movement in the United States had elements of Marxism. The leaders of the large unions, such as the American Federation of Labor (AFL) and the Congress of Industrial Organizations (CIO), usually tried to steer clear of the radical political agendas. The work of German American union leaders eventually led to many reforms in the workplace in the areas of benefits, pensions, working conditions, and safety. The well-known president of the United Automobile Workers (UAW) from 1946 to 1970, Walter Reuther (1907–1970), was German American.

The World Wars and German Americans

In 1871, after a series of wars, Prussian prime minister Otto von Bismarck (1815–1898) brought about the union of the German states (with the exception of Austria) into the

The Haymarket Square Riots of Chicago

In the 1880s the rise of trade unions nationwide had given voice to the long-suppressed complaints and demands of the workers. The result was widespread striking across the nation in the attempt to obtain better working conditions and pay. Big businesses were not pleased with the labor movement, fearing that conceding to labor's demands would diminish corporate profits and the system of free trade. Many wanted to stop the unions and went to great lengths to thwart them at every possible opportunity. One of the businesses' best weapons was the press, which could stir up the public against the workers.

After the newly organized union, the Knights of Labor, won a significant victory against the railroads in 1885, other organizations prepared to join the fight. On May 1, 1886, hundreds of thousands of workers participated in a general nation-wide strike in an attempt to make the employers agree to a standard eight-hour workday. Three days later, the atmosphere got violent. At a related strike in Chicago at the McCormick Reaper Works, a bomb was thrown at the police in Haymarket Square, killing one policeman and two civilians, and wounding many more.

Eight men were arrested for the bomb-throwing murders, although there was no evidence linking any of them to the bombing. Apparently some of them had not even been present at the rally. Of the eight arrested, six were German Americans. The Chicago press and business and political leaders united in turning the public against these men. Their trial was full of improprieties that were allowed to pass because of the public furor over the incident. The prosecution focused mainly on the previous political statements of the eight accused, rather

Second Empire, or Reich. Germany quickly became the strongest military, industrial, and economic power in Europe. While Bismarck governed, an elaborate system of alliances (unions among groups for a special purpose) with other European powers was created. In 1888, however, Wilhelm II (1859–1941) took over the rule of Germany and the delicate international balance was disturbed. After a series of crises, in 1914 World War I began. Despite initial successes, the German armies—allied with Austria-Hungary and Turkey against the Allies (United Kingdom, France, Russia, and eventually the United States)—were defeated in 1918. About 1.6 million Germans died during the war. In the Treaty of Versailles

than on any crime. All were convicted of murder. The trial was seen by many as unjust. Labor leaders throughout the nation protested, but the general mood of intolerance prevailed. Four of the accused were hanged and one committed suicide while in jail. The other three remained in jail.

In 1892 German-born American John Peter Altgeld (1847–1902) was elected to the governor's office in Illinois. Altgeld had risen through the ranks by means of successful investments and a strong sense of adventure. He was very wealthy and very politically ambitious—anyone might have thought at the time of his election that he would help to preserve the existing state of affairs. Altgeld knew very well that the powerful business interests in Illinois would end his political career if he brought justice to the three men who had been languishing in prison cells since the Haymarket riots. Nevertheless, he signed pardons for them and, along with the pardons, released a report exposing the shocking misdeeds of their trials. The three men went free after seven years in jail. Altgeld, on the other hand, was attacked on all fronts. According to Robert D. Sampson in "Governor John Peter Altgeld Pardons the Haymarket Prisoners," the *Chicago Tribune* proclaimed that the governor had not "a drop of true American blood in his veins. He does not reason like an American, does not feel like one, and consequently does not behave like one." The *Washington Post* declared that this was what was to be expected from someone who was "an alien himself." Altgeld, with personal knowledge of what it meant to be an outsider because of one's origins, continued to protect the poor. By 1896, as he had suspected, his political career was finished.

(1919) following the war, the Allies stripped Germany of its colonies (many of them in Africa), demanded the nation's almost complete disarmament, and imposed harsh reparations (payments to the other side for damages and expenses attributed to the war). Germany became a republic, governed under a liberal constitution. But the nation was devastated by the serious economic and social dislocations caused by the military defeat and by the subsequent economic depression.

Despite the harassment of the Know-Nothings and the business elite, German Americans had, as a whole, settled quietly into American life, often creating large German Amer-

During World War I, anti-German hysteria was directed at German Americans at home. This propaganda poster issued by the U.S. government depicts the wartime view of evil Germans (called "Huns," a negative word for German soldiers). *Created by Henry Patrick Raleigh. Reproduced by permission of © Corbis.*

ican enclaves (distinct ethnic communities within a city or other social environment) in which they could maintain their language and culture. Their days of peaceful obscurity in the United States were numbered, however. With the start of World War I, German Americans suddenly became the face of the enemy in the United States, and they suffered through violent harassment. Anything remotely "German" was attacked and/or destroyed. Books were burned, street names changed, and German businesses boycotted. Music by German composers like Ludwig van Beethoven (1770–1827) was removed from public performances. Hamburgers, sauerkraut, and dachshunds were renamed "liberty burgers," "liberty cabbage," and "liberty hounds." German Americans were physically attacked, tarred and feathered, and even killed. Robert Paul Prager, a German-born coal miner who was lynched by a mob in 1918, became the symbol of anti-German violence. On April 5, 1992, the first annual Prager Memorial Day was held in remembrance of all the victims of anti-German hysteria during World War I.

After World War I ended, thousands fled the resulting economic disaster in Germany. Between 1919 and 1933, some 430,000 Germans immigrated to the United States. Many were Jewish people fleeing from the anti-Semitism of the rising Nazi Party. (For more information, please see chapter 15 on Jewish immigration.) As a result of the anti-German sentiment in the United States, German Americans started to hide their ethnicity, attempting to blend in as much as possible. Many Americanized their names. German heritage festivals were suspended for a number of years. New immigrants arriving from Germany joined in the drive to be assimilated, losing their German characteristics as quickly as possible.

When Nazi leader Adolf Hitler (1889–1945) came to power in Germany, another surge of intellectuals, many of them Jewish, fled his regime and came to the United States. A total of 130,000 Germans immigrated between 1933 and 1945. It is worthwhile noting that although the United States understood that the Jews who were fleeing Nazi Germany were in grave danger, the government hesitated to change the number of German immigrants it would allow to enter the country. Some fleeing Jews were turned back at American ports and forced to face the cruel conditions in Germany. During World War II (1939–45), the freedom and rights of thousands of German American citizens were restricted. Certain citizens were labeled enemy aliens and required to carry identification cards. Their property was often searched or seized. They could not travel freely, and some were placed in internment camps as possible enemies. Although not as many German Americans or Italian Americans were interned as Japanese Americans, it was a very difficult time for many.

Still, German Americans made up one-third of U.S. armed forces during the war and served bravely in the war.

Although the wartime hostilities toward German Americans passed quickly after the world wars, it has not been until recent decades that German Americans began to reclaim their ethnic heritage in large numbers nationwide. The 1990s brought about a climate of multiculturalism in the United States.

German American culture

Until World War I, many German Americans lived in German-speaking communities throughout the United States. The communities ranged from tiny rural villages to city districts. Although they are far too numerous to list, a small sampling demonstrates the wide scope. The village of Maeystown, Illinois, was settled exclusively by German immigrants of the forty-eighter movement. New Braunfels, Texas, was established by one of the princes of Prussia for German settlement. Shipshewana, Indiana, was settled by the German Amish. Frankenmuth, Michigan, was founded by German Lutheran missionaries in 1845. The German colonists who established farms in Frankenmuth pledged to keep the community exclusively German Lutheran and to remain faithful to Germany and the German language. German communities or "Little Germanies" developed in many large cities, such as New York, New York; Chicago, Illinois; Milwaukee, Wisconsin; Baltimore, Maryland; St. Louis, Missouri; and Cincinnati, Ohio.

Although not all Germans lived in a German-speaking environment, it was very important to many of them to maintain their native language. German Americans took political action to make sure their children could be educated in the German language. Parochial (religious-based) schools, whether Lutheran or Catholic, taught students in German and English, or only in German. In the public schools, the German American parents succeeded in several states to get laws passed that mandated German instruction when a quota of parents in the community wanted it.

Another means for German Americans to maintain their culture was their sophisticated and widespread press.

The "March King," German-Portuguese American John Philip Sousa (1854–1932), composer of "Stars and Stripes Forever." *Courtesy of the Library of Congress.*

There were more German American newspapers than any other foreign papers in the country. The forty-eighters had come from a tradition of journalism, and many of the papers were liberal, intellectual, and very well written.

Germany has always been known for its brilliant musicians, such as Johann Sebastian Bach (1685–1750), Georg Frederic Handel (1685–1759), Franz Joseph Haydn

A couple in Sparta, New Jersey, drinking at Oktoberfest. *Reproduced by permission of © Corbis.*

(1732–1809), Wolfgang Amadeus Mozart (1756–1791), Ludwig van Beethoven (1770–1827), Franz Schubert (1797–1828), Felix Mendelssohn (1809–1847), and Robert Schumann (1810–1856). German Americans established a multitude of music halls, opera societies, and choral festivals after arriving in the New World. The symphony orchestras in Philadelphia, New York City, and Boston were founded by German Americans. In 1890 eighty-nine of the ninety-four performers with the New York Philharmonic Orchestra were German born. *Sängvereine,* or singing societies, across the nation provided a forum for amateurs to gather for sophisticated musical entertainment and competitions.

German Americans were abundant in the arts not only in large cities but also in small rural Midwestern towns as well. Unlike many immigrants at the time, many Germans came to the United States well educated and steeped in the cultural achievements of the German people. In fact, non-German Americans often accused them of snobbery.

In the years during and after World War I, anti-German backlash was severe, causing German Americans to lose many of the cultural traditions they prized. Roger Daniels comments in *Coming to America: A History of Immigration and Ethnicity in American Life,* that the sudden end of German instruction in schools "hastened the death of most of the other cultural institutions of German America." Nonetheless, German language and culture have had an obvious influence on U.S. vocabulary. German words now in common usage in the United States include kindergarten, gesundheit, ouch, delicatessen, blitz, sauerkraut, and wiener. Many of the Christmas traditions now seen as standard in America, such as Christmas trees (tannenbaum) and Santa Claus (Kris Kringle), were introduced by German Americans, as were New Year's Eve festivities. Early German settlers also brought with them a much more relaxed attitude toward the Sabbath (the day of rest and worship; for Christians, Sunday; for Jews, from Friday evening to Saturday evening) than that preached by the Puritans. German Americans transformed Sundays in America from days of rigid observances to days of rest and relaxation.

German Americans love to gather to eat and drink. Beer, a German specialty, has become one of the favorite beverages in America. Most of the big American brewing companies were founded by German Americans. Foods introduced by German Americans that are now common fare in the American diet include frankfurters, hamburgers, sauerkraut (although some credit Polish Americans with this addition), potato salad, bratwurst, liverwurst, and pretzels.

German American holidays and celebrations

In the middle of September each year, German Americans and many non-German Americans in Philadelphia, New York City, Chicago, and a variety of small towns nationwide gather for the Steuben Day Parade. Baron Friedrich von Steuben (1730–1794) was a German general in the time of the American Revolution (1775–83). He offered his services to George Washington. He is credited with transforming the untrained group of rebels into a disciplined military force and thus helping the Americans win their battle against England. The popular parade features German music, dancing, marching, costumes, and elaborate floats.

German American Day was officially proclaimed by President Ronald Reagan (1911–) in 1987 to be celebrated on October 6, the date on which Germantown, Pennsylvania, was founded in 1683. Oktoberfests and other cultural festivals help promote an understanding of German American heritage and traditions among German and non-German Americans alike.

For More Information

Books

Daniels, Roger. *Coming to America: A History of Immigration and Ethnicity in American Life.* New York: HarperCollins, 1990.

Frost, Helen. *German Immigrants, 1820–1920.* Mankato, MN: Blue Earth Books, an imprint of Capstone Press, 2002.

Hoobler, Dorothy, and Thomas Hoobler. *The German American Family Album.* New York and Oxford: Oxford University Press, 1996.

Web Sites

Sampson, Robert D. "Governor John Peter Altgeld Pardons the Haymarket Prisoners," *Illinois Labor History Site.* http://www.kentlaw.edu/ilhs/prisoner.htm (accessed on February 26, 2004).

Wurst, Klaus, and Norbert Muehlen. "Forty-eighters and Nativists," Part 3. *German Corner.* http://www.germanheritage.com/Essays/1848/forty-eighters_part3.html (accessed on February 26, 2004).

Irish Immigration

10

Irish Americans made up about 11 percent of the U.S. population in 2000, with a reported population of 30.5 million. They were the fourth largest ancestral group in the United States, after German Americans, Hispanic or Latino Americans, and African Americans. Irish Americans have spread throughout the United States and have long been assimilated (absorbed) in the mainstream culture. It is difficult, therefore, to imagine that 150 years ago, Irish Catholic immigrants faced severe discrimination (unfair treatment based on racism or other prejudices) when they arrived in the country. Many of the early immigrants suffered wretched living conditions and performed backbreaking work for low wages in the hope that their children would have a better life. Some historians have observed that the experience of the 4.5 million Irish immigrants in the nineteenth and twentieth century was typical of the American immigrant experience in general. The American Immigration Law Foundation, for example, asserts that "Irish immigration to America represented the first mass immigration to the United States and set the stage for all future immigrating ethnic minorities."

Historical background of Ireland

The story of Irish migration to the United States stems from Ireland's long-standing and bitter conflict with England, which ruled Ireland off and on from the twelfth century until the twentieth century. The Irish were a Gaelic culture, predominantly consisting of Celts (pronounced KELTS), a tall red-haired population that had come to Ireland from Europe sometime around the fifth century B.C.E. Ireland has been Christian since the fifth century C.E., when several missionaries, St. Patrick notably among them, set up churches and monasteries throughout the land. The island was divided into five provinces, Ulster, Connacht, Leinster, Meath (North Leinster), and Munster. Each had its own king or lord. Ireland was taken over by British invaders in the twelfth century, but the invaders tended to settle in among the Irish and lose their ties to England. England had only nominal (in name, but not in fact) rule in Ireland for several centuries.

In the 1530s Englsih King Henry VIII (1491–1547) broke with the Roman Catholic Church and placed himself at the head of the Church of England. Most Irish people continued to believe that the pope, not King Henry, was the head of their church. This division was to become a major focus of conflict between the two peoples, as England's national church became Protestant and much of Ireland remained Catholic. The British monarchs, beginning in the early sixteenth century, wanted a stable and loyal Protestant population in Ireland and began taking large tracts of land away from Irish Catholic owners and distributing them to English nobles and settlers, especially in Northern Ireland. The Irish fought these new English colonists, sometimes successfully. But in 1601 they lost the Battle of Kinsale and their attempts to stop the British colonization of Ulster were squashed. After the defeat, the English sent wave after wave of settlers, mainly Scottish Presbyterians, into Ulster.

Civil war broke out in England in the early 1640s as the result of a struggle for power between England's King Charles I (1600–1649) and its Parliament. In 1641, just prior to the war, the Irish had mounted a ferocious attack on the thirty-year-old Protestant colony at Ulster, killing an estimated ten to fifteen thousand people. The English were unable to respond because of their civil war, which ended in 1649 with the beheading of the king. Protestant parliamentarian

Fact Focus

- In 1691 the British enacted the first of the Penal Laws in Ireland, which prohibited Irish Catholics from receiving an education, entering a profession, purchasing land, voting, holding public office, owning any kind of weapon, or owning a horse of greater value than five pounds. The Penal Laws remained in effect until 1829, ensuring that Irish Catholics were impoverished and powerless to rebel against their oppressors.

- Starting in 1845 a mysterious disease killed Ireland's potato crop. Because the tenant farmers of Ireland had little besides potatoes to eat, within just a few years an estimated 1.5 million people died of starvation or related diseases.

- In 1847, as the potato famine raged, Parliament legislated that the Irish poor were the responsibility of the landowners. After that, when landlords evicted the tenant farmers from their land, they either paid to have them placed in workhouses or sent them off to the New World. An estimated two and a half million Irish Catholics entered the workhouses during the potato blight, while an estimated one to one and a half million obtained inexpensive one-way passage on rickety ships heading for the New World.

- Irish Catholic immigrants in the United States tended not to move inland to the rural areas but stayed in East Coast cities and towns.

- By the 1840s nativist organizations were gaining strength. The American Party, later known as the Know-Nothing Party, claimed that immigrants—primarily the Irish and Roman Catholics—were threatening to destroy American values and democracy.

- As the Irish American population grew in the northeastern cities, its growing numbers gave it increasing voting capacity. Urban Irish Americans across the country organized into political machines made up of precincts working under a boss whose power depended on his ability to deliver up the district's votes. Because they manipulated the voting system by granting favors, political machines always had some criminal element, but the extent varied greatly.

- In 1850, 75 percent of Irish women in the United States were domestics. Second-generation Irish American women, anxious to escape the household-help business, were determined to get an education. At the turn of the century, Irish American women stayed in school longer than Irish American men.

- The St. Patrick's Day parade is a U.S. tradition, not an Irish one. The first parade is said to have taken place in Boston in 1737. In Ireland St. Patrick's Day is a holy day, and until 1995 there were no St. Patrick's Day parades in Ireland.

Words to Know

Assimilation: The way that someone who comes from a foreign land or culture becomes absorbed into American culture and learns to blend into the ways of its predominant, or main, society.

Bishop: A Catholic clergyman of a higher ranking than a priest, who has the authority to ordain priests and usually has the responsibility of governing the diocese, a district established by the church.

Celtic: pronounced KEL-tick; Relating to an ancient race of European people—the Celts whose descendants live today in Ireland, the Scottish Highlands, Wales, and Brittany, a part of France. *Celtic* also refers to the language spoken by these people.

Chain migration: A process of immigration in which a person or persons from one location in the Old World migrates to a location in the New World and then brings over more people from their home. The relatives come, settling close to the first immigrant. They write to more people back home and send money when possible for their close ones to join them. In many cases, an entire neighborhood within a U.S. city, town, or farming region has been populated by people from one village or neighborhood in the old country.

Clachans: Small, close-knit communities in rural Ireland.

Discrimination: Unfair treatment based on racism or other prejudices.

Emigration: Leaving one's country to go to another country with the intention of living there. "Emigrant" is used to describe *departing from* one's country—for example, "she emigrated from Ireland." "Immigrant" is used to describe *coming to* a new country—for example, "she immigrated to the United States."

Ethnic: Relating to a group of people who are not from the majority culture in the country in which they live, and who keep their own culture, language, and institutions.

Exiles: People who have been sent away from their homeland.

and army commander Oliver Cromwell (1599–1658) took power and immediately rushed off to Ireland. Cromwell's army of twelve thousand men attacked the city of Drogheda in northeast Ireland, killing more than three thousand people there. From Drogheda Cromwell attacked Wexford, killing hundreds more. Other towns simply surrendered to him when they learned of the massacres.

Gaelic: The language spoken in Ireland, the Highlands of Scotland, and on the Isle of Man.

Grassroots: Arising from common people, rather than politicians, corporations, or others in power.

Immigration: To travel to a country of which one is not a native with the intention of settling there as a permanent resident. "Immigrant" is used to describe *coming to* a new country—for example, "she immigrated to the United States." "Emigrant" is used to describe *departing from* one's country—for example, "she emigrated from Ireland."

Industrialization: The historic change from a farm-based economy to an economic system based on the manufacturing of goods and distribution of services on an organized and mass-produced basis.

Laissez faire: French for "let it be"; A belief that the government should not interfere in the economy more than absolutely necessary.

Mass migration: A time in history when thousands—or even millions—of people from one country in the Old World immigrated to the New World within a relatively short period of time.

Migration: To move from one place to another, not necessarily across national borders.

Nationalist movement: Struggle for independence from the rule of another country.

Nativism: A set of beliefs that centers around favoring the interests of people who are native-born to a country as opposed to its immigrants.

Nostalgia: Remembering one's home with longing; homesickness.

Quarantine: Enforced isolation from the public to prevent the spread of an infectious disease.

Parish: Local church community.

Populist: Oriented toward common people, or democratic.

Workhouses: Institutions in which people in desperate poverty went to reside, and in which they worked for food and other aid.

As the leader of the new Republic of England, Cromwell decided to pay his soldiers for their part in the civil war by granting them land in Ireland. Irish landowners were exiled (sent away) from Munster and Leinster to be resettled on inferior land while their land was given to English Protestants. Cromwell, who hated Catholicism, expelled one thousand priests from Ireland and severely limited land ownership among the Irish Catholics.

The Penal Laws

In 1689 English political conflicts erupted into battle on Irish soil. The English King James (1633–1701), a Catholic, lost his throne to his Protestant brother-in-law, William of Orange (1650–1702), who had the support of English Protestants and Parliament. James fled to Ireland, where he could count on the help of the Catholics. There he and William fought the Battle of the Boyne. James lost the battle and with it, the English throne; and William became William III, king of England. England revenged itself by forcing Ireland to enter the Treaty of Limerick in 1691, which included the first of the Penal Laws. Under these laws, no Irish Catholic could receive an education, enter a profession, purchase land, vote, hold public office, own any kind of weapon, or own a horse of greater value than five pounds. Many Irish converted to the Church of England because the consequences of remaining Catholic were so severe. Irish Catholics as a whole had been reduced to poverty and had little political power to help themselves.

Many of the Protestant colonists in Ireland came to regard themselves as Irish and resented Britain's rule. In 1783 they forced the establishment of an independent Irish Parliament, but it was short lived. In 1800, after more conflicts, the Act of Union was passed, which created the "United Kingdom of Great Britain and Ireland," a union of England, Wales, Ireland, and Scotland to be ruled by one parliament in London. In the United Kingdom, Ireland would have representation in Parliament, but Irish government representatives could not pass laws on their own. The Penal Laws remained in effect for a time but were finally repealed in 1829, but only after a major political struggle with England.

The rural population of Ireland tended to live in small, close-knit villages called *clachans* (pronounced CLAH-kens), which often farmed their holdings of land as a community. People in a clachan lived and worked very closely together and helped each other through hard times. Most Irish Catholics were, by the nineteenth century, living in extreme poverty, particularly in rural areas. About 95 percent of Irish land was owned by British Protestants, who rented it out in small parcels. Ireland had undergone a tremendous population explosion and had not yet become industrialized (made the change from a farm-based economy to an economic system based on the manufacturing of goods and distribution of

services on an organized and mass-produced basis). There was not enough land or work to provide for the large population. Thus, the rented land parcels became smaller and smaller, with tenants leasing to subtenants who usually ended up with less than 5-acre lots. The tenant farmers did not have modern equipment or the money to buy it. Their lots could support only a tiny garden to feed their families—perhaps 1.5 acres to feed a family for the year. With this lack of space, equipment, and capital, most of the clachans had come to rely on only one food source for survival—the potato. An acre of potatoes produced more food and was more reliable than any other crop, and although a diet of only potatoes is not balanced, the nutritional value was enough to sustain a family.

The potato famine

In 1845 about three to four million of Ireland's eight million people were rural poor. Although they were responsible for growing Ireland's abundant export crops, the tenants were forced to deliver everything they grew to their landlords to pay their rent. This food—meat and grains—was shipped out of Ireland to be sold in foreign ports. Potatoes barely sustained the Irish farmers throughout the year.

In 1845 a mysterious disease, a fungus called *Phytophthora infestans,* hit Europe's potato crops, destroying about one-third of Ireland's potatoes. It was clear that many of the poor would starve unless they got help. That year the British prime minister had corn shipped in from the United States. With this aid, although many suffered terribly, no one died of starvation in 1845. Ireland's other crops prospered and continued to be shipped out of the country, even though the food was so badly needed by the very people who had grown it. There was a strong faction in the Parliament in London that believed in a "laissez faire" (let it be) approach to economy and government. They strongly opposed government interference in the economy. Some of these people believed that economic booms and crises, even a famine, were God's way of shaping the world. British politicians voiced their feelings that the Irish were a lazy people and might become dependent on relief, if it were offered.

In the summer of 1846 the potato crop in the Irish fields looked healthy and abundant. Some relief operations had been underway to feed the Irish people in case of another crop failure, but the British shut them down as the new crops came in. At the end of the growing season, though, the blight struck again; all the potatoes of Ireland blackened and rotted. There was no food left and no relief operations were in place. People began to starve by October. As the unusually cold winter of 1846 to 1847 began, tens of thousands of people starved to death or, weakened from malnutrition, died of infectious diseases like cholera and typhus that raged through the land. The misery in some of the rural areas of Ireland is hard to imagine today. Whole families could be found dead together, having starved in their homes. The government belatedly set up jobs digging roads to employ some of the starving farmers. But men lucky enough to get one of the road jobs frequently died from hunger before they received their first wages. The churches quit using coffins to bury the dead because they could not afford to pay for so many of them if they were going to try to help the living. This was "Black '47," the

very worst season of starvation in the potato famine. Because of a lack of seed potatoes (the plant that bears the seeds) after Black '47 to plant more crops, the famine continued through 1849 and would claim an estimated one to one and a half million lives. It was the worst famine in history up to the twentieth century. In places like Skibbereen, in County Cork, and many other rural areas on the western seaboard of Ireland, the signs of death and dying were visible at every corner.

Irish peasants generally rented their land on six-month leases. When they failed to pay their rent in the famine years, the landlords frequently evicted them (terminated their rent agreement and forced them to move away from the rented land), often burning down their homes to make sure they left. In 1847 Parliament legislated that the Irish poor were the responsibility of the landowners. Under this provision, the landlords continued to evict their starving tenants, and then generally took one of two methods to take care of them, neither of which was humane. The first was to crowd them into one of the

Starving peasants clamor at the gates of a workhouse during the potato famine.
Reproduced by permission of © Hulton Getty/Liaison Agency.

173 poorly run, disease-infested workhouses, also called poor-houses, that had been built around the Irish countryside for this purpose. A poor person had to live within the workhouse to receive aid and was required to exchange labor for food. It is estimated that two and a half million people entered the workhouses, and approximately two hundred thousand died in them, during the potato blight. The other choice, which may have been cheaper for the landlord, was to purchase an inexpensive ticket for the tenant on a rickety ship heading for Canada. An estimated one to one and a half million Irish Catholics left Ireland during the potato famine, with their passage paid by the landlord or with money they scraped together themselves.

Passage to America

Many of the hundreds of thousands of desperate passengers who emigrated from Ireland during the famine years found cheap passage to Canada and went there with the intention of traveling from Canada to the United States. The ships they boarded were called "coffin ships" because so many people died during the voyage from infectious disease. The dead were thrown overboard. For the living, the conditions aboard were often nightmarish. The ships were generally old timber ships not meant for passengers at all, and the ship owners would overload the ship with too many passengers. Roger Daniels, in *Coming to America: A History of Immigration and Ethnicity in American Life,* estimates that in the worst famine year, 1847, about seventeen thousand people died while at sea and another twenty thousand died after landing due to diseases picked up onboard. Other estimates of the death toll are even higher.

Once in Canada, the ships were generally quarantined (subject to enforced isolation from the public to prevent the spread of infectious disease) at an island near Montreal called Grosse Isle. The island was quickly overwhelmed by the huge number of immigrants, many of whom were near death and carrying disease. According to Terry Golway in *The Irish in America,* as many as fifteen thousand people may have died on Grosse Isle in their flight from the potato famine. Other Irish people made their way to the ports of Boston, Philadelphia, Baltimore, and New York.

The first Irish Catholic migrations to America

Irish immigration to North America had begun well before the potato famine. There were Irish among the colonial settlers in the seventeenth and eighteenth centuries. Others continued to arrive after the United States was formed in 1783. The mass migrations (times in history when thousands, or even millions, of people from one country in the Old World immigrated to the New World within a relatively short period of time) did not begin, though, until the early nineteenth century. Between 1815 and 1845, the grim condition of the Irish economy, a population explosion in the country, and the poor treatment of the Catholics initiated mass migration. It is estimated that about 1 million Irish Catholics immigrated to the United States in that pre-famine period. In 1840 Irish immigrants made up about one-half of all immigrants to the United States. Another 1.5 million Irish Catholic immigrants arrived in the United States in the potato famine years. Another 2.6 million came from 1860 to the present. When discussing the Irish immigration to the United States it is necessary to distinguish between the Catholic and Protestant Irish immigrants because their experiences differed significantly. Irish Protestants (many were the Scotch-Irish who had been colonists in Northern Ireland; see chapter 6 on the Scots and Scotch-Irish) faced less discrimination and tended to come to the new country with job skills and with some money to get started. This chapter deals mainly with the millions of Irish Catholic immigrants who came to the United States.

The early Irish Catholic immigrants

The early nineteenth-century Irish Catholic immigrants were mostly male and usually poor, illiterate, and unskilled. Whether it was because they lacked the funds to travel further or to buy land or because the famine had given them a strong distaste for farming, these immigrants tended not to move inland to the rural areas. Many made their way from Canada down to New England and New York. They stayed mainly in the East and South, in cities such as Baltimore, Maryland; Philadelphia, Pennsylvania; and Charleston, South Carolina. The Irish immigrants who made it away from the eastern seaboard, especially those who made it to the West Coast, did not have the same experiences as the majority that remained in the East. Out West, they tended to assimilate more quickly and find more success and less discrimination.

When they arrived in the New World, the young Irish immigrants got to work in low-paying, heavy-labor jobs quickly. As soon as it was possible, they sent their earnings back to Ireland to bring their families over to the United States. This pattern of migration is called chain migration and has been practiced by many groups of immigrants since the Irish. Chain migration works in this way: An individual or group of immigrants goes to a new land and gets established with a job and a place to live. He or she then helps to bring over friends and family, who come, get established near the earlier immigrants, and then help bring their own kin and friends over. The earlier

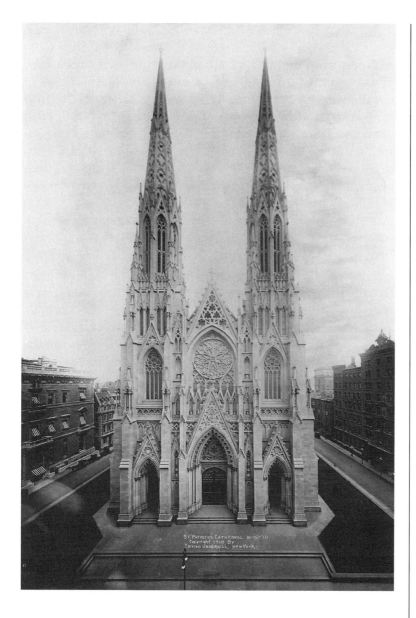

immigrants help the new ones to settle, and before long a new community of people who had connections in the old country has arisen in the new country. In cities, whole neighborhoods have formed made up of people from a particular village in the Old World. After the 1850s, the migrations from Ireland were no longer made up of single young males. Most Irish immigrants came over as families. After 1880, slightly more women than men were immigrating.

The immigrants were not Ireland's poorest people, since the poorest could not afford the passage, but they often arrived without much more than the clothes on their backs. Those coming from rural Ireland especially were not used to the industrial society or big cities, but they adapted. The Irish tended to live in tenement houses (apartment buildings in cities that were poorly made and lacking in safety and sanitation features), because that was all they could afford. They often lived very close together, as they had done in their clachans at home. Houses built for one family often housed several Irish families. The conditions in the city tenements and slums were often unhealthy, with poor sewage and no running water. To some unsympathetic onlookers, the early Irish immigrants seemed dirty or contemptible.

The transition from the rural parts of Ireland to the city neighborhoods of New York or Philadelphia would have been nearly unthinkable had it not been for the Catholic church parish (local church community), which served almost as an Irish village within the American city. Within the Catholic parish, the Irish immigrants found most of the services required for daily life and a sense of safety and familiarity in the midst of a strange land.

Religious discrimination and nativism

The Irish migration to the United States set the stage for future immigrants: They were met with vicious discrimination. During the first decades of the nineteenth century, there had been relatively few Catholics in the predominantly Protestant United States. When the Irish Catholics began to arrive in great numbers, a movement of anti-Catholicism swept the nation. By the 1830s a large and steady influx of Irish Catholic immigrants, along with German Catholics, had made Catholicism one of the major U.S. religions. Before they came to be accepted as part of the American culture, the Irish Catholics were often attacked.

In the 1830s sensational books were being published in the United States. Usually written in the format of tell-all memoirs, these books told wild and unfounded stories of depraved priests kidnapping and molesting nuns and scandalous behavior taking place within the Catholic church walls. The books, a product of Protestant hostility towards

Catholics and foreigners, were aimed at rousing the community against the newcomers. One of these books was so effective that it inspired an angry anti-Catholic mob to storm a Catholic convent in Charlestown, Massachusetts, and burn it to the ground. One of the instigators of this violence was the Congregational (a Protestant church) minister Lyman Beecher (1775–1863), the father of abolitionist (person who favored the end of slavery) writer Harriet Beecher Stowe (1811–1896), the author of the 1852 antislavery novel *Uncle Tom's Cabin*.

By the 1840s the anti-Catholic, anti-immigrant hostilities had become organized by nativist groups (associations that promoted the rights of "natives" as opposed to immigrants; here, natives referred to people who had been in the country longer than the incoming Irish, but not to Native Americans, whose rights were not a concern of the nativists). One of the prime nativist organizations was the American Party, which promoted "traditional American ideals" and claimed that immigrants—primarily the Irish and Roman Catholics—were threatening to destroy American values and democracy. The American Party raised fears of a conspiracy to use the U.S. voting system to elect agents of the pope (the head of the Roman Catholic church) so that the pope could exert political control over the United States, or at least local governments. Members of the American Party came to be known as "Know-Nothings," because they kept the agenda of their organization secret. When asked about their activities, they would answer, "I know nothing about it." Know-Nothings worked to ensure that immigrants could not hold public office. Their campaigns, which worked up anti-immigration feelings, were highly successful in the 1840s and 1850s, with Know-Nothings gaining several political offices during the mid-1800s, including mayor of Philadelphia and control of the Massachusetts legislature.

In 1844 controversy arose in Philadelphia over whether Catholic children in public schools could be allowed to read from the Catholic version of the Bible rather than the King James version and other issues. Violent mob riots erupted with all Catholics being targets, but particularly the Irish. The riots lasted from May through July. People were killed and Catholic churches, schools, and hundreds of homes were burned. During the Philadelphia attacks, some of the anti-Catholic/anti-Irish groups made threats against the Irish in New York. John Hughes (1797–1864), fondly called "Dagger John," the tough

"Dagger John" Hughes, Archbishop of New York

John Hughes (1797–1864) grew up in poverty in County Tyrone, Ireland. Like other Irish Catholics, he bristled in anger at the treatment Irish Catholics received under British rule. His anger grew when his sister died and British laws prohibited the family's priest from entering the cemetery as she was buried. At the age of twenty, Hughes immigrated with his family to the United States. There, determined to become a priest, he got a job as a gardener and stonemason at the Catholic St. Mary's college and seminary (an institution that trains priests) in Maryland. Although he was initially denied admission to the school because he had no formal education, Hughes's obvious leadership abilities won him admission to the seminary in 1820. He was ordained a priest six years later. As soon as he took his first position in Philadelphia, Hughes became an outspoken champion of the Irish immigrants, crusading everywhere against bigotry. Challenged to a debate by Protestant clergyman John Breckinridge (1797–1841), who attacked Catholicism, Hughes stood his ground famously: "I am an American by choice, not by chance. I was born under the scourge of Protestant persecution, of which my fathers in common with our Catholic countrymen have been the victims for ages. I know the value of that civil and religious liberty, which our happy government secures for all" (quoted by Ken Concannon in the *Arlington Catholic Herald*).

In 1842 Hughes became the bishop of New York. (A bishop is a Catholic clergyman ranking above a priest, who has the authority to ordain priests and usually has the responsibility of governing a diocese, a district established by the church.) An avid proponent of education, he began reforming the public schools, which were teaching Protes-

Catholic archbishop of New York, let it be known that the Irish would defend the city's churches with whatever force was necessary. There were no attacks in New York.

During the 1850s the nativist groups continued to campaign for office. Their campaigns whipped up sentiments against the Irish Americans to further the nativists' careers, often resulting in violence and destruction. Catholic churches and priests were the most frequent nativist targets.

Jobs

Irish American people in the mid-nineteenth century worked in every category of jobs, but a large portion were

tant Christianity with a large dose of anti-Catholic prejudice. After helping to secure laws against religious teachings in the public schools, Hughes began to build Catholic school systems. In 1844, when nativists threatened to riot in New York as they had in Philadelphia, he lived up to his nickname "Dagger John." Hughes stationed armed forces around the city's Catholic churches, telling the mayor that if one Catholic church burned, the people in his district would respond with torches of their own. The nativist rally was promptly cancelled.

The potato famine brought tens of thousands of Irish to New York City. As the destitute, ill, and traumatized immigrants crowded into shanty towns (areas where people have erected crude huts to live in) and tenements in New York City, they ushered in a new age of city slums, considered to be the worst New York has ever seen. Gang warfare, crime, prostitution, alcoholism, and drug addiction were rampant. In city slums like Sweeney's Shambles and Five Points, where the poorest Irish resided, the death rate was seven times higher than in other parts of the city. Even many sympathetic reputable Irish Catholics turned away from the Irish slums in disgust. Hughes, who became archbishop (head of the bishops in his province) of New York in 1850, saw the latest Irish immigrants as victims and focused his energy on providing them with spiritual and social assistance. He worked tirelessly to provide aid in all phases of settling new immigrants—work, hospitals, orphanages, banks, groceries, and schools, to name but a few. By the time he died in 1864, the Irish in New York City had made great strides in getting out of the tormented slums and moving into more comfortable and productive American lives.

doomed to work as unskilled laborers because so many had come from Ireland with no skills appropriate to an industrial nation and no money to start businesses or farms. The Irish willingness to work for extremely low wages created hostility toward them among other American workers, especially African Americans, who competed against them for unskilled jobs. Prejudice and discrimination against the newcomers were widespread and harsh. The popular magazine *Harper's Weekly* featured regular cartoons that ridiculed "Paddy" and "Bridget" (common Irish names) as drunken, disorderly, ignorant brutes. Signs stating "No Irish need apply" were posted everywhere.

Despite the hostility, the United States benefited greatly from the presence of Irish American workers. The country was, in fact, in great need of labor in the mid- and late-1800s. It had just begun the process of building its extensive systems of canals, railroads, and bridges and expanded its mining industry. There was no motorized equipment to do the job, just picks and shovels. The work was dangerous, the hours were long, and the pay was lousy, but the Irish Americans had come to the country prepared to work hard. The Chesapeake and Ohio Canal, the Erie Canal, and New Orleans' New Canal were essentially built by Irish Americans. The Irish, along with large crews of Chinese Americans, also laid much of the railroad track and dug the roads across the United States. Irish women, who arrived in great numbers in the post-famine years, served as domestics (household help) for many American families. Many Irish workers died in construction jobs and in the mines.

Conditions in Irish American slums became intolerable in the mid-1800s. Epidemics of the infectious diseases typhoid, typhus, cholera, tuberculosis, and pneumonia claimed thousands of lives. In 1857 some 85 percent of the people admitted to New York City's hospital were Irish immigrants. Infant and child mortality (death rates) were so high among Irish Americans that immigrant children were expected to live no more than fourteen years on the average after arrival in the United States. Gangs rose up in most of the cities and crime was rampant. Many Irish Americans turned to alcohol. When gold was discovered in California in 1849, thousands of Irish Americans joined the rush West. A few struck it rich. The rest returned to the East and Midwest or settled in the cities of the West.

By the time of the American Civil War (1861–65), many Irish Americans were tired of being considered one of the lowest class of citizens in the United States. They organized in a variety of ways to bring about social changes, but by 1863, the frustration level was high. In that year, President Abraham Lincoln (1809–1865) issued a military draft, requiring young men to join the fighting against the Confederates. African Americans were not required to fight and wealthy men could buy their way out of the draft for three hundred dollars. Irish laborers did not have that kind of money and had no choice but to join. Most Irish Americans were not enthusiastic about fighting for the Union. The emancipation of the slaves from slavery, a major reason for the war, was a diffi-

Kids playing in an alley in the New York City slums.
Reproduced by permission of AP/Wide World Photos.

cult issue for them because they dreaded the competition that the freed slaves would present in the job market. To be compelled to fight for this particular cause—and the unfairness of the draft—enraged them. Demonstrations broke out across the country to protest the draft. On June 12, 1863, when the draftees were publicly named in New York City, a mob of nearly fifty thousand people stormed the east side of the city, burning, looting, and killing. Many of the leaders and partici-

An American Dream in Butte, Montana

Not every Irish immigrant in the last half of the nineteenth century encountered years of poverty and discrimination when they arrived in the United States. Those who made it west of the Mississippi generally fared better than those who stayed in the East. Butte, Montana, was a tiny outpost in the mountains until the 1870s, when copper was found there. Instrumental in the discovery was Marcus Daly (1841–1900), an Irish immigrant who had been employed by a large mining company to investigate the potential of mining silver there. Daly, finding copper, quietly organized his own company, Anaconda Copper Company, and bought as many mines in the area as he could. Soon, his business was supplying a large portion of the nation's copper and Daly was a very wealthy man. He built up a political machine (a group of neighborhood units, or precincts, that, when working together under a single "boss" or machine, create a large political force) and managed to overwhelm a powerful business rival in the town. From that point, Daly ruled almost as king. Building up the industries around his own company in Butte, Daly was responsible for a tremendous influx of Irish immigrants to Butte. By 1900 there were about twelve thousand Irish people, nearly half the city's population.

Many of the laborers of Daly's time were recent immigrants from Cork, Ireland. In Butte, they worked an eight-hour day and earned nearly twice the hourly rate of other workers in the United States. Butte had the first trade union of the western United States. The trade unions and the self-help organizations there helped new immigrants, widows, and old-timers. Bigotry was not such a factor as it was in most eastern cities. Besides Irish, there were significant Chinese and Jewish populations; in fact, the town's first mayor was Jewish. Immigrants flocked there, usually receiving work and decent treatment when they arrived. The per capita (per person) income in Butte was one of the highest in the United States around the turn of the century. With saloons open twenty-four hours a day to accommodate the different work shifts, Butte was not a place where the timid or the prim would necessarily want to live, but it suited many Irish immigrants. Irish historian and writer Peter Quinn told Maureen Dezell in an interview quoted in her book, *Irish America: Coming into Clover,* that "if the Irish had ever had the numbers, the strength, and the power to re-create the world, it probably would have looked a lot like Butte."

pants of the riots were Irish Americans. They targeted black people in particular to vent their rage; African Americans were lynched, drowned, beaten, or otherwise killed. A black orphan asylum and church and hundreds of houses and businesses were burned down in the three-day riot before it was stopped by federal troops.

The Irish would not be at the bottom of the economic spectrum for long. As American cities grew, their governments and services needed manpower and the Irish moved into white-collar municipal positions that were low paying but secure and respectable. In Boston, Philadelphia, New York, Chicago, St. Louis, and many other cities, Irish Americans occupied an extraordinary share of the city government and administrative jobs, such as clerk, secretary, and inspector. The police and fire departments often had a majority of Irishmen in their ranks. In fact, one-quarter of New York City's police force in 1855 was Irish born.

Politics

The Irish living in the cities of the Northeast developed strong social networks within their parishes. Churches formed one bond; social organizations another. Another was the neighborhood saloon (often called a "grog shop"), a popular meeting place for the Irish. There were two thousand Irish saloons in downtown New York City by 1840 and the number grew quickly. In jobs and in politics in the Northeast, the Irish gained a reputation for being both "street-smart" and excellent administrators and organizers.

The political machine

The Irish American community began to make itself known in politics before the mid-nineteenth century, especially in the northeastern cities where its growing numbers gave it increasing voting capacity. Urban Irish Americans across the country organized into unofficial power blocks called "political machines." The machines were made up of neighborhood units, or precincts, that, when working together under a single "boss" and his staff, or the "machine," created a large political force. Each neighborhood had a ward captain (or "heeler") who was in communication with the residents. He could deliver the votes of his area to the leaders of the political machine; in turn, he would elicit favors for the people—jobs, licenses, contracts—from the machine. The political machines could then promise votes to elected political officials. Because they manipulated the voting system by granting favors, political machines always had some criminal element. The extent of criminal activity, however, greatly varied.

Political machines operated on a grassroots level (in which common people, rather than politicians, corporations, or others in power, raise the issues and initiate the political activities), and almost all of them were affiliated with the Democratic Party. By the mid-1800s, Irish Americans had, in fact, taken over the Democratic Party and city hall in several major cities. They were becoming a voice to be reckoned with in American politics. As a rule, Irish Americans aimed to replace the powerful elite classes in the United States with a more populist (oriented toward common people, or democratic) government and they were responsible for many important features of modern American politics.

New York City's Tammany Hall, the powerful political machine in Manhattan, was one of the most significant political arenas for Irish Americans in the 1800s. William Marcy "Boss" Tweed (1823–1878), an Irish American, became its leader and ruled the city, exercising heavy influence in state and federal politics from his political throne. Tweed and other Irish American politicians used their positions to promote the welfare of other Irish Americans, providing employment (particularly in blue-collar city jobs), food, and services. Sometimes the machine bosses worked within the law, and often they did not. Corruption and fraud were fairly common. Boss Tweed himself was imprisoned in 1873 for illegal activities. Machine boss and Boston mayor James Michael Curley (1874–1958) also spent time in prison. Nevertheless, Curley was responsible for great improvements in the poor and working person's lot in life. He built hospitals, schools, and recreational buildings and brought about expansion of workmen's compensation, shorter working hours, more fair state taxes, and much more.

Links with Irish liberation movement

In the 1870s and 1880s Ireland experienced more crop failures, and another mass migration from Ireland to the United States began. Second- and third-generation Irish Americans raised money for the new immigrants and helped them get set up in

Finley Peter Dunne and Mr. Dooley

Finley Peter Dunne (1867–1936) grew up in a family of Irish immigrants on Chicago's West Side. He began working as a newspaper writer in 1884, and after working for several dailies, took an editorial job at the *Chicago Evening Post*. There, he began a column, written in the voice of his narrator and character, Mr. Martin Dooley, a highly opinionated Irish American bar owner who lives and works on the South Side of Chicago in an Irish working-class neighborhood called Bridgeport. In Dunne's column, Dooley spouts off in Irish brogue (accent), naively criticizing the leaders of the country without always appearing to do so. The satire was biting and unmistakable, but the effect was very funny and delighted Dunne's growing readership. Through the naive and bumbling voice of his barkeeper, Dunne took on a number of hot political issues such as foreign policy, racism, and the American legal system.

Chicago, and eventually the whole nation, loved Mr. Dooley. Without offending, Dunne used his narrator to explore the nation's ethnic communities from within, an important step in American journalism. Literary critic Charles Fanning writes in the *Heath Anthology of American Literature*:

Dunne takes the late-nineteenth-century journalistic phenomenon of urban local color and extends it, through his feeling for place and community, to evoke Bridgeport as the most solidly realized ethnic neighborhood in nineteenth-century American literature.... Place, community, and character are all embodied in the vernacular voice of a sixty-year-old, smiling public-house man, the first such dialect voice to transcend the stereotypes of "stage-Irish" ethnic humor.

A few brief examples of the wisdom of Mr. Dooley, from Dunne's column *Mr. Dooley's Opinions,* are provided below:

- A fanatic is a man that does what he thinks th' Lord wud do if He knew th' facts iv [of] th' case.

- A man that'd expict to thrain lobsters to fly in a year is called a loonytic; but a man that thinks men can be tu-rrned into angels be an iliction is called a rayformer an' remains at large. (Translates: A man that would expect to train lobsters to fly in a year is called a lunatic; but a man that thinks men can be turned into angels by an election is called a reformer and remains at large.)

- Ye can lead a man up to the university, but ye can't make him think.

their new home. Ties to the old country were invigorated by the newcomers. Irish Americans began to organize in support of the growing nationalist movement (a struggle for independence from the rule of another country) in Ireland, where politician Charles Stewart Parnell (1846–1891) and many other nationalists were fighting to rid the country of British rule. Irish Americans founded the Land League of America, an organization that raised huge sums of money to help the effort in Ireland. It was later replaced with the Irish National League of America.

Irish American newspapers served to connect the Irish Americans with events in Ireland. Most Irish newspapers in the United States originated in order to advocate the liberation of Ireland from the British. The papers were especially popular with new immigrants in search of news of home, while also serving to remind second-generation immigrants of the troubles in the old country. The papers often raised funds for the Land League and other Irish causes. The first Irish American newspaper was the *Shamrock*, established in New York in 1810. The *Shamrock* made New York seethe with Irish nationalism. The *Boston Pilot,* the *Chicago Citizen,* Philadelphia's *Irish Press,* and many others soon followed. There were many outstanding Irish American journalists from the start, as there are today, with Jimmy Breslin (1930–), Anna Quindlen (1953–), Maureen Dowd (1952–), and Eileen McNamara (1952–), as just a few of the well-known examples. There are quite a few Irish American newspapers in circulation in the early twenty-first century. The *Irish Echo* is the largest and most national. It was founded in 1928 and prints separate Boston and New York editions.

Labor unions

The politics and vocations of many Irish Americans led to their strong involvement and leadership in the labor movement of the 1870s through the 1930s. During the 1880s, the Knights of Labor, led by Irish Americans, became the first national industrial union. It had more than seven hundred thousand members in 1886 and hundreds of thousands were Irish American workers. By 1900 over 50 of the 110 unions in the American Federation of Labor (AFL) had Irish American presidents. Mary Harris "Mother" Jones (1837–1930), a powerful leader of the labor movement, was an Irish immigrant.

Mainstream national politics

By the beginning of the twentieth century, Irish Catholic Americans had taken political offices at almost all

levels. Being Catholic was still a factor in the predominantly Protestant country, but by 1860, there were 3.5 million Catholics in the country. Although Catholics were still in the minority, Roman Catholicism had become the largest religious denomination in the nation, and it continued to grow. The presidency, however, was thought to be off limits to Catholics. Irish American governor of New York Al Smith (1873–1944), who had gotten his start through affiliations with Tammany

President John F. Kennedy visiting his ancestral home in Dunganstown, Ireland, in 1963. *Reproduced by permission of © Bettmann/Corbis.*

Hall, became the first Catholic to win the Democratic nomination for the presidency in 1928. He was defeated in the election by Republican Herbert Hoover (1874–1964). As governor, Smith had been responsible for many long-reaching reforms and had won the respect of both parties. Many believe that Catholicism was the reason he lost in the presidential race. During his campaign, he received approximately ten million pieces of hate mail, most directed at his religion.

It was not until 1961 that an Irish Catholic American would become president of the United States. John F. Kennedy (1917–1963) was the great grandson of Bridget Murphy Kennedy and Patrick Kennedy, who fled County Wexford in Ireland during the potato famine. During the Kennedy administration, Irish Catholic Americans filled many of the country's top political positions: speaker of the House of Representatives, majority leader of the Senate, chair of the Democratic National Committee, and president of the AFL-CIO.

Irish American women

Single Irish women immigrated to the United States in much larger numbers than were common with other nationalities. In fact, at the turn of the twentieth century, about 60 percent of Irish immigrants were single women. The reason for this was the situation in Ireland. The system of inheritance (the passing on of assets from one generation to the next) there provided that only one son could inherit the family farm and only one daughter would receive a dowry. With no jobs and few prospects, a large segment of Ireland's young people simply did not marry. When women did marry, it was often to men who were significantly older than them. Without employment, there was little choice for a young single woman in Ireland but to live with her parents and help out with the household. Many chose to scrape together the money for passage to America. Irish women traveled across the sea with female friends or relatives or arrived alone.

Once in the United States, Irish women almost immediately went out in search of work. They generally became domestic servants. In fact, in 1850, 75 percent of Irish women in the United States were domestics. The pay was very poor and the work was hard, but it was safe—they lived in the homes of their employers and had regular meals—and it was respectable. Americans called Irish domestics "Bridget," a common Irish name, no matter what their names were; this became one of the major stereotypes of Irish women.

From the start, Irish women were active in the social world of the new country. There were, for example, many Irish women in the labor movement. Second-generation Irish American women, anxious to escape the household-help business, were careful to get an education. Historians note that Irish American women stayed in school longer than Irish American men at the turn of the century. They became nurses, nuns, teachers, and secretaries, among other professions. About 80 percent of single Irish American women had jobs.

Irish American population

When Irish independence was declared in 1921, immigration to the United States virtually ceased. Small numbers of

Irish have continued to come to the United States since that time, but the mass migration was over. Ireland lost more of its population to the United States than to any other country. In 1860 there were only five Irish persons left in Ireland for every Irish person in the United States (compared with thirty-three Germans in Germany for every German American, and forty-two British in Britain for every British American).

In 2000 the U.S. Census reported that there were 30,528,492 people claiming Irish ancestry in the country—about ten times the number of Irish people in Ireland and 10.8 percent of the U.S. population. There are about forty-four million people in the country who have some Irish descent. More than half of Irish or part-Irish Americans in the United States today are Protestant, and a good portion of those are the Scotch-Irish (see chapter 6 on Scotch-Irish), leaving about twenty million Irish Catholics. Irish Americans live throughout the nation. The states with the largest populations of Irish Americans are California, New York, Pennsylvania, Florida, and Illinois.

Irish Americans today have become part of established mainstream U.S. culture. Most are from families that have been in the United States for many generations; only a small fraction of 1 percent of the Irish American population today is foreign born. There was a rise in the 1980s and 1990s of illegal immigrants from Ireland. Escaping a severe job shortage in Ireland, many sidestepped immigration quotas by acquiring visitor visas (documents allowing foreigners to stay in the United States for a limited period of time) and then stayed beyond the expiration of the visa. Because it was fairly easy for them to blend in, few were caught. In the early twenty-first century Ireland's economy was doing very well, and many of the new or undocumented immigrants could possibly return.

Irish American culture

Although many Irish people immigrated to the United States before or after the potato famine, the involuntary nature of the mass migration that occurred in the 1840s and 1850s left a mark on Irish American culture as a whole. Many Irish immigrants longed for Ireland once they were settled in the New World. They often blamed the British rule for their exile from their beloved home. Feeling deep loss and nostalgia (remembering one's home with longing; homesickness) for their past, Irish Americans have at times had trouble defining themselves as both Irish and Americans. Though they spoke the language and looked like the dominant culture in the United States, many Irish Americans kept themselves just slightly apart from the mainstream for several generations after immigration. Irish American arts, celebrations, and customs often reflect these tendencies.

Venues of the nineteenth century

As the worst anti-Irish discrimination passed in the nineteenth-century United States, Protestant Anglo America affectionately accepted the Irish but tended to think of Irish Americans in broad stereotypes. One classic stereotype is the sentimental, street-fighting, fast-talking, beer-guzzling, working-class young man of stage and the movies. Irish Americans often played on these stereotypes in their roles in vaudeville shows (nineteenth-century variety shows with comic acts and song and dance); they also dressed up in blackface in minstrel shows and played on African American stereotypes. For comedy, the audiences loved the sound of the Irish accents.

From the Irish American vaudeville acts, the comedy team of Ned Harrigan (1845–1911) and Tony Hart (1855–1891) developed extremely popular shows in the 1870s and 1880s resembling today's musicals. Their *Mulligan Guard* shows were set in shabby New York City neighborhoods, featuring Harrigan as an Irish saloon keeper and Hart as an African American washerwoman. In his book *History of the Musical Stage, 1879–1890: The First Musical Comedies,* John Kenrick describes the strong appeal of these musical comedies to a working-class, immigrant-based audience: "The plots focused on such real-life problems as interracial tensions, political corruption and gang violence, but there was always enough clownish humor to keep everyone laughing. Since every class and ethnic group was treated as fair game and often depicted with surprising sympathy, nobody took offense."

At about the same time, Irish Americans loudly rejected the serious theater that was coming from Ireland around the turn of the twentieth century, when the Irish

Players brought the dramas of playwrights William Butler Yeats (1865–1939) and John M. Synge (1871–1909) to American stages. In these plays common Irish people were often depicted as dirty, uneducated, and impoverished. Since they had been stereotyped by Americans in this way, the Irish Americans did not want to see it, preferring to indulge in sentimentality (false or extravagant emotion) rather than in harsh realism. The romanticized musical comedies and Hollywood movies to come were more comfortable for mainstream America as well.

George M. Cohan (1878–1942), the song and dance superstar of the first years of the century, was born into an Irish American family and spent his childhood touring the country with the Four Cohans, his family's vaudeville act. Cohan is credited with having taken the Irish step dancing—the jibs, reels, and hornpipes performed in soft shoe or hard shoe—that he had learned from his parents and popularizing it in the song and dance of the American stage. In 1904 he wrote and starred in *Little Johnny Jones,* which featured the popular tunes "Yankee Doodle Dandy" and "Give My Regards to Broadway." Cohan wrote more than forty musicals, but is most remembered today for his patriotic, sentimental songs, such as "You're a Grand Old Flag," "Harrigan" (about comic Ned Harrigan), and "Over There."

Irish American popular songs at the turn of the century, many of which came from stage shows, were highly sentimental, idealizing dear old Ireland and motherhood, among other things. Songs like "Danny Boy" (with lyrics written by a British attorney, Fred Weatherly [1848–1933]), "My Wild Irish Rose," and "When Irish Eyes Are Smiling" (written for the musical *The Isle O' Dreams* [1912] by Chauncey Olcott [1860–1932]) had little to do with Ireland and much to do with the sweet nostalgia of people who had not been there for many decades, if ever.

Film and drama to the 1950s

In 1938 two of the nominations for best actor in the Academy Awards were Irish American actors playing Irish Americans: James Cagney (c. 1899–1986) for *Angels with Dirty Faces* (1938) and Spencer Tracy (1900–1967) for *Boys Town* (1938). Both movies worked on themes of Irish American street and parish life. Both movies feature a priest (actor Pat O'Brien [1899–1983] in *Angels* and Tracy in *Boys Town*) who is trying to guide youngsters out of the criminal life common in the city streets. The Irish American flavor, with Catholicism, gangsterism, and tough, misguided street kids overcoming the past and turning good, were becoming part of Hollywood's list of classic films as Irish Americans were assimilating into the mainstream. Golway writes that Cagney managed to portray the "menacing urban Irishman, an image that had frightened or repulsed America for nearly a century, while exuding a magnetism and charm that were also particularly urban Irish American. That he did so was a tribute to his magnificent talent, but it was also a sign of the times."

Along with the popular fare, one of the top U.S. playwrights of all time was writing serious drama in the 1930s. Eugene O'Neill (1888–1953) was the son of stage actor James O'Neill, who had grown up in a very poor Irish immigrant home. James had left a Shakespearean stage career to act on the popular stage because he feared the poverty he had known in his childhood. His son, Eugene, rejected the popular plays that had paid his father's salary. Among his many award-winning plays, O'Neill wrote a beloved but very realistic and dark autobiographical play, *A Long Day's Journey into Night,* in 1939. This is his true story of a family of Irish immigrants in the generations following the migration. This was not drama about the stereotypical Irish pub-keep or the street-fighting tough guy. Although the public did not often view O'Neill as Irish American, he did. O'Neill, as quoted by William Shannon in *The American Irish,* said that "the critics have missed the most important thing about me and my work, the fact that I am Irish."

In the twentieth century, there have been many great Irish American artists in all genres. They did not form their art around their ancestral roots. Rather, they wrote, painted, or danced in whatever form of modern American expression they chose, as assimilated people generally do.

The New Irish in the United States

For many years, people in Ireland have been rolling their eyes at the Irish American culture, often denying there

Holiday: St. Patrick's Day

St. Patrick (died c. 460 C.E.) is the patron saint of Ireland. He was born in Britain but was captured by Irish raiders at the age of sixteen and taken to Ireland. He escaped after six years there. After leaving Ireland, he spent many years in religious training. Hearing voices that instructed him to go back to Ireland, St. Patrick returned as an ordained priest and began a very successful mission converting the Irish to Christianity. In the legends about St. Patrick, he used the three-leafed shamrock to explain the Trinity (the union of the Father, Son, and Holy Ghost in one Godhead) to the Irish people; he is also said to have driven all the snakes out of the land. He died on March 17, and that has long been his feast day in Ireland.

The St. Patrick's Day parade is a U.S. tradition, not an Irish one. The first parade is said by many to have taken place in Boston in 1737, sponsored by the Irish Charitable Society. Soon Philadelphia and New York had parades sponsored by the Friendly Sons of St. Patrick and the Ancient Order of Hibernians. (Other people claim the first St. Patrick's Day parade was in 1762 in New York and was staged by Irish soldiers in the English military.) As the potato famine brought in millions of immigrants from Ireland, the parade became more and more popular among Irish Americans, as a show of devotion to Ireland. It has never been a very religious holiday in the United States.

St. Patrick's Day parades today take place in at least one hundred U.S. cities. Some of the biggest parades are in Chicago, Illinois; Boston, Massachusetts; New York City, New York; and Savannah, Georgia. Ireland did not have parades until very recently. There, St. Patrick's Day is a holy day in which Irish families attend church in the morning and celebrate in the afternoon with music and a meal, perhaps Irish bacon and cabbage. In 1995, however, St. Patrick's Day parades were organized in an attempt to draw tourists to Ireland. Dublin now hosts a very large parade.

is any Irishness to it at all. From some corny Bing Crosby (1904–1977) movies to "Danny Boy," green beer, phony Irish pubs in shopping malls, and greeting cards featuring leprechauns (elves of Irish mythology), the American culture has departed from its roots in Ireland, sometimes past the point of recognition. But in the 1980s and 1990s, a new wave of Irish immigrants entered the United States, bringing with them a taste of the vibrant cultural scene taking place in Ireland, called the "New Irish." Interest in the genuine Irish culture revived within the nation. Since travel to and from Ire-

land has become quick and more affordable, people interested in traditional Irish arts can study them at the source. In the United States, Irish rock bands, movies, and artists have been very popular in the 1990s and twenty-first century. In San Francisco there is now a large annual Celtic Arts Festival.

Traditional Irish music has come into favor in the last few decades. Immigrants to the United States brought with them a variety of forms of traditional music that originated in western Ireland. The musical instruments of traditional Irish music were fiddles, pipes, wooden flutes, whistles, accordions, banjoes, guitars, pianos, drums, and even bones. Along with slower songs and marches, the music included jigs, polkas, reels, flings, and waltzes. For many years, the immigrants gathered in the nation's cities and played together, mixing the variations of the music into new and innovative forms, which then blended with the wide variety of other American music forms. Over the years, Americans lost interest in traditional Irish music, and it has only been since the

The St. Patrick's Day Parade making its way past St. Patrick's Cathedral in New York on March 17, 2001. *Reproduced by permission of AP/Wide World Photos.*

1960s that it is being seriously studied and played here again, with a great deal of exchange between Ireland and the United States. *Riverdance,* the traditional and innovative Irish dancing revue that swept Europe in 1993, came to the United States in 1996, where it has been a huge, money-making smash. Two of its principal dancers and innovators were Irish Americans. Many Irish musicians have been very popular in the United States: the Chieftains, the Pogues, U-2, Sinead O'Connor (1966–), Enya (Eithne Ni Bhraonain, 1961–), the Cranberries, and the Black '47, to name a few.

Movies and literature about Irish people and Ireland have also changed from the idealized or stereotyped images of the past. Among popular films about the Irish conflict with Britain have been *Michael Collins* (1996), *The Crying Game* (1992), and *In the Name of the Father* (1994). Films about Irish life and family include *My Left Foot* (1989) and *The Secret of Roan Innish* (1995). A film about nineteenth-century Irish American gangs in the Five Points area and the Bowery in New York is *Gangs of New York* (2002). A film about immigrating to the United States in the twenty-first century is *In America* (2002).

For More Information

Books

Daniels, Roger. *Coming to America: A History of Immigration and Ethnicity in American Life.* New York: HarperCollins, 1990.

Dezell, Maureen. *Irish America: Coming into Clover.* New York: Doubleday, 2000.

The Irish in America. Edited by Michael Coffey, with text by Terry Golway. New York: Hyperion, 1997.

Shannon, William. *The American Irish.* Amherst, MA: University of Massachusetts Press, 1990.

Web Sites

Concannon, Ken. "Dagger John and the Gangs of New York." *Arlington Catholic Herald,* March 20, 2003. http://www.catholicherald.com/articles/03articles/dagger-john.htm (accessed on February 26, 2004).

Fanning, Charles. "Finley Peter Dunne." In *Heath Anthology of American Literature.* 4th ed. Edited by Paul Lauter. Boston: Houghton Mifflin. http://college.hmco.com/english/lauter/heath/4e/students/

author_pages/late_nineteenth/dunne_fi.html (accessed on February 26, 2004).

"Immigration, Irish." *Library of Congress: American Memory.* http://memory. loc.gov/ammem/ndlpedu/features/immig/irish.html (accessed on February 26, 2004).

Kenrick, John. "History of the Musical Stage, 1879–1890: The First Musical Comedies." *Musicals 101.com.* http://www.musicals101.com/ 1879to99.htm (accessed on February 26, 2004).

Scandinavian Immigration

11

Scandinavia is a region in northern Europe composed of the countries Sweden, Norway, and Denmark. Finland and Iceland are often included as part of the region as well, and immigration from these five countries will be discussed in this chapter. The Scandinavian Peninsula, on which Norway and Sweden are located, lies north of the Baltic Sea. Denmark is situated on the Jutland Peninsula, which is bordered on the south by Germany and by a group of islands in the Baltic Sea lying across a narrow strait from Sweden. To the west of Sweden and south of Norway lies Finland, which shares its eastern border with Russia. Iceland is an island nearly 600 miles west of Norway between the North Atlantic and the Arctic oceans. The northernmost portions of Norway, Sweden, and Finland are in the Arctic Circle. The Arctic Circle is a parallel of latitude at 66.5° north of the equator that marks the northern frigid zone.

In the 2000 U.S. Census, 10.5 million people claimed descent from one of the Scandinavian countries: approximately 4.5 million from Norway, 4 million from Sweden, 1.4 million from Denmark, 623,573 from Finland, and 42,716 from Iceland. Most of the emigration (leaving one's country to go to another country with the intention of living there) from the Scandinavian countries took place during the eighty-year period from 1840 to 1920. During that period of time, one-third of the total population of Scandinavia immigrated to the United States. In 2000 the number of people of Norwegian descent in the United States was greater than the total population of Norway.

The people of Sweden, Norway, and Denmark descended from the Nordic peoples who have lived in the region for at least ten thousand years. Each of these three countries has its own language, but the languages of the Danes and the Norwegians are similar enough that they can communicate with each other while speaking in their own languages. The ancestors of the Finns arrived in their country around the year 1 C.E. from the Ural Mountain region in Russia. They speak a language that is very different from the Scandinavian languages. In fact, their language is similar only to that of Estonia. Iceland was settled by the Norwegians in about 900 C.E. The official language of Iceland is Icelandic, which stems from the language of the Vikings who settled the island in the ninth century.

Historical background

For several centuries beginning about 700 C.E., the Swedes, the Norwegians, and the Danes became seafaring warriors who raided and conquered lands far and wide throughout Europe and into Russia and Asia. The kings of these nations became Christians in about 1000, and the Norwegians converted (changed someone from one set of beliefs to another) the people of Iceland to Christianity. In the thirteenth century the Swedes conquered Finland and converted its people to Christianity as well. In 1397 the Scandinavian countries of Sweden, Norway, and Denmark formed a union (a political unit joined together by agreement). Their agreement actually created a union of five countries, since Finland remained under the rule of the Swedish, and Iceland was ruled by Norway. The five countries remained united until Sweden broke away in 1523. Norway and Denmark remained united until 1814, when Sweden conquered Norway. Norway was then ruled by Sweden until 1905. Finland became a part of the Russian empire in 1809, achieving its independence in 1917 during the Russian

Fact Focus

- In 1638 Sweden attempted to establish a colony called New Sweden in the area around the Delaware Bay (present-day New Jersey, Maryland, Delaware, and Pennsylvania). About one-third to one-half of the settlers in New Sweden were Finns.

- In 1825 a group of fifty-two Norwegian religious dissenters pooled their resources to immigrate to America. By the years 1834 and 1835, the group had migrated west to Illinois. There they established the Fox River settlement, which became the base camp for future Norwegian immigrants to the United States.

- The first large wave of Scandinavian immigration in the 1850s most often consisted of middle-class people moving to the Midwest to establish farms.

- In the mid-1840s the Church of the Latter-Day Saints, or the Mormons, sent three missionaries to Scandinavia. The missionaries were particularly successful in Denmark because the laws were lenient toward their work. About twenty thousand Danes were converted by Mormon missionaries and immigrated to the United States during the second half of the nineteenth century.

- Unlike the Swedes, Norwegians, and Finns, the Danes did not establish many tightly knit Old World communities in the United States. Because fewer Danish women emigrated than Danish men, the young male immigrants often married women from other ancestries and after a few generations lost touch with their national roots.

- The World War I era (1914–18) was a hard time in the United States for new immigrants, and Scandinavian Americans became targets of an anti-immigrant trend. During the excessive patriotic hysteria of these years, many Scandinavian Americans chose to hide their ethnicity and become as "American" as possible.

- In 1980 almost 30 percent of Swedish Americans claimed pure Swedish ancestry, which is a very high percentage. Most Swedish Americans lived in relative isolation in Swedish American farming communities or urban enclaves (distinct cultural or nationality units within a foreign city or region). Because of their isolation, and the low rate of ethnic intermarriage, Swedish Americans retained their ethnic language longer than many other American immigrant groups.

Revolution. Iceland had remained in the union with Denmark but became a separate country within the union in 1918. It became an independent nation in 1944. All the Scandinavian

Words to Know

Arctic Circle: A line of latitude at 66° 33′ North that marks the northernmost point at which the sun is visible on the northern winter solstice and the southernmost point at which the midnight sun can be seen on the northern summer solstice. In the Arctic regions, the winters are continuously dark and the summers are continuously light.

Assimilation: The way that someone who comes from a foreign land or culture becomes absorbed into American culture and learns to blend into the ways of its predominant, or main, society.

Chain migration: A pattern of immigration in which an individual (or group of individuals) immigrates to a new country. Once the first immigrant is settled and communicates to people back home about the new country, he or she is followed by family members and friends, who settle nearby in the new community. They are then followed by their family and friends, and soon there is a small community from a particular village or neighborhood in the homeland within the new community.

Colony: A group of people living as a political community in a land away from their home country but ruled by the home country.

Conservative: Resisting change; staying with traditional values.

Discrimination: Unfair treatment based on racism or other prejudices.

Emigration: Leaving one's country to go to another country with the intention of living there. "Emigrant" is used to describe *departing from* one's country—for example, "she emigrated from Ireland." "Immigrant" is used to describe *coming to* a new country—for example, "she immigrated to the United States."

Enclave: A distinct cultural or nationality unit within a foreign city or region.

Ethnic: Relating to a group of people who are not from the majority culture in the country in which they live, and who keep their own culture, language, and institutions.

Exiles: People who have been sent away from their homeland.

Great Depression (1929–41): A period of economic hard times worldwide that began with the stock market crash of 1929 and continued through the 1930s.

Immigration: To travel to a country of which one is not a native with the intention of settling there as a permanent resident. "Immigrant" is used to describe *coming to* a new country—for example, "she immigrated to the United States." "Emigrant" is used to describe *departing from* one's country—for example, "she emigrated from Ireland."

Indentured servants: Servants who agreed to work for a colonist for a set period of time in exchange for payment of their passage from Europe to the New World. At the end of the service term (usually seven years), the indentured servant was given goods or a small piece of land to help set up a new life in the colony.

Industrialization: The historic change from a farm-based economy to an economic system based on the manufacturing of goods and the distribution of services on an organized and mass-produced basis.

Intellectuals: People given to creative speculation and rational thought about life rather than accepting traditional values.

Labor unions: Organizations that bring workers together to advance their interests in terms of getting better wages and working conditions.

Mass migration: The movement of thousands—or even millions—of people from one country to another within a relatively short period of time.

Migration: To move from one place to another, not necessarily across national borders.

Multiculturalism: A view of the social world that embraces, or takes into account, the diversity of people and their cultures within the society.

Nativism: A set of beliefs that centers around favoring the interests of people who are native-born to a country (though generally not concerning Native Americans) as opposed to its immigrants.

New World: The Western Hemisphere, including North and South America.

Old World: The regions of the world that were known to Europeans before they discovered the Americas, including all of the Eastern Hemisphere—Europe, Asia, and Africa—except Australia.

Persecution: Abusive and oppressive treatment.

Quaker: A member of the Society of Friends, a radical Protestant sect in England founded by George Fox (1624–1691) in the late 1640s.

Reparations: Payments to the other side for damages and expenses attributed to the war.

Socialist: Believing in a society in which no one owns private property, but rather, the government or public owns all goods and the means of distributing them among the people.

Temperance movement: The drive to stop people from drinking alcohol.

countries have had a central Lutheran (Protestant) Church, established in the sixteenth century.

Early migrations

There was not much emigration from any of the Scandinavian countries until the nineteenth century, with some very notable exceptions. Norway has claim to having been the first European nation to "discover" the New World. Legendary Norwegian explorer Leif Eriksson (c. 971–1015) is said to have set foot on the shores of North America, probably in Newfoundland, Canada, sometime around 1000 C.E. (for more information, see chapter 3 on pre-Columbian migrations.)

In 1639 Danish sea captain Jonas Bronck set out to establish a settlement in the New World. He brought his wife and a group of indentured servants (people who agree to work for a colonist for a set period of time in exchange for payment of their passage from Europe to the New World and at the end of their term are usually given land or goods) from Germany, Denmark, and the Netherlands to a 500-acre parcel of land he had purchased between the present-day Bronx and Harlem Rivers in New York. The area was part of the Dutch New Netherlands colony (a group of people living together as a political community in a land away from their home country but still ruled by the home country), but the Dutch had not attempted to settle there. Bronck established a large farm and built an elegant home, stocked with a collection of about fifty books—an unusual luxury in colonial times. But his time in the New World was short: He was killed in Indian raids in 1643. The Bronck's (or Bronx) River was named after him.

In 1638 Sweden attempted to establish a colony called New Sweden in North America. At that time Sweden was a very powerful European kingdom that included Finland and portions of Norway, Russia, modern Poland, Latvia, Estonia, Lithuania, and Germany. The first Swedish colonial expedition sailed up the Delaware Bay in 1638 and built Fort Christina at the site of present-day Wilmington, Delaware. It was the first permanent European settlement in the Delaware River Valley. Over the next two decades, twelve more expeditions arrived from Sweden with Finnish and Swedish settlers (in fact, about one-third to one-half of the settlers in New Sweden were

A map of Norway, Sweden, Finland, Denmark, and other countries in 1939.
Reproduced by permission of the Gale Group.

Finns). The colonists established farming communities in an area that included parts of present-day Delaware, New Jersey, Pennsylvania, and Maryland. The Swedes might have maintained rule of the colony, but in the 1650s the governor of New Sweden attempted to take over a part of the Dutch New Netherland colony. The Dutch were stronger than the Swedes and responded by taking over all of New Sweden. This ended Swedish rule forever in the New World, but the Swedes and Finns stayed in the colony and maintained a Swedish culture there. Although other Scandinavians joined these early settlers from time to time in the Delaware Valley, there were no large migrations from Scandinavia for nearly two centuries.

Nineteenth-century migrations

During the nineteenth century, the population of the Scandinavian countries began to increase at a very rapid rate. The rise in population happened before the industrial revolution (the historic change from a farm-based economy to an economic system based on the manufacturing of goods on an organized and mass-produced basis) could bring industry and new jobs into the cities. Many rural people took a severe financial hit, with no land to farm and no jobs available. As immigration to the United States began, according to Dorothy and Thomas Hoobler in *The Scandinavian American Family Album,* a case of "American fever" spread through Norway and then the other nations. Beginning about 1840, the first immigrants in North America had settled in and were able to write to family and friends in Scandinavia and describe their new homes. Then newspapers began to report on the wonders of the New World. They reported that the U.S. government was giving away land to farmers who promised to farm the land for several years. The promise of free land drew large groups of immigrants. Recruiters looking for laborers in mines and logging camps drew more.

With the exception of the Danes, most Scandinavian immigrants formed communities in the United States in which they could continue to speak their own language, practice their own customs, and educate their children as they chose. After the first few families from a village or a town in the old country had become established in the United States, more families from the same village would immigrate and settle near them. Many Scandinavian American communities were made up almost entirely of people who had known each other and lived near one another in the old country.

As a general rule, the further north Scandinavian Americans lived in their native country, the further north they tended to live within the United States. Many Scandinavian immigrants were drawn to the United States by the availability of farmland, and they tended to move to the Midwest and, later on, to the Pacific Northwest. Others came for jobs, to work as shipbuilders, miners, and lumbermen.

On farms, Scandinavian women shared almost all aspects of the work, raising animals and tending crops. In many cases, farmers would go off to work at a job in a logging camp or elsewhere during the winter, leaving their wives and children to take care of the farm. Because of their self-sufficiency and ability to work hard, Scandinavian American women were sought after as domestic (housekeeping) servants in U.S. homes. By the turn of the twentieth century, single Scandinavian women were immigrating to the United States and finding work—many as domestic servants, but others in factories and textile mills.

Norwegian immigration

In the early 1800s Norway's population increased by 50 percent. The country had relatively little land that was good for farming. When the population soared, more than half the people owned no land and there were no jobs for them.

The first expedition of Norwegian settlers to immigrate to the United States in the beginning of the nineteenth century consisted of fifty-two religious dissenters, people who chose to practice their religion in a way that the official Lutheran church did not approve. Some were Haugeans, followers of the teachings of peasant preacher Hans Nielsen Hauge. Starting in about 1796, Hauge traveled throughout Norway preaching in the homes of farmers and distributing his intense and homespun devotional literature. Another group that experienced oppression in Norway were the Quakers, members of the Society of Friends, a radical Protestant sect that rejected formal methods of worship because they believed that the Holy Spirit dwells within each person and that a person who yields to the prompting of their own "inner light" will be saved. Because the Lutheran church would not accept the Haugeans and the Quakers, some of these believers chose to emigrate. Norway was fairly isolated from the rest of the world, and not much was known there about the United States. Knowing little about what to expect in the New World, the first group of dissenters seeking to emigrate sent its leader, Cleng Peerson (1782–1865), ahead to see if the United States would be a good place to establish a new colony.

After Peerson had returned with an encouraging report, the group of dissenters pooled their resources to outfit a small sloop (a boat with sails) called the *Restauration* to take them to America in 1825. They came to be known as the "Sloopers." When they arrived in the United States, the Sloopers first settled in New York, near Lake Ontario. The land was difficult to farm there, though, so in 1834 and 1835, they moved west to Illinois, where land was cheaper

The sod roofs of old houses in Roros, Norway, a mining town founded in 1646.
Reproduced by permission of © Richard T. Nowitz/Corbis.

and easier to till. There they began the Fox River settlement, which became the base camp for future Norwegian immigrants to the United States.

A second group of Norwegian immigrants came to America in 1836, settling in Fox River and Chicago. Norwegian immigrants came yearly after that, settling first in Illinois, then spreading north and west to Wisconsin, Minnesota, Iowa, North and South Dakota, and eventually to the Pacific Northwest. A few settled in Texas, and some stayed in New York, near where they first landed, rather than traveling west. Most Norwegians were deeply opposed to slavery, which discouraged them from settling in the South. Some of those Norwegians in Texas did own slaves, but for the most part, Norwegian Americans opposed slavery and fought on the side of the Union Army in the American Civil War (1861–65).

Norwegian immigration to the United States peaked between 1866 and 1914. Over six hundred thousand Norwegians came to America during these years. In contrast to earlier Norwegian immigrants who came to America with the intention of settling permanently, many of the immigrants of the peak years were single young men hoping to earn enough money to return to Norway in better circumstances. As many as 25 percent did return, but the rest stayed. Norwegian immigrants continued to come to the United States after World War I (1914–18; a war in which Germany fought against many other countries, including the United States), but their numbers have declined steadily since that time.

In 2000 about 4.5 million people in the United States claimed Norwegian ancestry, in addition to 425,099 people who simply claimed Scandinavian ancestry. The states with the largest populations of Norwegian Americans are Minnesota, Wisconsin, California, Washington, and North Dakota. North Dakota is by far the most "Norwegian" state in the United States, with Norwegian Americans making up 29 percent of the total state population.

Swedish immigration

Between 1851 and 1929, 1.2 million Swedish immigrants entered the United States. Only Ireland and Norway (and perhaps Iceland) lost a higher percentage of their populations to North America. Several factors in Sweden encouraged emigration. Like Norway, Sweden had experienced a population explosion, mainly in its rural areas. It is estimated that the population of Sweden had more than doubled in the century before the emigration. Industrialization had not yet taken hold, so there were few jobs to be found off the farm, even in the capital city of Stockholm. A series of droughts and floods created a famine during the 1860s, and soaring prices made what little cash people had worth less and less. Political upheavals, a cruel government, religious oppression, a rigid class system, and mandatory military service made life uneasy for some in Sweden. It was illegal to belong to any but the official Lutheran church. Because the Lutheran church in Sweden was very strict and conservative (staying with traditional values), there were often conflicts between the church and political reformers or intellectual groups (people given to creative speculation and different thoughts about life rather than acceptance of traditional values). Many immigrated seeking more freedom, but most were seeking economic opportunity.

In 1846 a Swedish religious dissenter named Eric Janson (1808-1850) brought a group of 148 religious immigrants to the New World, seeking to set up a religious society there. By the time Janson and his followers arrived at the port in New York, troubles had already started among them. Janson claimed to be a prophet (someone who has a special spiritual gift or has obtained knowledge directly from God) and had told the group that they would not get sick on the trip across the Atlantic. He had also said that as soon as they landed in New York they would instantly know the English language. He was wrong on both counts, and several people abandoned the expedition upon landing. Janson's troop set up a colony in Illinois, naming it Bishop Hill. They faced many hardships as they struggled to make shelter before the winter set in. An infectious disease, cholera, caused an epidemic that killed a large portion of the new settlers. More settlers kept arriving, however, and the colony grew in area and population. Bishop Hill was a communal colony—that is, all its people owned the land in common and worked it together. Janson was an extraordinarily rigid ruler who believed that anyone who contradicted him was led by the devil. He was murdered in 1850. After his death, Bishop Hill continued to function as a communal society until 1861, when it collapsed because of financial problems. Some of Bishop Hill's residents stayed, working their own farms there, and others moved on. Most Jansonists later became Methodists, a Protestant denomination characterized by a concern for high moral standards and social justice. The town continued to serve as an important gateway for other Swedish immigrants moving into the Midwest.

The first big wave of Swedish immigration to the United States began in the 1850s. It was largely middle class and consisted of entire farming families. They settled in the Midwest, where the terrain (land) was much like what they had known in Sweden. At that time, the United States was expanding westward and promoted settlement by offering acreage at low prices. The Homestead Act of 1862, which offered free land to those willing to farm it for a certain number of years, drew huge numbers of Swedes to the United

States. The descendants of some of the original Swedish American homesteaders continue to work those farms today.

A second major wave of Swedish immigrants from the late 1870s to early 1890s included many more urban Swedes who settled in cities and industrial areas of New York and New England. Others joined earlier immigrants in Chicago. Swedish farmers continued to immigrate as well and began spreading westward, all the way to California. A number of Swedish Mormons, who had been converted in Sweden by Mormon missionaries, settled in Utah, the center of the Mormon community. The Mormons, members of the Church of the Latter-day Saints, had been founded by Joseph Smith Jr. (1805–1844) in the 1830s. Smith had experienced revelations from God, which he transcribed (wrote down what was said to him) into the *Book of Mormon* and then set out with his followers to found "Zion," a place where true believers would all gather one day. After being evicted from Ohio and Missouri, the Mormons settled in Utah in 1847.

The last major wave of Swedish immigration to the United States began in the early 1900s and lasted until 1929. With the onset of the stock market crash of 1929 and the Great Depression (1929–41; a period of economic hard times worldwide) that followed, economic opportunities were no better in the United States than in Sweden. Many of Sweden's repressive government measures had been lifted by this time. There was no longer any compelling reason to leave Sweden, and emigration virtually ceased. Since 1930, only a very small number of Swedes have immigrated to the United States.

In 2000 the U.S. Census reported 4.3 million Americans who claimed Swedish ancestry. There were also about a half million who simply claimed Scandinavian ancestry. The states with the largest Swedish American populations were Minnesota, California, Illinois, Washington, and Michigan.

Danish immigration

In Denmark there was relatively little religious or political repression compared with Sweden and Norway. One of the motivations for Danish emigration in the nineteenth century was the prodding of the Church of the Latter-day

Mormon family assembled in front of a log cabin, spinning wheel to the left, in Utah, in 1875. *Reproduced by permission of © Bettmann/Corbis.*

Saints, or the Mormons. When the Mormons sent missionaries to Europe in the mid-1840s and 1850s, they sent three to Scandinavia. The missionaries had an easier time in Denmark than in other countries because its government had a relaxed attitude about their work. Their recruitment was highly successful: The Mormons drew about twenty thousand Danish converts to their center in Utah in the second half of the nineteenth century. The church had an emigration fund, which paid for the passage of many Danes who would not otherwise have been able to go.

Even before the Danish Mormon converts immigrated to the United States, about two thousand Danes had arrived between 1820 and 1850. The Danish immigrants were composed mainly of middle-class families who could pay their way to the United States. But like Sweden and Norway, by 1859 Denmark was experiencing the economic strain of sudden overpopulation. Tales of fertile lands and plenty of job opportunities in the United States brought hope to many in the old country. Three hundred thousand Danes had emigrated by 1920. In the year 1900, one-tenth of Denmark's total population immigrated to the United States. Most of these immigrants were young and male and came from the lower economic classes.

The 2000 United States Census lists 1,430,897 persons of Danish ancestry. The states with the largest Danish American communities include California, Utah, Minnesota, Wisconsin, and Washington. Unlike Swedes, Norwegians, and Finns, the Danes did not establish many tightly knit Old World communities in the United States. Because fewer Danish women emigrated than Danish men, the young male immigrants often married women from other ancestries and were quickly assimilated into (blended into) the American culture. While Swedes and Norwegians maintained strong cultural communities in areas where their populations were concentrated, Danes tended to scatter around the nation.

Finnish immigration

Mass migrations from Finland to the United States took place a little later than those of the other Scandinavian countries, in the early years of the twentieth century. Small numbers of Finns had been coming over since the colonial days. Finland, which had been ruled by Sweden until 1809 (when Sweden ceded it, or gave it up, to Russia), had been well represented among the Swedes who had settled New Sweden. Some say as many as half the settlers sent to the colony by Sweden were Finnish. After coming under Russian rule, a small population of Finns immigrated to Alaska, which was being managed by the Russian American Fur Company. Some of the Finns who worked there under the Russians married native Aleut women and stayed there even after the United States bought Alaska in 1867.

Before 1850 the majority of Finnish immigrants to the United States were sailors who left their ships and either joined the rush to California in search of gold or found a home in one of the big eastern cities. Then, in the 1860s, mining companies began recruiting among the Finns, particularly those who were living in northern Norway, to come to work in the copper mines in northern Michigan. After the first Finns had made the trip, found work, and reported home about it, more of their countrymen followed, especially when farming conditions deteriorated in Finland in the 1870s. Between 1870 and 1920, about 340,000 Finns immigrated to the United States. They primarily went to Michigan, Minnesota, and New York, and many lived in predominantly Finnish communities where they could preserve their language and customs. The last large migration of about twelve thousand Finns occurred in 1923.

Today, Michigan still has a high percentage of Finnish Americans. They came originally to mine copper in northern Michigan, but they soon spread out throughout the state. In 1990 about 40 percent of the population of the Copper Country in the north was Finnish American. Other Finns were recruited to be lumbermen in Michigan. Many of the miners and lumbermen eventually saved some money and purchased small farms. A significant number of Finns moved south to work in the automobile industry as it grew in Detroit.

In 2000 the U.S. Census reported 623,573 persons of Finnish ancestry. The states with the largest Finnish American populations were Michigan, Minnesota, California, Washington, and Wisconsin.

Icelandic immigration

Iceland experienced a series of disasters in the eighteenth and nineteenth centuries, including disastrous volcanic eruptions, widespread disease, a sheep epidemic, and widespread starvation. At a time when the other Scandinavian countries were experiencing population explosions, Iceland's population was decreasing because many people had not survived the catastrophes. The country was still part of a union with Denmark, but when Icelanders emigrated, most preferred to go to Canada and the United States. About 15,000 came to the United States between 1855 and 1914—a huge proportion of Iceland's total population, which was 78,000 people in 1900. Most Icelanders in the United States settled in North Dakota and Washington, or in New York and Los Angeles.

In 1855 the Mormons established a city at Spanish Fork, Utah, and for the next five years Icelandic Mormons

flowed into the new settlement, making it the first Icelandic settlement in the United States. Many of the city's current population are of Icelandic descent. In 1918 Iceland won its independence from Denmark. Since that time, there has been little immigration to the United States from Iceland.

There were 42,716 persons claiming Icelandic ancestry in the United States in 2000. The states with the largest Icelander populations include Washington, California, Utah, Minnesota, and North Dakota. One Icelander settlement was founded on Washington Island in Lake Michigan in Wisconsin in 1870. Another settlement was then established in North Dakota.

Backlash

Most Scandinavian Americans had little when they entered the country. Like many newly arriving immigrants, they worked very hard as farmers, laborers, miners, lumbermen, domestic servants, factory workers, or craftsmen. Unskilled workers earned a meager living even though their work was exhausting and dangerous and the hours were long. Many Scandinavian Americans, wanting to fight for a better and more fair work life, became actively involved in labor unions (organizations that bring workers together to advance their interests in terms of getting better wages and working conditions). One famous example was labor-union activist Joe (Häglund) Hill (1879–1915). Hill was a Swedish immigrant who wrote popular songs for one of the most radical unions, the Industrial Workers of the World (the IWW, nicknamed the Wobblies), which sought to unite all workers in one union. Some of the big U.S. businesses felt threatened by the radicals and exerted pressure on important politicians and law enforcers to apply pressure to political activists. Hill was convicted of murder and executed in 1915, and many believed he was framed because of his political activities and beliefs. By that time, the American public was lashing out at people it viewed as subversive (intending to overthrow the establishment). When the IWW helped Finnish American miners in the iron mines of Minnesota organize a strike, Americans began to associate Finns, and Scandinavian Americans in general, with radical causes.

The World War I (1914–18) era was a hard time in the United States for most people who were viewed as foreign. As the nation was drawn into World War I, a wave of anti-immigrant prejudice swept the country. German Americans took the brunt of it, but even though the Scandinavian countries remained neutral in the war, Scandinavian Americans also became targets. The use of their own languages, for some reason, made them the target of angry native-born Americans. During the excessive displays of patriotism during these years, many Scandinavian Americans chose to hide their ethnicity and become as "American" as possible. Parents spoke only English with their children at home. They Americanized their names: Svenson became Swanson, Nilsson became Nelson, and Bengtson became Benson.

When the war was over, the United States entered into a period known as the first "Red Scare" of 1919 and 1920, when the American people became convinced that communists were secretly conspiring to take over the United

States. Many Scandinavian Americans—particularly those who were actually involved in political activism, but also many who were simply viewed as foreign and therefore suspicious—were made the target of this hysteria. By the time the mania had subsided, some of the culture and language that Scandinavian Americans had hoped to maintain in the United States was lost to them.

Scandinavian American culture

In the early twenty-first century most Scandinavian Americans have assimilated into U.S. culture. Millions of the Swedes, Norwegians, and Finns are several generations removed from the U.S. communities established by their ancestors in which their native language was spoken and their customs practiced. They have married people from other national backgrounds and lost touch with their roots. Millions of other Scandinavians, though, have remained in the areas in which their ancestors settled, especially in parts of Minnesota, Iowa, Illinois, Wisconsin, and North and South Dakota. Although the native languages are generally not spoken today, the foods, holiday traditions, religion, and many other aspects of the culture have been retained and have mixed with other traditions to form unique Scandinavian American traditions. At the same time, the mainstream of American culture today has been firmly imprinted by the Scandinavian influences.

Norwegian American culture

Norway is divided into *bygds,* or districts, each of which has developed its own culture with distinctive clothing, customs, folk songs and dances, stories, and language dialect. Immigrants to America tended to settle among others from the same bygd, creating small cultural enclaves. In 1902 Norwegian Americans who wanted to maintain their ethnic identity began to form bygdelags, or district societies. Within twenty years, fifty bygdelags had been established, with a total of more than seventy-five thousand people involved. Many urbanized Norwegian Americans chose not to participate in the societies, believing Norwegian Americans would be more successful in their home if they blended into mainstream society. There was some tension over this issue within the Norwegian American community.

Most Norwegian Americans were rural in the early days of immigration. They came from peasant farming families in Norway and clung to what they knew, recreating their old environment in their new home. Most Norwegian Americans have continued to resist urbanization (becoming citified, or part of the city), right up through the present. Many of the old family farms are still run by descendants of the original settlers.

Because Norwegian and English are both in the Germanic family of languages, Norwegian immigrants to the United States found English relatively easy to learn. Early immigrants added many English words into their spoken language so that later immigrants, even those who spoke the same original dialect, often could not understand them. Because Norwegian Americans tended to live in isolated farming communities surrounded by other Norwegian speakers, they retained their native ethnic language longer than many other U.S. immigrants. Even third-generation Norwegian Americans were often fluent in Norwegian. In recent years, however, only a very few elderly folks in the Norwegian American communities still speak in the Norwegian tongue.

The Norwegian Lutheran Church in America was formed in 1917 when the three major Norwegian American churches—the Norwegian Synod, the Haugean Synod, and the United Norwegian Lutheran Church (NLCA)—merged. Many Norwegian Americans were outraged when the NLCA decided to hold its services in English rather than in Norwegian, but the new, merged church recognized that later generations of Norwegian Americans had become more American and chose to minister to their needs. In 1946 the NLCA further enraged conservative Norwegian Americans by dropping "Norwegian" from the church name, becoming the Lutheran Church in America (LCA). The LCA absorbed German and Danish Lutherans in 1960 and recently united with the American Lutheran Church to become the Evangelical Lutheran Church in America (ELCA). Two Norwegian-speaking congregations still exist in the early twenty-first century, both named "Minnekirken" (meaning "Memorial Church"), in Chicago and Minneapolis.

The Norwegian Lutheran Church tended to be fairly conservative. Many Norwegian Americans supported the temperance movement (the drive to stop people from drinking alcohol). U.S. Congressman Andrew Volstead (1860–1947), the son of Norwegian immigrants, introduced the Prohibition Act, also known as the Volstead Act, to Congress in 1919. The act prohibited the manufacture, transportation, and sale of intoxicating beverages.

The first Norwegian American writer to become well known in the United States was Ole E. Rölvaag (1876–1931), who had been a fisherman in Norway before immigrating in 1896. Rölvaag worked as a farmhand in the United States before entering college. He received a graduate degree from St. Olaf College in Minnesota, where he became a professor of Norwegian. Rölvaag wrote several novels dealing with Norwegian settlers in South Dakota. His novels took a very grim view of the immigration process, but they were highly acclaimed and widely read. The book *Giants in the Earth* (1927) was selected by the Book of the Month Club and sold almost 80,000 copies by the end of its first year in print. A critic for the *Nation* called the book "the fullest, finest and most powerful novel that has been written about pioneer life in America." Rölvaag dedicated the book "To Those of My People Who Took Part in the Great Settling, To Them and Their Generation."

Norwegian Americans have made significant contributions to the music world. Early Norwegian Americans founded many choral societies, some of which still exist today. The St. Olaf College Choir of Northfield, Minnesota, has achieved international renown since its beginnings in the early 1900s. Founding director F. Melius Christiansen (1871–1955) wanted to develop a cappella singing (singing without accompaniment by musical instruments). Christiansen created the first chorus of its kind in the United States. Norwegian folk dances are still performed by Norwegian American dance groups around the country.

Skiing was relatively unknown in the United States in the 1800s. When Norwegians immigrated, they brought with them their love of skiing, both as a sport and as a mode of transportation during the long, snowy winters. Cross-country skiing and ski-jumping were Norwegian American specialties. Telemarking (named after a district of Norway), involving a particular way of turning, later became popular.

Swedish American culture

For many years Swedish Americans rarely intermarried with people of other ethnic backgrounds. In 1980 almost 30 percent of Swedish Americans claimed pure Swedish ancestry, which is a very high percentage considering how few new immigrants had arrived since 1930. Because of their relative isolation in Swedish American farming communities or city enclaves, and the low rate of ethnic intermarriage, Swedish Americans retained their ethnic language longer than many other American immigrant groups. However, in 1925 the Augustana Synod, the largest Lutheran denomination among Swedish Americans, began conducting its church services in English. Although this angered conservative Swedish Americans, by 1935 all Swedish American Lutheran church services were in English. Americanization eventually took its toll: fluency in Swedish was largely lost in the United States.

The Swedish Lutheran Church, in Sweden and in the United States as well, was known to be quite conservative, urging people to lead very disciplined and serious lives. Like Norwegian Lutherans, the Swedish Lutherans were active in championing temperance, or self-control. But certainly not all Swedish Americans were church oriented. During the late nineteenth and early twentieth century they tended to split between two camps: one church oriented and usually fairly conservative and the other more politically active and freethinking.

Chicago had a very large Swedish American enclave. In an area of the city known as Andersonville, there were about 150,000 Swedish immigrants by 1900. In Andersonville the Swedish language was spoken, the stores and restaurants were owned and operated by Swedes, and many of the goods sold came from Sweden. In their book *The Scandinavian American Family Album,* Dorothy and Thomas Hoobler quote Swedish American journalist Isador Kjellberg. Kjellberg described Andersonville in 1890: "The liveliest section of the busy Chicago Avenue shows, its entire length, a large mass of exclusively Swedish signs, that Anderson, Petterson, and Lundstrom were here conducting a Swedish general store, a

Swedish bookshop, a Swedish beer saloon.... And wherever one goes one hears Swedish sounds generally, and if one's thoughts are somewhat occupied, one can believe one has been quickly transported back to Sweden."

A famous cycle of novels on Swedish immigration to the United States was written not by an immigrant at all but rather by Swedish author Vilhelm Moberg (1898–1973). As a child growing up in the Swedish province of Smaaland, Moberg was aware that many people were leaving his country for the New World. Before he had even started school, he was eagerly reading the weekly newspaper stories about the New World and the Swedes who had gone there. He became utterly fascinated with the idea of America. Through the years his curiosity grew. He gathered information concerning the Swedish people who had departed for America wherever he could find it—from parish registers, contemporary diaries, brochures, newspaper articles, letters from emigrants in America, and his communications with his own relatives. Ultimately he decided to experience the trip himself. In 1948 Moberg made his first visit to the United States. There he continued his search for the fates of those who came before, piecing together information from diaries and tombstones.

A girl and boy, dressed in traditional Swedish-style outfits, stand together at a festival. *Reproduced by permission of © Raymond Gehman/Corbis.*

The result of Moberg's years of toil was a four-volume work of historical fiction that has come to be known as the *Emigrant* novels (in translation, they are: *The Emigrants* [published in Swedish, 1949; English translation, 1950], *Unto a Good Land* [Swedish, 1952; English, 1953], *The Last Letter Home* [volumes 3 and 4, Swedish, 1956 and 1959; English, 1961]. The cycle chronicles the nineteenth-century immigration of Karl Oskar and Kristina Nilsson to America. The Nilssons settle on a small farm in Minnesota, where Karl Oskar works very hard to survive, but finds the life as a pioneer farmer satisfying and independent. Kristina never stops missing her home. They

The Smorgasbord

All Scandinavian countries have a tradition of the "cold table"—a buffet from which diners may pick and choose the dishes they wish to eat. The Danish and Norwegians call it a *koldt bord* and the Finnish call it *voileipäpöytä*. The Swedish call it smorgasbord.

In Swedish, the word "smorgasbord" means "bread-and-butter table," which sounds simple but is in fact a great feast. The smorgasbord is a buffet that is sometimes served in several courses and sometimes put out all at once. It consists of many small dishes from which you can pick and choose the ones you want.

The first two courses are made up of cold foods: the main one is herring prepared in a variety of ways—pickled, baked, jellied, and stewed—and served with onions, potatoes, or dill. There may also be rye bread and butter, hard-boiled eggs, caviar (eggs from a sturgeon, a cold-water fish), cheeses, pickles, sausages, and cold meats. Next come hot meats, such as Swedish meatballs in lingonberry (also called mountain cranberry) sauce, ham, pickled cabbage, boiled potatoes with dill and onions, beets, salads, and many other dishes. Ginger snaps and other cookies are favorite sweets.

live among fellow Swedish emigrants in Minnesota who experience different levels of success and despair, the results—shown in individual human lives—of the mass migration from Sweden in the late nineteenth century. The novels were very popular in the United States and in Sweden. In fact, several members of the Swedish rock band ABBA created a musical called *Kristina from Duvemåla* from Moberg's novels. The musical was performed in Sweden in 1998 and 1999. Moberg, who was a successful journalist, playwright, and novelist in Sweden, came back to the theme of emigration in his later novel *A Time on Earth* (Swedish, 1962; English, 1965), in which an aging Swedish American man lives out the later years of his life in a California hotel room, lonely and unfulfilled. A play based on this novel was very popular in Sweden.

Danish American culture

Denmark's official national church was the Evangelical Lutheran Church, usually known as the Danish National Church. In 1849 Denmark created a constitutional, democratic government that advocated freedom of religion. But even after the new constitution, Danish Baptists and Mormons wanted the freedom of religion they believed America would provide. A significant number of Danes who immigrated to the United States did not belong to a church.

Even among Danish Lutheran immigrants there were divisions. One group of Danish Lutherans known as the Grundtvig faction called for Danish communities and schools to preserve the Danish language and culture in the United States. Opposing the Grundtvigs were the Inner Mission, another Lutheran group that advocated assimilating (blending) into the American culture quickly in order to be able to compete and succeed in the New World.

Danish immigrants brought several innovations in science to U.S. farming. One Danish immigrant brought an egg incubator with him when he established a farm in California. (An egg incubator is an apparatus that allows for hatching eggs artificially.) Another Danish immigrant started the use of a milk separator, which separated the cream from the milk, in Iowa in 1882.

A Danish American changed the American perception of the role of photography. Jacob Riis (1849–1914) became a celebrated journalist and a reformer of the terrible urban slum conditions to which many immigrants were subjected. Riis was born and grew up in Denmark, the son of a teacher. When he was thirteen years old, he discovered in his native town a tenement house (an apartment building that is below normal standards and is usually found in a city neighborhood) that had been built over a sewer and was infested with rats. Horrified by the terrible conditions the inhabitants of the building had to live with, the boy began his own program of killing the rats and washing the building to bring some cleanliness and decency to the homes of the poor.

Riis immigrated to the United States in 1870. He eventually found work at the *New York Tribune,* where he was assigned to the police beat. The building in which he worked was surrounded by tenements, and Riis translated the miserable scenes he witnessed there into human-interest stories. He chose to make it his life's work to clean up New York's slums and help the people in them; from then on he worked at this mission tirelessly. In newspaper and magazine articles, lectures, and books, he described and photographed the life of the poor, especially the children. His illustrated articles brought unceasing publicity to the plight of the poor on the Lower East Side of New York and crusaded for school playgrounds, better working conditions, and restrictions on the sale of liquor. Frequently it was the pictures of human misery that did the job, where words had not been effective. His illustrated book *How the Other Half Lives* (1890) caused a tremendous public outcry and motivated people to action. In a culture that was still oriented to the printed word, Riis showed in this book the power of the documentary photograph in shaping public opinion. The book also brought Riis to the attention of up-and-coming reform politician (and future U.S. president) Theodore Roosevelt (1858–1919). Riis became Roosevelt's good friend and later his biographer.

Finnish American culture

The Finnish language has no relation to the English language, and many Finnish immigrants did not know English when they arrived in the United States. Because the two languages were so different, it often took longer for Finns to become comfortable with English than for people from Norway or Denmark, whose languages had Germanic roots, like English. Thus many Finns settled into communities with other Finns. Within these communities, they spoke Finnish and maintained a strongly Finnish culture. Over time, a new language called "fingliska," part Finnish and part English, developed within the Finnish American communities. Two important centers of many of the Finnish communities were the Lutheran church and Finnish societies.

Like most immigrant groups, Finnish Americans gradually stopped speaking Finnish, but there are places in the United States where the Finnish language and traditions are being revived. For example, in a high school in Hancock, Michigan, in the heart of Copper Country in Michigan's Upper Peninsula of Michigan, the curriculum includes courses in the Finnish language and culture. All students are taught about the experiences of Finnish immigrants. Hancock was settled by Finns and continues to have a very large population of Finnish ancestry. The town is the site of Suomi University, which was founded in

1896 by Finnish immigrants. A Hancock city government committee was established in the 1980s to preserve and increase the Finnish presence within the city landscape.

The Lutheran Suomi (Finland) Synod was founded in 1890 as the Finnish American church. It maintained strong ties to the Finnish Lutheran Church. In 1962 the Suomi Synod merged into the Lutheran Church in America (LCA), signaling the Americanization of the church and of Finnish Americans. While many Finnish immigrants were deeply religious Lutherans, others arrived with a more political perspective and they did not necessarily belong to a church. Those with a more conservative, religious orientation were often at odds with those with a more leftist (advocating political reform and change) and labor-oriented focus. Finns interested in the politics of reform and the labor movement often met in "halls." In Brooklyn's "Finn Town," for example, there were a variety of Finnish activities ongoing at Imatra Hall.

Finland has a distinctive tradition in architecture. During the early part of the twentieth century Finnish architecture profoundly influenced American buildings. Two immigrants from Finland who had a tremendous impact on architecture in the United States and worldwide were Eliel Saarinen (1873–1950) and his son Eero Saarinen (1910–1961). Eliel Saarinen first received international attention when he and his partners designed the Finnish pavilion for the Paris Exposition of 1900. Drawing upon the theories and designs of several architectural movements, Saarinen and his partners used the forms of Finnish medieval castles, stone churches, and log structures. Their style has come to be called Finnish National Romanticism. In the pavilion, the form recalled Finnish medieval churches while the interior of the central hall was dominated by frescoes (paintings on plaster) illustrating the mythical events portrayed in Finland's national epic, the *Kalevala.* (The *Kalevala,* an ancient Finnish oral [spoken] tradition, was transcribed in the Finnish language and published in the nineteenth century.) The pavilion reflects the desire in Finland for an independent national identity, after centuries of Swedish rule, but it also incorporates great architectural movements from around the world.

In 1922 Eliel Saarinen won the second prize in the Chicago Tribune Tower competition, and that year he moved to the United States. He taught for a short while at the University of Michigan and then built the Cranbrook Academy of Arts in Bloomfield Hills, Michigan. At Cranbrook, he headed the Department of Architecture and City Planning. Eliel's son Eero won the competition for the Jefferson National Expansion Memorial in St. Louis, Missouri, which was built in the early 1960s. The memorial is a stainless-steel arch in St. Louis. Eero designed the Kresge Auditorium and Chapel at the Massachusetts Institute of Technology, Cambridge. The auditorium was the first major shell construction in the United States. (This auditorium contains a little theater, a concert hall, and rehearsal rooms. It is noted for its graceful white dome: one-eighth of a sphere anchored on hidden abutments at three points. On the three faces between, glass walls arch upward to meet its thin concrete shell.) He also designed the Trans World Airlines terminal at Kennedy Airport, New York, and many other large projects. Though very different, both Saarinens produced designs that were customized to express something about the culture. Eliel's graduate program at Cranbrook has a continuing impact on the architecture of the United States.

In the early part of the twentieth century, Finnish entertainment troupes (companies) were very popular in Finnish American communities, performing plays and music that provided much-needed recreation and entertainment. One of the most renowned performers of the 1920s and 1930s was the Finnish American accordionist Viola Turpeinen (1909–1958). She began her career playing for dances and local celebrations with a male violinist, but by the end of the 1920s she and another female accordionist Sylvia Pölsö toured the Midwest, drawing eager audiences.

The United States has received many cultural contributions from the Finns. One favorite is the sauna, a steam bath, often created by throwing water on hot stones, an invention that is more than a thousand years old in Finland. In areas where Finnish Americans congregate in the United States, eating customs have been inspired by Finnish cookery, including the "cold table," or voileipäpöytä, a buffet of fish, meat, cheeses, and fresh vegetables eaten with bread and butter. Hot dishes include *kalakukko,* a pie made with small fish and pork; Karelian rye pastries stuffed with potatoes or rice; and reindeer stew. A popular delicacy is *viili,* similar to yogurt.

Icelandic American culture

In 1885, the Icelandic Lutheran Synod was established. Icelanders also joined other Protestant churches, such as the Unitarian Church and the Mormons.

Icelanders in the United States usually try to preserve their native identity. Many Icelanders have a strong sense of the Icelandic heritage and look upon the Vikings as pioneering heroes who originally settled Iceland and became the first Europeans in America. This aspect of American history has long been ignored and is only slowly entering into the U.S. school curriculum.

Vilhjalmur Stefansson (1879–1962), the son of Icelandic immigrants, was an influential and highly acclaimed Arctic explorer. Among his many accomplishments, he was the last explorer to discover new lands in the Arctic. He ad-

Many states have an annual Norwegian parade on May 17th, commemorating the signing of the Norwegian Constitution in 1814.

Reproduced by permission of the Norwegian Tourist Board.

vanced the study and appreciation of cultures other than one's own, and above all, in his books and works, he educated the world about the Arctic.

Icelanders brought a very simple diet to North America—basically meat and potatoes, since the cold climate of their native land made it difficult to grow most vegetables or fruit. The Icelanders did keep cows for dairy products, and their milk was used to make *skyr*, a smooth, nonfat creamy curd that looks like yogurt but is really a form of cheese. Skyr has been one of Iceland's national foods since the days of the Vikings. It is very popular in Iceland today because it is known as a health food.

Scandinavian American holidays

Many Swedish Americans continue to celebrate the traditional twenty days of Swedish Christmas, beginning on

December 13 with St. Lucia's Day. On Christmas Eve, they serve the traditional foods of lutefisk, dried cod soaked in lye, and rice porridge. Another traditional Swedish food still enjoyed by Swedish Americans is limpa, a type of rye bread.

For a time in the nineteenth and early twentieth centuries, Norwegian Americans celebrated *syttende mai,* or May 17, commemorating the signing of the Norwegian Constitution in 1814. Huge centennial celebrations were held in 1914, but then the anti-immigrant hysteria of the World War I years suppressed ethnic festivities. The multicultural movement that began in the 1960s, however, allowed syttende mai to reemerge for its sesquicentennial in 1964. Today, many Norwegian American communities hold parades and other cultural festivities on May 17 each year. Two of the traditional Norwegian foods served at these feasts and on other special occasions are lutefisk, made from specially prepared cod, and lefse (pronounced LEF-suh), a flatbread usually made from potatoes and rolled out paper-thin with a grooved rolling pin.

For More Information

Books

Hoobler, Dorothy, and Thomas Hoobler. *The Scandinavian American Family Album.* New York and Oxford: Oxford University Press, 1997.

McDonald, Julie. *Definitely Danish.* Iowa City, IA: Penfield Books, 1992.

Melchisedech Olson, Kay. *Norwegian, Swedish, and Danish Immigrants, 1820–1920.* Mankato, MN: Blue Earth Books, an imprint of Capstone Press, 2002.

Web Sites

Spiegel, Taru. "The Finns in America." *Library of Congress: European Reading Room.* http://www.loc.gov/rr/european/FinnsAmer/finchro.html (accessed on February 26, 2004).

Westward Migration: 1783–1912

12

When the American Revolution (1775–83; a war fought between Great Britain and the American colonies in which the colonies won their independence) ended in 1783, Great Britain ceded (formally gave) to the new United States all the territory between the Atlantic Ocean and the Mississippi River except New Orleans and Spanish Florida. In theory, the new country stretched for more than a thousand miles in every direction. However, with the exception of outposts along navigable inland rivers, most Americans lived along a tiny ribbon of settlement along the Atlantic seaboard. In fact, at the time of the revolution, about 95 percent of the total U.S. population resided east of the Appalachian Mountains. Tens of thousands of Indians occupied their ancestral lands within U.S. territory. Many Native American tribes were friendly to newcomers—trading with them and guiding them to new lands. Other tribes, however, were prepared to fight the advances of European Americans onto their lands. The threat of Indian attack as well as the inaccessibility of the western lands presented enough of a threat to keep many people from heading west. Although many fortune seekers, farmers, and adventurers were eager to migrate to the open

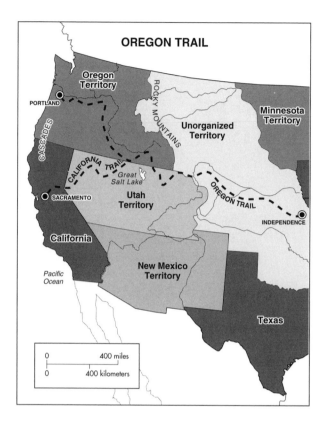

OREGON TRAIL

Oregon Territory

PORTLAND

ROCKY MOUNTAINS

CASCADES

Unorganized Territory

Minnesota Territory

CALIFORNIA TRAIL

Great Salt Lake

OREGON TRAIL

SACRAMENTO

Utah Territory

INDEPENDENCE

California

Pacific Ocean

New Mexico Territory

Texas

| 0 | 400 miles |
| 0 | 400 kilometers |

A map of the western half of the United States, showing the route of the Oregon Trail from Independence, Missouri, to Portland, Oregon.

Reproduced by permission of the Gale Group.

frontier, the expansion that was to come within the next century probably would have been unimaginable to even the most forward-thinking pioneers.

If you compare a map of the United States today with a map of the continent at the end of the eighteenth century, it is clear that most of the continent was not part of the nation in 1783. Spain laid claim to vast areas: It held Florida, as well as Texas, New Mexico, Arizona, and California. Beyond that, France had ceded the huge but vaguely defined Louisiana Territory to Spain in 1762, which extended from the Mississippi River to the Rocky Mountains. Then there was Oregon Territory—a loosely defined but very large region of North America that extended from the southern border of Alaska down to the northern border of California, stretching from the Pacific Ocean eastward to the Rocky Mountains. Oregon Territory included the present-day states of Oregon, Washington, and Idaho as well as parts of Montana and Wyoming. Several countries originally laid claim to parts of the territory, but Spain gave up its claim in 1819 and Russia followed suit in 1825. That left Great Britain and the United States claiming the same land; however, under a treaty signed in 1818, and renewed in 1827, they effectively agreed to share it.

Migrations from the eastern states

At the close of the American Revolution, the original thirteen British colonies were overflowing with people heading for the frontier (the area at the farthest border of a settled territory). At that time families that had been living for generations in the eastern states were running out of land. Many farming families' sons picked up and moved over the mountains into the Old Northwest or the New South. Many who left Virginia and North Carolina headed into central Ken-

Fact Focus

- Between 1805 and 1840, mountain men trapping for beaver opened up the roads that would open the West to U.S. expansion and settlement.

- In 1843, 1,000 people with 120 wagons and huge herds of cattle and oxen met in Missouri to start their journey overland on the Oregon Trail. The following year, more than 1,500 people made the trip, arriving either in Oregon or California. In 1845, 2,760 pioneers set off for Oregon or California. During the years of wagon migration, about 14,000 people traveled overland to the Pacific Coast.

- After gold was discovered in California in 1848, California's population quadrupled, reaching nearly 380,000 by 1860. The state's population continued to grow at a rate twice that of the nation as a whole in the 1860s and 1870s.

- In 1862 Congress subsidized (financially supported) two railroad companies to finish the transcontinental railroad. The Central Pacific Company was to start laying tracks in Sacramento, California, and cross the Sierra Nevada Mountains. The Union Pacific Railroad started its project in Omaha, Nebraska, to meet with Central Pacific somewhere in between. The actual meeting of the two projects in Promontory Point, Utah Territory, on May 10, 1869, marked the achievement of the nation's first transcontinental railroad.

- The Homestead Act of 1862 touched off a mass migration from 1870 to 1900, when 4.3 million acres were settled, mainly in the prairie and High Plains regions of North and South Dakota, Nebraska, Kansas, Oklahoma, Colorado, Wyoming, and Montana. Overall, the amount of farmland under cultivation doubled.

tucky and Tennessee. Other pioneers spilled into what is now Ohio and quickly built homes, farms, and towns there. In the next decade many settlers poured into Mississippi and Alabama in the New South.

Roads to the west were crowded from early spring to late fall with settlers moving westward, singly, by families, or in groups. The typical migrating unit was the family, moving to a new home farther west, with their belongings in a single covered wagon and with perhaps a cow or two. Some well-to-do farmers or plantation owners relocated with all their belongings loaded into a long train of well-equipped wagons. A two-wheeled cart, pulled by a horse or an ox, was the only vehicle of many. Others made the journey on horseback or on foot.

Road-building had been slowly connecting the thirteen colonies and beyond even prior to the American Revolution. The Wilderness Road was established in 1794, creating an easy route through the Cumberland Gap, a pass through the Allegheny Mountains at the junction of the present-day state borders of Kentucky, Tennessee, and Virginia. The new nation began the labor-intensive task of laying roads stretching to every corner it sought to settle. Smaller overland roads, such as the Philadelphia and Lancaster Turnpike Road of 1795 and the 95-mile-long Catskill Turnpike (also called the Susquehanna Turnpike, started in 1801 and completed 1806), which connected New England with the Great Lakes in the Midwest, the United States quickly set the stage for the mass departure to the West.

Thousands of settlers placed their possessions, often including livestock, on flatboats on the upper Ohio River. They floated to their destination along the Ohio River or continued down the Ohio to the Mississippi River. Similarly, the canal boats on the Erie Canal, after its completion in 1825, were often crowded with people migrating to western New York or to Michigan and northern Ohio, Indiana, and Illinois. Pioneers also had the option to travel on the many navigable bodies of water in the United States, such as the Mississippi-Missouri-Ohio river systems and the Great Lakes.

Steamboats later played a large role in transporting settlers upstream to lands along the Mississippi and the Missouri Rivers. In 1807 the first steamboat chugged up the Hudson River from New York City to Albany. Soon, steam-powered rivercraft were carrying people and goods along many of the nation's arteries. In 1812 a steamboat went from Pittsburgh to New Orleans; even more important, in 1815 a steamboat left New Orleans and ascended the Mississippi River to Louisville, Kentucky. The Ohio and Mississippi river systems bore seventy steamboats by the early 1820s and five hundred by 1840. The success of these new steam-powered crafts led to the disappearance of the slower keelboats, but flatboats, another familiar form of river transportation, continued to carry people and goods down river. Thousands of pioneers loaded their possessions, often including livestock, on flat-

Words to Know

Assimilation: The way that someone who comes from a foreign land or culture becomes absorbed into a culture and learns to blend into the ways of its predominant, or main, society.

Colony: A group of people living as a political community in a land away from their home country but ruled by the home country.

Emigration: Leaving one's country to go to another country with the intention of living there. "Emigrant" is used to describe *departing from* one's country—for example, "she emigrated from Ireland."

Exiles: People who have been sent away from their homeland.

Immigration: To travel to a country of which one is not a native with the intention of settling there as a permanent resident. "Immigrant" is used to describe *coming to* a new country—for example, "she immigrated to the United States."

Migration: To move from one place to another, not necessarily across national borders.

Overlanders: People traveling west by land rather than by sea.

Topography: The surface features of a region, such as mountains, plateaus, or basins.

boats on the upper Ohio. They floated down that river highway to their destination in the West or traveled down the Mississippi River.

In the early nineteenth century private interests built small canals in the United States. In 1825 the Erie Canal—connecting the Great Lakes to the Hudson River (and, thus, to New York City)—was finally completed. The Erie Canal carried more than one million tons of cargo in 1845, and for two decades the United States went through a "canal-mania." State governments rushed to connect cities and regions with rivers and lakes, and canals appeared throughout the Northeast and the Midwest.

The movement into the Old Northwest immediately following the Revolutionary War led to the admission of quite a few new states. Between 1790 and 1812, the western states of Kentucky (1792), Tennessee (1796), Ohio (1803), and Louisiana (1812) were admitted to the union. After the

United States defeated Great Britain in the two-year War of 1812, the British agreed not to give any more aid to the Native Americans in the area between the Appalachian Mountains and the Mississippi River. It was a devastating blow to the Indians. Without supplies to help in their fight against the United States, the Indian nations east of the Mississippi River fell entirely under the control of the U.S. government. Western migration increased rapidly. Indiana was admitted to the Union in 1816 and Illinois in 1818. In the New South, Mississippi was admitted in 1817 and Alabama in 1819. Missouri had been part of the Louisiana Territory until 1812, when the Missouri Territory (including present-day Arkansas) was established.

A flood of settlers between 1810 and 1820 more than tripled Missouri's population from 19,783 to 66,586, leading Missourians to petition Congress for statehood in 1818. The nation was, by that time, deeply divided over the slavery issue. People who opposed slavery did not want new states entering the union to allow the institution; people from the southern slave states generally wanted enough slave states in the Union to maintain their share of representation in the federal government. Congress finally approved statehood for Maine and Missouri under the terms of the Missouri Compromise (1820), which sanctioned slavery in the new state but banned it in the rest of the former Louisiana Territory north of Arkansas. Missouri became the twenty-fourth state in 1821. The slavery issue would affect westward expansion until the end of the American Civil War (1861–65; war fought between the Union [North] and the Confederacy [South]).

By 1820 about 20 percent of the U.S. population lived west of the Appalachians. The area where the population had settled formed a vast triangle with its base along the Atlantic Ocean and its tip roughly at the meeting place of the Ohio River and the Missouri River with the Mississippi. Along both sides of the triangle, people were spilling over—north to the upper Great Lakes and south to the Gulf of Mexico. And the overland westward migrations had only begun.

The Louisiana Purchase and the Lewis and Clark expedition

In 1803 France regained possession of the Louisiana Territory from Spain and sold the whole territory to the United States for fifteen million dollars. The purchase more than doubled the size of the United States, adding to it what are now the states of Louisiana, Oklahoma, Arkansas, Missouri, Kansas, Nebraska, Iowa, Minnesota, and North and South Dakota, as well as a large part of Wyoming, most of Colorado, and parts of New Mexico and Texas. A large section of this vast territory had never been explored by any known European Americans.

Even before the Louisiana Purchase, President Thomas Jefferson (1743–1826), an enthusiast for westward expansion, had established a team that he called the Corps of Discovery to explore the continent from the Mississippi River to the West Coast. Jefferson placed his secretary Meriwether Lewis (1774–1809) in charge of this large and well-funded expedition. He particularly wanted the Corps to search for the mythical and long-sought Northwest Passage—a water route through the con-

Mandan Villages

In the westward migration of the nineteenth century, explorers and pioneers were much more frequently helped by American Indians than attacked by them. One of the early frontier havens for fur trappers, explorers, and pioneers was a large settlement, called the Mandan Villages, found along the Missouri River in what is now North Dakota. There were actually three tribes living there: the Mandan, the Minnetaree, and the Amahamis. The Mandan Villages consisted of five settlements, with about forty-four hundred Indians living there—a larger population at that time than St. Louis or Washington, D.C.

The Mandan Villages were centers of trade for many Indian tribes, who traveled from far and wide to trade their wares for the Mandans' farm goods, mainly corn, beans, squash, and tobacco. Every fall traders from other tribes and Europeans arrived in the Mandan Villages to trade. For the mountain men, the Mandan Villages were friendly places to stay as well as to trade. The earth-houses in the villages were comfortable and warm places to take shelter from the frigid Plains winters. The people, too, were friendly and helpful. Without the help of the Native Americans, it would have been difficult or impossible for these early expeditions that opened the West.

tinent that would lead to the Pacific Ocean. Lewis invited his old friend William Clark (1770–1838) to be co-leader and they assembled an expedition party. They never found a water route through the continent—such a route did not exist—but their exploration had a stimulating effect on westward expansion.

The Corps of Discovery began its historic journey on May 14, 1804, moving up the Missouri River in a fifty-five-foot keelboat and two pirogues, or dugout canoes. Averaging about fifteen miles a day, by the end of October the expedition reached the villages of the Mandan, Minnetaree (or Minitari), and Amahamis Indians near the mouth of the Knife River in present-day North Dakota. There the explorers built a log fort and spent the long, frigid winter making many notes in their journals, drawing maps of their route, and taking counsel with Native Americans about the territory to be crossed.

On April 7, 1805, the expedition resumed its journey. By that time they had added an interpreter (someone who

can translate one language to another) named Charbonneau, with his Shoshoni wife Sacajawea (c. 1786–c. 1812) and her baby. Passing through country never before visited by white men, by August 17 the expedition reached the end of the navigable (passable by boat) part of the Missouri River. With Sacajawea's help, Lewis and Clark purchased horses from Indians who lived nearby and made the difficult trip across the Rocky Mountains. From there, the explorers descended the Clearwater, Snake, and Columbia Rivers to arrive at the Pacific Ocean in mid-November.

The expedition spent its second winter on the south side of the Columbia River in Oregon Territory (which included present-day Washington and much of Montana, Idaho, and Wyoming) before heading home. They arrived back in St. Louis on September 23, 1806. The explorers had covered somewhere between six and eight thousand miles in twenty-eight months. The route they had taken would never be useful to the overlanders (people traveling west by land rather than sea), but their trip triggered a century of westward expansion.

Mountain men and fur trading in the West

The Lewis and Clark explorers took very careful and detailed notes about the lands they crossed, reporting back on the climate, animal life, vegetation, topography (the surface features of a region such as mountains, plateaus, or basins), and Indian populations. A large group of hardy adventurers took keen interest in their report that the West was teeming with beavers.

In Europe, the beaver hat was all the fashion for men. Beaver hats were made of slick beaver fur that had been processed into felt. They came in a variety of shapes and sizes, but the broad-brimmed "stovepipe" hats in particular were seen in the most sophisticated social circles. Europe, which had run out of beavers, provided an excellent market for the plentiful American beaver. Hunting for beaver in the almost unexplored American West was nearly impossible and very dangerous. Thus, when the Lewis and Clark expedition was completed, it was the rugged "mountain men" who put to use what the expedition had learned, forging pathways through the western wilderness in search of beaver.

The first mountain men had been members of the Lewis and Clark expedition employed by a Spanish fur trader named Manuel Lisa (1772–1820). By 1808 the Missouri Fur Trade Company was in business and more forts followed. Then John Jacob Astor (1763–1848), already a millionaire from the fur trade in the East, organized the Pacific Fur Company. In 1811 he founded Astoria, the first permanent American settlement in the Pacific Northwest. The venture was not a success and Astor sold it three years later to British interests, but some of the Astor party stayed, becoming Oregon's first permanent white residents. The British, who shared a claim on the Oregon Territory with the United States, established a very successful fur trading post there through the Canadian North West Company. Later, the British Hudson's Bay Company would take over that operation. Although Britain and the United States had agreed to a treaty of joint occupation of Oregon Territory in 1818, the de facto (actual) governor of the territory from 1824 to the early

1840s was Dr. John McLoughlin (1784–1857), the chief of the Hudson's Bay Company at Fort Vancouver in Washington.

St. Louis, Missouri, quickly became a center of the fur trade. In 1822, businessman and frontier entrepreneur William Henry Ashley (1778–1838), the lieutenant governor of Missouri, placed a newspaper advertisement calling for one hundred "Enterprising Young Men … to ascend the river Missouri to its source, there to be employed for one, two, or three years." The men who responded to this ad became known as "mountain men." Probably no more than fifteen hundred men ever held this position. In time, the mountain men split into two groups. Most worked for Ashley and received only a portion of the proceeds of their catch, but in turn received the equipment necessary for the venture. The other group, his "free trappers," received no wages and had no obligation to him, but he guaranteed to meet them in the mountains and buy their furs at fixed prices. As his mountain men moved into the beaver-rich Rocky Mountains, Ashley initiated the *rendezvous* (French for "get-together"). The rendezvous served as a means to collect furs and resupply the trappers. Every summer from 1825 to 1840, a four- to six-week rendezvous was held in a carnival-like atmosphere, combining trade with recreation. Supply trains of mules and wagons came from Missouri, and a year's trading was accomplished efficiently without trading posts. However, many mountain men would spend most of the money they received for their furs while they were drinking and enjoying themselves at this wildly festive event.

Mountain men led a rugged and dangerous existence: Many died from accidents, Indian warfare, or exposure to the elements. The work they did took them far away from most European American settlements. Many of them married Indian women and learned a great deal about Native American life and customs. Generally mountain men were rough and looked it. They wore their hair long, grew beards, and had the weathered features of people who live in very harsh elements. Their clothes were usually made of buckskin. The mountain men did such a good job of trapping that the American beaver had nearly disappeared by 1840. By that time, beaver hats went out of style and the fur trade was finished.

During their years of trapping, the mountain men had become very familiar with paths through the West and knew the trading posts and forts in key locations along the way. When people began to migrate west, the newly unemployed mountain men became their guides, leading the pioneers over roads they had created themselves through the mountains and wilderness. They were instrumental in opening up the West for U.S. migrations.

Spanish territory

In 1700 Spain dominated more territory in North America than any other European power, including England, which controlled only a relatively narrow band of colonies along the Atlantic seaboard. What the Spanish regarded as the northern territory of New Spain included all of what we now call the American Southwest: Texas, New Mexico, Arizona, Utah, Nevada, and parts of Colorado and Wyoming. California was settled by Spain, and Spain had also claimed Oregon Territory. In addition, Spain had possession of Florida, its original foothold in North America. In 1763 Spain added the Louisiana Territory to its North American holdings. Florida and Louisiana were soon ceded, but Spain held claim to a significant portion of the continent.

Then, in 1810, a revolution broke out in Mexico. It was at first suppressed, but other rebellions followed, and in 1821 Mexico won its freedom from Spain. Mexico quickly developed into a federal republic in 1824 with a constitution similar to that of the United States. Mexico took over the control of the northern colonies, but it was difficult for the new nation to govern the northern territories because its capital, Mexico City, was hundreds of miles to the south. California nearly governed itself from 1821 to 1830. In addition, it became increasingly difficult to persuade Mexicans to migrate north and settle the potentially rich lands of Texas.

Texas

Until the nineteenth century, the United States showed little interest in Texas. But the purchase of Louisiana Territory in 1803 made Texas a next-door neighbor. "Filibusters" (military adventurers) began to filter across the U.S. borders to enter Texas, although it was Spanish territory and they were not officially welcome there. Because Texas needed settlers to survive as a colony, the Mexican Republic took a gamble and allowed certain Americans to settle in Texas if they became Catholics and Mexican citizens. The first to take up this offer was Moses Austin (1761–1821), who received a land grant from the Spanish in 1821, just before the Mexican Revolution. He died before he could bring his group of settlers to Texas, but his son, Stephen F. Austin (1793–1836), took over and brought three hundred American families into Texas, establishing a huge colony of which he was the leader.

Thousands of "Anglos" (white, non-Hispanic U.S. citizens) quickly followed Austin to Texas, many illegally. In 1825 Mexico loosened its policies further, granting more land to foreigners; seven thousand of them almost immediately poured into the Mexican province. Most new settlers were Anglos who, unlike the earlier Anglo settlers, tended to remain aloof from the Mexican culture of the region they had moved into. They disliked Mexican culture and government; and the Protestants among them disliked the dominance of the Roman Catholic Church. Quickly seeing that the Anglos wanted more and more control over Texas, in 1830 Mexico forbade any more Americans to immigrate into Texas, but it was too late. In 1835 Texas had about thirty thousand Anglo-Texan settlers, vastly outnumbering the Mexicans and the Native Americans there.

In 1835 a force of Anglo-Texans, attempting to force Mexico to give Texas more freedom, seized the town of San Antonio from the Mexican army. In 1836 the Mexican forces of General Antonio Lopez de Santa Anna (1794–1876) laid siege to the Alamo, a mission in San Antonio where some 188 Anglo-Texans had taken refuge. On March 2, a group of Anglo-Texans drew up their "Texan Declaration of Cause for Taking Up Arms," essentially a declaration of independence. Four days later, Santa Anna's forces attacked the Alamo and killed everyone within. The Anglo-Texans rallied, though, and after a couple of deadly battles, the Mexican general was forced to recognize Texas's independence. Although the Mexican government did not recognize its independence, Texas began to function as an independent nation. In 1845 the United States annexed (took possession of) Texas, claiming the Rio Grande River to be the border between the United States and Mexico. Mexico still considered Texas to be its own territory. Even if Mexico agreed to give up Texas, the nation was angered by the border set by the United States, which encroached on lands it considered to be 150 miles south of Texas.

New Mexico

Meanwhile, Americans were making inroads into New Mexico. In 1821, William Becknell (c. 1797–1865) pioneered the Santa Fe Trail from Independence, Missouri, to the Mexican capital of New Mexico. He was soon followed by a steady stream of Americans anxious to profit from trade with the Mexican territories. The urge to push beyond the borders of the United States seemed almost unstoppable.

Manifest Destiny

In 1845 journalist John O'Sullivan (1813–1895) coined the term "manifest destiny" in an article he wrote for the *United States Magazine and Democratic Review.* Manifest destiny was, in his words, the God-given American right to "overspread the continent allotted by Providence for the free development of our yearly multiplying millions." Many Americans agreed that, despite the Native American tribes who had lived on their ancestral lands for centuries or the Spanish who had gotten there first among Europeans, the United States had a divine mission to open the continent to their (supposedly) superior form of culture and government.

The concept of expanding the country's borders to include such a large amount of territory was by no means shared by all. The Whig political party believed that trying to govern too much territory might, in the long run, destroy the new government. Many believed it was nearly a suicidal venture to try to reach the West overland. Bringing women and children through the rough wilderness was considered savage by many. The lack of civilization at the frontier was also a concern. But there was strong political pressure to push westward. A pro-expansion faction was led by Thomas Hart Benton (1782–1858), a prominent United States senator from 1821 to 1851. Benton, like many other supporters of manifest destiny, had a racist justification for taking the land. "It would seem that the White race alone received the divine command to subdue and replenish the earth, for it is the

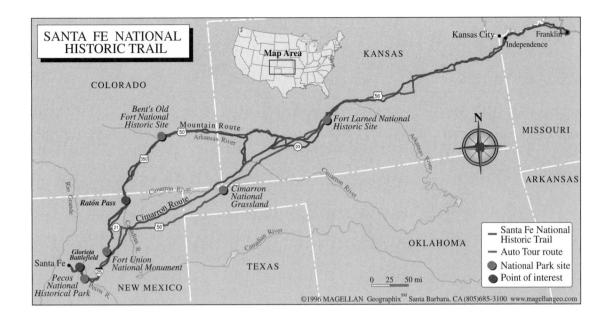

A map showing the Santa Fe National Historic Trail.
Reproduced by permission of © Maps.com/Corbis.

only race that has obeyed it," he wrote in 1846, as quoted by Page Stegner in *Winning the Wild West: The Epic Saga of the American Frontier, 1800–1899*. He went on to say that unless Native Americans could adapt to the civilization brought by the Americans, they faced certain extinction. The subject of expansion of the United States always brought up the issue of slavery, and whether new states would enter the union as slave states or free states.

A publicity campaign began in the 1830s to draw people to migrate out to the West—to Oregon and California in particular. At that time, the two sparsely populated areas were ruled by other nations: Oregon was governed by Britain and California was under Mexican rule. This situation did little to dampen the interest of the American public. Both regions were portrayed by propagandists (people who spread information about something with a particular purpose, rather than the simple truth, in mind) as potential utopias (ideal places). American writer Richard Henry Dana Jr. (1815–1882) wrote glowingly of California in his account of his life at sea, *Two Years Before the Mast* (1840). Dana's descriptions as well as those of many others captured the American imagination. "California fever" and "Oregon fever," rushes to move to these areas, struck. The writings of the early settlers in California painted it as a paradise, with perfect climate and won-

An illustration from "Life on the Oregon Trail," written by Gary Blackwood. The illustration shows pioneer women performing normal, everyday household chores while on the Oregon Trail, such as hanging laundry and cooking. *Courtesy of the Library of Congress.*

derful vegetation. Oregon "boosters" painted the Pacific Northwest as a garden state with a mild climate perfect for farming.

The Oregon Trail

The overland route taken by the Lewis and Clark expedition could never be traveled by wagon and so was useless for migration. The mountain men who came after Lewis and Clark discovered the essential mountain passes that made the Oregon Trail more accessible. But the mountain men traveled on foot and with packhorses. Most people believed that it would be impossible to cross the Rocky Mountains with wagons. The two thousand-mile Oregon Trail started from the Missouri River at Independence, Missouri, crossed the Great Plains, crested the Continental Divide at South Pass, Wyoming, and traversed the semiarid Great Basin to the Columbia River in the Pacific Northwest. People whose destination was California turned south off the Oregon Trail in present-day eastern Idaho to follow the California Trail through the Great Basin and across the Sierra Nevada into California. The importance of the Oregon-California Trail to the westward expansion of the United States cannot be overstated. Without it, most of the western territory was inaccessible by overland route from the United States.

Since the mid-1820s the United States and Great Britain had struggled for possession of Oregon Territory. For the most part the struggle focused on the Columbia River and the region between the Columbia and latitude 49° north, including the great harbor of Puget Sound. In 1827 the two powers reconfirmed their joint occupation of the territory and policy of free entry for American and British subjects into Oregon without damaging the claims of either power.

Among the British, the first overland traveler to arrive in Oregon was Alexander Mackenzie (1764–1820), leader of the North West Company, a fur trading enterprise based in Montreal. Mackenzie reached the Pacific Coast in 1793, the first white man known to have crossed the continent north of Mexico. Other traders, particularly representatives of the British Hudson's Bay Company, followed. In the years 1807 to 1810, the company set up a chain of trading posts on the western slope of the Rocky Mountains. In 1825, the Hudson's Bay Company established its trading post, Fort Vancouver, on the Columbia River (across from present-day Portland, Oregon). Its director was Dr. John McLoughlin (1784–1857), a Quebec-born physician of Scottish descent who would use his great energies and talents to make Fort Vancouver and the Hudson's Bay Company the center of power in this region. Trading posts soon were situated at important points and a fairly well-established route was laid down.

In 1826 Mexican settlers in California were amazed that the mountain man and explorer Jedediah Strong Smith (1799–1831) had made his way across the mountains and into their isolated land. Smith had rediscovered the South Pass, a twenty-mile-wide pass through the Rocky Mountains at the border between the United States and Oregon Territory. The South Pass made it possible for wagon traffic to cross the Rockies. Smith was not welcomed by the Mexican officials, who were concerned that Anglos might try to take over this sparse-

Jedediah Strong Smith, Mountain Man

Jedediah Strong Smith (1799–1831) was twenty-two years old when he went to St. Louis, Missouri. He was hired by William Henry Ashley (1778–1838), the founder of a fur-trading company. Smith went on Ashley's expedition to the West between 1822 and 1823 with the first large group of trappers to venture into that region.

In 1823 Smith led an eleven-man expedition to trap in the central Rockies and Columbia River areas. While crossing the Badlands the party nearly died of thirst. In the Black Hills, Smith was attacked by a wounded grizzly bear that almost crushed his head between its jaws. One of Smith's men sewed up the wounds with a needle and thread and reattached his ear. After that incident Smith always wore his hair long to cover up the scars. Smith's expedition continued on their way across the continent, spending the winter of 1823 to 1824 at a Crow Indian village in what is now Wyoming. They left in late February 1824, crossing the continental divide into the Green River Valley in mid-March. The trail they pioneered through the mountains was named South Pass; it later became the main passageway for Americans moving west.

Smith had sent word back to Ashley about the rich fur country he had found. In early July 1825 Ashley traveled up the Missouri from St. Louis to meet Smith on the Green River. This was the first major rendezvous of fur trappers and traders that was to become an annual event for over twenty years. The following October, Smith and Ashley took their large supply of furs back down the river to St. Louis, where Smith then concluded an agreement with Ashley to become his partner.

In 1826 Smith headed toward the Great Salt Lake, which he had seen in 1824, in order to investigate reports that the lake was linked with the Pacific Ocean by the legendary Buenaventura River. The river did not exist. In his exploring, Smith led a party to the Great Salt Lake and then to Utah Lake. They followed the Virgin River downstream to the Colorado River and then crossed the Mojave Desert by following the course of the Mojave River. The party reached Mission San Gabriel in what is now a suburb of Los Angeles on November 27, 1826, becoming the first Americans to travel overland to California. This major achievement ultimately removed the obstacle to the American settlement of California.

ly populated province for the United States. Despite the Mexican governor's fears, other Americans soon followed Smith.

The first people to travel the Oregon Trail in a covered wagon were Presbyterian missionaries Marcus (1802–1847) and Narcissa (1808–1847) Whitman, who made the trip with three other missionaries in 1836 and developed a mission among the Cayuse Indians in the Walla Walla River Valley in the southwestern corner of present-day Washington. The Methodist Church sent missionaries to Oregon in 1837 and 1840. Although the missionaries had little success in changing the religious beliefs of the Native Americans, their success in getting to Oregon and living there made a large impact on friends and family back home. In 1841 and 1842 small wagon trains set off from Independence, Missouri, on the Oregon Trail. According to Frank McLynn in his book *Wagons West: The Epic Story of America's Overland Trails,* 34 people made it overland to California in 1841 and 125 made it to Oregon in 1842. Although the British policy was to discourage U.S. migrants from entering Oregon, they were usually very helpful to those who arrived.

As the decade progressed and Americans responded to the westward expansion fever, the Oregon Trail became heavily traveled. In 1843, 1,000 people with 120 wagons and huge herds of cattle and oxen met in Missouri to start their long, difficult journey overland on the Oregon Trail. Of these, 875 people made it to the Pacific Northwest, where they settled in the fertile Willamette Valley. The following year, more than 1,500 people made the trip, arriving either in Oregon or California. In 1845, 2,760 pioneers set off for Oregon or California. In the years before 1849, the majority of the migrants were on their way to Oregon's Willamette Valley. According to McLynn, more than 14,000 people traveled overland to the Pacific Coast. Of that total, only 2,735 went to California, while 11,512 went to Oregon.

In 1845 many Americans believed it was the manifest destiny of the United States to expand from coast to coast. This expansion could not be accomplished without gaining control of California and the Oregon Territory. The United States became eager to annex the Oregon Territory early in the decade and made constant offers to the British to divide the territory. Britain was not interested in what is now the state of Oregon but wanted to keep its interests in Vancouver and its access to the Columbia River in what is now the state of Washington. In 1845, war with Britain over the disputed area seemed likely. However, the main British presence in the Oregon Territory, the Hudson's Bay Company, had lost interest in the area because the beaver population had been depleted. The company moved its headquarters out of the region. With so many Americans already living in the Willamette Valley, the British could not defend it. In 1846 Britain accepted the U.S. proposal to set the border between the United States and British interests in Canada at the forty-ninth parallel. Oregon and Washington had become a part of the United States.

It would not be so easy to win California. Mexico had many reasons for bitterness toward the United States and its pursuit of manifest destiny. In 1846 the Mexican-American War (1846–48) began. In January 1847, the Mexican forces in California surrendered. More than a year later, after a long period of fighting in central Mexico, a treaty of peace was signed at Guadalupe-Hidalgo in February 1848. Under the terms of the Treaty of Hidalgo, Mexico ceded California and other territories to the United States in exchange for fifteen million dollars and the acquisition by the United States of some three million dollars in claims by Mexican citizens.

California Gold Rush

Just nine days before the Treaty of Guadalupe-Hidal-go was signed, gold was discovered in northern California. The news of the gold discovery soon spread around the globe, and a massive rush of people poured into the region. By the end of 1848, about six thousand miners had arrived and obtained ten million dollars' worth of gold. During 1849, about forty thousand to fifty thousand more gold seekers had poured into the foothills of the Sierra Nevada; gold production was two or three times as great but spread among more miners. In 1850 an estimated eighty thousand more miners arrived. In 1852, the peak year of production, about eighty million dollars in gold was mined in the state.

To get to California as quickly as possible to participate in the rush for riches in the mid-1800s, there were just a few routes available from within the United States, and all of them took months. People came overland, on horseback or with a small wagon, often by the Oregon-California Trail. They also came by sea. Coming from the East Coast, they sailed down around Cape Horn at the southernmost part of South America or through the Strait of Magellan in Argentina and then sailed back up along the West Coast. This trip also took about five months and was fairly expensive. There were other ocean routes that brought the traveler part way down the Atlantic shores of South America and then required overland routes across that continent and boarding a ship on the Pacific side. There were many fortune seekers coming in from Europe and South America, and Asia was also represented among the newcomers.

California's population quadrupled during the 1850s, reaching nearly 380,000 by 1860, and it continued to grow at a rate twice that of the nation as a whole in the 1860s and 1870s. The new population of California was remarkably diverse, coming from many different backgrounds. The 1850 census found that nearly a quarter of all Californians were foreign-born, while only a tenth of the national population had been born abroad. In succeeding decades, the percentage of foreign-born Californians increased, rising to just under 40 percent during the 1860s.

An African American gold miner panning for gold in 1852 in California during the gold rush. *Reproduced by permission of Hulton Archive/Getty Images.*

Most of the migrants who rushed to California to pan for gold were young males who had no intention of staying there. In fact, the 1850 census records that 92 percent of California's population was male. They simply wanted to get rich and go home. Many did leave within a year or two. Most were disappointed, broke, and unhappy, having survived the lawless, violent, frontier conditions but not having found the fortune they sought.

One of the most serious problems facing California in the early years of the gold rush was the absence of adequate government. Miners organized more than five hundred "mining districts" to regulate their affairs; in San Francisco and other cities, "vigilance committees" were formed to combat widespread robbery and arson. Violence was rampant during the Gold Rush. In the gold camps where miners stayed, there was drinking and fighting, and many arguments were resolved with guns. Although there were many murders among the European Americans who had arrived in California's gold camps, the Chinese and Native Americans in particular were victimized by the cruelty and lawlessness of the gold miners. Immigrants from China, arriving with gold fever like everyone else, were physically abused, denied basic rights, and prohibited from working. The treatment of California's Native Americans by the gold seekers (called "forty-niners," because they began to arrive in the year 1849) is an appalling segment of American history. Men viciously hunted down Native Americans and shot them as if in sport. Some newspaper writers actually advocated the annihilation (the killing of everyone in a particular group) of California Indians. It is estimated that there were about 150,000 Native people in California in 1848, before the Gold Rush. According to historian James Sandoz, as quoted by Stegner, by 1860 there were only about 30,000 Indians left in California. Some died from infectious diseases, but murder by migrating Europeans killed most of the population.

On the move: life on wagon trains

Before the railroads traversed the continent, some people made the trip out West in a stagecoach. There were numerous independent stagecoach lines, with stops throughout the West. People could book passage and be driven to their destination with other travelers, but this was not as easy as it may sound. The trips were dusty, crowded, long, and very difficult. The cost to customers for the trip was about seven cents a mile and often severe physical discomfort, as the ride could brutally shake passengers. In fact, the most popular slang terms for stagecoaches on the western routes were the "shake guts" and "spankers."

Most pioneers elected to obtain their own wagon. Many set out on their journey to the West with their farm wagon filled with belongings and covered with a canvas tent. Others bought wagons specifically designed for the overland trails. They often joined a wagon train, which was an organized caravan of wagons with a captain to lead the way across the continent.

People starting from points east in the years between 1843 and 1869 generally started their trip on the Missouri

River, which runs from west to east from present-day southern Montana at the far west, through the Dakotas, Nebraska, Iowa, and Kansas. The Missouri River then crosses Missouri, where it meets the Mississippi River. Most migrants boarded their wagon on a steamship somewhere on the eastern part of the river and then got off the ship at a "jumping off point"— usually Independence, St. Joseph, or Westport in Missouri, or Omaha or Council Bluffs in Nebraska. Each spring in these towns, thousands of wagons would gather to await the departure of the wagon train. On an agreed-upon day, the journey would begin, but very slowly. The route would become so congested with wagons that the first several days could be spent simply getting all the wagons on the road.

The wagon trains usually had a hired guide, generally a mountain man who knew the route well. They usually elected leaders and formed a simple government so that decisions could be made throughout the trip. People did not always act in harmony, however. Pioneer diaries reveal that quarreling and hostility were very common among the participants of a wagon train.

Like immigrants from overseas, the migrants pushing west were generally people of middle income: neither the wealthiest nor the poorest of Americans. The wealthy probably did not often go because they were well enough off where they were. The poor simply could not afford to go. The cost of the wagon, supplies, and setting up in the West would be prohibitive. It is said that the very least amount of starting money to make the trip would have been about $500, but $1,000 was more reasonable and many spent much more than that. A wagon, if the pioneer was not using his or her own farm wagon, and a team of oxen or mules might cost between $300 and $600. At the time these were very large amounts of money. In 1850 the average wage for a laborer was about 25 cents per day (this usually included room and board) and for a skilled laborer about 62 cents a day. To spend $1,000 in 1850 would be equivalent to spending more than $22,000 today. Most people leaving for the West sold their farm or their home and just about everything else they owned. Some people who did not have enough money to pay their own way offered to work for pioneer families and received their passage in that way.

Two types of covered wagons dominated in the overland trips of the pioneers in the mid-nineteenth century:

Conestoga wagons and prairie schooners. Conestoga wagons were developed in the eastern United States to haul heavy cargo. At about twenty-three feet long, they were so big it was impossible for animal teams to pull them over the treacherous roads of the Oregon Trail. Prairie schooners were about half the size of Conestoga wagons and were useful on the Oregon Trail, where they could be hauled by a smaller team of animals. They featured a hoop frame to hold the bonnet over the wagon bed. Wagons on the Oregon Trail were almost always pulled by mules or oxen. Horses were not able to travel long enough without grass and water. The wagons needed to hold an immense amount of supplies for the pioneers to survive the trip. The wagons had to be as light as possible so they would not overexert the animals on the rugged trip.

Participants in wagon trains were urged not to carry furniture or anything else they would not need on the trip. Most of the tremendous load in their wagon was in very basic foods. According to McLynn, a family of four would need at least:

- 800 pounds of flour per person
- 400 pounds of bacon per person
- 300 pounds of beans, rice, and dried fruit
- 75 pounds of coffee
- 200 pounds of lard
- 25 pounds of salt and pepper

They would also need simple tools to fix their wagon, shoes, clothes, cooking utensils, pots and pans, and dishes.

Once they were on the road, the pioneers settled as best they could into a daily routine, though they were often beset by challenges (river crossings, bad weather). People slept either in their wagons, though these were often too crowded with supplies, or in tents. They woke early in the morning. Men would herd the cattle that had strayed during the night, break camp, and yoke their teams, while the children gathered buffalo chips (dung, that is, dried manure droppings left by the herds of buffalo on the plains) to burn for fires. Women cooked the breakfast and by 7:00 A.M. everyone was continuing to travel. Many people walked most of the day. The trains plodded on at a walking pace, usually covering fifteen to twenty-five miles on a good day. The person who drove the team was often the only one on the wagon, although in the afternoons sometimes others would nap in the back. The wagon train guide chose the spot for encampment in the evening. The wagons in the train would form a large circle, with the livestock inside the circle, as protection from Indian raids or wandering off. Then tents were pitched outside the circle. Children once again gathered the buffalo chips for the evening fires and women began cooking the evening meal. After dinner, there was talk and even singing and storytelling around the fire, while the women were generally left with the cleanup.

In the division of labor that prevailed, women may have worked the hardest on the trail, according to many historians. When the caravan stopped at mealtime, the women could not just relax; they were expected to prepare and serve a hearty if simple meal. They baked bread daily—even pastries were on most families' menus. All this was done with the difficulties of cooking outside, keeping bugs and dirt out of the food, using a makeshift oven, and dealing with all kinds of weather. Besides cooking and childcare, women were responsible for laundry—a grueling job that required quite a few hours at the riverside. Because no one wanted to hold up the day's travel for laundry, the chore usually had to be done on Sunday, the only day the train did not travel. Thus, while others rested, women were often pounding out the family's filthy clothes on the rocks of a frigid river.

It is said that about one in ten pioneers died while crossing the continent in a wagon train. The greatest dangers were drowning and wagon accidents. Exposed to the weather and each other, there were many outbreaks of infectious disease, especially cholera, an often fatal disease of the intestines. Although much has been written about the dangers posed by Native Americans, in fact, most tribes were very helpful to the emigrants. In many cases the wagon trains relied on Native Americans for survival, either for the goods they could trade or for their help in emergencies.

Railroads

In the 1830s steam railroads began to appear in the nation. Most railroad lines merely joined major waterways as people continued to rely on water transportation. However,

Construction engineers of the transcontinental railroad line celebrating in Utah on May 10, 1869.
Reproduced by permission of AP/Wide World Photos.

investors began to develop new routes, and by 1853 seven routes connected the eastern seaboard with the interior West. Although no railroad connected the East Coast with California until 1869, by 1860 the United States possessed more than thirty thousand miles of rails, most of it east of the Missouri River. In 1862 the U.S. Congress decided to go forward with long-discussed plans for a transcontinental railroad, a railroad that stretched from coast to coast. Two railroad companies were given the job. Central Pacific Company was to start laying tracks in Sacramento, California, and cross the Sierra Nevada Mountains, while the Union Pacific Railroad started its project in Omaha, Nebraska, to meet with Central Pacific somewhere in between. The actual meeting of the two projects in Promontory Point, Utah Territory, on May 10, 1869, marked the achievement of the nation's first transcontinental railroad.

Before the 1870s, cities and towns could arise only on coasts and major waterways. Water provided the only means to deliver the food and goods to be consumed by the population and transport the goods produced there. After 1870, thousands of miles of rail connected even the most remote areas to the rest of the country, and communities sprouted up rapidly all over the nation.

Mail systems

In the nineteenth century, migrating westward meant leaving many aspects of civilization behind, but people still needed to be able to send and receive mail. Some mail was delivered to California by boats that made the trip around South America from the East Coast. Stagecoaches, though independently owned, were often paid by the government to handle the mail on regular schedules. The government even improved the roads that were used for this purpose and sometimes posted troops to guard the mail-bearing coaches. The first government contract with an independent stagecoach was in 1858.

By 1860 a company called the Pony Express had formed to take on mail delivery in the West. For a little over a year, the Pony Express riders delivered mail in an area spanning between St. Joseph, Missouri, and Sacramento, California. The company hired young riders to do the job. Each rider changed horses every ten or fifteen miles at the 190 stations the service established. After about seventy-five miles a new rider took over. Many of the two hundred riders employed by the Pony Express were teenagers, and the company gave them Bibles and made them promise not to drink or swear. The first run of the Pony Express in April 1860 proved successful, reaching California in only ten days. The service operated once a week at first, then twice weekly. In November 1860 the riders carried a telegraph report of the election of Abraham Lincoln (1809–1865) to the presidency from Fort Kearny, Nebraska, to Fort Churchill, Nevada, in six days, their fastest ride yet. But in 1861 the company folded as the first transcontinental telegraph line reached San Francisco. The railroads soon took over the mail delivery.

Homestead Act

During the 1830s and 1840s, the notion of free land for settlers attracted powerful support from labor organizations around the country. People like Horace Greeley

(1811–1872), the editor of the powerful *New York Tribune,* campaigned for the distribution of homestead parcels to anyone who wanted them. For decades, though, a political coalition of Easterners and Southerners managed to block a free land policy. Southerners suspected that antislavery settlers would populate the territories. The conservative Easterners who allied themselves with the slaveholding Southerners on this issue were generally opposed to westward migration.

After years of conflict, in 1862, Abraham Lincoln signed the Homestead Law. Under the provisions of the bill, a settler twenty-one years of age or older who was, or intended to become, a citizen and who acted as the head of a household could acquire a tract of 160 acres of surveyed public land free of all but minor registration payments. Title to that land went to the settler after five years of continuous residence. The act immediately drew people from all over the world to the interior of the United States.

Cowboy culture

From the first wagon trains in the early 1840s to the rise of the transcontinental railroad in 1869 about five hundred thousand people migrated West. After the rush to California of the early 1850s, people began to settle in other points along the westward trail. One of these places was the Great Plains. The Great Plains is a flat and treeless area that lies east of the Rocky Mountains from Canada down to Texas and includes present-day North and South Dakota, Nebraska, and parts of Oklahoma, Texas, and Kansas. In the early 1800s, explorer Zebulon Pike (1779–1813) informed the American public that the Plains were uninhabitable for humans. This would have been news to the Sioux, Apache, Comanche, Arapaho, Kiowa, Cheyenne, and many other Indian tribes living there at that time. For many years settlers tended to look for other destinations. But in time, pioneers traveling through the Plains via the Oregon Trail in the north or the Santa Fe Trail (a trail extending from Missouri to Santa Fe, New Mexico) in the south took interest in the vast region, particularly when they saw the vast herds of buffalo grazing there.

Cattle raising had become a prosperous business in Texas, where untended longhorn cattle had multiplied by the millions and ranged freely. Because there were so many cattle

A cowboy with lasso readied looks at the herd on the open range circa 1902. *Reproduced by permission of the National Archives and Records Administration.*

in Texas, the price of beef there was very low. Cattlemen were looking for a way to get their product out into the American markets nationwide, without having to drive their herds through the nation's difficult terrain.

In 1867 an Illinois businessman decided to hire people to drive herds of cattle from the Nueces River Valley in South Texas eight hundred miles north to the tiny town of Abilene, Kansas. There, the cattle could be held for railroad shipment to the eastern markets, where they could bring in a much higher price. This began the era of huge cattle drives. The drives took place in the spring, usually taking a couple of months at about twelve miles per day. For a herd of two thousand cows, there was generally a crew of about ten or eleven cowboys.

In four years after the first cattle drive, about 500,000 cows made the trip to Abilene and then were shipped out to faraway markets on the railroad. Abilene, located at the northern end of the Chisholm Trail, a route that ran right through the Indian Territory (now Oklahoma), soon grew into the greatest of the cow towns. Within a few years, herds of 2,000 to 2,500 heads of cattle were being driven to Abilene and other Kansas cow towns. Mature animals were shipped eastward for slaughter and processing. Younger stock and breeding cattle were driven farther north and west into the grasslands of the Dakotas, Montana, and Wyoming. By 1870, 500,000 head a year were being herded north along the Chisholm Trail and other great cattle trails.

At that time, people began to start up their own ranches on the Plains. It took little to establish a large operation because of the "open-range" system. Cattle were simply branded by the owner and left on the range to graze wherever they chose. Each year, stray cattle were brought home by means of a roundup. This event covered thousands of square miles of the range. Hundreds of skilled cowboys located and drove home all the cattle out there, eventually separating them out for their owners. For a decade, the range had a very strong and distinct cowboy culture. It was sparsely populated and the rules of the range were understood and followed by most of the ranchers.

In 1880 the price of beef rose dramatically with a new demand for it on American tables and a rapidly growing U.S. population. People from all over the world raced to the Great Plains to start cattle ranches. Along with a new population of wealthy landowners dressed up in the latest cowboy fashions, the range became overcrowded with livestock. As the Plains became overgrazed, people began to fence in their ranches with barbed wire. Large herds of sheep also ranged the West during the nineteenth century. Soon cattlemen, sheepmen, and a swelling population of homesteaders were in conflict. By the 1880s, the scarcity of good grasslands and the never-ending shortage of water led to an escalation of range warfare, including theft of livestock, fence-cutting, intimidation, and occasional violence. The rapid spread of barbed-wire fencing after 1875 doomed the open-range cattle industry.

Life was already not going well for ranchers when, in the winter of 1885 to 1886, one of the worst winters in history hit the Great Plains. In the bitterly cold temperatures, cattle died by the hundreds of thousands. Cattle ranchers by the thousands were financially ruined. The open range was no

The Dust Bowl and the Okie Migration

In April 1934, in the midst of a severe drought, a dust storm hit the Great Plains, affecting a 300,000-square-mile area that included Kansas, Texas, western Oklahoma, eastern Colorado, and New Mexico. Since farmers had long been grazing livestock on the plains, there was little grass left and no root systems to hold down the dry soil. The winds picked up massive clouds of dust. The next month, after a long spell of unusually high temperatures, a second windstorm hit the same area. It is estimated that these two dust storms alone blew 650 million tons of topsoil off the involved area of the Great Plains, which came to be known as the Dust Bowl.

The tenant farmers and small farmowners of the Dust Bowl who watched these storms wipe out their livelihoods were often called "Okies." With their crops gone, they could not afford to pay their mortgages (home or farm loans) and it wasn't long before the banks foreclosed (took their property away). Most Okies packed up their trucks and headed west. A total of 2.5 million people left the Great Plains states in the 1930s. Most moved to neighboring states, but some 460,000 people moved to the Pacific Northwest, where they found jobs in lumbering or building the Bonneville and Grand Coulee Dams. More than 300,000 more moved to California.

Most of the Dust Bowl refugees quickly discovered that California's large-scale agribusiness (corporations whose business is farming) left no room for a family farm. Many settled in California's major cities, but they received little welcome there. Los Angeles authorities were already busy shipping Mexican Americans back to Mexico, and they balked at the prospect of yet another burden on their charity rolls.

About 110,000 Okies joined California's population of migrant farmworkers, mainly working as pickers in the fruit and produce farms in the San Joaquin Valley. Many farmers had chosen to migrate to the valley because the agribusiness managers had sent out leaflets to lure them there. The large, corporate farms wanted temporary labor—usually called migrant labor—and the Okies soon made up almost half of California's farm labor. Working as families, they traveled up and down the state, from the southern Imperial Valley to the northern Sacramento Valley. They lived in squalid shacks in communities called ditch camps, located on the sides of the road where water ditches ran. Hardly fit for human habitation, ditch camps were filthy and disease-ridden. Wages were too low to get these families out of poverty.

In 1936 the federal government created twelve new camps in the San Joaquin Valley for the migrant farmworkers. They had modern sanitation and recreation facilities and the metal shelters were rented as homes to many needy people for the cost of a penny a day. Unfortunately, many could not get in. The plight of these Okies was made famous by Nobel Prize-winning author John Steinbeck (1902–1968) in his 1939 novel *Grapes of Wrath*.

The End of the Buffalo

When Europeans arrived on the North American continent it is estimated that there were at least thirty million buffalo (also called American bison) living on the Great Plains. The accounts of most explorers tell of herds numbering in the tens of thousands of animals and ranging as far as the eye could see. The buffalo easily supported the basic survival needs of most Plains Indians. Its meat provided food; its skin provided clothing, tepee covers, bedding, riding gear, and containers. Its sinews (tendons) became bowstrings and thread; its bones were used as tools. Even its dried dung served as fuel in a treeless environment. Not surprisingly, the buffalo was sacred to the Plains tribes.

There were plenty of buffalo to support the thousands of migrants who arrived in the Plains in the late nineteenth century. By the early 1870s, although white hunters had killed many buffalo, the supply was still strong. Three factors led to the near-extermination (killing) of the species. The first was a belief held by many politicians and military officials that the way to subdue Native Americans and force them to move onto reservations was to completely eliminate the buffalo on the Plains.

The second factor was the new railroad system, which brought amateur hunters from all over the country to hunt the buffalo. For example, in 1872 a passenger train rolled into the station in Dodge City, Kansas, where it was held up by a huge herd of buffalo crossing the tracks. The passengers on the train began shooting at the animals just for fun, killing 500 animals while they waited to pass and leaving them there to rot. The third factor was the development of a tanning process that allowed buffalo hide to be made into useful leather in 1871. Suddenly there was money in buffalo hides, and the slaughter was unceasing. People migrated onto the Plains to enter into the buffalo-hide business.

In 1894 laws against killing buffalo were finally passed but by that time there were only a few hundred left. In 1902 the U.S. government placed forty captive and wild buffalo under protection in Yellowstone National Park. This protected herd grew into the one that exists in the park today. In the early twenty-first century there are about twenty-five herds of American buffalo, mainly in Yellowstone, but also in other U.S. and Canadian wildlife reserves. The species now numbers around sixteen thousand animals.

longer a way to do business. The cowboy era ended at that time, but cattle raising in the Great Plains went on to become a large and more scientific and stable business.

At the same time, promoters of westward expansion—mainly steamship and railroad companies—were using heavy propaganda (a campaign of information, often misinformation, intended to persuade people to believe in or agree with something) to urge people to move out to the Great Plains. People from all over the world were told that there was fertile land and a great climate, which was certainly not always the case, and free land to those willing to farm it. The Homestead Act had touched off a new mass migration. Advancing settlement, expansion of the railroad network, and the development of labor-saving agricultural machinery fueled an unparalleled boom in American agriculture. From 1870 to 1900, 4.3 million acres were settled, mainly in the prairie and High Plains regions of the Dakotas, Nebraska, Kansas, Oklahoma, Colorado, Wyoming, and Montana. Overall, the amount of farmland under cultivation doubled. It was not until 1935 that the remainder of the public lands was withdrawn from distribution under the Homestead Act. By then some 285 million acres had been homesteaded.

Home on the range

Life on the Plains was never easy. There were many obstacles to be overcome before the land could be used for farming. Because the Plains were largely without trees, log cabins could not be built. Instead settlers cut strips of sod (surface dirt and grass) from the ground and made houses by piling them one on top of the other. Door and window openings were outlined with poles and the structure was covered with cow or buffalo hides. When built properly sod structures could keep out the wind and the rain. Unfortunately many of them were not built properly, and the farmers and their families had to live in drafty houses that leaked whenever it rained. The lack of wood on the prairies also meant a lack of fuel for heating, so the first settlers used buffalo chips and slow-burning hay. These heating methods were not efficient, and the problem was eventually solved when the railroads brought coal to the Plains.

Despite the propaganda that had drawn people from Norway, Germany, and Great Britain to farm on the Plains, the tough matted sod resisted the farmer's plow. Although John Deere (1804–1886) had produced a steel plow that would cut deep, clean furrows through the tough sod, it was too expensive for most new settlers. The early Great Plains farmers often had no choice but to hire professional teams of men with the plows that would break the soil. Once broken, the soil could be more easily plowed in subsequent years. Even so, the average farmer could hardly cultivate more than 40 acres of his quarter section (160 acres). In the early years of the westward movement this was enough for many settlers who had moved to the Plains to establish a simple and independent way of life.

The Great Plains were dry and arid. There was an almost perpetual scarcity of water. Rivers and streams were few and far apart. Settlers dug wells at least two hundred to three hundred feet deep, but then had difficulty getting the water to the surface. Windmills driven by the near continuous winds of the prairie provided power, but windmills cost more money than most settlers had. Some settlers stored water in great barrels in their yards. Humans and animals drank from the same barrels and before long "prairie fever," or the infectious, often fatal, bacterial disease typhoid, swept through the country, killing many people. Rain was generally scarce, but in the 1870s the Great Plains experienced a period of generous rainfall. This encouraged settlers to remain despite other hardships. However, by the 1880s several natural disasters fell upon them: drought (lack of rain), blizzard, grasshoppers by the millions, cyclones, and scalding heat waves. By 1900 two-thirds of all farmers had given up and moved away or lost their property to foreclosure (when a bank takes back property because payments have not been made).

Although the Great Plains settlers lived largely isolated lives, there were occasions when they got together for community activities. In the scattered, small towns the farmers would come to work together to build a church or a community hall. Frequently, neighbors cooperated in putting up new sod houses or repairing old ones. In times of sickness, death, or natural disaster, people commonly helped one another. No matter how strong the desire for an independent existence, the unrelenting harshness and unpredictability of life on the Plains meant that survival often depended on turning to others for help. Nevertheless, only the most determined, obstinate, and hardy pioneers were able to survive and ultimately carve out a new existence for themselves.

The end of the frontier

In 1893 a young history teacher at the University of Wisconsin named Frederick Jackson Turner (1861–1932) called attention to a statement in the bulletin of the Superintendent of the United States Census for 1890. The statement said that the American frontier had closed. For many years the Census Bureau had maintained a definition of the "frontier" as an area containing not less than two nor more than six inhabitants to the square mile. Lines were drawn on the census map each decade to indicate the location of this frontier, and by 1890 one line extending westward from the Prairie states and a second eastward from the Mountain states converged and overlapped in the Great Plains. When he noticed this overlapping, Turner, intrigued, concluded that the close of the frontier symbolized the end of a great historic movement. At the meeting of the American Historical Association in Chicago in 1893, Turner read a paper he had prepared entitled, "The Significance of the Frontier in American History."

Turner held that American society and institutions were unique, resulting from the existence here of "an area of free land, its continuous recession, and the advance of American settlement westward." According to Turner, the European came to America with his cultural baggage, but in the process of adjusting to, and ultimately overcoming, the primitive environment in which he found himself, the immigrant was transformed into something new—an American living in an American social setting with distinctly American institutions.

For More Information

Books

Davis, William C. *The American Frontier: Pioneers, Settlers, and Cowboys, 1800–1899*. New York: Smithmark, 1992.

Lavender, David Sievert. *The Rockies*. Revised ed. New York: HarperCollins, 1975.

McLynn, Frank. *Wagons West: The Epic Story of America's Overland Trails*. New York: Grove Press, 2002.

Stegner, Page. *Winning the Wild West: The Epic Saga of the American Frontier, 1800–1899*. New York: Free Press, 2002.

Web Sites

"Louisiana Purchase Map Analysis." *Louisiana Digital Library.* http://louisdl. louislibraries.org (accessed on March 3, 2004).

Trinklein, Mike, and Steve Boettcher. "The Oregon Trail." http://www.isu. zedu/%7Etrinmich/Oregontrail.html (accessed on March 3, 2004).

Where to Learn More

Books

Adovasio, J. M., with Jake Page. *The First Americans: In Pursuit of Archaeology's Greatest Mystery*. New York: Random House, 2002.

Barrett, Tracy. *Growing Up in Colonial America*. Brookfield, CT: Millbrook Press, 1995.

Brogan, Hugh. *The Longman History of the United States of America*. 2nd ed. London and New York: Addison Wesley Longman, 1999.

Ciongoli, A. Kenneth, and Jay Parini. *Passage to Liberty: The Story of Italian Immigration and the Rebirth of America*. New York: Regan Books, 2002.

Clark, Jayne. *The Greeks in America*. Minneapolis: Lerner Publications, 1990.

Daley, William W. *The Chinese Americans*. New York: Chelsea House, 1996.

Daniels, Roger. *Coming to America: A History of Immigration and Ethnicity in American Life*. New York: HarperCollins, 1990.

Davis, William C. *The American Frontier: Pioneers, Settlers, and Cowboys, 1800–1899*. New York: Smithmark, 1992.

Dezell, Maureen. *Irish America: Coming into Clover*. New York: Doubleday, 2000.

Dolan, Sean. *The Polish Americans*. New York: Chelsea House, 1997.

Dubofsky, Melvyn. *Industrialism and the American Worker, 1865–1920*. 3rd ed. Wheeling, IL: Harlan Davidson, 1996.

Fagan, Brian M. *Kingdoms of Gold, Kingdoms of Jade: The Americas Before Columbus.* London: Thames and Hudson, 1991.

Ferry, Steve. *Russian Americans.* Tarrytown, NY: Benchmark Books, 1996.

Fitzhugh, William W. "Puffins, Ringed Pins, and Runestones: The Viking Passage to America." In *Vikings: The North Atlantic Saga.* Edited by William W. Fitzhugh and Elisabeth I. Ward. Washington and London: Smithsonian Institution Press in association with National Museum of Natural History, 2000.

Fixico, Donald L. *Termination and Relocation: Federal Indian Policy, 1945–1966.* Albuquerque: University of New Mexico Press, 1986.

Freedman, Russell. *In the Days of the Vaqueros: The First True Cowboys.* New York: Clarion Books, 2001.

Frost, Helen. *German Immigrants, 1820–1920.* Mankato, MN: Blue Earth Books, 2002.

Gernand, Renée. *The Cuban Americans.* New York: Chelsea House, 1996.

Gonzalez, Juan. *Harvest of Empire: A History of Latinos in America.* New York: Viking, 2000.

Grossman, James R. *Land of Hope: Chicago, Black Southerners, and the Great Migration.* Chicago: University of Chicago Press, 1989.

Hawke, David Freeman. *Everyday Life in Early America.* New York: Harper & Row, 1988.

Hertzberg, Arthur. *The Jews in America: Four Centuries of an Uneasy Encounter.* New York: Simon and Schuster, 1989.

Hoobler, Dorothy, and Thomas Hoobler. *The Chinese American Family Album.* New York: Oxford University Press, 1994.

Hoobler, Dorothy, and Thomas Hoobler. *The German American Family Album.* New York and Oxford: Oxford University Press, 1996.

Hoobler, Dorothy, and Thomas Hoobler. *The Scandinavian American Family Album.* New York and Oxford: Oxford University Press, 1997.

Howe, Irving. *World of Our Fathers: The Journey of the East European Jews to America and the Life They Found and Made.* New York: Simon and Schuster, 1976.

The Irish in America. Coffey, Michael, ed., with text by Terry Golway. New York: Hyperion, 1997.

Jackson, Robert H., and Edward Castillo. *Indians, Franciscans, and Spanish Colonization: The Impact of the Mission System on California Indians.* Albuquerque: University of New Mexico Press, 1995.

Johnson, Paul. *A History of the Jews.* New York: Harper & Row, 1987.

Kitano, Harry. *The Japanese Americans.* New York: Chelsea House, 1996.

Kitano, Harry H. L., and Roger Daniels. *Asian Americans: Emerging Minorities.* Englewood Cliffs, NJ: Prentice Hall, 1995.

Kraut, Alan M. *The Immigrant in American Society, 1880–1921.* 2nd ed. Wheeling, IL: Harlan Davidson, 2001.

Lavender, David Sievert. *The Rockies*. Rev. ed. New York: HarperCollins, 1975.

Lee, Lauren. *Japanese Americans*. Tarrytown, NY: Marshall Cavendish, 1996.

Lehrer, Brian. *The Korean Americans*. New York: Chelsea House, 1996.

Loewen, James W. *Lies My Teacher Told Me: Everything Your American History Textbook Got Wrong*. New York: Touchstone Books, 1996.

Magocsi, Paul R. *The Russian Americans*. New York: Chelsea House, 1996.

McLynn, Frank. *Wagons West: The Epic Story of America's Overland Trails*. New York: Grove Press, 2002.

Middleton, Richard. *Colonial America: A History, 1565–1776*. 3rd ed. Oxford, UK: Blackwell, 2002.

Monos, Dimitris. *The Greek Americans*. New York: Chelsea House, 1996.

Nabokov, Peter, ed. *Native American Testimony*. New York: Thomas Crowell, 1978.

Odess, Daniel, Stephen Loring, and William W. Fitzhugh. "Skraeling: First Peoples of Helluland, Markland, and Vinland." In *Vikings: The North Atlantic Saga*. Edited by William W. Fitzhugh and Elisabeth I. Ward. Washington and London: Smithsonian Institution Press in association with National Museum of Natural History, 2000.

Olson, Kay Melchisedech. *Norwegian, Swedish, and Danish Immigrants, 1820–1920*. Mankato, MN: Blue Earth Books, 2002.

Palmer, Colin A. *The First Passage: Blacks in the Americas, 1502–1617*. New York: Oxford University Press, 1995.

Petrini, Catherine. *The Italian Americans*. San Diego: Lucent Books, 2002.

Phillips, David, and Steven Ferry. *Greek Americans*. Tarrytown, NY: Benchmark Books, 1996.

Piersen, William D. *From Africa to America: African American History from the Colonial Era to the Early Republic, 1526–1790*. New York: Twayne, 1996.

Pitt, Leonard. *The Decline of the Californios: A Social History of the Spanish-Speaking Californians, 1846–1890*. Berkeley: University of California Press, 1966.

Portes, Alejandro, and Rubén G. Rumbaut. *Immigrant America: A Portrait*. 2nd ed. Berkeley: University of California Press, 1996.

Press, Petra. *Puerto Ricans*. Tarrytown, NY: Benchmark Books, 1996.

Schmidley, A. Dianne. *U.S. Census Bureau, Current Population Reports, Series P23-206, "Profile of the Foreign-Born Population in the United States": 2000*. Washington, DC: U.S. Government Printing Office, 2001.

Scott, John Anthony. *Settlers on the Eastern Shore: The British Colonies in North America, 1607–1750*. New York: Facts on File, 1991.

Shannon, William. *The American Irish*. Amherst: University of Massachusetts Press, 1990.

Stegner, Page. *Winning the Wild West: The Epic Saga of the American Frontier, 1800–1899*. New York: The Free Press, 2002.

Suro, Roberto. *Strangers Among Us: How Latino Immigration Is Transforming America*. New York: Knopf, 1998.

Takaki, Ronald. *Strangers from a Different Shore: A History of Asian Americans*. Boston: Little, Brown, and Company, 1989.

Tonelli, Bill, ed. *The Italian American Reader: A Collection of Outstanding Fiction, Memoirs, Journalism, Essays, and Poetry*. New York: William Morrow, 2003.

Wepman, Dennis. *Immigration: From the Founding of Virginia to the Closing of Ellis Island*. New York: Facts on File, 2002.

Williams, Jean Kinney. *The Mormons: The American Religious Experience*. New York: Franklin Watts, 1996.

Wood, Peter H. *Strange New Land: African Americans, 1617–1776*. New York: Oxford University Press, 1996.

Periodicals

Hogan, Roseann Reinemuth. "Examining the Transatlantic Voyage." Parts I and II. *Ancestry Magazine* (Part 1: November/December 2000): vol. 18, no. 6; (Part II: March/April 2001): vol. 19, no. 2. These articles can be found online at http://www.ancestry.com/library/view/ancmag/3365.asp and http://www.ancestry.com/library/view/ancmag/4130.asp (accessed on April 1, 2004).

Peck, Ira. "How Three Groups Overcame Prejudice." *Scholastic Update* (May 6, 1998): vol. 6, no. 17, p. 12.

Rose, Jonathan. "Organized Crime: An 'Equal-Opportunity' Employer; Every American Ethnic Group Has Had Its Fingers in Organized Crime—a Fact That the Dominance of Italian-American Crime Rings Tends to Mask." *Scholastic Update* (March 21, 1986): vol. 118, p. 12.

Web Sites

"About Jewish Culture." *MyJewishLearning.com*. http://www.myjewishlearning.com/culture/AboutJewishCulture.htm (accessed on April 1, 2004).

"Africa: One Continent, Many Worlds." *Natural History Museum of Los Angeles*. http://www.nhm.org/africa/facts/ (accessed on April 1, 2004).

"The American Presidency State of the Union Messages." *The American Presidency*. http://www.polsci.ucsb.edu/projects/presproject/idgrant/site/state.html (accessed on April 1, 2004).

"American West: Transportation." *World-Wide Web Virtual Library's History Index*. http://www.ku.edu/kansas/west/trans.htm (accessed on April 1, 2004).

"Austrian-Hungarian Immigrants." *Spartacus Educational*. http://www.spartacus.schoolnet.co.uk/USAEah.htm (accessed on April 1, 2004).

Bernard, Kara Tobin, and Shane K. Bernard. *Encyclopedia of Cajun Culture.* http://www.cajunculture.com/ (accessed on April 1, 2004).

"A Brief History of Indian Migration to America." *American Immigration Law Foundation.* http://www.ailf.org/awards/ahp_0203_essay.htm (accessed on April 1, 2004).

Chinese American Data Center. http://members.aol.com/chineseusa/0cen.htm (accessed on April 1, 2004).

"Coming to America Two Years after 9-11." *Migration Policy Institute.* http://www.ilw.com/lawyers/immigdaily/letters/2003,0911-mpi.pdf (accessed on April 1, 2004).

"French Colonization of Louisiana and Louisiana Purchase Map Collection." *Louisiana Digital Library.* http://louisdl.louislibraries.org/LMP/Pages/home.html (accessed on April 1, 2004).

Guzmán, Betsy. "The Hispanic Population: Census 2000 Brief." *U.S. Census Bureau, May 2001.* http://www.census.gov/prod/2001pubs/c2kbr01-3.pdf (accessed on April 1, 2004).

"Haitians in America." *Haiti and the U.S.A.: Linked by History and Community.* http://www.haiti-usa.org/modern/index.php (accessed on April 1, 2004).

"A History of Chinese Americans in California." *National Park Service.* http://www.cr.nps.gov/history/online_books/5views/5views3.htm (accessed on April 1, 2004).

Immigration: The Living Mosaic of People, Culture, and Hope. http://library.thinkquest.org/20619/index.html (accessed on April 1, 2004).

"Landmarks in Immigration History." *Digital History.* http://www.digitalhistory.uh.edu/historyonline/immigration_chron.cfm (accessed on April 1, 2004).

Le, C. N. "The Model Minority Image." *Asian Nation: The Landscape of Asian America.* http://www.asian-nation.org/model-minority.shtml (accessed on April 1, 2004).

Logan, John R., and Glenn Deane. "Black Diversity in Metropolitan America." *Lewis Mumford Center for Comparative Urban and Regional Research, University at Albany.* http://mumford1.dyndns.org/cen2000/BlackWhite/BlackDiversityReport/black-diversity01.htm (accessed on April 1, 2004).

Lovgren, Stefan. "Who Were the First Americans?" *NationalGeographic. com.* http://news.nationalgeographic.com/news/2003/09/0903_030903_bajaskull. html (accessed on April 1, 2004).

Mosley-Dozier, Bernette A. "Double Minority: Haitians in America." *Yale–New Haven Teachers Institute.* http://www.yale.edu/ynhti/curriculum/units/1989/1/89.01.08.x.html (accessed on April 1, 2004).

RapidImmigration.com. http://www.rapidimmigration.com/usa/1_eng_immigration_history.html (accessed on April 1, 2004).

The Scottish History Pages. http://www.scotshistoryonline.co.uk/scothist.html (accessed on April 1, 2004).

Simkin, John. "Immigration." *Spartacus Educational.* http://www.spartacus. schoolnet.co.uk/USAimmigration.htm (accessed on April 1, 2004).

Spiegel, Taru. "The Finns in America." *Library of Congress: European Reading Room.* http://www.loc.gov/rr/european/FinnsAmer/finchro.html (accessed on April 1, 2004).

"The Story of Africa: Slavery." *BBC News.* http://www.bbc.co.uk/world service/africa/features/storyofafrica/9chapter9.shtml (accessed on April 1, 2004).

Trinklein, Mike, and Steve Boettcher. *The Oregon Trail.* http://www.isu. edu/%7Etrinmich/Oregontrail.html (accessed on April 1, 2004).

"U.S. Immigration." *Internet Modern History Sourcebook.* http://www.ford ham.edu/halsall/mod/modsbook28.html (accessed on April 1, 2004).

Virtual Museum of New France. http://www.civilization.ca/vmnf/vmnfe. asp (accessed on April 1, 2004).

Index

Illustrations are marked by (ill.)

Anaconda Copper Company, *1:* 266

Anagnostopoulos, Michael, *2:* 481

Anarchy, *2:* 442

Anasazi, *1:* 63, 76–77

Ancient Order of Hibernians, *1:* 278

Andersonville, Chicago, Illinois, *1:* 304–5

Angel Island, *1:* 33, 45–47, 45 (ill.); *2:* 399–400

Angelou, Maya, *1:* 216

Angels with Dirty Faces, 1: 276–77

Anglican religion, *1:* 118–19, 135, 140

Anglo-Texans, *1:* 327; *2:* 618–19

Animism, *1:* 193

Anna in the Tropics, 2: 663

Anticommunism, *2:* 487, 512–13, 666–67

Anti-Defamation League, *2:* 442

Anti-immigrant sentiments, *1:* 285. *See also* Discrimination
German Americans, *1:* 235–42
Italian Americans, *2:* 468–69
Jewish Americans, *2:* 442–45
Scandinavian Americans, *1:* 300–301
unemployment and, *2:* 521–22

Anti-Mexican movement, *1:* 24–25. *See also* Mexican Americans

Antimiscegenation laws, *2:* 419, 597

Anti-Semitism, *2:* 423–24
in Germany, *2:* 433–36
Jewish immigrants and, *2:* 434, 442–45, 447
Russian Jews and, *2:* 448–49
in Spain, *2:* 424–25, 428

Antislavery movement, *1:* 208–9. *See also* Abolition of slavery

Antiterrorism and Effective Death Penalty Act of 1996, *2:* 572–73

Antiterrorist policies, *1:* 28–29; *2:* 556–57, 572–74

Antiwar demonstrations, *1:* 265–67

Anza, Juan Bautista de, *1:* 106–7

Apache Indians, *1:* 104–5

Arab Americans, *1:* 18; *2:* 547–80
culture of, *2:* 547–48, 576–77
discrimination against, *2:* 570–76, 572 (ill.)

history and, *2:* 548–54
religion of, *2:* 549

Arab Anti-Discrimination Committee (ADC), *2:* 571

Arab-Israeli conflict, *2:* 554, 559–61, 560 (ill.), 577, 579

Arabian Jazz, 2: 578–79

Arabic language, *2:* 547–48

Arawaks, *1:* 88–89, 92, 95

Archaeology, pre-Columbian life and, *1:* 62–63, 62 (ill.)

Architecture
Finnish, *1:* 310–11
Greek, *2:* 482

Arctic exploration, *1:* 311–12

Aristide, Jean-Bertrand, *2:* 678, 679

Aristocracy, English, *1:* 116

Arizona, *1:* 104–5; *2:* 622–23

Arkwright, Richard, *1:* 139

Armenia, *2:* 490 (ill.)

Armstrong, Louis, *1:* 217, 218 (ill.)

Arranged marriages, *2:* 408–9, 477, 611

Arrival in United States, *1:* 42–44

Arte Público Press, *2:* 646

Arts. *See also* Literature; Music
dancing, *2:* 482–83
Finnish architecture, *1:* 310–11
folk dances, *1:* 303; *2:* 482–83, 495, 516
Greek architecture, *2:* 482
Mexican American, *2:* 648–49
photography, *1:* 307–8

Ashkenazim Jews, *2:* 428, 430

Ashley, William Henry, *1:* 325, 332

Asian American immigration, *1:* 17; *2:* 381–422, 581–616. *See also* specific Asian countries
by country, *2:* 582
Hawaii and, *2:* 401

Asian Indian immigration, *2:* 583, 586–95

Asian Indian languages, *2:* 592

Asiatic Barred Zone, *2:* 582–83

Asiatic cholera, *1:* 40

Asiatic Exclusion League, *2:* 407

Aspira, *2:* 660

Assassination, of Trujillo Molina, *2:* 675

Assembly camps. *See* Internment

Assembly lines, *2:* 528, 536 (ill.)

Assimilation, *1:* 1–2, 4
  of African Americans, *1:* 191
  of Asian Indians, *2:* 589
  of Cambodian Americans, *2:* 610
  of Chinese Americans, *2:* 395
  of Danish Americans, *1:* 285, 297, 307
  of Dutch Americans, *1:* 183–84, 186
  of French Americans, *1:* 175
  of German Americans, *1:* 229–30, 241
  of Greek Americans, *2:* 477, 479
  of Hungarian Americans, *2:* 494
  of Irish Americans, *1:* 247, 274
  of Italian Americans, *2:* 462, 467, 469–72
  of Japanese Americans, *2:* 408, 411, 414
  of Jews, *2:* 431–32, 434–36, 439, 453–54
  of Native Americans, *2:* 352, 354, 539–45
  of Norwegian Americans, *1:* 301–2
  of Russian Americans, *2:* 512, 516
  of Scandinavian Americans, *1:* 290, 300–301
  of Scottish Americans, *1:* 154
  of Swedish Americans, *1:* 304
  of Turkish Americans, *2:* 562
Astor, John Jacob, *1:* 324
Astoria, *1:* 324
Atatürk, *2:* 562
Atlantic slave trade, *1:* 194–97, 195 (ill.)
Auctions, slave, *1:* 36, 200 (ill.), 201 (ill.)
Augustana Synod, *1:* 304
Austin, Moses, *1:* 327
Austin, Stephen F., *1:* 327
Austria-Hungary, *2:* 486–92
Autobiographies, *2:* 614
The Autobiography of Malcolm X, *1:* 203
Automotive industry, *2:* 528–29, 567
Avilés, Pedro Menéndez de, *1:* 166
Aztecs, *1:* 73 (ill.), 95–96; *2:* 643–44

B

Babalaos, *2:* 671
Babaluaye, *2:* 671
Baca, Judith, *2:* 648
Bach, Johann Sebastian, *1:* 243
Bagpipes, *1:* 154, 156 (ill.), 157
Bahía de Cochinos, *2:* 667–68
Balalaikas, *2:* 516
Balboa, Vasco Náñez de, *1:* 91
Baldwin, James, *1:* 216
Balkan Wars, *2:* 475–76
Baraka, Amiri, *1:* 217
Barbed-wire fencing, *1:* 344
Barnhart, Edward N., *2:* 375
Barrios, *2:* 658, 659–60
Bartholdi, Frédéric-Auguste, *1:* 177
Baseball, *2:* 412–13
Basset, Andre, *1:* 39 (ill.)
Batista, Fulgencio, *2:* 665
Battle of Culloden, *1:* 144, 149
Battle of Kinsale, *1:* 248
Battle of Puebla, *2:* 643
Battle of the Boyne, *1:* 252
Bavaria, *2:* 433
Bay of Pigs, *2:* 667–68
Beaver hats, *1:* 324, 325
Becknell, William, *1:* 328
Bedloe, Isaac, *1:* 177
Beecher, Lyman, *1:* 261
Beer, *1:* 245
Beethoven, Ludwig van, *1:* 241, 244
Before the Flames, *2:* 578
Behind the Mountains, *2:* 681
Benet, Stephen Vincent, *1:* 46
Benton, Thomas Hart, *1:* 328
Beringia, *1:* 66–67
Berra, Yogi, *2:* 472
BIA (Bureau of Indian Affairs), *2:* 539 (ill.), 540–41
Bilingual education, *1:* 33, 55, 58, 242; *2:* 639–40, 664
Bilingual Education Act of 1968, *1:* 58
Birds of passage, defined, *1:* 9
Bishop Hill, Illinois, *1:* 294
Bishops' Wars, *1:* 146
Bismarck, Otto von, *1:* 237–38
Black '47, *1:* 254–55, 280
Black creoles, *1:* 210; *2:* 371
Black Oath, *1:* 151
Black Plague, *1:* 85–86

Charles I (King of England), *1:* 128, 134, 146–47, 150–51, 248

Charles II (King of England), *1:* 147, 227 (ill.)

Charlesfort, *1:* 165–66

Charleston, South Carolina, *1:* 138, 167

Charlestown, Massachusetts, *1:* 261

Charros, *1:* 100

Charter companies, *1:* 112, 114–15

Chaul Chnam, *2:* 613–14

Chávez, César, *2:* 641 (ill.), 642

Chávez, Denise, *2:* 646

Cherokees, *2:* 357–61

Chicago, Illinois, *1:* 214; *2:* 534, 536

Chicano literature, *2:* 644–47

Chickasaws, *2:* 361

Chief Joseph, *2:* 366, 367–68, 367 (ill.)

Chief Powhatan, *1:* 121

Chieftains (music group), *1:* 280

Child labor, *2:* 519, 525–26, 526 (ill.)

Children of Cambodia's Killing Fields: Memories of Survivors, *2:* 613

Children of a Desired Sex, 2: 594

China
history of, *2:* 382–86
immigration from, *1:* 16, 33, 336; *2:* 381–403
languages of, *2:* 401

Chinatowns, *2:* 394–95, 394 (ill.)

"Chinese cheap labor," *2:* 386 (ill.)

Chinese Consolidated Benevolent Association, *2:* 390

Chinese Exclusion Act of 1882, *1:* 6, 16, 21, 42–43, 45; *2:* 398, 399, 584, 629

Chinese New Year, *2:* 402

Ch'ing Dynasty. *See* Manchus

Chisholm Trail, *1:* 343–44

Choctaws, *2:* 357–58

Cholera, *1:* 40

Choral societies, *1:* 303

Choudhury, Sarita, *2:* 595

Christianity. *See also* Catholicism
anti-Semitism and, *2:* 424
Arab Americans, *2:* 555, 557–58, 564

conversion to, *1:* 94
Korean Americans and, *2:* 600
Muslims and, *2:* 565
slavery and, *1:* 206–7

Christiansen, F. Melius, *1:* 303

Christmas traditions
German Americans and, *1:* 245
Polish, *2:* 503
Swedish, *1:* 312–13

Chrysler, Walter Percy, *1:* 186

Church of England. *See* Anglican religion

Church of God in Christ, *1:* 220

Church of Scotland, *1:* 145

Churches, Korean American, *2:* 600

CIA (Central Intelligence Agency), *2:* 675

Cigar manufacturing, *2:* 662–64

Cinco de Mayo, *2:* 643

CIO (Congress of Industrial Organizations), *1:* 237

Cisneros, Sandra, *2:* 646–47

Cities. *See* Urbanization

Citizenship, *2:* 585
children of citizens, *2:* 398–99
Filipinos and, *2:* 419–20
Korean Americans and, *2:* 598
Mexican Americans and, *2:* 621–22
Naturalization Act, *2:* 383, 405, 411, 583, 589
for Puerto Ricans, *2:* 657

City populations, *2:* 527

Civil disobedience, *1:* 212

Civil rights. *See also* Discrimination
of Arab Americans, *2:* 570–76, 575 (ill.)
of Mexican Americans, *2:* 625

Civil rights movement, *1:* 212–13

Clachans, *1:* 252–53

Clans, Scottish, *1:* 149, 154

Clark, William, *1:* 322–26, 323 (ill.)

Class system, in New Spain, *1:* 99

Clermont, 1: 50

Cliff Palace (Anasazi house), *1:* 77 (ill.)

Clotel, or the President's Daughter, *1:* 216

Clovis culture, *1:* 70–72, 70 (ill.)

Clovis points, *1:* 70–72, 70 (ill.)

Coahuiltecan, *1:* 72

Desegregation. *See* Segregation

Deseret, *2:* 373

Desire, 1: 202

Detention camps. *See* Internment

Detroit, Michigan, *2:* 528–29, 567

DeWitt, John L., *2:* 375–76

Dezell, Maureen, *1:* 266

Díaz, Porfirio, *2:* 627

"Didn't Live Nowhere," *2:* 522 (ill.)

Diego, Juan, *2:* 642

DiMaggio, Joe, *2:* 472

Discovery of new worlds. *See* Exploration and discovery

The Discovery of the Potato Blight, 1: 253 (ill.)

Discrimination, *1:* 2, 4, 6
    Arab Americans, *2:* 570–76, 572 (ill.), 577–78
    Asians, *1:* 17; *2:* 382, 405, 588–89
    Chinese Americans, *2:* 390–91, 389 (ill.), 395–98
    Filipinos, *2:* 418–20
    German Americans, *1:* 56, 236–37, 238–41, 240 (ill.), 245
    Haitian Americans, *2:* 682
    Irish Catholics, *1:* 247, 249, 252, 260–62, 263–64
    Italian Americans, *2:* 468–69
    Japanese Americans, *2:* 407–8, 410–11
    Korean Americans, *2:* 596–97
    Mexican Americans, *2:* 622, 624, 629, 631
    Native Americans, *2:* 359
    Puerto Rican, *2:* 660
    Russian Americans, *2:* 511–13

Diseases
    Asiatic cholera, *1:* 40
    bubonic plague, *1:* 85–86
    infectious, *1:* 40–41, 264; *2:* 530
    on transatlantic journeys, *1:* 40–41

Displaced Persons Act of 1948 and 1950, *2:* 496, 501, 512

Ditch camps, *1:* 345

Diversity
    in Austria-Hungary, *2:* 487
    in German Americans, *1:* 221–22
    in Pennsylvania, *1:* 135–36

Domestic servants, Irish Americans and, *1:* 273

Dominican Americans, *2:* 651–53, 672–76, 676 (ill.)

Dominican Republic, *2:* 672–75, 681

Domino, Antoine "Fats," *1:* 219

Dooley, Mr. Martin. *See* Dunne, Finley Peter

Dorset culture, *1:* 82

Dorsey, Thomas A., *1:* 217

Douglass, Frederick, *1:* 208, 216

Dowd, Maureen, *1:* 270

Dowries, *2:* 594

Draft, military, *1:* 264–65

Dragon dance, *2:* 402

Dress, Asian Indian, *2:* 593–95

Drop-out rates, for Mexican Americans, *2:* 640

Druze, *2:* 557, 566

Du Bois, W. E., *1:* 213; *2:* 536

Dunkards. *See* German Brethren

Dunne, Finley Peter, *1:* 269

Dust Bowl, *1:* 345

Dutch Americans, *1:* 162, 177–87

Dutch East Indies Company, *1:* 177–78

Dutch language, *1:* 186

Dutch Reformed Church, *1:* 181–82, 184

Dutch West Indies Company, *1:* 178, 180–82

Duvalier, François (Papa Doc), *2:* 677–78

Duvalier, Jean-Claude, *2:* 678

E

East India Company, *1:* 114

Easter, *2:* 482

Eastern European immigrants, *1:* 16–18; *2:* 485–516

Eastern European Jews, *2:* 425, 432, 436–39, 451

Eastern Orthodox religion, *2:* 481, 564

Economic depression, *2:* 521. *See also* Great Depression

Economic sanctions against Iraq, *2:* 564

Edict of Nantes, *1:* 166

Edison, John, *1:* 186

Edison, Thomas Alva, *1:* 186
Editorial Quinto Sol, *2:* 645
Education
  of African Americans, *2:* 532
  of Arab Americans, *2:* 569–70
  of Asian Indian Americans, *2:* 592
  bilingual, *1:* 33, 55, 58, 242; *2:* 639–40, 664
  of Cambodian Americans, *2:* 610–11
  of Filipinos, *2:* 417, 421–22
  of Greek Americans, *2:* 479–80, 479 (ill.)
  Jews and, *2:* 431 (ill.), 432
  kindergartens, *1:* 234–35
  of Korean Americans, *2:* 599
  of Mexican Americans, *2:* 639–41
  of Native Americans, *2:* 543–44
  public schools, *1:* 53–54, 242, 262–63
  of Puerto Ricans, *2:* 660, 661
  of Vietnamese Americans, *2:* 607
Educational reform, *1:* 53–54, 262–63
Edward VI (King of England), *1:* 118
Egg incubators, *1:* 307
Egyptian Americans, *2:* 561
Eid al-Fitr, *2:* 579
El grito de Dolores, *2:* 645
El Salvador, *2:* 684–85
ELCA (Evangelical Lutheran Church in America), *1:* 302
Elizabeth I (Queen of England), *1:* 118–19
Ellington, Duke, *1:* 217, 218 (ill.)
Ellis Island, *1:* 17 (ill.), 33, 40 (ill.), 43–44, 43 (ill.); *2:* 439–40
Ellison, Ralph, *1:* 216
Emergency Quota Act of 1921, *1:* 18; *2:* 469
Emigrant novels, *1:* 305–6
Emigration Canyon, *2:* 373
Employment. *See* Workers
Employment discrimination. *See* Discrimination
Encomiendas, *1:* 32, 93–94
Engels, Friedrich, *2:* 507
England. *See also* United Kingdom
  colonialism, *1:* 32

Ireland and, *1:* 248–51
New Netherland and, *1:* 182
Northern Ireland and, *1:* 150–51
religion in, *1:* 117–19, 140
Scotland and, *1:* 146, 147–50
English as a second language (ESL), *2:* 639–40
English Church, *1:* 118–19
English Civil War, *1:* 147, 248
English immigration, *1:* 111–41, 119 (ill.)
  after colonial period, *1:* 138–40
  financing, *1:* 112–15
  motivation, *1:* 115–19
English language requirement, *1:* 55–56
English-only schools, *1:* 56–58; *2:* 640
Enlightenment, Jewish. *See* Haskala
Entertainment. *See also* Arts; Movies; Music
  Finnish Americans, *1:* 311
  Italian Americans, *2:* 474
Entrepreneurs
  Arab American, *2:* 567–69, 568 (ill.)
  Asian Indian Americans, *2:* 590–91
  Chinese American, *2:* 393–94
  Greek American, *2:* 477
  Korean American, *2:* 583, 600
  Vietnamese American, *2:* 606–7
Enya, *1:* 280
Epiphany (Three Kings Day), *2:* 661
Episcopalians, *1:* 140
Equal Education Opportunity Act of 1974, *2:* 639
Erie Canal, *1:* 51, 318–19, 320 (ill.)
Erik the Red, *1:* 80–81
Erik the Red's Saga, *1:* 80
Eriksson, Leif, *1:* 63, 81–82, 288
Escandón, José de, *1:* 106
ESL (English as a second language), *2:* 639–40
Ethnic identity. *See* specific ethnicities
Europe. *See* specific European countries
European Jews. *See* Ashkenazim Jews

H

Joint stock companies, *1:* 32, 114, 125–26
Jones, John Paul, *1:* 151
Jones, Mary Harris "Mother," *1:* 270
Jones Act of 1917, *2:* 657
Joplin, Scott, *1:* 217
Jordanian Americans, *2:* 560–61
Judah, *2:* 423–24
Judaism, *2:* 435–36. *See also* Jews
    African Americans and, *1:* 220
    Muslims and, *2:* 565
    today, *2:* 453–54
Jump blues, *1:* 218–19
Jutland Peninsula, *1:* 283

K

Kaffiyehs, *2:* 570
Kalakaua, David (King of Hawaii), *2:* 412
Kalevala, 1: 310
Kanellos, Nicolás, *2:* 645–46
Karamu, *1:* 219
Karenga, Maulana, *1:* 219
Karma, *2:* 611
Kawkab Amirka, 2: 554–55
KCOR-TV, *2:* 648
Kearney, Dennis, *2:* 396
Kemal, Mustafa, *2:* 562
Kennedy, John F., *1:* 46, 272, 272 (ill.); *2:* 586, 667–68
Kennedy, Patrick, *1:* 272
Kennewick Man, *1:* 68, 69
Kenney, Bridget Murphy, *1:* 272
Kenrick, John, *1:* 275
Key West, Florida, *2:* 662, 664
Khmer language, *2:* 610
Khmer Republic, *2:* 608–9
Khmer Rouge, *2:* 583, 608–9, 611, 612–14
Kieft, Willem, *1:* 184
Kievan Rus', *2:* 504
The Killing Fields, 2: 613
Kilts, *1:* 149
Kinara, *1:* 219
Kindergartens, *1:* 234–35
King, B. B., *1:* 217
King, Martin Luther Jr., *1:* 212 (ill.), 213
Kino, Eusebio, *1:* 104
Kinte clan, *1:* 203

Kjellberg, Isador, *1:* 304
Knickerbocker, Diedrich, *1:* 184–85
Knights of Labor, *1:* 238, 270
Know-Nothing party. *See* American Party
Knox, Henry, *1:* 151
Knox, John, *1:* 144–45
Koledy, *2:* 503
Koran, *2:* 549, 565, 570, 579
Korean Americans, *2:* 583, 586, 595–602
Korean language, *2:* 598
Korean War, *2:* 597
Koreatown, Los Angeles, California, *2:* 599, 599 (ill.)
Kosciuszko, Tadeusz, *2:* 500
Kraut, Ala M., *1:* 41
Krefeld, Rhineland, *1:* 228
Kresge Auditorium and Chapel, Cambridge, Massachusetts, *1:* 310
Krik? Krak!, 2: 681
Kristallnacht, *2:* 444, 445
Krushchev, Nikita, *2:* 508
Ku Klux Klan, *1:* 4, 153, 211–12; *2:* 532
Kulaks, *2:* 509
Kwangtung Province, *2:* 384, 386, 391
Kwanzaa, *1:* 219
Kyes, *2:* 601

L

La Isabela, *1:* 92
"La Nouvelle Yorck," *1:* 39 (ill.)
La Salle, Sieur de (Robert Cavelier), *1:* 162, 171, 173
Labor movement, *1:* 238–39
    Cuban Americans in, *2:* 664
    Finnish Americans in, *1:* 309
    Jewish Americans in, *2:* 442
    Mexican Americans in, *2:* 641 (ill.), 642
    in Poland, *2:* 502
Labor unions, *2:* 418 (ill.)
    Filipinos in, *2:* 418 (ill.), 419
    German Americans in, *1:* 237
    Irish Americans in, *1:* 266, 270
    Jewish Americans in, *2:* 440–41
    Scandinavian Americans in, *1:* 300

Martí, José, *2:* 664
Martin, Dean, *2:* 472
Martin, Sallie, *1:* 217
Marx, Karl, *1:* 237; *2:* 507
Mary (Queen of England), *1:* 118
Maryland, *1:* 134–35
Mass migrations, *1:* 8
   Austria-Hungary, *2:* 491
   Chinese, *2:* 383
   defined, *1:* 11
   Germans, *1:* 231–32
   Irish Catholics, *1:* 257–60,
     268–69
   Italian, *2:* 464
   Italian and Greek, *2:* 455–56
   Turks, *2:* 562–63
   to western states, *1:* 316–21
Massachusetts, *1:* 127–32, 138,
   190, 204
Massachusetts Bay Company, *1:*
   128
Matchmakers, *2:* 409
Matson, Floyd W., *2:* 375
May, Someth, *2:* 614
Mayan refugees, *2:* 683
Mayflower, 1: 125 (ill.), 126
Mayflower Compact, *1:* 126
Mayombera, *2:* 671
Mayorazgo, *1:* 99
McCarran-Walter Act of 1952, *1:*
   21; *2:* 584–85
McCarthy, Joseph, *2:* 512
McDonald, Daniel, *1:* 253 (ill.)
McKay, Claude, *1:* 216
McLoughlin, Dr. John, *1:* 324–25,
   331
McLynn, Frank, *1:* 333, 338
McNamara, Eileen, *1:* 270
Meadow Cove site, *1:* 81–82, 81
   (ill.)
Mecca, *2:* 566
Meiji Restoration, *2:* 403–4
Melkites, *2:* 564
Melting pot. *See* Assimilation
Melville, Herman, *1:* 186
Mendelssohn, Felix, *1:* 244
Mendelssohn, Moses, *2:* 431
Menehunes, *1:* 80
Menino, Thomas, *2:* 474
Mennonites, *1:* 226, 228–29; *2:* 510
Mesa Verde National Park, *1:* 77
   (ill.)
Mesoamericans, *1:* 76
Mestizos, *1:* 99

Metropolitan Opera, *2:* 474
Mexican-American War, *1:* 108,
   334; *2:* 618 (ill.), 619–23
Mexican Americans, *2:* 617–49,
   637 (ill.), 646 (ill.), 651–52
Mexican immigrant workers, *1:* 9
Mexican Revolution, *2:* 627–28
Mexican War of Independence, *1:*
   108; *2:* 618
Mexico
   history of, *2:* 618–23
   independence of, *1:* 326; *2:* 643
   Texas and, *1:* 326–28; *2:* 618–19
Mexico City, *1:* 86, 95–96
Mexico-U.S. border, *1:* 24–26. *See
   also* United States Border Pa-
   trol
Meyer, Margarethe, *1:* 234–35
Miami-Dade County, Florida, *2:*
   653, 680
Michael Collins, 1: 280
Middle class, *1:* 86
Middle passage, *1:* 197–98
Migrant workers
   defined, *1:* 11
   Filipino, *2:* 417
   Mexican American, *2:* 627, 632,
     634, 636, 642
   Okies, *1:* 345
Migration. *See also* Forced migra-
   tions; Mass migrations
   eras of, *1:* 9–22
   to Hawaii, *1:* 80
   vs. immigration, *1:* 10–11
   Okie, *1:* 345
   Puerto Rican, *2:* 651–53,
     655–62
   from Scandinavia, *1:* 289–91
Military draft. *See* Draft, military
Milk separators, *1:* 307
Milloudon Sugar Plantation, *2:*
   386 (ill.)
Ming Dynasty, *2:* 382
Minhag America, 2: 435
Mining industry, *2:* 627
Minstrel shows, *1:* 275
Minuit, Peter, *1:* 162, 179–80
Mission Concepcion, *1:* 105 (ill.)
Mission San Xavier de Bac, *1:* 97
   (ill.)
Missionaries, Christian
   in Arab world, *2:* 552
   Jesuit, *1:* 167–68
   western migration and, *1:* 333

Missions, *1:* 86, 96–98, 97 (ill.)
  California, *1:* 106–8; *2:* 623–24
  Florida, *1:* 101–2
  Jesuit, *1:* 168
  secularization of, *2:* 623–24
Mississippi, *2:* 532
Mississippi Masala, 2: 594–95
Mississippi River, *1:* 171, 318
Mississippian cultures, *1:* 74–75, 75 (ill.)
Missouri, *1:* 320–21
Missouri Compromise, *1:* 320–21
Missouri Fur Trade Company, *1:* 324
Missouri River, *1:* 318
Missouri Territory, *1:* 320
Mr. Dooley's Opinions, 1: 269
Moberg, Vilhelm, *1:* 305–6
Mogollon, *1:* 76
Moksha, *2:* 593
Molina, Alfred, *2:* 595
Molokans, *2:* 510, 511
Monk's Mound, *1:* 74
Monolingualism, *1:* 56–58
Monsoon Wedding, 2: 595
Moors, *1:* 88; *2:* 424–25
Morales, Esai, *2:* 647
Mormon Trail, *2:* 373
Mormons, *1:* 296 (ill.); *2:* 371 (ill.)
  Danish, *1:* 285, 295–96
  forced migration of, *2:* 352, 372–73
  Icelandic Americans, *1:* 298–99
  Swedish, *1:* 295
  westward expansion and, *1:* 48–49
Morrison, Toni, *1:* 216
Mosaicism. *See* Multiculturalism
Mosques, *2:* 555 (ill.), 566 (ill.)
Motown, *1:* 219
Moundbuilders, *1:* 63, 74–75, 75 (ill.)
Mountain men, *1:* 324–26
Mouvement Ouvrier Paysan (Peasant Workers Movement), *2:* 678
Movies
  Arab American stereotypes and, *2:* 571
  Asian Indian, *2:* 594–95
  on Cambodia, *2:* 613
  Irish Americans and, *1:* 276–77, 280

Italian Americans and, *2:* 471, 474
  on Scottish history, *1:* 156–57
Moving, *1:* 31–32
Mozart, Wolfgang Amadeus, *1:* 244
Muddy Waters, *1:* 217
Muhammad, *2:* 548–49, 566–67, 579. *See also* Muslims
Mulattoes, *1:* 99
Mulligan Guard shows, *1:* 275
Multiculturalism, *1:* 2
Multilingualism, *1:* 54–58. *See also* Bilingual education
Murals, Chicano, *2:* 648
Muscovy, *2:* 504–5
Music
  African American, *1:* 217–19
  Arab American, *2:* 576–77
  German American, *1:* 243–44
  Irish, *1:* 279–80
  Mexican American, *2:* 649
  Norwegian American, *1:* 303
  Polish Americans and, *2:* 504
  Russian, *2:* 516
  Scottish, *1:* 154–56
Musical comedies, *1:* 275
Muslims, *2:* 548–50, 552, 557, 564–66, 566 (ill.). *See also* Nation of Islam
  in Africa, *1:* 193–94
  Asian Indian, *2:* 589
  Ramadan, *2:* 566, 579–80
  schools, *2:* 570
  Turkish, *2:* 562–63
Mutsuhito (Emperor of Japan), *2:* 403–4
Mutual protection societies, *2:* 467
My Left Foot, 1: 280
My Own Country, 2: 595
"My Wild Irish Rose," *1:* 276
Myer, Dillon S., *2:* 540–41

N

NAACP (National Association for the Advancement of Colored People), *1:* 212
NAGPRA. *See* Native American Graves Protection and Repatriation Act of 1990 (NAGPRA)

Nair, Mira, *2:* 594–95
Nanak, *2:* 588
Naples, Italy, *2:* 457
Napoleon I (Emperor of France), *2:* 506
Napoléonic Code, *1:* 175
Narrative of the Life of Frederick Douglass, an American Slave, Written by Himself, 1: 216
Narváez, Pánfilo de, *1:* 91
A Nation of Immigrants, 1: 46
Nation of Islam, *1:* 220
National Association for the Advancement of Colored People (NAACP), *1:* 212
National Baptist Convention of the U.S.A., Inc., *1:* 220
National Council of La Raza, *2:* 647
National Farm Workers Association. *See* United Farmworkers Union
National Origins Act of 1924, *1:* 18; *2:* 400, 411, 445, 469, 477, 555, 582–83, 631, 657. *See also* Quota system
National politics, Irish Americans in, *1:* 270–72, 271 (ill.), 272 (ill.)
National Road, *1:* 50
National Tartan Day, *1:* 157
Nationalism
  Asian Indian, *2:* 586
  Hungarian, *2:* 497
  Irish, *1:* 268–70
  Korean, *2:* 596, 597
Nationals, U.S., *2:* 417
Nation-states, German, *1:* 223, 226
Native American Graves Protection and Repatriation Act of 1990 (NAGPRA), *1:* 69
Native Americans
  African Americans and, *1:* 191
  buffalo and, *1:* 346
  in California, *1:* 107–8, 336; *2:* 623–24
  in Caribbean Islands, *2:* 653–55
  Catholic missions and, *1:* 96–98
  in cities, *2:* 517–18, 519
  Columbus, Christopher and, *1:* 90, 90 (ill.), 92

consensual unions and, *1:* 98–99
  culture of, *2:* 542–43
  effect of European migration on, *1:* 11–12, 83–84, 92–95
  forced migrations of, *2:* 351–68, 357 (ill.)
  Great Plains, *1:* 77, 79
  Jesuits and, *1:* 167–68
  Lewis and Clark expedition and, *1:* 322–23, 323 (ill.)
  Manhattan and, *1:* 179–80
  manifest destiny and, *1:* 328–29
  mountain men and, *1:* 325
  Northeast, *1:* 79
  origins of, *1:* 61–62
  Our Lady of Guadalupe and, *2:* 642–43
  Pilgrims and, *1:* 126–27
  pre-agricultural culture, *1:* 71–73
  rise of agriculture and trade, *1:* 73
  slavery and, *1:* 92–95
  Southwest, *1:* 76–77
  urbanization of, *2:* 538–45
  vaqueros, *1:* 98 (ill.), 100–101
  westward migration and, *1:* 20, 47–48, 315, 320
Nativism, *1:* 2, 4, 6, 235–37, 249, 260–61; *2:* 396. *See also* Discrimination
Natural resources, English immigrants and, *1:* 116–17
Naturalization Act of 1790, *2:* 383, 391, 411, 583, 589
Nauvoo, Illinois, *2:* 372
Nava, Gregory, *2:* 647
Navajo Nation Reservation. *See* Treaty Reservation
Navajos, *2:* 353, 363–65, 540
Naval blockade, of Cuba, *2:* 668
Navigation, *1:* 33–34, 34 (ill.). *See also* Water transportation
Nazi Germany, *2:* 425, 445
Neeson, Liam, *1:* 157
Netherlands. *See* Dutch Americans
Neve, Felip de, *1:* 107
New Amsterdam, *1:* 166, 179 (ill.), 181, 201 (ill.); *2:* 428. *See also* New York City

New Brunswick, New Jersey, *2:* 495

"The New Colossus," *1:* 3, 6

New England, *1:* 128–30, 133–34, 199–200, 202. *See also* specific states

New England Confederation, *1:* 133–34

New France, *1:* 168–69, 170 (ill.)

New Irish, *1:* 277–80

New Mexico, *1:* 102–4, 328; *2:* 622

New Netherlands, *1:* 162, 178–82, 202, 288; *2:* 428

New Orleans, *1:* 217

New Paltz, New York, *1:* 167 (ill.)

New Spain, *1:* 95–96, 98–99

New Sweden, *1:* 285, 288–89

New Year
    Cambodian, *2:* 613–14
    Chinese, *2:* 402
    lunar, *2:* 402
    Vietnamese, *2:* 604

New York City, *1:* 39 (ill.), 40 (ill.), 42–44, 52 (ill.), 138. *See also* Ellis Island; New Amsterdam
    Dominican Americans in, *2:* 653
    Irish Catholics in, *1:* 263, 265 (ill.)
    Italian Americans in, *2:* 465–66
    Jewish immigrants in, *2:* 428–29
    Puerto Ricans in, *2:* 660
    Russian Americans in, *2:* 514
    slums in, *1:* 307–8
    St. Patrick's Day Parade in, *1:* 279 (ill.)

Newfoundland, Canada, *1:* 81–82, 81 (ill.)

Newport, Rhode Island, *1:* 133, 138

Newspapers, Chicano, *2:* 645. *See also* Press

Nez Perce, *2:* 366–68

Ngangas, *2:* 671

Nicaraguan Americans, *2:* 653, 682, 683–84

Nicholas II (Czar of Russia), *2:* 507

Nirvana, *2:* 390, 606, 611

Nisei, *2:* 408, 410, 412–13

NLCA (United Norwegian Lutheran Church), *1:* 302

No Day, *2:* 481

Nomads, *1:* 68

Nonquota immigrants, *1:* 23; *2:* 585

Norse explorers, *1:* 80–83

The North (American), *1:* 203–4. *See also* New England

North Carolina, *1:* 138

North Dakota, *1:* 299 (ill.)

North Korea, *2:* 597

North Vietnam, *2:* 602

North Virginia group. *See* Plymouth Company

Northeast Indians, *1:* 79

Northern Ireland, *1:* 144, 150–51, 248

Northern Italian foods, *2:* 474

Northern School (Buddhism). *See* Mahayana Buddhism

Northward migration. *See* Great Migration

Northwest Passage, *1:* 177–78, 321–22

Northwest Territory, *1:* 49 (ill.)

Norway, *1:* 284–89, 289 (ill.)

Norwegian Constitution, *1:* 312 (ill.), 313

Norwegian immigration, *1:* 291–93

Norwegian language, *1:* 302

Norwegian Lutheran Church in America, *1:* 302–3

Norwegian Synod, *1:* 302

Nova Britannia: Offering Most Excellent Fruites by Planting in Virginia, *1:* 116–17

Nova Scotia, Canada, *2:* 368–69

Nureyev, Rudolf, *2:* 513

O

Obatala, *2:* 671

O'Brien, Pat, *1:* 277

Occupational safety, *2:* 525–26

Ochi Day, *2:* 481

Ochun, *2:* 671

OCNA (Orthodox Church in North America), *2:* 514–15

O'Connell, William, *2:* 444

O'Connor, Sinead, *1:* 280

PZPR (Polish United Workers' Party), *2:* 501

Q

Qing Dynasty. *See* Manchus
Quakers, *1:* 135–36
  in Germany, *1:* 226
  Norwegian, *1:* 291
  Pennsylvania and, *1:* 227–28
  slavery and, *1:* 202
Queue, *2:* 391
Quindlen, Anna, *1:* 270
Quinn, Peter, *1:* 266
Quota immigrants, *1:* 23
Quota system, *1:* 3, 21; *2:* 445–47, 469, 583–85, 586. *See also* National Origins Act of 1924
Quotations about immigration, *1:* 46
Qur'an, *2:* 549, 565, 570, 579

R

Rabbis, *2:* 432, 448
Racial segregation. *See* Segregation, racial
Racism, *1:* 4, 6, 211–13. *See also* Anti-Semitism; Discrimination
  Japanese Americans and, *2:* 375–76, 406, 408, 412–13
  Korean Americans and, *2:* 601
Ragtime, *1:* 217
Rahman, Omar Abdel, *2:* 571
Railroads, *1:* 51, 317
  buffalo and, *1:* 346
  Chinese Americans working on, *2:* 387–88, 392–93, 397 (ill.)
  economic growth and, *2:* 463
  Irish Americans working on, *1:* 264–66
  Mexican Americans working on, *2:* 627
Raleigh, Walter, *1:* 112–13
Ramadan, *2:* 566, 579–80
Rancheros, *2:* 619, 624
Ranching. *See* Cattle ranching
Ranchos, *2:* 623

Rap music, *1:* 219
Rastafarianism, *1:* 220
Reagan, Ronald, *1:* 26, 246
Recife, Brazil, *2:* 428
Reconstruction (American South), *1:* 211; *2:* 531–33
Red Fort, Calcutta, India, *2:* 587 (ill.)
Red Scare, *1:* 300–301; *2:* 487, 511–12. *See also* Anticommunism
Redpath, Jean, *1:* 155–56
Reed, Ishmael, *1:* 216–17
Reform Judaism, *2:* 435–36, 453
Reformation. *See* Protestant Reformation
Reformed Presbyterian Church, *1:* 155
Refugee Act of 1980, *1:* 21; *2:* 604, 679
Refugee Relief Act of 1953, *2:* 478, 559
Refugees
  Cambodian, *2:* 609–10
  Cuban, *2:* 653, 667–69
  defined, *1:* 11–12
  Guatemalan, *2:* 683
  Haitian, *2:* 653, 679–80, 682
  Laotian, *2:* 614–15
  Lebanese, *2:* 558
  Mexican, *2:* 628
  Palestinian, *2:* 559–61, 560 (ill.)
  Vietnamese, *2:* 583, 602–4
Registered aliens, defined, *1:* 12–13
Registration of immigrants, *1:* 22–23
Reglas, *2:* 671
Regulations, shipping, *1:* 40–41
Reincarnation, *2:* 592–93
Religion. *See also* specific religions
  African, *1:* 193–94
  African Americans, *1:* 220
  Arab, *2:* 548–49, 550
  Arab Americans, *2:* 548–49, 554–55, 564–66, 565 (ill.)
  Asian Indian, *2:* 588–89, 592–93
  Cambodian Americans, *2:* 611
  Caribbean, *2:* 671
  Chinese, *2:* 388–89
  Danish Americans, *1:* 306–7
  Dutch Americans, *1:* 181–82, 184–85
  in England, *1:* 117–19, 140

of English immigrants, *1:*
140–41
Filipino Americans, *2:* 421
Finnish, *1:* 309
in France, *1:* 162–67
German Americans, *1:* 232–33
Greek Americans, *2:* 481
Haitian Americans, *2:* 682
Hungarian Americans, *2:* 497
Icelandic Americans, *1:* 311
Japanese Americans, *2:* 414
Korean Americans, *2:* 599–600
in Lebanon, *2:* 558
Mexican Americans, *2:* 642–43
in Northern Ireland, *1:* 150–51
Norwegian Americans, *1:* 302–3
Polish Americans, *2:* 503
in public schools, *1:* 262–63
Puerto Ricans, *2:* 661
Russian Americans, *2:* 510, 511,
514–15
Scotland, *1:* 144–45
slavery and, *1:* 206–7
Swedish American, *1:* 304
Vietnamese Americans, *2:*
605–6
Religious conflicts and persecu-
tion. *See also* specific reli-
gions and countries
in France, *1:* 162–67
in New England, *1:* 130–33
in Northern Ireland, *1:* 150–51
Norwegian, *1:* 285, 291
in Russia, *2:* 510
Swedish, *1:* 294
Religious freedom
Jewish Americans and, *2:* 430
in Massachusetts, *1:* 130–32
Ulster Scots and, *1:* 151
Religious schools. *See* Parochial
schools
Religious settlers and refugees, *1:*
13–14. *See also* specific reli-
gious groups
defined, *1:* 12
Pilgrims, *1:* 124–27
Puritans, *1:* 127–28
Relocation, of Native Americans,
2: 540–42
Renaissance, *1:* 86–87
Rendezvous, *1:* 325, 326
Rensselaer, Kiliaen Van, *1:* 180
Rensselaerswyck, *1:* 180

Reparations, for Japanese Ameri-
can internment, *2:* 379
Repatriation, *2:* 631–32
Repatriation Act of 1935, *2:* 419
Republic Day (Turkey), *2:* 563
Requierimento, *1:* 94
Reservations, Native American, *2:*
352, 353, 538, 539 (ill.)
Resettlement camps, for Viet-
namese refugees, *2:* 603–4
Restauration, *1:* 291
Resurrection Boulevard, *2:* 647
Retail trades, *2:* 557, 567–68, 568
(ill.), 587 (ill.), 599 (ill.)
Reuther, Walter, *1:* 237
*Revista Chicano-Riqueña (Chicano-
Rican Review)*, *2:* 645–46
Revocation of the Edict of
Nantes, *1:* 166
Rhee, Syngman, *2:* 596, 597
Rhode Island, *1:* 132–34
Rhythm and blues, *1:* 219
Ribault, Jean, *1:* 165
Rideout, Bonnie, *1:* 155
Riis, Jacob, *1:* 307–8; *2:* 466, 522
(ill.)
Rio Grande River, *2:* 619–20
Riots
anti-Catholic, *1:* 261–62
anti-Chinese, *2:* 395–96
anti-draft, *1:* 265–66
anti-Filipino, *2:* 418
Los Angeles, *2:* 601
Zoot Suit, *2:* 633
"Rip Van Winkle," *1:* 185
The Rise of David Levinsky, *2:* 440
Riverdance, *1:* 280
Rivers, transportation on, *1:* 318
Rizal Day, *2:* 421
Rizal, José, *2:* 421
Roads, *1:* 317, 318
Roanoke Island, *1:* 112–13
Rob Roy, *1:* 156–57
ROCE (Russian Orthodox Church
in Exile), *2:* 515
Rock and roll, *1:* 219
Rocky Mountains, *1:* 331–32
Rogers, Will, *1:* 46
Rolfe, John, *1:* 121, 122–23
Rölvaag, Ole E., *1:* 303
Roman Catholic Church. *See*
Catholicism
Romero, Oscar, *2:* 685

Spanish colonialism, *1:* 13, 32, 85–109, 89 (ill.)
  African slaves and, *1:* 191, 194
  vs. British, *1:* 111, 114
  Caribbean and, *2:* 653–55
  Cuban independence and, *2:* 662–65
  exploration and discovery, *1:* 88–90
  Filipinos and, *2:* 416, 420
  Hispaniola and, *2:* 672
  Mexican independence and, *2:* 643
  Native Americans and, *2:* 363–64
  Puerto Rican independence and, *2:* 656–57
  settlements in present-day U.S., *1:* 99–108
  Spanish territory, *1:* 326–28
  in western U.S., *1:* 316
Spanish Fork, Utah, *1:* 298–99
Spanish Inquisition, *2:* 425
Spanish Jews. *See* Sephardic Jews
Spanish language, *1:* 55, 58; *2:* 638–39, 648, 661
SPARC (Social and Public Art Resource Center), *2:* 648
Spiritual music, *1:* 217
Sports
  Japanese Americans in, *2:* 412–13
  Norwegian, *1:* 303–4
  Scottish, *1:* 157–59, 158 (ill.)
Squanto, *1:* 126–27
Stagecoaches, for mail, *1:* 341
Stalin, Joseph, *2:* 508–9, 511, 512
Stark, John, *1:* 151
"Stars and Stripes Forever," *1:* 243
Starvation. *See* Famine
States, new Western, *1:* 319–21
Statue of Liberty, *1:* 3, 6, 7 (ill.), 177; *2:* 437
Steam railroads, *1:* 334–35
Steamships, *1:* 41, 50, 318
Steel production, *2:* 528
Steerage, *1:* 37, 39–41, 231; *2:* 388
Stefansson, Vilhjalmur, *1:* 311–12
Stegner, Page, *1:* 329
Steinbeck, John, *1:* 345
Stereotypes
  of Arab Americans, *2:* 571
  of Irish Americans, *1:* 275
Steuben, Baron Friedrich von, *1:* 245

Steuben Day Parade, *1:* 245
Stimson, Henry L., *2:* 376
Storytelling, *2:* 681
Stowe, Harriet Beecher, *1:* 209, 261
Strikes, labor, *1:* 238; *2:* 393
Stuarts (royal family of England), *1:* 146–47
Stuyvesant, Peter, *1:* 182, 184
Suburbs, *2:* 471–72, 537
Sugar plantations, *1:* 93–94, 198; *2:* 386 (ill.), 387, 405–6, 417, 596, 656–57
Sumo, *2:* 412
Sung, Kim Il, *2:* 597
Sunnis, *2:* 549, 566
Suomi University, *1:* 308–9
Sushi, *2:* 415 (ill.)
Susquehanna Turnpike, *1:* 318
Swamis, *2:* 593
Swastika, *2:* 446 (ill.)
Sweden, *1:* 284–89, 289 (ill.)
Swedish Americans, *1:* 285, 293–95
Swedish language, *1:* 304
Swedish Lutheran Church, *1:* 304
Syllabary, Cherokee, *2:* 358
Symphony orchestras, *1:* 244
Synagogues, *2:* 429–31
Synge, John M., *1:* 276
Syria, Greater, *2:* 555
Syrian Americans, *2:* 557–59
Syttende Mai celebrations, *1:* 312 (ill.), 313

T

Taft, William Howard, *2:* 444
Tagalog language, *2:* 420
Taiping Rebellion, *2:* 384
Tammany Hall, *1:* 271–72
Tampa, Florida, *2:* 663, 664
Tanabata, *2:* 415
Taoism, *2:* 389–90, 606
Tartans, *1:* 149
Taxi driving, *2:* 591 (ill.)
Telemundo, *2:* 648
Television, Mexican Americans and, *2:* 647–48
tenBroek, Jacobus, *2:* 375
Ten Years' War, *2:* 662–64

Tenant farmers. *See also* Share-
cropping
Irish Catholics, *1:* 252–53,
255–56
Italian, *2:* 460
Scottish, *1:* 150
Tenement housing, *2:* 530
Tenochtitlán, *1:* 95–96
Terrorist attacks, September 11,
2001, *1:* 28–29; *2:* 549,
556–57, 571–72, 572 (ill.),
574–76, 577–78
Tet, *2:* 604
Texas, *1:* 105–6, 105 (ill.), 326–28
cattle ranching in, *1:* 342–43
Mexican-American War and, *2:*
619–23
Mexican Americans in, *2:* 619,
638
Textile industry, *1:* 139; *2:* 524,
526 (ill.)
Thai Americans, *2:* 614, 615 (ill.)
Thanksgiving, *1:* 127
Theravada Buddhism, *2:* 611
Thief Treaty, *2:* 366, 367
Third wave of immigration, *1:*
21–22
Thirteen colonies, *1:* 119 (ill.). *See
also* Colonial era, 1492–1796
Thirteenth Amendment to the
Constitution, *1:* 210
Thirty Years' War, *1:* 226–27
Three Kings Day (Epiphany), *2:*
661
*Through and Through: Toledo Sto-
ries, 2:* 578
Thule culture, *1:* 82
Thurman, Uma, *2:* 595
A Time on Earth, 1: 306
Tindley, Charles Albert, *1:* 217
Tobacco plantations, *1:* 122–24
Togoda Satsanaga Society, *2:* 593
Tomei, Marisa, *2:* 595
Tontons macoutes, *2:* 677–78
Torah, *2:* 429, 432, 435
Toscanini, Arturo, *2:* 474
Totalitarianism, *2:* 509
Tracy, Spencer, *1:* 276–77
Trade, *1:* 86–88
Africa and, *1:* 194
Dutch immigration and, *1:*
177–78
embargo, *2:* 667
English colonialism and, *1:* 114

Europe and China, *2:* 382–84
Native Americans and, *1:* 322
Trade unions. *See* Labor unions
Trading companies. *See* Joint
stock companies
Trading posts, *1:* 331. *See also* Fur
trade
Trail of Tears, *1:* 20; *2:* 353,
360–61, 360 (ill.)
Trans World Airlines terminal,
Kennedy Airport, *1:* 310
Transatlantic journeys, *1:* 36–41,
231–32, 256–57
Transcontinental railroad, *1:* 317,
340–41, 340 (ill.); *2:* 393, 397
(ill.), 522
Transportation, *1:* 49–51. *See also*
Railroads; Water transporta-
tion
for California Gold Rush, *1:*
334–35
from China, *2:* 387–88
in colonial era, *1:* 32–38
in westward migration, *1:*
317–19
Travel modes, *1:* 49–51. *See also*
specific types of travel
Treaties, Native American, *2:* 352,
353, 356–58, 366–67
Treaty of Dancing Rabbit Creek,
2: 357–58
Treaty of Guadalupe Hidalgo, *1:*
55, 334; *2:* 618, 619, 621–22,
625–26
Treaty of Limerick, *1:* 252
Treaty of Paris of 1898, *2:* 657
Treaty of Tordesillas, *1:* 90, 114
Treaty of Utrecht, *2:* 368–69
Treaty of Versailles, *1:* 238–39
Treaty Reservation, *2:* 365
True Lies, 2: 571
Trujillo Molina, Rafael Leonidas,
2: 674–75
Truth, Sojourner, *1:* 208, 209 (ill.)
Tubman, Harriet, *1:* 209
Turkey, *2:* 478, 490 (ill.)
Turkish Americans, *2:* 562–63
Turner, Frederick Jackson, *1:* 349
Turpeinen, Viola, *1:* 311
TWA Flight 800, *2:* 574
Tweed, William Marcy "Boss," *1:*
268
Twiller, Wouter Van, *1:* 184
Two Years Before the Mast, 1: 329

Tydings-McDuffie Act of 1934, *2:* 418–19

Typhus, *1:* 40

U

U-2, *1:* 280

Ulster, Northern Ireland, *1:* 150–51, 248

Uncle Tom's Cabin, 1: 209

Underground Railroad, *1:* 208–9

Undocumented immigration, *1:* 23–29

Undocumented workers. *See* Illegal aliens

Unemployment, *2:* 521
  Dominican immigration and, *2:* 675
  Great Depression and, *2:* 535, 631–32
  Korean immigration and, *2:* 598
  Puerto Rican migration and, *2:* 656, 656 (ill.), 657

Union Pacific Railroad, *1:* 317, 340; *2:* 392

Union of the Parliaments (United Kingdom), *1:* 147

Union of Soviet Socialist Republics. *See* Soviet Union

United Colonies of New England. *See* New England Confederation

United Farmworkers Union, *2:* 418 (ill.), 641 (ill.), 642

United Kingdom, *1:* 147, 252
  Acadians and, *2:* 368–70
  Arabs and, *2:* 553–54
  India and, *2:* 586
  Oregon Territory and, *1:* 331, 333–34
  trade with China, *2:* 382–84

United Nations, *2:* 554

United Norwegian Lutheran Church (NLCA), *1:* 302

United States. *See also* Second wave of immigration; specific laws and states
  American dream, *1:* 1
  Asian American immigration, *1:* 17; *2:* 381–422, 581–616

Asian Indian immigration, *2:* 583, 586–95

Caribbean immigration, *2:* 651–81

Central American immigration, *2:* 651, 653, 682–85

Danish immigration, *1:* 295–97

English immigration, *1:* 111–41, 119 (ill.)

Filipino immigration, *2:* 381–82, 383, 416–22

Finnish immigration, *1:* 297–98

German immigration, *1:* 15–16, 56, 221–46

House Committee of Immigration, *1:* 43

immigrant arrival in, *1:* 42–44

importance of immigration in, *1:* 1

Irish immigration, *1:* 15, 247–81

Italian immigration, *2:* 455–75, 465 (ill.)

Jewish immigration, *2:* 423–54

Latino immigration, *2:* 651–53

manifest destiny and, *1:* 19, 328–30

Norwegian immigration, *1:* 291–93

occupation of Dominican Republic, *2:* 673

occupation of Haiti, *2:* 677

Scandinavian immigration, *1:* 283–313

South American immigration, *2:* 651

Southeast Asian immigration, *1:* 21; *2:* 581–82, 586

Third wave of immigration, *1:* 21–22

undocumented immigration, *1:* 23–29

United States Border Patrol, *1:* 3, 24 (ill.), 25; *2:* 629, 636–37

United States Constitution, *1:* 204
  Fourteenth Amendment, *2:* 383, 391, 531
  Thirteenth Amendment, *1:* 210

Univisíon, *2:* 648

Urbanization, *1:* 20–21; *2:* 517–45
  of African Americans, *2:* 531–38
  growth of cities, *1:* 51–53
  of Native Americans, *2:* 538–45

Urista, Alberto. *See* Alurista

U.S. Diversity Immigrant Visa
Lottery, *1:* 23
USA PATRIOT Act of 2001, *2:* 573
USSR. *See* Soviet Union
Utah, *1:* 295
Utah Territory, *2:* 373

V

Valentino, Rudolph, *2:* 474, 571
Vaqueros. *See* Cowboys
Vassey, France, *1:* 164–65
Vaudeville shows, *1:* 275
Vedanta Society, *2:* 593
Vedas, *2:* 592
Verdi, Giuseppe, *2:* 474
Vermont, *1:* 190, 204
Vhalidze, Valery, *2:* 513
Viceroys, Spanish, *1:* 99
Victor Emmanuel II (King of
Italy), *2:* 458
Victoria (Queen of Britain), *2:* 586
Vienna, Austria-Hungary, *2:* 494
(ill.)
Vietnamese Americans, *1:* 21, 22
(ill.); *2:* 583, 602–8, 603 (ill.),
608 (ill.)
Vietnamese language, *2:* 583, 605
Vietnamese New Year, *2:* 604
Vietnamese War, *2:* 602
Vigilance committees, *1:* 335–36
Vikings, *1:* 79–83, 81 (ill.), 311–12
Villa, Pancho, *2:* 627
Vinland, Newfoundland, Canada,
1: 63, 81–82
The Vinland Sagas, 1: 80
Violence
anti-African Americans, *2:*
532–33
anti-Catholicism and, *1:* 261
anti-Chinese Americans, *2:*
395–96
anti-Korean Americans, *2:* 597,
601
anti-Mexican Americans, *2:* 633
California Gold Rush and, *1:*
335–36
Viollett, Roger, *1:* 165 (ill.)
Viramontes, Helena María, *2:* 646
Virginia, *1:* 112, 199, 200–202
Virginia Company, *1:* 114–15,
116–17, 122

Visas, *1:* 23; *2:* 583, 591–92
Vishnu, *2:* 592
Vivekanada (Swami), *2:* 593
Volstead Act. *See* Prohibition Act
of 1919
Volstead, Andrew, *1:* 303
Voodoo, *2:* 671, 682
Voting rights
of African Americans, *1:* 211,
213; *2:* 531–32
of Mexican Americans, *2:* 622

W

Wages, increasing, *2:* 528–29
Wagner-Rogers bill, *2:* 447
Wagon trains, *1:* 336–39
*Wagons West: The Epic Story of
America's Overland Trails, 1:*
333
Wakamatsu Tea and Silk Colony,
2: 409
Wald, Lillian, *1:* 53
Walesa, Lech, *2:* 502
Walker, Alice, *1:* 217
Walker, T-Bone, *1:* 217
Wallace, William, *1:* 156
Wallowa Valley, *2:* 367
Walter, Thomas, *2:* 482
Wampanoag Indians, *1:* 126–27
Waqfa, *2:* 579
War brides, *1:* 112, 140; *2:* 597
War Brides Act of 1945, *1:* 140; *2:*
400
War of 1812, *1:* 320
War on Terrorism, *2:* 572–73
Warren, Earl, *2:* 375
Warwick, Rhode Island, *1:* 133
Washington, Booker T., *1:* 213
Washington, D.C.
African Americans in, *1:*
214–15
Capitol building, *2:* 482
Washington, Denzel, *2:* 595
Water scarcity, on Great Plains, *1:*
348
Water transportation
boat people, *1:* 9; *2:* 583, 603
(ill.), 604, 679
to California, *1:* 334–35
on rivers, *1:* 318

Russia in, *2:* 507
Scottish immigration after, *1:* 153
World War II
  African American migration after, *2:* 536
  Chinese in, *2:* 400
  Dutch immigration after, *1:* 183
  Hungarian Americans and, *2:* 496
  Japanese Americans and, *2:* 374–79, 411–14
  Jewish refugees and, *2:* 445–48
  Mexican workers during, *2:* 632, 634
  Native Americans in, *2:* 540
  Poland during, *2:* 501
  Russian Americans and, *2:* 512–13
Wright, Richard, *1:* 216

Y

Yamato Colony, *2:* 409–10
"Yankee Doodle Dandy," *1:* 276
Yarmulkes, *2:* 454
Ybor, Vicente Martinez, *2:* 663

Yeats, William Butler, *1:* 276
Yekl: A Tale of the New York Ghetto, *2:* 440
Yemaya, *2:* 671
Yemeni Americans, *2:* 561–62, 579
Yeshivas, *2:* 432
Yiddish, *2:* 428, 451–53
Yoga, *2:* 583, 593
Yogananada (Swami), *2:* 593
Yom Kippur, *2:* 452
Yong-man, Park, *2:* 596
Yonsei, *2:* 408, 414
Young, Brigham, *2:* 371 (ill.), 372–73
Young Chief Joseph. *See* Chief Joseph
Youth clubs, *2:* 413

Z

Zakat, *2:* 566
Zapata, Emiliano, *2:* 627
Zawadi, *1:* 219
Zion (Mormons), *2:* 372
Zionism (Jewish), *2:* 449, 553, 554
Zoot Suit Riots, *2:* 633
Zydeco music, *1:* 210